Contents

Preface

The *College Administrator's Handbook* provides an overview of administration at the college level for individuals entering the field. It should be useful for in-service purposes whether it becomes a base for formal orientation and in-service activities or is used for independent reading. It should be of particular assistance to faculty who find themselves moving into positions as program directors, division and department chairpersons, and assistant and associate deans. Its broad overall coverage should also make it appropriate for use as a textbook for introductory courses in the administration of higher education.

It has become obvious that the roles of college and university administrators are becoming increasingly complex. A number of influences are responsible. Among these are the changing economic and social conditions, collective bargaining, and the pressures from faculty for a greater voice in decision making.

In past years, it was not unusual to find deans, associate and assistant deans, and chairpersons entrenched in positions where they remained until retirement. In some institutions, the status of chairpersons has been altered by collective bargaining agreements that call for their election and place limitations upon the length of time they may serve. Other administrators often are appointed on a short-term basis. Then there are the individuals who decide to leave administration and return to the classroom with its accompanying benefits of greater flexibility and time for reading and research. The result is frequent turnover in administrative personnel and a constant flow of inexperienced administrators as faculty members move into and out of administrative positions.

Because there are so many different forms of organization in institutions of higher education, it is not possible to be prescriptive in a book of this type. Instead, an overview of administrative activities and concerns is presented as well as some of the recent thinking and ideas of others in the field. The approach used here makes the material applicable to two and four year undergraduate institutions as well as colleges within a university setting.

There has been no intention to take a particular philosophic stand. Bureaucracy and collegiality are discussed as well as what appears to be decreasing autonomy, specifically among those institutions supported to some extent by public funds. One might say there is a negative tone throughout the *Handbook*. If this is the reaction of the reader, so be it. Higher education is finding itself in difficult straits and there is no way to provide simple solutions to many complex problems. Just as each institution must find the most effective balance between collegiality and bureaucracy for its own purposes, so must each utiliize its own resources to the fullest extent to find its own solutions to the problems being faced.

It is hoped that the information and ideas presented herein will be helpful and that, in addition, the reader will further pursue many of them through the more extensive readings suggested in the footnotes and bibliography.

Appreciation is extended to the following institutions that provided illustrative materials: University of Illinois, Kansas State University, Temple University (particularly the School of Business Administration and the College of Education), Gloucester County College (New Jersey), Somerset County College (New Jersey), Reed College, Mt. Holyoke College, and the University of Kentucky.

CHAPTER 1

Setting the Scene

While the 1960s will long be remembered in colleges and universities for campus demonstrations, often violent, these were also the years of greatest academic expansion. During that period, enrollments more than doubled so that by 1969, there were 7.9 million enrolled in colleges and universities as compared to an earlier 3.6 million. At the same time, institutional spending tripled. Suddenly, these same institutions found themselves with tremendous financial difficulties, a situation that some foresaw, but whose dire predictions were largely ignored. The long range impact of the rapid growth of the 1960s has been finally felt and college and university administrators are seeking ways to handle a situation that for most of them is unique.

During the 1970s, higher education has been struggling with reform and reorganization as it tries to respond to the many stresses from both internal and external sources. It now faces a situation where it is being expected to do more with less and where change is most likely to take place through substitution and contraction rather than through growth and expansion. Periods of stress and strain have been met before and many institutions have been strengthened by the experiences. It is obvious, however, that strong administrative leadership is more important than ever.

This introductory chapter provides a brief description of some of the influences having an impact upon higher education. Subsequent chapters focus upon leadership characteristics, administrative functions, and the implications of recent developments for the college-level administrator. Included among the latter are staffing considerations, collective bargaining, changing governance structures, planning and budgeting, and accreditation.

SOCIAL STRESSES

Among the social conditions to which institutions have been responding are the problems inherent in urban settings, changes in patterns of race relations leading to a new consciousness of ethnic backgrounds, and major changes in the role of women. The pressures impinging upon colleges and universities are reflected in their statements of institutional mission, the curriculum, and day to day systems for change.

Meeting Societal Needs

Because colleges and universities in the United States are many things to many people, numerous demands for new and varied services are made upon them. A variety of problems is awaiting attention particularly in the urban areas. These include transportation, general deterioration of the cities, and poverty. Energy conservation and environmental problems are also requiring increased attention. Comprehensive research efforts needed in these areas are being limited by the decreasing availability of support money for research from the federal government, foundations, endowments, and private business and industry. Resources as well as creative interdisciplinary approaches are needed if colleges and universities are to play the leadership role expected of them.

In a study to assess institutional effectiveness, the Carnegie Commission on Higher Education identified five basic functions for American colleges and universities. These may be summarized as follows:

1. Provision of opportunities for the intellectual aesthetic, ethical, and skill development of individual students, and the provision of campus environments which can assist students in their general developmental growth
2. Advancement of human capability in society at large
3. Enlargement of social justice for the postsecondary age group
4. Transmission and advancement of learning and wisdom
5. Critical evaluation of society—through individual thought and persuasion—for the sake of society's renewal [1]

The Commission rated institutional performance as satisfactory or better in the first, second, and fourth areas only. Thus, it becomes apparent that higher education still faces an enormous task if it is to meet the needs of society implicit in the five basic functions.

Another report from the same commission describes a number of trends that are expected to continue having an impact upon higher education. Among these are the challenges to inhumanity by young people leading to respect for all other persons as equals. The report suggests that the loss of privacy that has been developing will require a more honest and more realistic approach to interpersonal relationships. As expressed in the Commission's report, the future and its implications for relationships between higher education and society require some high-powered decisions both within the campus gates and without. These decisions will determine the kinds of teaching and research activity in which higher education will engage. There will always be some dedicated individuals who will work away at what they believe to be important regardless of what society wants. While these efforts may be slowed down because society is paying for our system of education, a better understanding of one another and the universe should emerge.

Changing Student Clientele

Higher education is no longer a privilege reserved only for the elite. It must provide for a clientele with more variations in levels of academic ability and preparation and cultural backgrounds than has existed before. As an example, the Federal Office for Civil Rights conducted a survey of approximately 3,000 campuses and found that the "number of minority-group students attending colleges and universities in the United States rose 11.7 percent between 1972 and 1974, while total enrollments in the same two-year period increased by less than 2 percent. Census Bureau figures show that "blacks made up 9 percent of the total college enrollment in 1974, compared to 5 percent in 1964." The Office of Civil Rights' study "shows that in 1972 minority group students represented 11.9 percent of the country's full-time enrollment. Two years later, that proportion had risen to 13.1 percent." [2] In addition to proportional shifts in minority enrollments, there is also a wider range in age among the student body, as well as a larger proportion of women.

Increasing numbers of students are shifting their enrollments from full to part-time status several times during the course of working toward their degrees. Many who are already employed return to school for the purpose of working toward improving their skills and updating their knowledge base. It is not uncommon to find employers covering tuition bills in these instances.

Many older students are enriching their lives through formal study which, in many instances, is pursued on a noncredit basis. The decrease in the work week, which for some has already been reduced from the standard forty hours to thirty-five, provides time to pursue course work in which they are interested. For others whose jobs may be dull and boring, the concept of lifelong education provides the challenge and opportunity to pursue vocational interests. Finally, institutions have discovered the "senior citizen" and vice versa.

The average age of students in colleges is shifting and as stated in the Carnegie Commission report, needs continue to expand and evolve:

For educating greater proportions of the population
For educating citizens over more of their lifetimes
For broader ranges and alternative choices in types of training
For higher levels of training
For expertise that aids in solving today's social problems
For manpower training geared to the state's changing employment patterns [3]

The changing nature of the student body has led to tremendous growth in student personnel services. As higher education has opened its doors to the nontraditional populations including the disadvantaged, counseling services of numerous kinds as well as remedial programs for those lacking the basic skills needed for success have had to be organized. The very nature of these populations requires low student/faculty ratios with the attendant high costs of instruction.

Institutions are finding it necessary to adjust their programs to accommodate changing student concerns, interests, and choices. In the 1960s, students clamored for "relevant" courses and curricula. Today, employment opportunities and the increasing emphasis on career education are affecting their choices. Students must be educated for an ever accelerating rate of change along with being assisted in developing a personal flexibility and a comprehensive value system that will stand them in good stead.

TECHNOLOGICAL INFLUENCES

Many technical innovations have appeared in business and industry, some of which are appropriate for adaptation and adoption by colleges and universities. Among these are developing instructional systems, highly developed communications media, and the massive field of computer technology. Most affected have been the fields of research and institutional administration, particularly where computers are bringing about substantial changes in administrative structure and operation with an increased emphasis upon institutional research and centralization of information. Despite the potential for it, there has been relatively little advancement in instructional programs, although large campus libraries have been expanding their capabilities.

Administrative Applications

Technology, particularly computerization, has added a sophistication to administration not only in control and monitoring activities but also in providing information and completing transactions for day to day operation. Student registration, record keeping, and payroll operations have become more efficient and flexible. Budget administration has undergone radical change. Great strides have been made in routinizing the acquisition of information. The Higher Education General Information Survey (HEGIS) forms, which were developed for collecting information needed by the U.S. Office of Education, have led toward more efficient procedures for collecting information as well as triggering an acceleration in the development of a national system of management information. The efforts of the Western Interstate Commission for Higher Education (WICHE) have made it possible for institutions to obtain comparable data from others similar to themselves in mission and complexity to use as a basis for evaluating the efficiency and effectiveness of their own internal operations.

In addition to an external integration of management decision information, HEGIS and WICHE have provided valuable guidance for the development of institutional information systems. As a result, technology has become a tool for day-to-day operations and control as well as an invaluable resource for short- and long-term planning. Further discussion about information systems and planning is found in Chapter 9.

While the introduction of technological approaches may result in higher costs initially, the results can pay off in added efficiency based on information that has been retrieved in formats never thought possible. Also, the use of technological tools should eventually reduce costs in some areas of administration, library operation, and instruction. Caution is needed to prevent the production of voluminous reports containing masses of unnecessary information. While potential for providing invaluable data exists, people must know how to precisely define the information needed and then interpret the data when it is received.

Instructional Applications

In contrast, very little has been done in the instructional area, particularly in the individualization of student learning experiences. The possibilities of learning through television, films, tapes, and video-cassettes are endless. Computers can be of assistance in cataloging materials and in curriculum design. In the latter area, the computer may be used to match cassettes and chains of cassettes with the individual student's objectives. There is a need to examine the total array of instructional materials including those commercially produced. Most important of all, high quality instructional programs and learning materials developed by colleges and universities should be shared with other institutions. Failure to do so will lead to unnecessary and wasteful duplication of effort.

In addition to utilizing technological capacities, flexible time arrangements may be established to help increase instructional productivity. By individualizing learning experiences, it becomes possible to decrease the time required by faculty and some students for achieving a given instructional objective while prolonging the time during which instruction is available for those who need it.

Individualization of learning experiences does not mean that students should be working independently all of the time. Interaction in group situations is a vital part of the educational process. Discussion is a means for exchanging ideas and strengthening the learning of concepts, both of which are important. Such participation also provides opportunities for the improvement of verbal skills as well as the ability to articulate one's ideas and beliefs. There are times, too, when the lecture method is most appropriate. The available technologies should be integrated with other instructional methods in working towards the achievement of instructional objectives.

ECONOMIC STRESSES

Much is being said and written about the financial difficulties of colleges and universities. Cost-cutting has become a necessity. Some colleges have merged with others while some have even gone out of existence. The pressures of inflation accompanied by changing enrollment patterns, decreasing governmental aid, and demands for increased services have taken their toll. Increased tuition charges are obviously not the answer. An uncertain financial outlook makes for an uncertain future.

Changing Enrollment Patterns

At one point, statisticians believed that the traditional student enrollment would continue to grow until the year 2000. That prediction now appears to have been false. The decline in the birth rate which began in 1958 is being felt in the elementary and secondary schools and it has been predicted that by 1993, there will be a decrease of more than three million college-age people. Table 1–1 illustrates this trend with projections to 1985–1986 at which point the number of high school graduates is expected to decline dramatically.

In addition to the diminishing birth rate, a number of other reasons account for the decline. Among these is the questioning of the value of a college education that leads to a decreasing interest among traditional college-age students in programs which culminate in an academic degree. The instability and unpredictability of the job market provide an uncertainty about the possibility of jobs after the expense of college. A degree no longer guarantees increased earnings and many graduates are finding themselves in jobs for which they are actually overqualified. For this reason, some parents have become reluctant to make large financial outlays for their children's future. Financial aid funds have not kept up with tuition increases, thus forcing many students to attend public rather than private institutions. Many private schools will be unable to continue without additional federal and state aid. Also, some students have elected to attend two-year institutions rather than four because of the former's thrust toward career education accompanied by lower costs.

While enrollments went up unexpectedly in 1974 and 1975, they dropped in 1976 which was the first no-growth year since 1951.[4] The most recent complete figures from the National Center for Education Statistics show total college enrollment for Fall 1977 did not meet the projected 12,146,000 in Table 1–2. An increase of 2.6 percent over the previous year resulted in an actual total of 11,415,020 full-

Table 1–1 **High-School Graduates**

	1965–66	*1971–72*	*1977–78*	*1979–80*	*1981–82*	*1983–84*	*1985–86*
Public	2,334,000	2,706,000	2,825,000	2,770,000	2,631,000	2,417,000	2,371,000
Private (Estimated)	298,000	300,000	310,000	310,000	310,000	310,000	310,000
Total	2,632,000	3,006,000	3,143,000	3,080,000	2,941,000	2,727,000	2,681,000

Chronicle of Higher Education, 19 September 1977, p. 8. Reprinted with permission.

TABLE 1–2 Enrollments in Two-Year and Four-Year Institutions

	1965	*1971*	*1977*	*1979*	*1981*	*1983*	*1985*
TWO-YEAR INSTITUTIONS							
Full-time	642,710	1,290,548	1,905,000	2,077,000	2,209,000	2,269,000	2,248,000
Part-time	530,242	1,195,363	2,559,000	2,926,000	3,325,000	3,431,000	3,431,000
Public	1,041,264	2,365,867	4,323,000	4,856,000	5,290,000	5,543,000	5,580,000
Private	131,688	120,044	141,000	147,000	154,000	157,000	157,000
Degree-credit	841,000	1,725,000	2,834,000	3,130,000	3,361,000	3,480,000	3,470,000
Nondegree-credit	332,000	761,000	1,630,000	1,873,000	2,083,000	2,220,000	2,267,000
Total	1,172,952	2,485,911	4,464,000	5,003,000	5,444,000	5,700,000	5,737,000
FOUR-YEAR INSTITUTIONS							
Full-time	3,439,547	4,786,684	5,315,000	5,408,000	5,406,000	5,276,000	4,995,000
Part-time	1,308,365	1,676,049	2,367,000	2,517,000	2,627,000	2,667,000	2,628,000
Public	2,928,332	4,438,442	5,393,000	5,608,000	5,722,000	5,689,000	5,490,000
Private	1,819,580	2,061,976	2,289,000	2,317,000	2,311,000	2,254,000	1,133,000
Degree-credit	4,685,000	6,391,000	7,589,000	7,832,000	7,940,000	7,850,000	7,530,000
Nondegree-credit	63,000	72,000	93,000	93,000	93,000	93,000	93,000
Total	4,747,912	6,462,733	7,682,000	7,925,000	8,033,000	7,943,000	7,623,000

Note: Figures for 1977–1986 are projected.
Chronicle of Higher Education, 19 September 1977, p. 8. Reprinted with permission.

TABLE 1–3 College and University Enrollments

	1965	*1971*	*1977*	*1979*	*1981*	*1983*	*1985*
Full-time*	4,082,257	6,072,389	7,220,000	7,485,000	7,615,000	7,545,000	7,243,000
Part-time*	1,838,607	2,871,412	4,926,000	5,443,000	5,862,000	6,098,000	6,117,000
Public	3,969,596	6,804,309	9,716,000	10,464,000	11,012,000	11,232,000	11,070,000
Private	1,951,268	2,144,335	2,430,000	2,464,000	2,465,000	2,411,000	2,290,000
Degree-credit	5,526,000	8,116,000	10,423,000	10,962,000	11,301,000	11,330,000	11,000,000
Nondegree-credit	841,000	1,725,000	1,723,000	1,966,000	2,176,000	2,313,000	2,360,000
Total	5,920,864	8,948,644	12,146,000	12,928,000	13,477,000	13,643,000	13,360,000

* Estimated for 1965
Chronicle of Higher Education, 19 September 1977, p. 8. Reprinted with permission.

time and part-time students.[5] Overall enrollment for Fall 1978 was reported at 11,354,765 students, reflecting a drop of 0.5 percent.[6] With the decline in the traditional college population, enrollment of the nontraditional students is expected to increase, but the total enrollment will eventually reflect a loss as shown in Tables 1–2 and 1–3.

The implications of the changes in enrollment patterns cannot be ignored. As the traditional college age group declines in number, colleges and universities are looking for new markets and innovative ways to serve new social demands. The size of this additional market will be an important factor in their future financial health.

Inflation

Most financial difficulties can be related to inflation. While the rate may slow down at times, the inflationary trend is expected to continue in the foreseeable future. Inflation has been particularly destructive because it has not been accompanied by any offsets such as large increases in income from tuition, endowments, gifts, and increased appropriations from state and federal governments.

There will be no relief from higher costs, most of which are in the salary area. As general wage inflation continues, these costs will continue to rise. A high percentage of faculty are tenured, which means they are in the higher salary brackets. Costs of services in areas such as food and maintenance will increase as a result of the same wage inflation. In addition to increasing salary costs, the rapidly escalating cost for energy is creating concern. Increasingly larger proportions of available funds are being used to operate the physical plant which, in turn, decreases the amount of available funds for other vital services.

Decreasing Government Aid

Federal aid began to level off in the 1970s after doubling in the 1960s. As much as 14 percent and, in some places, 20 percent of an institution's total income has come from the federal government. Funds are being shifted to student grants and loans rather than previously emphasized programs and construction. Cutbacks in research funding are affecting graduate schools. At the same time, "total expenditures for higher education climbed from $5.2 billion in 1957–58 to about $17.2 billion in 1967–68 and were estimated at $41 billion in 1976–77."[7]

Primary responsibility for higher education has belonged to the states, which have provided both initiative and funds. The state colleges and universities along with the more recently established two-year community colleges are examples of state efforts. Legislators and the public they represent have become dollar conscious and education must compete more and more with other institutions and agencies for its share of funds.

The picture becomes more complicated by the numerous funding formulas used by the various states. Any number of the following components may be found:

1. Number of students enrolled;
2. Geographical location of campuses;
3. College status of development in terms of campus and curriculum;
4. Type of curricular program and/or distribution of instructional discipline enrollments; and
5. College program functions: (a) instruction and research, (b) extension and public service, (c) library and learning resources, (d) student services, (e) administration and institutional support, and (f) plant operation and maintenance.
6. Responsive mechanism to adjust to inflationary trends;
7. Categorical funding—for faculty and staff development;
8. Cost differences involving maintaining an existing program vs implementing a new one;
9. Plant funding.[8]

Need for Financial Efficiency

Tuition fees are rising, but tuition alone is not sufficient to fill the gap between income and expenditures. At the same time, endowments and endowment income are rising very little, corporate giving is decreasing, and tax incentives for private donations are diminishing. For some colleges, bankruptcy is obvious; for others, programs will be cut and staff reduction accompanied by pressure for increased faculty productivity is inevitable.

State and federal governments are forcing administrators to account for the allocation of public money in more detail and in standard formats. Decisions for spending must be rigorously justified. In the long run, greater institutional efficiency should result, although some emergency cost-cutting may affect quality.

Among the systems being adopted by institutions in an effort to improve efficiency are the planning, budgeting, programming approach (PPBS) initially introduced in the Department of Defense and zero-based budgeting. Of course, these kinds of approaches must be modified in some way to make them more appropriate for use in college and university settings. They do, however, make it possible for administrators to gain greater control over costs and to rationalize cutbacks in programs and services.

In practice, a number of general approaches in various combinations were found in a study by the Carnegie Commission. The report describes six approaches being used in various combinations, thus making funds available for expansion in some programs and the development of new programs while achieving cutbacks in others. The approaches found were: (1) selective cutbacks, (2) across-the-board percentage cuts in budgets, (3) consolidation of existing programs, (4) readaptation of existing programs, (5) application of Harvard's "every tub on its own bottom" approach, and (6) central reassignment of vacated positions.[9]

As one views the problems created by declining student enrollments occurring simultaneously with a serious recession in the general economy, it becomes clear that improved management and administrative techniques are needed. The decline in the demand for faculty members, decreased opportunities for advancement of younger faculty members, reductions in government support for research, and the failure of increases in faculty salaries to keep pace with the rise in the cost of living reflect the changing conditions. A 1974 study by the Carnegie Council on Policy Studies in Higher Education disclosed that 10 percent of the 1200 colleges and universities surveyed expected to respond to the situation by undergoing radical change such as merger, consolidation, or closure by 1980. At the same time, colleges and universities are being urged to improve their productivity by increasing student-teacher ratios, eliminating esoteric courses, adopting more efficient administrative procedures, and cooperating with neighboring institutions on academic programs.[10] Another possible alternative to be added to those just listed is instructional cooperation through joint use of faculty within and between institutions.

LEGISLATIVE AND LEGAL RESTRAINTS

Pressures from external sources are being felt in addition to the financial restraints with which institutions must cope. State governments are examining institutional operations in detail and emphases in funding by the federal and state governments are changing accompanied by demands for a closer accounting. The growing number of court decisions affecting higher education make for an increasingly turbulent environment with which administrators must cope. Many necessary decisions will be financial ones, and because administrators are responsible for fiscal control, there will be increasing authority in the administrative hierarchy. It is inevitable that academic situations will become more structured.

State and Federal Influences

Paul Dressel and William Faricy make a strong statement when they say, "Autonomy fathered irresponsibility" and proceed to explain further:

> Autonomy, fed by federal grants and contracts as well as state funds, became virtually synonomous with academic freedom and with professional competency. Since professional competence clearly rests in the faculty, the role of administration, boards, legislators (in the faculty conception) was not to reason why but simply find the cash. . . . This is inconsistent with the view that the university (whether public or private) exists to carry out certain purposes delegated by society and must fulfill these purposes as effectively and economically as possible.[11]

As costs continue to rise at a rate of 7 to 10 percent and income is unable to keep up, state legislators are looking at institutional operations more closely than ever. Tenure, professional load, programs, and budget are all coming under their close scrutiny. State legislatures and the public they represent are becoming increasingly concerned about obtaining a maximum return on the dollars spent for education. To illustrate, legislatures in Arizona, Kansas, Missouri, and other states have set student/faculty ratios.

State subsidization carries with it state review of the quality of institutions. New York, for example, has moved toward a state coordinated assessment of the quality of programs. Outside consultants are used in addition to the institutions' self-assessments. If the state feels a program is no longer justified, it must be discontinued. Precedent developed for supporting state authority in a program area when the New York Supreme Court ruled that the New York Education Department has the authority to close doctoral programs offered by the State University of New York. The state department evaluation has already resulted in the closing of a number of programs throughout the state.

An important developing trend at the state level is the shift from institutional subsidies to student subsidies. Providing grants directly to students not only permits them greater choices in selecting the schools they wish to attend but also gives students a larger role in deciding which institutions will survive. This change indirectly assists the private institutions, which are needed to balance the kinds of educational opportunities available.

State coordinating boards are being established to develop and maintain state plans for higher education. They are generally of two types. In the first, individual boards of various state institutions of higher education are replaced by a single statewide board of control. This type of organization may be found in approximately fifteen states including Florida, Iowa, and Kansas. Unfortunately, little statewide coordination takes place with this arrangement because internal institutional management is so time consuming. The second type is the master board placed above individual local boards, examples of which may be found in Oklahoma, California, Texas, Illinois, and Wisconsin.[12]

Brubacher and Rudy identify two dimensions in state coordination. The vertical aspect deals with educational programs from the baccalaureate through the doctorate. A horizontal approach has to do with the geographical distribution of academic programs over the state. There has even been some regional activity such as the Southern Regional Education Board established in 1948, The Western Interstate Commission for Higher Education (WICHE) in existence since 1953, and the New England States organization dating back to 1954. The scope of their activity is illustrated by the

Southern Regional Board consisting of sixteen states working together to coordinate their systems of higher education so as to avoid uneconomical duplications of services and make possible more effective use of joint facilities.[13]

Dressel and Faricy observe that such moves inevitably tend toward

1. designation of institutional and departmental roles to avoid unnecessary duplication within a state,
2. approval of new programs and degrees to ensure that they are actually needed and that funds are available for their support,
3. development of an appropriations formula based upon instructional load, and
4. both position and salary control.[14]

Other effects, not undesirable, might be a more equitable distribution of resources, a more diverse system of higher education, and institutional improvement resulting from the external pressure for self-examination and development of long-range plans. Some middle ground is needed that will provide institutions with the autonomy necessary for effective operation and, at the same time, yield the greatest return for the funds expended.

Federal agencies are having an impact not only by reducing available funds but also by increasing requirements for justification for obtaining funds and accounting for them afterwards. Obtaining grants for research requires formulation of related policy statements and accreditation by the appropriate approval agencies. Affirmative action requirements are another way in which the government has imposed restrictions. Faculty, staff, and student personnel policies are subject to federal scrutiny. As a result, institutions desiring to receive federal money, among other requirements, present for approval their plans for correcting any existing discriminatory practices in hiring, promotion, and salary rewards for women and minorities. A third example of federal influence is the famed Buckley Amendment which made it necessary for colleges and universities to examine their procedures for handling student records and, in many instances, to establish new ones which included newly formulated restrictions on access to student information.

Both state legislatures and federal government agencies can affect institutional operation and expenditures by the patterns through which they make money available. Questions they raise, data they request, and recommendations they make in the process all have an influence. The large number of laws and regulations has led to a proliferation of paper work that has become "staggering."

While colleges and universities need state support and protection, they also need to be protected from state intrusion into academic and other matters that should be the responsibility of the institution. In other words, guidelines defining limitations on state regulation are needed. The same might be said of federal regulation.

Legal Restrictions

Administrators have the responsibility to create and maintain an appropriate environment for education. They must be reasonable and fair in carrying out this responsibility. However, their professional autonomy is being increasingly diluted by legal decisions made in the courts. The dominant issues have been summarized as access, participation, representation, and extended privilege. At this point, faculty members have acquired property rights on the conditions of employment, the right to unionize and engage in collective bargaining, and representation in most matters of policy and decision directly affecting their civil and property rights.[15]

The student protest activities of the 1960s led to a number of court decisions that grew out of the dismissal and suspension of students. As O'Neil states, these decisions defined "the range of student conduct protected by the first amendment" and "procedures to be followed in punishing student transgressors." Resort to the courts will probably increase as colleges and universities seek protection against external influences and pressures and as excluded groups seek to participate in decision making. An increasingly strict standard of review by the courts will follow challenges to departures from neutrality in admissions and employment policies while fiscal problems may provide additional incentives for litigation.[16]

Judicial rulings have already extended beyond the area of student activism. The California Supreme Court upheld an earlier decision that declared a preferential admission program using racial quotas as a basis for admission to special programs unconstitutional. In the same case, now identified as the Bakke case, the United States Supreme Court ruled that Alan Bakke was illegally denied admission to medical school because he did not have the opportunity to compete for sixteen of the one hundred spaces available which had been reserved for black applicants. While the University of California at Davis was ordered to admit Bakke in September, 1978, admission programs using race as one factor when considering applicants were not considered illegal. Time is needed to fully interpret the seemingly contradictory decision. Meanwhile, the decision did result in a careful examination of admission policies by many colleges and universities. As mentioned earlier, the New York State Supreme Court ruled that the State Department of Education did have the authority to close doctoral programs offered by the State University of New York. The courts have also contravened actions dealing with nonreappointment of faculty members. The question of institutional autonomy versus state authority is expected to be raised in a number of ways as well as the whole question of public funding for both public and private schools.

Demands for Accountability

Administrators and faculty members must deal with the demands developing from taxpayers' pressure for increased accountability. In other words, they must be responsible for the "outputs" as related to the resources or "inputs." Governmental agencies are requiring closer screening with more statistics and more frequent reports. Laissez-faire operations are no longer tolerated. Faculty members are demanding accountability from their institutions and, in return, institutions are demanding faculty accountability. Performance standards and methods for measuring effectiveness are becoming increasingly important for everyone at all levels in the educational enterprise including the board of trustees.

NEW MANAGEMENT TECHNIQUES

Colleges and universities are being charged with inefficiency and accused of ineffectiveness in their efforts to cope with changing societal demands. In some instances, state legislatures and boards of trustees are pressuring them to adopt the operational procedures of other organizations believed to be more efficient. As a result, entire institutions are seeking to develop more effective and efficient operational procedures, but caution must be exercised so that quantitative measures do not take precedence over the qualitative. Efficiency may be defined as the "capacity to achieve results with a given expenditure of resources" and effectiveness as the "degree of success an organization enjoys in doing whatever it is trying to do."[17] There is a need to find ways to increase effectiveness and, at the same time, reduce costs in order to improve efficiency. Human productivity as an essential resource must be increased, but it must be accompanied by objective evaluation of job performance. Finally, waste through poor maintenance and utilization of space and physical plant can no longer be tolerated.

Not all new techniques necessarily save money but they do help to avoid costly mistakes and to make more rational decisions. They should be used with discretion and expertise; otherwise, they could have the opposite effect and result in decreased effectiveness and efficiency.

Goals and Planning

Edward Gross and Paul V. Grambsch submitted questionnaires to presidents, vice-presidents, deans, and directors plus a carefully selected sample of department chairpersons and faculty at eighty major universities in the United States. They summarized their major findings on goals as follows:

> The top goals of American universities revolved about support functions, led by the goal of protecting the academic freedom of the faculty, as well as related goals having to do with the careers of the faculty. Students and teaching of undergraduates were generally assigned places near the bottom of the list of 47 goals. The overall findings suggested that output goals in universities were being taken for granted and that attention was being given to institutionalizing the internal operations of the organization. When respondents were asked which goals they felt should be emphasized, students and teaching occupied higher positions, suggesting a guilty conscience, a conclusion supported by feelings about "sins of omission." There was a feeling that students deserved more attention, that there should be more loyalty to the institution on the part of the faculty, and less emphasis on cosmopolitan values.[18]

More self-examination of the kind described above is needed. The rapidly changing environment in which education finds itself is forcing institutions to establish statements of mission and goals. The period of growth for the sake of growth and growth without planning has passed. Institutions and all those connected with them must develop a clear idea of what they are attempting to accomplish and a means for assessing their accomplishment. Vagueness in goals will result in a lack of evaluation.

Educators have been unable to agree upon the major goals of education for a long time. It is becoming apparent that they must work toward some agreement even though some may have to compromise to do so. In addition, institutional goals must fit in with the goal system of the state and federal governments, alumni, parents, students, and other sources of funding if the institutions are to continue obtaining funds.

FACULTY AND STUDENT INVOLVEMENT

Until the early 1960s, many decisions were made solely by administrators and then announced or, unfortunately, they were sometimes not announced yet implemented. Students and faculty began demanding participation in governance and their participation rapidly increased so that by the early 1970s the decision-making process became one that involved wide participation and could be characterized as decentralized. Tripartite committees composed of administrators, faculty, and students became an accepted model for policy development and decision making as well as for the selection of administrators including department chairpersons, deans, student affairs administrators, and others. The whole area of governance has become much more complex to organize and manage, particularly since the extent of involvement and role of students has never been completely clarified. Finally, the full impact of the collective bargaining movement has not yet been felt.

Implications of Faculty Unionism

Unionization of the faculty provides a power base from which pressures are exerted through the collective bargaining process. As retrenchment efforts increase and personnel are laid off or denied tenure, it is only natural that this power base will become increasingly active. Work load, salary adjustments, promotion policies, and fringe benefits will continue to be issues. In addition, the advent of collective bargaining on a campus makes necessary a redefinition of the role of existing faculty structures, such as the senate, so that the two may complement one another.

The Student Voice

The widespread student activity of the years past has led to student membership on numerous committees and participation in widespread decision making that, in some instances, may have been not only irrelevant to students but also unrelated to their areas of knowledge and expertise. Once the high enthusiasm of their initial victories waned, students tended to lose interest and withdraw; they tend to concentrate their efforts in those areas that affect them most.

Areas most pertinent at the collegial level include the evaluation of faculty members and courses. At the institutional level, conduct codes, housing, special services, and recreational programs, for example, open a much broader area for student involvement. As tuition increases are implemented and financial aid becomes more difficult to obtain, increased activity from students can be expected not only at the local level but also at the state level as they bring pressure upon legislators.

THE CHALLENGE

What lies ahead? During the 1960s, growth in higher education was phenomenal. Dramatically increasing enrollments and availability of seemingly endless financial resources resulted in a quantitative expansion never before experienced. Higher education is demonstrating vitality and ability to adapt to the changes and grow in quality as it

> . . . is attempting to develop new products, i.e., new courses, programs, degrees; new methods of production, i.e., improving instructional and noninstructional productivity; new markets, i.e., new sources of students; new productive factors, i.e., dollar resources; and is reorganizing and restructuring the enterprise.[19]

SUMMARY

Numerous factors provide a new challenge to college and university administrators. Among these factors are the changing patterns of race relations, a new consciousness of ethnic backgrounds, and changes in the role of women. Problems of the urban areas and the environment cannot be ignored, yet restrictive pressures resulting from economic, legislative, and legal restraints exist. It is more important than ever that administrators utilize the talents and efforts of faculty and students as well as appropriate technical innovations and new management techniques in meeting the challenges posed by the need for reform and reorganization in higher education.

The remaining chapters provide more detail

about the implications of these challenges as well as describing the kinds of administrators needed to meet them.

ENDNOTES

1. "Report Card on U.S. Higher Education," *Intellect* 102 (1973): 4.
2. Ellen K. Coughlin, "Minority Enrollments Up 11.7 Pct. in Two Years," *The Chronicle of Higher Education,* 8 November 1976, p. 7.
3. Used with permission. *A Digest of Reports of the Carnegie Commission on Higher Education.* Copyright © 1974 by The Carnegie Foundation for the Advancement of Teaching (New York: McGraw-Hill, 1974), p. 57.
4. From an address by Patricia Carry Stewart at the 14th Biennial Workshop of the Eastern Association of College and University Business Officers, New York City, March, 1977.
5. *The Chronicle of Higher Education,* 26 June 1978, p. 7.
6. *The Bulletin* (Philadelphia), 19 December 1978, p. 15.
7. Used with permission. *A Digest of Reports of the Carnegie Commission on Higher Education.* Copyright © 1974 by the Carnegie Commission for the Advancement of Teaching, p. 65.
8. Marvin A. Rapp, "Community Colleges: Coming Years of Uncertainty" (A paper prepared for the New Jersey Business Officers Annual Conference, May 1977), pp. 12–13.
9. The Carnegie Commission on Higher Education, *The More Effective Use of Resources* (New York: McGraw-Hill Book Co., 1972), p. 94.
10. Ford Foundation, *Paying for Schools and Colleges* (New York: Ford Foundation, 1976), p. 32.
11. Paul L. Dressel and William H. Faricy, *Return to Responsibility: Constraints on Autonomy in Higher Education* (San Francisco: Jossey-Bass, 1972), p. 2.
12. John S. Brubacher and Willis Rudy, *Higher Education in Transition,* 3rd ed. rev. (New York: Harper and Row, 1976), p. 386.
13. *Ibid.,* p. 408.
14. Dressel and Faricy, *Return to Responsibility,* p. 155.
15. Cameron Fincher, "On the Rational Solution of Dominant Issues in Higher Education," *Journal of Higher Education* 46 (1975): 494.
16. Robert M. O'Neil, "The Colleges and the Courts: A Peacetime Perspective," *Liberal Education* 59 (1973): 176–177.
17. Francis E. Rourke and Glenn E. Brooks, *The Managerial Revolution* (Baltimore: The John Hopkins Press, 1966), p. 11.
18. Used with permission. *Changes in University Organization, 1964–1971* by Edward Gross and Paul V. Grambsch. Copyright © 1974 by The Carnegie Foundation for the Advancement of Teaching (New York: McGraw-Hill, 1974), p. 197.
19. Larry L. Leslie and Howard F. Miller, Jr., *Higher Education and the Steady State* (Washington, D.C.: American Association for Higher Education) ERIC/Higher Education Research Report No. 4, 1974, Foreword.

CHAPTER 2

Collegial Administrative Roles

Collegial administrative structures may range from rather simple organizations to ones that are part of a more complex university structure. Regardless of the complexity of an organization, similarities may be found in many of the relationships, duties, and functions expected of and assumed by deans and other administrative personnel within a collegial organization. Some basic concepts related to these administrative roles are presented in this chapter. Emphasis is placed upon roles and relationships within the collegial organization itself rather than within the context of any larger, more complex organization of which the college may be a component.

ADMINISTRATION AND ORGANIZATIONAL EFFECTIVENESS

Administrators must remain flexible enough to respond constantly to the many changing characteristics of their environments while working toward achievement of the goals of their particular institutions. The task becomes increasingly burdensome as institutions grow in complexity. In addition, administration becomes more difficult during a time of decline or even a steady state period than it is during periods of rapid expansion. Administrators are now performing more functions and are faced with an ever increasing technological sophistication that tends to foster centralization of functions. As a result, the growing emphasis on organizational effectiveness, development, and change makes the future of any organizational pattern uncertain.

A Goal-Oriented Approach

Organizations are developed for specific functions expressed in their goals and objectives. Obviously, these goals and objectives cannot remain static if the organization is to be a vital one. A major responsibility attached to educational leadership is establishing some vehicle for a continuous review and revision of the statements of the direction for that institution's efforts towards self-renewal and keeping abreast of the changing needs of its constituency. Included also is the need to plan for the achievement of established goals. Who is to do what, when, and where must be determined. Decisions including financial ones must be made. Financial planning is a most important part of the overall planning process for achieving the purposes of the institution as they relate to students, the various constituencies, and the curriculum. Whatever the goals and planning for their ultimate achievement may be, the primary concern must be the extent to which students will benefit.

A constant problem in any organization is that of obtaining agreement upon organizational goals that are congruent with the personal goals of individuals in that organization. Any changes must be based upon consideration of what has been and currently is as the starting point. To "start from scratch" when an organization already exists is not feasible. Change for the sake of change is not acceptable. The administrator's task is to find collaborative ways for members of the organization to work toward common goals through carefully planned change. The cooperation, knowledge, and experience of all concerned is essential.

Need for Organization

When an essential task becomes too great for one person, some kind of organization must be developed to accomplish it. As a result, the larger the task, the greater the number of individuals who become involved, each with responsibility for some segment. Coordination of the activities becomes more difficult. Communication systems must be developed so that people know who is doing what, why and how it is being accomplished, and where it is being accomplished. An organization consists of people, procedures, and resources which function as a unit (even though it may consist of a number of subunits) to accomplish specific goals. The success or effectiveness of the organization is determined by how well it succeeds in accomplishing its goals.

Increasing attention is being given to the organizational development concept and approaches sometimes referred to as OD. Among the concerns of organizational development is the interaction between and among an organization's leaders and its members and the direction the organization will take in response to environmental factors. Organizations can become more effective and vital through active organizational development.

Basically, organizational development is a concept applied to bringing about planned organizational change. It encompasses the fields of psychology, sociology, and education in the attempt to deal with people and their interpersonal relationships. Its ultimate objective is to create a climate of trust and cooperation in which both personal and institutional goals may be achieved. The concept is being applied to higher education in an attempt to bring individuals to a point where they will work well together. Unless this happens, any change in the system will be difficult to implement.

McGannon describes the complexity of the task as follows:

> . . . the organization of a college or university involves many devices for review and concurrence which might frustrate a person whose experience has been in industry. Not only must the organization of a college promote response to ideas emanating from the central academic leadership but it must be open to ideas from other sources and ensure sensitivity to widely diverse points of judgment. The sources of ideas and the loci of judgments occur in every school, department, and program as well as in a broad spectrum of functional and status categories: the general faculty (both collectively and individually), administrative officers, staff, student body, alumni, trustees, donors and even government.[1]

Colleges and universities face a unique problem. As educational institutions, they are composed of professionals who work together in a mode quite different from that of a government agency or a business firm. Their aim is effective education and research. Their structures are more horizontal than vertical and their activities centralized. While the structures in higher education are not those usually found in a business enterprise, there is still a need for organization and management. Housing, food services, heat, light, equipment, housekeeping, and other services are all operational concerns that cannot be ignored.

Cohen and March offer an interesting viewpoint when they describe the American college and university as belonging to a class of organizations referred to as organized anarchies. They define an organized anarchy as "any organizational setting that exhibits the following general properties:

1. Problematic goals which are vague, ill-defined, a loose collection of changing ideas which are not a coherent structure
2. Unclear technology meaning it does not understand its own processes and operates on trial and error learning from the accidents of past experience, imitation, and the inventions born of necessity
3. Fluid participation where participants themselves vary and who also vary in the amount of time and effort they devote to the organization.[2]

As colleges and universities move toward organizational change and implementation of a management approach, difficulties arise because—

> Much of our present theory of management introduces mechanisms for control and coordination that assume the existence of well-defined goals and technology, as well as substantial participant involvement in the affairs of the organization. When goals and technology are hazy and participation is fluid, many of the axioms and standard procedures of management collapse.[3]

Some form of management structure is needed to make an institution effective in accomplishing its educational and operational tasks and accountable for that effectiveness. Institutional mission and goals, the nature of the people involved, resources available, and external environmental factors all play a part in determining that structure. Effective evaluative techniques are another important concern. Because of the variations in the factors above, there is no one organizational design that can be appropriate for every college.

Management or Administration

More and more the term *management* is applied to the operation of colleges and universities in place of the previously used term *administration*. There are differences in opinion about the definition and breadth of the two functions. Some view administration as leadership while management deals with day-to-day routine operations. Others see administration as the routine function focusing on implementation of policy and provision of administrative support to programs with management defined in broader terms. Richman and Farmer take the latter stance in their comprehensive definitions of the two.

> Management involves strategy, innovation, initiating and bringing out change, creative problem solving and decision making, actively seeking out alternatives and opportunities, reformulating goals and priorities, redeploying resources, negotiating, resolving conflicts, dynamic or active leadership, diplomacy, statesmanship, and a high degree of risk-taking and entrepreneurship. Administration implies more routine decision making and operations, and the implementation of goals, priorities, and strategies usually determined by others. It is more concerned with following predetermined policies, procedures, and regulations. It tends to be more adaptive, passive, and reactive than management and it is much more of a closed system concept primarily concerned with internal efficiency and operations. It is also more concerned with internal monitoring and control than with external environmental change and strategic planning.[4]

College administrators will continue to be called administrators not managers. They must, however, delegate routine administrative functions to others in the organization so as to be able to provide the kind of leadership described above as management. This broader comprehensive concept of administration will be applied throughout the remainder of this text.

Efficiency versus Effectiveness

A vital concern is articulated by Henderson and Henderson.

> It is essential in college administration that a distinction be maintained between the concept of efficiency and that of effectiveness. A janitor can be judged by his efficiency; a learning experience or the investigation of a hypothesis must be judged by its effectiveness—the degree to which the objectives have been achieved.[5]

There is no way to assess either efficiency or effectiveness. Efficiency is often time related and equated with a quantitative measure of output, particularly in industry. Some individuals view larger class size as a means for improving efficiency. While increasing class size might produce financial savings, it may not be efficient because the resulting learning situation may be less effective. Instead, policies that save money and avoid duplication of effort are needed and may have to be enforced by the dean or even some figure in the central administrative hierarchy. There is a real need to examine the issues of resource allocation in particular.

Questions such as the following might be asked: Would a centralized clerical operation be better than one dispersed throughout departmental offices? What duplications in course offerings are there throughout the institution? How can the duplication be eliminated? How may faculty resources be most effectively used? Is the current system for faculty involvement in decision making the most efficient for utilizing faculty talent and time? In view of decreasing enrollments in a particular area, would collapsing a division of several departments into a single department provide a more efficient organizational structure? These are but a few possibilities for a serious self-examination.

Determining the level of effectiveness becomes more difficult. It may be necessary to determine whether the ends or the means for achieving them are of greater value. Goals are often so long range that it becomes difficult to measure the level of achievement at any particular point. For this reason, short-term objectives become important for assessing effectiveness.

Some assessment of morale, absenteeism, level of employee turnover, and group cohesiveness may be helpful in determining effectiveness in areas such as support staff. In-service activities might be instituted in an attempt to improve the effectiveness of teaching.

Caution must be exercised to prevent an overemphasis on efficiency since this could result in low morale, staff and faculty recruitment problems, impaired quality of performance, and cynicism and even dishonesty on the part of some individuals. There is a need to try to increase productivity and operating efficiency without seriously hindering academic effectiveness.

Ways have been developed and instituted for achieving greater efficiency in areas such as the business operations, student record keeping, and day-to-day institutional operations through the use of new developments in technology, particularly the computer. Unfortunately, the same cannot be said for instructional situations. While some educators find the application of the concept of efficiency to classroom situations abhorrent, it becomes difficult to argue against the concept of finding the most efficient means for developing the most effective learning situation and accomplishing the established objectives. The educational enterprise has a difficult task ahead.

The Need for Policies

One of the means for achieving organizational consistency and continuity is a comprehensive set of policies, which are then undergirded by appropriate procedures. Policies facilitate the delegation of authority and serve as a means and a guide for efficient and consistent decision making. Bogue and Riggs identify three levels of policy for colleges and universities:

1. Governing policies: Those policies of mission and program and general operating conditions set by governing agencies.
2. Executive policies: Those policies of fiscal, facility, and personnel management established by the president and the chief executive officers in response to governing policy.
3. Operating policies: Those policies of work environment and expectations set by deans and directors of activities in response to executive policy.[6]

Policies at one level must often be supplemented at the next lower level. For example, an institutional policy might state that funds will be allocated to support faculty attendance at professional conferences. At the college and department levels, this must be supplemented by policies that guarantee equitable distribution of the available funds and be accompanied by a set of procedures for distributing the funds.

It is common to find statements labeled policies that are actually combinations of policy and procedures as is the one below taken verbatim from a negotiated contract.

POLICY ON SABBATICAL LEAVE
(as found in
Faculty–Board Agreement)

Sabbatical leaves shall be granted by the Board, subject to the following conditions:

a. A faculty member will be eligible for sabbatical leave after completion of 7 years of continuous service at the college, or after 7 years since his sabbatical leave at the college.
b. Such leaves must be applied for during the first semester of the preceding year, with the specific study or research purpose clearly stated in the application.
c. Applications shall be submitted to the President.
d. After careful consideration of all applications, the President shall make his recommendation to the Board. Final decision on granting sabbatical leaves shall rest with the Board.
e. Sabbatical leave may be for 1 or 2 semesters at half pay.
f. Sabbatical leaves are not subject to the grievance procedures of this agreement.

The policy might be stated simply as:

> The Board shall grant study leaves for one or two semesters at half pay. To be eligible, faculty members shall have completed seven years of continuous service at the college or seven years since their last sabbatical leave at the college.

The remaining items are actually procedures that have been agreed upon through the collective bargaining mechanism.

Policies should be stated simply and be as few in number as possible. They must not be overly restrictive, but should provide leeway for administrative judgment where warranted. Also, policies should be stated in positive rather than negative terms. Constant feedback from the operating level is needed so that policies are reviewed and revised as needed. Too often, written policies become obsolete and are replaced by informal policies that have developed out of operational procedures which could easily lead to abuses.

Development and implementation of policies require two-way communication. Those who are to be affected by a policy should be involved in its formulation in some representative way. Procedures must be communicated to those who are involved in the implementation of a particular policy and, as previously mentioned, constant feedback from the operating level is needed. In this way, policies will be more acceptable to those affected and will be more responsive to changing circumstances. The faculty role in policy development is discussed in greater detail in Chapter 7.

Authority and Power

Authority in institutions of higher education is based on both the bureaucratic structure of the institution and the nature of its collegiality. In the formal bureaucratic structure, individuals are responsible for specific areas. Each area with its organization is responsible to the next larger domain. An orderly, reasonable structure is essential. Relationships within the bureaucratic structure must be well defined, as well as relationships between that structure and the other authority base emanating from officially created groups including committees, task forces, advisory boards, and study groups. Unless authority lines are clearly defined, chaos will result. Finally, authority beyond that assigned must not be assumed by any individual or group. To do so creates problems and will lead to decreasing effectiveness, accompanied by increasing conflict.

While an organizational chart may depict line and staff relationships on paper, the power structure of a college or university reflects the way things really are. Various groups, internal and external, are constantly vying for power so that it becomes an administrative task to understand the nature of the power struggle and minimize conflicts so that the progress of the institution is not hindered. These conflicts tend to increase when serious financial problems develop.

Gross and Grambsch, who conducted a study on changes in university organization between 1964 and 1971, found the power structure of 1971 unchanged from that of 1964 and reported that:

> The examination of university power structures has led to the conclusion that the major cleavage in power to influence university goals is one that pits "outsiders" against "insiders," rather than the celebrated split between faculty and administrators.[7]

"Insiders," of course, are deans, chairpersons, faculty, and students while "outsiders" are composed of legislators, state and federal governments, regents, and citizens. Unless groups are cohesive, their power is dissipated. Deans are viewed as wielding power and some individuals do because of strong personal traits but, in most instances, deans are not a powerful group because they are vying for resources. Chairpersons are also competing for budget resources in addition to which their differing academic orientations set the stage for competition.

Henderson and Henderson describe four types of power, one or more of which form the power structure of an institution. The first of these is power derived from the delegation of authority by those who have the legal authority to confer it, which is recognized as legitimate authority. The second is that derived as a result of the expertise of faculty, administrators, and staff who possess certain kinds of expertise and "want to be consulted when a problem involves their sphere of interest." As the writers point out, "When any of these experts are consulted, their advice and recommendations may be so influential as to control the decisions."

A third kind of power is that used by individuals or groups whom administrators might use as informal consultants for a discussion of problems and possible solutions. The last is power attained by individuals as a result of a "charismatic personality," or a kind of "missionary zeal for some cause," or because they have been "successful in building a power block." The first of the four types of power might be described as power belonging to and/

or emanating from the formal structure of the organization while the remainder are of an informal nature.[8]

Ultimately, both power and authority rest in the board of trustees, the state governing board, or whatever the governing body of the institution might be. The authority of these bodies results from the original charter of the institution but their power, in reality, results from their veto power.

Role of Administrators

Providing broad, general direction to the organization is a primary responsibility of administrators. Clearly specified objectives, an identification of alternative routes to those objectives, and a choice among those alternatives are needed to develop that direction. Administrators also bear the responsibility for making available and managing human and material resources so that they will be effectively applied toward achieving the goals and objectives of the institution. This means that an administrator must have a clear picture of the organization to which he or she belongs and be constantly aware of the nature of that institution.

In educational institutions, it is more common for ideas and recommendations to be formulated by faculty and move upwards for administrative approval and implementation rather than move downward from the administration as directives. The administrator must encourage others in such a way as to release their creativity and initiative toward accomplishing the purposes of the institution. In other words, a climate must be established that is conducive to an orderly developmental process rather than a series of disruptive innovations. Yet, administrators with ideas must be free to initiate a flow of those ideas in the appropriate direction.

The role of the administrator is diversified in that it involves numerous activities including organizing, planning, directing, coordinating, and evaluating. The areas of responsibility to which these activities are related will vary according to the pattern of delegation of responsibility. Throughout, a most important activity will be dealing with the budget since it is through development of the budget that resources are made available for the accomplishment of institutional purposes. In summary, the administrators must not only make decisions as individuals but also help others make decisions as well, for administrators bear the ultimate responsibility for what happens within their own units.

THE DEAN

The dean is ultimately accountable for the college organization, but serves more as a leader and motivator than as a ruler by utilizing student and faculty participatory processes for the achievement of institutional purposes. It is a dean's responsibility to utilize all available resources to the fullest in translating these purposes into an organized program feasible of implementation within budgetary restraints. A formal structure must be maintained through which the division of work is defined, delegated, and coordinated. Within that structure, the dean is the key figure for moving the institution forward.

The dean's position involves problematic situations related to both personnel and resources. The successful dean learns to work effectively with colleagues rather than doing something for or to them. To do so, he or she must be viewed as absolutely honest, frank, and impartial, as well as one who can be trusted and is devoted to the welfare of the institution and the preservation of academic freedom. Finally, a dean must possess a high level of executive skill and make recommendations and decisions only after the most careful consideration. Rules, policies, and procedures must be administered uniformly since handling each case or situation individually will ultimately lead to chaos. The nature of the position and situations with which the dean must deal has a constant effect upon the individual's understandings, beliefs, perceptions, and attitudes. Deans are under constant scrutiny and frequently criticized, thus their role is an extremely complex and difficult one.

Leadership Responsibilities

A leadership style must be developed that will lead to the most effective utilization of available resources, most particularly those resources found among faculty. The age old question of authoritarianism versus a democratic approach arises, but either approach in its extreme will be unacceptable and ineffective. If both institutional and employee needs are to be met, a combination of the two should be utilized. The exact pattern of the combination will be determined by the nature of the situation and the individuals involved. Martha A. Brown in her study of eighteen public colleges and universities in four states found that professors prefer "a leader who presents problems, gets suggestions, makes decisions or defines limits, and asks his colleagues to help him make decisions, as opposed to more authoritarian decision-making arrangements." [9] While an individual has little control over those aspects of style governed by personality traits, the successful administrator must utilize a style that is acceptable to those above and below in the hierarchy.

Administration and leadership are synonomous. Administration that copes with daily problems and keeps the institution functioning is not enough nor will responding to complaints or using a "greasing the squeaky wheel" approach move an institution forward. The true educational leader provides ideas and direction while aiming for simplicity, efficiency, and coherence. Such an individual must also be capable of mediating conflict and attaining concurrence of the academic community in the determined direction and means for achieving the established objectives. Necessary resources must be made available as well as establishment of a climate within which people feel they are able to work effectively.

While descriptions of educational leadership are commonplace, ways are still being sought to determine factors making up leadership. Armand J. Galfo, following completion of his formal study of the topic, says, "In summary, the study supports the notion that neither the early researches, which merely focused on personality traits, nor the more recent ones, which have turned to leader behaviors and situational variables, are entirely satisfactory." [10]

The overriding question is whether the dean should really be a leader or only a catalyst of faculty opinion and decision making. While faculty opinion and participation in decision making are vital, particularly in the area of curriculum, strong educational leadership is needed if an institution is to move forward and keep abreast of rapidly changing times. Goals, programs, and resources, including human resources, are elements for which leadership must be provided. Leadership must lead. Mediating conflict or differing interests is not sufficient; decisions do have to be made and, all too frequently, they must be made quickly.

Tasks

Deans are the executive officers of their own divisions and, as such, are directly responsible to the next administrator in the hierarchy who may be a vice president for academic affairs or the president depending upon the size and nature of the institution. Deans' offices with their staffs have become facilitating operations and, in addition, have assumed many of the duties previously belonging to the presidents of small colleges. The exact tasks of a particular deanship and dean's office will vary

> with the nature and size of the institution, presidential assignments, local custom, written regulations, a dean's own qualities of mind and character and skill, the individual twist and group impact of faculty members, and the opinions of other academic deans which a particular dean absorbs into his own conception of office and profession.[11]

Common functions involve those related to goals of collegial education, the program for achieving the goals, and resources for implementation and evaluation of the effort. While more variation than standardization may be found, commonalities do exist. Variation is likely to be more in the degree of responsibility than in the actual nature of the responsibility.

John L. Cramer lists seven functions of administration with more specific activities under each. While his discussion is related to community colleges, the functions are descriptive of the general tasks faced by any dean (p. 24).

Other specific activities may be added to the functions listed that include obtaining data from department chairpersons, faculty, and students for use in planning and moving the organization toward achievement of its goals. Responsibility involves not only providing resources but also allocating them equitably and expediting repairs and alterations. Besides developing the college budget and securing the financial base, a dean is ultimately responsible for allocation of available funds, authorizing and approving expenditures, interpreting the fiscal situation and limits of fiscal possibility to faculty and department chairpersons, and, where necessary, convincing his or her constituency when there is no choice or alternative in times of financial stringency. The dean is accountable for determining who does what, how time is used, where the waste is, workload calculations, cost-effectiveness, etc.

While curriculum belongs to the faculty, the dean must see it in its totality and assure that it is achieving the agreed upon purposes of the college. The dean can spur discussion about stimulating issues and improve all over program by acting as a change agent through analyzing, questioning, challenging, stimulating, and persuading. To keep abreast of the field, the dean must read a wide range of current literature, and must review available institutional agenda, minutes, committee reports, grant applications, and program and course descriptions. The administrative role in curricular matters is discussed further in Chapter 8.

Another means for viewing the dean's responsibilities is to examine relationships with specific people and suborganizations, which would result in a pattern similar to that below.

- *President or Vice President:* Keeps them informed on major instructional projects, changes, and experiments under consideration; acts in an advisory capacity on academic and faculty matters; presents and justifies the college budget.
- *Central Support Offices:* Coordinates college procedures with central office requirements; maintains two-way communication; provides information upon request; serves in an advisory role for contemplated changes in policies and procedures at the central office level.
- *Departments:* Interprets administrative views and policies; stimulates growth and serves as an observer and resource person for program development; seeks ways to strengthen departmental functions while, at the same time, resolving competition between departments.
- *Faculty:* Acquaints faculty with institutional problems; tells them what they need to know; encourages them to broaden their competence by experimentation and research and yet retain their identity with the college and satisfy institutional requirements; pro-

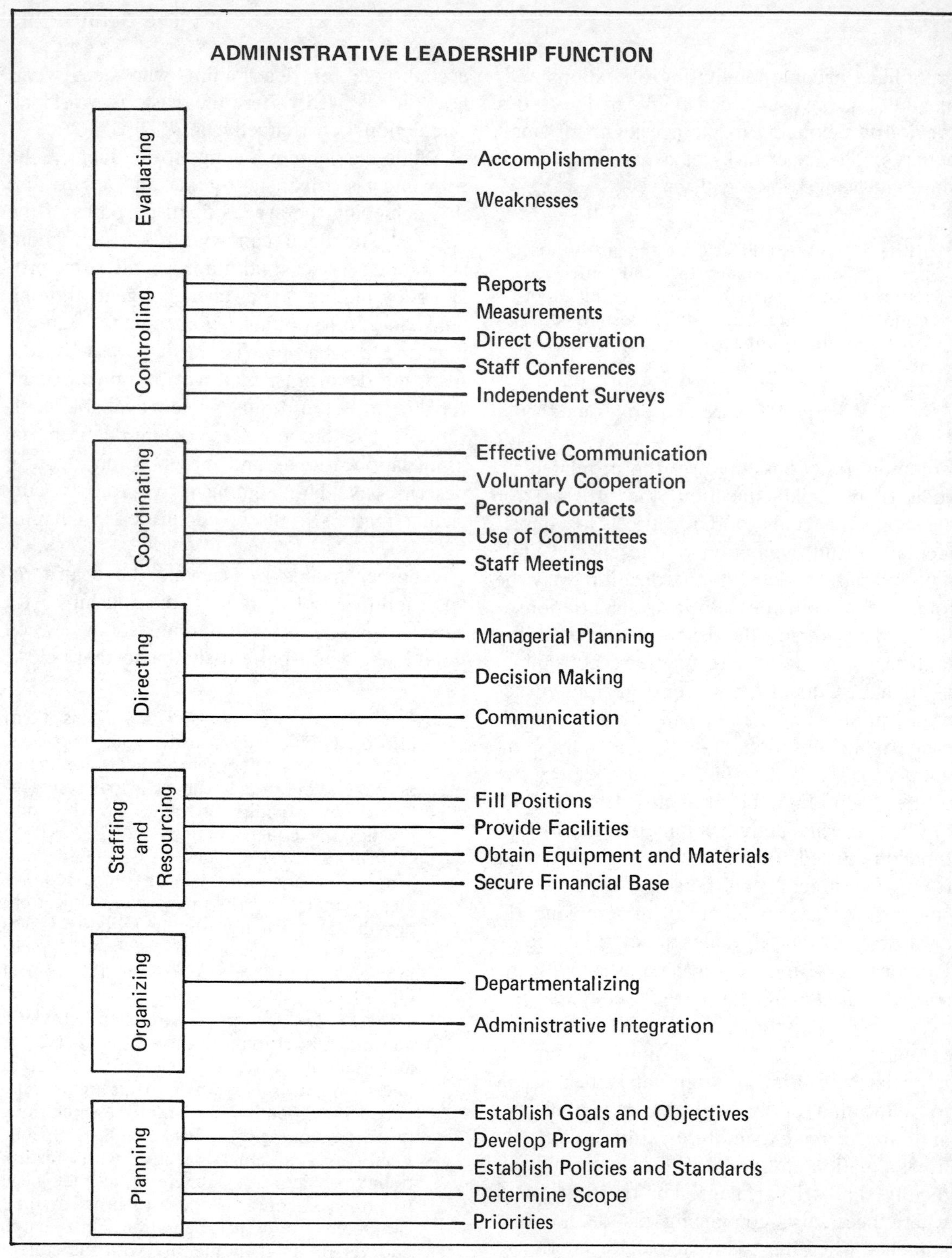

John L. Cramer, "Administrative Leadership," *Improving College and University Teaching,* 22 (1974): 92.

vides low key leadership and resources for faculty development activities; brings faculty together from various parts of the college; makes recommendations for hiring, tenure, and promotion; maintains morale through support, understanding their problems, and individual contacts and counseling.

- *Students:* Understands students in terms of "their world" and needs; explains policies; provides appropriate services; knows student mix and what it should be.

The responsibilities of deans as outlined by several institutions appear below. The first four were obviously developed for application within the larger context of university organizations, while the remainder represent position descriptions developed by two-year community colleges. Throughout, emphasis is on the dean's leadership responsibilities for the direction of the organization, its programs, and its resources as well as the ultimate responsibility for numerous decisions. The statements from the two-year colleges are much more definitive in outlining these responsibilities.

DEAN OF THE GRADUATE SCHOOL AND COORDINATOR OF RESEARCH

The Dean of the Graduate School and Coordinator of Research is chairman of the Graduate Faculty and the Graduate Council. Under the broad direction of the President and the Vice President for Academic Affairs, he provides general planning, guidance and review for all of the University's endeavors in graduate instruction and research. He bears responsibility for the total research activity of the University, including the University Research Foundation, and for the coordination of research and graduate education. He has direct administrative responsibility for the interdisciplinary research institutes. He appoints associate members of the Graduate Faculty and recommends the appointment of regular members for the approval of the President. He recommends on the appointment, promotion and granting of tenure to faculty members who may be involved in research and graduate programs of the University. He also recommends on budgets as they may affect research and graduate programs. The President, Vice President for Academic Affairs, and the Dean of the Graduate School and Coordinator of Research shall be ex officio members of all committees of the Graduate School.

DEAN OF UNDERGRADUATE STUDIES

The Dean of Undergraduate Studies has the function, under the purview of the Vice President for Academic Affairs, of integrating and strengthening those aspects of undergraduate education of common interest to those appropriate colleges in the University System. He serves as chairman of the Undergraduate Council. He administers offices and programs designed to provide more effective instructional resources. He also has general responsibility for those undergraduate programs of a University-wide nature such as the Honors Program and the Undergraduate Research and Creativity Program. He shall have the same authority and responsibilities as those of a dean of a college in the administration of educational units that might be transferred to or developed under his office.

DEANS OF THE COLLEGES

The dean of a college is the executive officer of his college. It is his function to see that the policies and regulations of the Board of Trustees, the Administrative Regulations, the Rules of the University Senate and the Rules of his college faculty are enforced. He is the chairman of his college faculty and is an ex officio member of all college committees. He is charged with overseeing the educational work of his college and its efficient conduct and management in all matters not specifically charged elsewhere. He is responsible for the curricula of his college, for the quality of instruction given therein, for the assignment of duties to all personnel and for the service rendered by the faculty of his college, individually and as a whole. He shall review the performance evaluations, submitted by the department chairmen, of members of his college. He shall be responsible for recommendations on salaries, salary changes, appointments, reappointments, terminal appointments, decisions not to reappoint, post-retirement appointments, promotions, and granting of tenure for members of his college or for ultimate action thereon when such authority has been delegated to him by the vice president to whom he reports or the President. He shall submit the budget request for his college and administer the budget when it is approved.

The dean of a college may have further administrative responsibilities delegated to him by the vice president to whom he reports or the President. These responsibilities may vary from college to college.

The dean is the spokesman for his college. In the event that he feels it necessary to depart from recommendations of his college faculty, he must communicate the college faculty's recommendation as well as his recommendation and notify the faculty of his action.

DEAN OF THE SCHOOL OF BUSINESS ADMINISTRATION

Direct curriculum, faculty, facilities, and budgetary activities of the School of Business Administration which includes 195 full-time faculty members, 120 part-time faculty and staff. The school has eleven academic departments, a Bureau of Business and Government Services, a Research Center, and International Business program, an Actuarial Science program, and publishes a triannual journal. Under the Bureau of Business and Government Services, there is a Real Estate Institute and a Court Reporting Program. The School offers programs leading to the degrees of Bachelor of Business Administration, Master of Business Administration and Ph.D. in Business Administration as well as an M.S. in certain fields. The budget for the School is $6.5 million a year. The dean reports to the Vice President for Academic Affairs.

DEAN OF ACADEMIC SERVICES

Scope

Reporting directly to the President, is responsible for the development, administration, and supervision of the Academic Services program of the College.

Examples of Responsibilities

- Responsible for developing and implementing academic programs that will serve the diverse needs of the students who attend the Community College.
- Responsible for initiating and maintaining an on-going process of curriculum improvement, revision and development, encouraging faculty participation and input.
- Responsible for preparation and administration of the budget for the Academic Services area.
- Responsible for making recommendations to the President for employment and retention of personnel assigned to the area of Academic Services in accordance with Affirmative Action Policy.
- Responsible for directing the development of viable instruments to implement relevant and effective staff evaluation procedures.
- Responsible for initiating and maintaining in-service projects to provide career development opportunities for faculty and academic supervisory personnel.
- Responsible for coordinating communication, articulation, and understanding among Academic Services personnel, Community Services, Student Services, and other College departments.
- Responsible for developing in supervisory staff and faculty a concern for the students and the teaching–learning climate, and for providing opportunities to initiate varietal innovative, and experimental teaching methods.
- Responsible for continuing professional self-growth and development through study, memberships, participation in educational seminars.
- Responsible for administration of agreements entered into between Academic Services staff and the Board.
- Responsible for articulation with the College Development Office to afford maximal exchange of ideas, information, and resources
- Responsible for fostering an institutional attitude and developing a team concept for College unity.
- Responsible for promoting and encouraging

an understanding of the College and its purposes and objectives for the community.

•Responsible for assuming leadership in the development of educational short and long range plans for the College.

•Responsible for keeping the President informed of all activities in the Academic Services area and innovations and new developments in the field of education.

•Responsible for recommending new policies or procedures for adoption.

•Responsible for representing the College at meetings and programs as assigned by the President.

•Responsible for maintaining confidential faculty personnel records.

•Responsible for performing related duties as assigned by the President.

DEAN OF BUSINESS, CAREER AND TECHNICAL PROGRAMS

Description

The Dean of Business, Career and Technical Programs is responsible to the Executive Dean of Academic and Student Affairs for the planning, organization, implementation, administration and evaluation of academic programs in the following areas: accounting, business career and business transfer programs, data processing, law enforcement, nursing, and secretarial science; as well as, cooperative programs with the County Vocational Technical Institute.

Responsibilities

1. To provide leadership in the planning and executing of the above programs while ensuring that these programs support the philosophy and objectives of the college.
2. To recommend to the Executive Dean of Academic and Student Affairs policies and procedures that will further the development of his/her areas of responsibility including:
   a. the recruitment, selection, and evaluation of professional staff in his/her area of responsibility.
   b. the organization of appropriate councils and committees to insure faculty and student participation in policy and program development.
   c. the development of new curriculum and special programs related to his/her area of responsibility.
3. To develop an intellectual, innovative and cooperative atmosphere conducive to the professional growth of faculty, and to provide faculty with opportunities commensurate with their abilities.
4. To plan and supervise internal budget operations for his/her designated budget classifications.
5. To coordinate the activities and services of designated college advisory committees.
6. To develop proposals for grant funds and for the implementation of funded projects.
7. To develop liaison with local business and industry and plan and develop new career programs.

THE DEAN'S STAFF

In a college of any size, it is not possible for the dean to perform all the necessary tasks alone. Those tasks that can possibly be delegated should be identified followed by a determination of the staffing needed to accomplish them. When establishing the required positions or reviewing the existing organization, consideration must be given to the status of the functions. As in the academic progression from assistant to associate professor, the title of associate dean reflects a higher status in the hierarchy than that of assistant. An organization that attaches the title of associate dean to positions dealing with program, research, and general administration and the title of assistant dean to the office responsible for student affairs implies a lower echelon status all too often accorded students. Some organizational patterns avoid these implications by establishing all positions at the associate level only or even as all assistant deanships.

Assistant and Associate Deans

The major consideration in selecting members of the dean's staff should be ability. The basic tenet of affirmative action programs must be followed, i.e., the best qualified individual should be selected without discrimination of any kind. Assistant and associate deans are sometimes selected through a comprehensive search mechanism similar to that used for higher ranking administrative posts. In addition to providing a wider range of candidates, this procedure has the potential for bringing in experienced people with new ideas and strength in a particular area that might be weak. Deans may also select members of their internal staff, which reduces the time needed for orientation to the position since the individual is already somewhat familiar with institutional policies and procedures.

Variations exist in the length of appointments. Some may be for indefinite periods of time which provides stability and continuity in the office. Another practice is limitation of terms to three to five years providing for rotation of the positions among numerous staff members. The latter practice is another means for bringing in new ideas and also serves as a means for making faculty aware of the reasons for what might be called an administrative viewpoint.

The individuals selected for the dean's staff must not only respect the dean as an individual but must also respect the dean's ideas. There must be a feeling of sharing administrative responsibilities but, at the same time, realizing that it may be necessary for the dean to bypass their offices in some situations. All must learn to anticipate problems and issues and work together as a team toward their resolution rather than to operate by means of constant last-minute consultations, clearances, and hasty decisions.

It is the dean's responsibility to provide direction and assign the necessary tasks if the dean's office is to be a well-organized effective operation. The tasks to be performed should be explicitly defined. Examples follow.

ASSOCIATE DEAN FOR CURRICULAR AND STUDENT AFFAIRS

Duties and Responsibilities

1. Development, implementation, and evaluation of degree curricula and other instructional programs in conjunction with College Curricular Committees.
2. Oversees all student affairs (recruitment, admissions, advising, registration, academic progress and status, graduation, appeals and grievances).
3. Liaison with Undergraduate and Graduate Curricular Committees of the College.
4. Participation in academic program and student services planning for each academic year.
5. Liaison with Department Chairpersons on academic program and student matters.
6. College representative on University Committees (Administrative Computer Policy Committee, Registration Planning Committee).
7. Liaison with student organizations.
8. Liaison with other University academic units for interdisciplinary program development.
9. Liaison with external academic institutions (Cluster, articulation).
10. Liaison with College Task Force on matters relating to above areas of responsibility.

ASSOCIATE DEAN FOR ACADEMIC AFFAIRS AND BUDGET

Duties and Responsibilities

1. Collaboration in budget preparation for each academic year with Dean and Departmental Chairpersons both individually and as a group.

2. Review of College submissions to University administration concerning faculty personnel, including merit, promotion and tenure, leaves, and released time.
3. Participation in planning regarding budget and personnel.
4. Liaison with budget, planning, personnel, research, steering, and other noncurricular College committees.
5. Encouraging and facilitating research efforts.
6. Review of final departmental semester scheduling.
7. Faculty Ombudsman.
8. Representation on Council of Deans in the absence of the Dean.
9. Chairperson, College Space Committee (representing College to University regarding allocation of space).
10. Liaison with College Task Force on matters relating to above areas of responsibility.

Responsibility should be given only in an area where the individual possesses competence and, with responsibility, corresponding authority must be delegated. While the associate and assistant deans must also provide initiative for carrying out their responsibilities, the dean should hold them accountable since the dean is ultimately accountable for their performance. Reports delineating the objectives for the area of responsibility and progress made toward achieving them should be required at regular intervals. The dean must also find time for meeting with the asssociate and assistant deans collectively and individually for discussion of problems, updating of all concerned about one another's activities, and to play the role of consultant as needed.

Administrative Assistants

Some deans find one or more administrative assistants to be a valuable addition to the office. Frequently, these positions assist in assuring a smooth office operation, and even provide a kind of continuity as administrators come and go. To be effective, appointments to such positions should be as permanent as possible. Some institutions make the mistake of utilizing only doctoral students who may be meeting residency requirements or are meeting internship requirements for degrees in higher education. Because the latter are one- or two-year assignments, the practice leads to constant turnover and instability. While such assignments may be desirable in some ways for both the individual and the institution, they should be limited and used in conjunction with appointments that will provide the needed continuity for a smooth efficient operation.

Appropriate responsibilities for administrative assistants include: keeping personnel files up to date, making transportation arrangements, assisting new faculty in finding housing, providing new faculty with appropriate information about the college and university, coordinating the college schedule of classes and confirming space, distributing and collecting grade sheets and other institutional forms, and providing everyday assistance to administrators and faculty wherever possible. A truly competent administrative assistant, whether in the dean's office or in a departmental office, eventually becomes nearly indispensable.

DIVISIONS, DEPARTMENTS, AND THEIR CHAIRPERSONS

The only purpose of any college organization is to facilitate achievement of the aims and purposes of the institution. The usual basic organizational operating units are divisions and departments. Whether the organization should involve divisions or departments or some combination of both will depend upon the specific situation and the underlying philosophy of the educational program. The importance of the role of division and department chairpersons has become more significant with the increasing influence of faculty members in the development of institutional policy. In fact, it has been estimated that 80 percent of all administrative decisions take place at the departmental level.[12] Department chairpersons are vital to optimum functioning at the collegial level, and their relationship with the dean must be one of confidence in each other.

Among the responsibilities delegated to departments, major emphasis should be placed upon curricular development and instruction. While some faculty seem to believe that colleges and universities exist for furthering faculty goals and activities, the major concern really is the education of students, undergraduate as well as graduate.

Divisions and Departments

Divisions are generally broader in their scope than departments. They are frequently found in community colleges where their orientation will include both the so-called pure and applied courses. As an example, a Division of Social Sciences might encompass education, social work, and police science and administration in addition to the traditional social sciences. Advantages of the divisional structure include: decreased administrative complexity within the college, encouragement for interdisciplinary cooperation, decreased departmental rivalry and flexibility in staffing. Caution must be exercised, however, since too large a division might become cumbersome and unwieldy.

It is also possible to have an organization in which several departments form a division. In this instance, each department has a chairperson who is responsible to the division chairperson. Then the division chairperson reports to the dean. While such an arrangement has the advantage of decreasing the number of individuals with whom the dean must deal, it does tend to create additional administrative complexity and an extensive hierarchy of administrators. It also tends to perpetuate departmental distinctions and competition so that other advantages of the divisional structure are lost. Whether it be divisions, departments, or some combination that is deemed most appropriate in an institution, basic purposes must be fulfilled to justify existence of the unit.

Balderston presents a precise definition of a department as "a coalition of faculty with mutuality of scholarly interest in the welfare and prestige of its members and of the field on campus."[13] The department controls the offerings in its field whether these be for students majoring in that field or whether they are complementary to programs for students in other departments. Departments

> provide a commonality of interests, and they relate more directly to curricular development than do other units. However, departments do have a specialized orientation, and they tend to develop an independent life and goals which are not always consonant with those of the institution, especially in regard to undergraduate education. Thus conflict—arising out of differences in goals, competition among departments for students and resources, and poor communication—is common. Administrators complain about departments, individually and collectively, and departments complain about administrators, also individually and collectively.[14]

While conducting a study at Michigan State University, Faricy developed a definition of a department as "(1) an administrative unit of the university, (2) to which personnel were assigned for salary and career management (promotion, tenure), and (3) which possessed and exercised authority to offer courses of instruction."[15] His definition emphasizes the department as an administrative unit rather than being discipline oriented. While departments organizationally may represent the lowest level in the administrative hierarchy, they really are the basic academic unit and the home for curricular development, basic teaching, research, and service that are the purposes of colleges and universities. Departments, therefore, have administrative and academic functions.

Departments are concerned about and seek the autonomy some feel is needed for effective operation. Autonomy without accountability leads to an expensive, ineffective, and inefficient operation. Although departmental affiliations tend to strengthen members' loyalty toward their discipline and department, there is an increasing need for viewing the larger institution as a whole and becoming involved in achieving its purposes. Departments should become more involved in educational and organizational planning, improving teaching and relationships between faculty and students, developing improved processes for promotion and tenure, relating more effectively to the larger organization, and putting forth renewed efforts toward innovation and experimentation.

Because the traditional departmental organization tends to emphasize specialization, it has inhibited the development of interdisciplinary and multidisciplinary approaches. A number of unique organizations for overcoming this are described by McHenry and others. Among them are the future-oriented problem-based departments whose focus may change from time to time that have been developed at the University of Wisconsin—Green Bay. Another is the residential college concept instituted at the University of California—Santa Cruz. Here, groups of disciplines are represented through "divisions," disciplines through "boards of studies," and the residential college is the basic unit of student and faculty identification.[16]

Departmental Organization

Robert K. Murray visited twenty-two universities ranging in size from 2,000 to 35,000 students and found five stages of departmental organizational development. He summarized that from stages one to five,

> Coming almost full circle, academic man thus substitutes the former arbitrary authority of a personal autocratic head with the equally arbitrary authority of an impersonal bureaucratic machine, run by almost nameless administrative assistants.[17]

To illustrate, departmental organizations range from very simple ones where the chairperson operates alone, arbitrarily and dictatorially with no committees to complex organizations with elaborate committee structures and full staff meetings. Department chairpersons may control virtually all departmental affairs from developing the budget to assigning teaching loads and hiring, rewarding, or even disciplining staff members with no consultation. At the other extreme is the chairperson who acts as a coordinator and obtains resources from the dean for implementing decisions made by the faculty. Along the same lines, participation by faculty may range from none to participation in departmental affairs by all faculty or perhaps only senior faculty being consulted.

There has been a move away from collegial decision making involving meetings of the total faculty to government by committees representing either the total faculty or specific segments. Departments frequently operate through faculty committees within identifiable policies and even by-laws. Where the department is large, faculty are generally involved in the selection of committee members to represent them and their interests thus providing a locus for their input and making the decision-making structures more acceptable.

Departments should continually examine themselves and look at the mechanisms for decision making and means for resolving the conflicts that inhibit implementation of needed change. Provision must be made for making decisions in relatively short periods of time so departmental policies and procedures do not become "blocks" to effectiveness rather than the facilitators they are meant to be. Departments that have formalized their decision-making processes and are well administered will enjoy greater prestige and influence. They will also be more successful in productive planning and achieving their goals, securing resources, and coping with restraints imposed upon them.

Role of the Chairperson

The role of a division or department chairperson is an ambitious and complex one. The prestige factors, or lack of them, institutional traditions, size, and complexity, all have an impact upon the importance of the position and potential effectiveness of the individual in the position. Specific authority most frequently delegated to the position is dealing with routine administrative matters with little or no authority outside the division or department. The ambiguity is heightened even further by the issue of whether the position is considered to be supervisory or nonsupervisory. Thus far, it has been classified in both ways depending upon the institution. In fact, the National Labor Relations Board evolved a policy in 1973 that the status of department chairpersons would depend on their powers at a particular institution.

The complexity of the role is emphasized by Peterson who, in a review of pertinent studies, found no less than ten and as many as forty-six areas in which faculty and administrators expect the department chairperson to play a role.[18] In addition, the chairperson often carries a teaching load, although it may be somewhat reduced, and it is not unusual to find no extra financial compensation for doing so.

The chairperson must respond to institutional officers in positions of authority as well as be responsive to the professional expertise and competence of the department's faculty. By virtue of both teaching and administrative experience, the chairperson stands between the faculty and the administration.

The role of the chairperson should be one of leadership and not domination; it is that of a colleague and peer, not a superior. The individual in the position must be acceptable to colleagues and also be a competent administrator who is able to communicate with the dean and represent departmental interests in order to obtain the necessary resources. The chairperson does much to establish the climate of the division or department, its emphasis, and to keep before the faculty the department's purposes. Implementation of institutional policies with major emphasis upon the improvement of teaching and learning is another function.

A special aspect of the role is responsibility for encouraging and providing opportunities that will foster the professional and personal growth of faculty members. The chairperson must know the faculty in the department as individuals to be able to identify their needs. It also means being aware of and making available the necessary resources for supporting and encouraging faculty growth. Much of this may be accomplished through effective utilization of promotion and tenure processes, merit and salary increases, travel money, research support, clerical assistance, assignment of graduate student resources, teaching assignments, and the recognition of individuals for specific accomplishments and contributions.

The chairperson is also responsible for course and space scheduling, securing equipment and teaching supplies, budget preparation, recruitment, recommendations for hiring, orientation of academic personnel, curricular improvement, two-way communication with students, faculty, administrators, alumni, and the community. The more routine operations should be delegated to an assistant, thus enabling the chairperson to provide the needed educational leadership.

An important aspect of the position is preparation of the budget, which should be based on long- and short-range planning. (A more detailed discussion of planning and the budget process appears in Chapter 9.) A real measure of a chairperson's effectiveness is the ability to develop a budget that provides for continued academic growth and is realistic in terms of the resources available. Finally, the chairperson must be able to defend or justify the proposed budget to the dean who then assumes responsibility for the next step in obtaining the needed funding.

There appears to be more emphasis in the community colleges upon the broader divisional view of the administrator as compared to the subject matter specialist orientation of the department chairperson in a four-year college. Nevertheless, there are some similarities in the responsibilities. The job descriptions on the following pages are representative examples of the chairperson's responsibilities as developed by a two-year college and two four-year institutions.

DIVISION CHAIRPERSON

With the advent of establishing division chairpersonships as twelve-month functions with minimal instructional responsibilities, the nature of the chairperson's assignments is proposed as follows:

1. Direct supervision of faculty performance with authority to correct inadequacies.
2. Providing assistance and recommendations in recruitment and selection of new faculty members.
3. Offering advice and recommendation regarding retention, promotion, and dismissal of faculty members within his division.
4. Responsibility for making recommendations to the President or his designated representative on textbooks and teaching materials requested by division members.
5. Responsibility for orientation and in-service programs for division members.
6. Responsibility for curriculum growth within the division, coordinating division curriculum plans with those of other divisions, and pursuing all appropriate steps for curriculum development through the college Curriculum Committee.
7. Responsibility for overall articulation between his division's plans and activities and those of all other divisions.
8. Responsibility for guiding the development of all division policies and obtaining any required approval from appropriate college administration.
9. Responsibility for initial preparation of the division budget and for subsequent budgetary recommendations to appropriate college administration.
10. Responsibility for coordination of scheduling and related activities for his division and for recommendation of division scheduling preferences to the appropriate college administration for incorporation in the total college schedule.
11. Responsibility for all materials and equipment assigned to the division.
12. Responsibility for recommending to the appropriate college administration or other college division all desired purchases, expenditures, or acquisitions.
13. Responsibility for recommending to the appropriate college administration all matters of teacher utilization within his division.
14. Responsibility for participation in the classroom supervision process and for follow-up conferences.
15. Responsibility for the continuing assessment of division programs and recommending to the appropriate college administration any indicated modifications.
16. Responsibility for helping to develop and maintain harmonious intercollege relationships of direct concern to his division.
17. Responsibility for supervising the de-

velopment of courses of study for all division offerings.

18. Responsibility for disseminating to division members significant contributions from literature, resource persons, other institutions, etc.
19. Responsibility for the development of increasing faculty participation in the role of program and course development.
20. Responsibility for working closely with the Office of Program Development in preparation and/or modification of courses and programs.
21. Responsibility for attendance at and planning for professional meetings of significance to the respective divisions.
22. Responsibility for increasing supervisory service with adjunct and other part-time personnel.
23. Responsibility for helping to prepare in-service programs and career development projects.
24. Responsibility for helping to develop the professional responsibilities attendant to the revised college calendar.
25. Responsibility for involvement in facility planning as applicable.
26. Responsibility for developing ever-closer relationships with the community services function at the County College.
27. Responsibility for helping to create an atmosphere of mutual respect among all divisions and levels of responsibility within the college.
28. Basic responsibility for creating a favorable climate for the teaching–learning situation.

DEPARTMENT CHAIRPERSON

Summary of Occupation

Develop long-run strategies, create necessary structures and oversee implementation in areas such as curriculum, publicity, governance, budget, staff.

Duties and Responsibilities

Irregular but Repeated Tasks: Student problems with enrollment, grades, complaints, waivers, admissions, independent study. Special faculty needs/problems such as project support, space/supplies, complaints. Respond to information requests from administration, outside agencies, companies, individuals.

Carry out special tasks for the dean or higher administration, e.g., accreditation, special budget study, tenure review. Entertain visiting firemen, job candidates, students, and faculty.

Governance Roles: Serve ex officio on all standing department committees—Undergraduate Affairs Committee, Graduate Affairs Committee, Scheduling, Promotion and Tenure, Merit and Inequity, Hiring, Graduate Advisors, Fellowships, and Research. Also on ad hoc committees as appropriate, e.g., budget and Graduate Program Publicity, Chairpersons Committee of School (Executive Committee). Frequently on Collegial Assembly Steering Committee.

Recurrent Tasks: Prepare, defend, administer and arbitrate department budget and space needs. Develop and defend staffing strategy, prepare notices, oversee vitae, arrange and carry out interviews, execute hiring. Organize, staff and oversee on-going committee functions. Schedule, staff, and review courses, including selection and oversight of "outside" faculty and book orders. Prepare and distribute course/program descriptions. Oversee and arbitrate for office staff. Organize and supervise advising for majors and graduate students. Develop, distribute and respond to graduate program information. Coordinate graduate admissions, fellowships, program administration, e.g., examinations, dissertations and placement. Acquire and distribute information on research opportunities, oversee development and submission, especially budget. Evaluate study leave requests. Collect and evaluate information for tenure/promotion, merit/inequity.

DEPARTMENT CHAIRMEN

The department chairman serves as chairman of the department faculty in the development by the department of policies on such matters as academic requirements, courses of study, class schedules, graduate and research programs and service functions. He presides over all departmental meetings, except as he may delegate this function, and is an ex officio member of all departmental committees. He has administrative responsibility for implementing the department's program within the limits established by the regulations of the University, policies of the University Senate and the rules of the college and of any school of which it is a part.

The department chairman is responsible for recommendations on the appointment of new members of the department, promotions, reappointments, terminal appointments, decisions not to reappoint, postretirement appointments and the granting of tenure. Procedures and criteria used in preparing recommendations shall be those established by the University, the college and the departmental faculty. As a minimum, the procedures must include consultation with all tenured members of the department and with all those with the rank of assistant professor or equivalent who have been members of the department for two years, except as noted below. All recommendations on matters listed above must include the written judgment of each consulted member of the department along with the recommendations of the chairman. The following exceptions may be made: (1) faculty members need not be consulted on recommendations for promotion affecting members with equivalent or higher rank, except that all faculty members with tenure shall be consulted on recommendations for granting tenure; (2) faculty members without tenure need not be consulted on recommendations for granting of tenure; (3) the right to make recommendations on temporary appointments and/or appointments at the assistant professor level or below may be delegated, with these appointments to be reviewed by the tenured faculty of the department during the second semester of the first year of appointment.

The department chairman is responsible for the periodic evaluation of department members by procedures and criteria established by the University, the college and the departmental faculty.

The department chairman submits the budget request for his department and administers the budget after approval. He is responsible for making recommendations on salaries and salary changes.

In connection with the major administrative functions of the chairman, he must seek the advice of members of the department, individually or as a group, or of advisory committees that he may appoint.

The chairman is the spokesman for the department. In the event that he feels it necessary to depart from the opinion of the departmental faculty, he must communicate the department opinion as well as his own, stating his reasons for differing from the departmental opinion, and notify the department of his action.

CHAIRMEN OF INTERDISCIPLINARY INSTRUCTIONAL PROGRAMS

The chairman of an interdisciplinary instructional program shall be a member of one of the academic departments participating in the program:

The chairman shall be responsible to the dean(s) of the college(s) in which the program is located and advise the dean(s) on staff and other needs of the program in connection with budget planning. He shall rely upon the advice of a committee of interested faculty drawn from the departments offering the courses composing the curriculum.

In summary, the importance of the chairperson's position cannot be ignored; it is illustrated by the findings of Dressel, Johnson, and Marcus in their study of fifteen institutions. Faculty ranked department chairpersons as having the greatest influence over departmental affairs followed by the department faculty as a whole, special department committees, the dean of the school, and the university administration in that order.[19] The chairperson may support and encourage departmental resistance to change or may, through creative leadership, assist the department in developing new policies, new directions, and renewed effectiveness. The same may be said of division chairpersons.

SUMMARY

An organization consists of people, procedures, and resources that function as a unit toward the accomplishment of specific goals. Although organizational structures in higher education differ from those found in industry, some concepts from business and industry are being applied to bring about planned change in a climate of trust and cooperation.

The college administrator must be a manager in the very broadest terms by providing dynamic leadership in initiating and bringing about change. At the same time, he or she is responsible for routine decision making and operations while following predetermined policies, procedures, and regulations.

The primary responsibility of an administrator is providing broad general direction to the organization. This includes making available and managing human and material resources for effective application toward achieving institutional goals and objectives. An administrator makes decisions as an individual and helps others to do the same. The total administrative role is an extremely diverse one that involves numerous activities including organizing, planning, directing, coordinating, and evaluating.

The dean is the key figure in moving a college forward and is responsible for defining, delegating, and coordinating the efforts of all concerned. While faculty opinion and participation in decision making are important, the dean has educational leadership responsibilities for the direction of the organization, its programs, and its resources as well as the ultimate responsibility for most decisions. Capable associate and assistant deans and administrative assistants can be invaluable to a dean for carrying out the responsibilities of the office.

A college organization may include divisions or departments or both. Whatever organization is used, the units serve both administrative and academic purposes in facilitating achievement of their aims and objectives as well as the larger goals of the institution. The chairperson's role may range from one where actions are taken alone arbitrarily and dictatorially to the other extreme where the chairperson is merely a coordinator for obtaining resources to implement decisions made by the faculty. Ideally, department and division chairpersons should lead a unit in developing new policies and new directions as well as renewed effectiveness.

ENDNOTES

1. J. Barry McGannon, "Academic Dean: Dimensions of Leadership," *Liberal Education* 59 (1973): 280.
2. Michael D. Cohen and James G. March, *Leadership and Ambiguity* (New York: McGraw-Hill, 1974), pp. 2–3.
3. *Ibid.*, p. 4.
4. Barry M. Richman and Richard N. Farmer, *Leadership, Goals, and Power in Higher Education* (San Francisco: Jossey-Bass, 1974), pp. 14–15.
5. Algo D. Henderson and Jean Glidden Henderson, *Higher Education in America: Problems, Priorities and Prospects* (San Francisco: Jossey-Bass, 1974), p. 204.
6. E. G. Bogue and R. O. Riggs, "Institutional Policy and Its Abuses," *Journal of Higher Education* 45 (1974): 357.
7. Used with permission. *Changes in University Organization, 1964–1971* by Edward Gross and Paul V. Grambsch. Copyright © 1974 by The Carnegie Foundation for the Advancement of Teaching. (New York: McGraw-Hill, 1974), p. 169.
8. Henderson and Henderson, *Higher Education in America,* p. 208.
9. Martha A. Brown, "What Kind of Leaders Do Faculty Members Want?" *College Management* 8 (1973): 26.
10. Armand J. Galfo, "Measurement of Group Versus Educational Leaders' Perception of Leadership Style and Administrative Theory Orientation," *Journal of Educational Research* 68 (1975): 314.

11. Arthur J. Dibden, ed., *The Academic Deanship in American Colleges and Universities* (Carbondale, Ill.: Southern Illinois Press, 1968), p. vi.
12. James H. L. Roach, "The Academic Department Chairperson: Functions and Responsibilities," *Educational Record* 57 (1976): 13.
13. Frederick E. Balderston, *Managing Today's University* (San Francisco: Jossey-Bass, 1974), p. 53.
14. Paul L. Dressel, F. Craig Johnson, and Philip M. Marcus, *The Confidence Crisis: An Analysis of University Departments* (San Francisco: Jossey-Bass, 1970), pp. ix–x.
15. William H. Faricy, "Grouping Departments," *Journal of Higher Education* 45 (1974): 100.
16. Dean E. McIlenry and Associates, *Academic Departments* (San Francisco: Jossey-Bass, 1977), pp. 63–116.
17. Robert K. Murray, "On Departmental Development: A Theory," *Journal of General Education* 16 (1964): 236.
18. Marvin W. Peterson, "The Organization of Departments," *Research Report Number Two,* American Association of Higher Education, December 1, 1970, p. 4.
19. Dressel, Johnson, and Marcus, *The Confidence Crisis,* pp. 60–61.

CHAPTER 3

Selection and Evaluation of Administrators

Competent administrators who, in addition to their service function, are able to provide leadership in the areas of resources, people, goals, and programs are needed if colleges and universities are to operate at an optimum educational and financial level. Change in an institution, however, is not brought about through one person's efforts. Instead, it is brought about through the ability of all administrators in the organization to obtain the collaborative efforts of people and channel their talents towards the development and achievement of appropriate goals. Personal qualities become important whether seeking an administrator to fill a position or evaluating an administrator already on the job. This chapter covers the qualities needed by the successful administrator as well as suggestions for selection and evaluation procedures.

QUALIFICATIONS AND DESIRABLE TRAITS

An examination of the literature describing traits considered desirable in deans and department chairpersons reveals a number of groupings of characteristics. Among these are educational background, prior experience, and personal characteristics. While programs for the development of administrators for higher education have been preparing graduates for some kinds of administrative positions, it is frequently necessary that individuals begin their careers in lower level positions and move upward. A question is beginning to arise whether some administrators for central office positions should come from the managerial or academic ranks. In addition to central administrative positions, the same question has been raised in relation to the academic deanship.

ACADEMICIAN OR PROFESSIONAL ADMINISTRATOR?

Even though it was developed more than fifteen years ago, Gould's description of the academic deanship is still valid. It emphasizes the enormous expectations of the individual in the position as both an academician and as an administrator.

> The dean's favored position calls for delicate balance and restraint. Like the European dean, he is expected to be a leading scholar and a leader of scholars; unlike the European dean, he is expected also to be a master of administrative technique, a pivotal man in the formation of policy, a maker of good decisions, and the self-sacrificing servant of the faculty.[1]

Faculty members generally believe that an administrator who comes from the academic ranks better understands the concepts of academic standards and academic freedom and would be more prone to defend them than one who was a successful leader in business, government or the military. The academic orientation of a respected scholar is preferred since the task involves utilization of tangible resources to achieve relatively intangible results. Opposition to business administration practices and preparation of nonacademic professional administrators is expressed by strong objections to "managerial techniques" and "deliberate management" in statements such as "a college cannot be run like a factory." Nevertheless, a successful academic administrator needs some of the same proficiencies as the business administrator, particularly in the areas of finance, personnel, policy implementation, and planning. In many ways, higher education has become big business as a result of the tremendous growth of the 1960s. If it is to remain healthy and vital, it must adopt some business principles and practices in place of the freer, more personalized informal academic approach.

Gross and Grambsch in their study for the Carnegie Commission found the role of management in American universities to be far from settled. Some of their respondents felt that management is overemphasized, over bureaucratized, and, in general, overwhelming. On the other hand, a number of their respondents indicated that "there has been entirely too much dabbling by faculty in administration and that, in general, universities should be run by professionals." [2]

It appears reasonable to project that administrators closest to the academic programs of an institution, particularly deans and division and department chairpersons, will continue to come from the academic ranks while those at the higher levels with supportive responsibilities rather than direct academic ones may be brought in with other than academic orientations.

Qualifications for the Deanship

There is little to be said about the educational background of a dean since he or she is expected to provide scholarly leadership and should thus be a scholar. Whether the expected degree level should be the master's or the doctorate is dependent upon the institution and its orientation. As community colleges proliferated, a number of deanships were filled by individuals without doctorates, some of whom had been administrators in area school districts. As the organizations have matured and the pressures of finding appropriate staffing have diminished, the doctorate has been increasingly required for deanships in two-year colleges similar to the expectencies of the majority of four-year institutions.

As for prior experience, the dean should be an educator with a background that provides the necessary professional insight into the processes of teaching and learning. Some experience is needed in the area of organizational structure and the responsibilities of an administrator. Deans frequently come from the ranks of chairpersons and associate and assistant deans since these positions provide a number of the experiences considered crucial to the development of a capable academic administrator.

The personal characteristics desired in a dean are so multitudinous that it is doubtful any one individual could possess them all. The ideal dean should be: objective and honest, logical, imaginative and creative, resourceful, dependable, self-confident, flexible, tactful and tolerant, courteous and congenial, patient, sincere, decisive, emotionally stable, and highly energetic. Also important are a strong personality, common sense, integrity, and a strong inner drive accompanied by perseverence. A dean must be able to: obtain the cooperation of others and develop morale; communicate effectively both orally and in writing; organize and delegate wisely; make sound judgments and decisions, often very quickly; work with a wide range of people as an enabler, catalyst, and facilitator, and, depending upon the situation, use a variety of the management skills described by McIntosh and Maier.

1. Participatory or democratic management
2. Consultative management so that subordinates understand the rationale behind unpleasant situations
3. Authoritarian decision making in absolute emergencies.[3]

An effective dean must have the respect of his or her peers and the faculty, be knowledgeable about and utilize group dynamics processes, and be a well-informed scholar with a solid commitment to the profession and the institution with an understanding of the financial aspects, structure, and organization of higher education.

Qualifications for Division and Department Chairpersons

A chairperson should possess many of the same qualities needed by a dean. Because the position is that of "the man (or woman) in the middle," a chairperson must have the ability to listen, be sympathetic and understanding, and yet, see things in perspective. There must be a willingness to move toward correcting a difficulty or resolving a problem when necessary, along with the good judgment to refrain from doing so when the situation warrants it. It is obvious that discretion, common sense, and independent thought are absolute necessities.

Roach succinctly describes the needed qualities and skills as follows:

> The successful department chairperson must: (a) possess certain personal qualities such as openness, integrity, objectivity; (b) be able to administer the departmental program; (c) possess and use certain job skills and certain human relations skills; and (d) at the same time maintain high professional competence. The necessary skills the chairperson must develop are: (1) planning; (2) communicating, representing, negotiating, coordinating, and facilitating functions; (3) problem solving; (4) organizing and administering.[4]

An effective chairperson understands and appreciates the role of administration in furthering college goals and is willing to accept administrative authority and responsibility.

In the human relations area, skills are needed in counseling, advising, the art of compromise, and democratic processes. Administrative and managerial skills are needed for preparing agendas and chairing meetings; organizing; delegating and directing the work of secretaries, administrative assistants, and graduate student assistants, preparing schedules; maintaining departmental records; obtaining and providing information requested by the dean; reviewing the research proposals submitted by faculty; and budget preparation and implementation.

The chairperson must have the confidence of the faculty and be respected for his or her ability as a teacher and scholar so that effective leadership for faculty development and curriculum improvement may be exercised. Finally, an effective chairperson understands and appreciates the role of administration in furthering college goals and is willing to accept administrative authority and responsibility.

SELECTION AND APPOINTMENT

Many variations will be found in the processes for selecting administrators. At the dean's level, the most prevalent is use of the search committee. Associate and assistant deans may be identified through the same process or be appointed at the pleasure of the dean. In the latter procedure, appointments are generally made from the internal staff. Division and department chairpersons may assume their roles through any one of several routes including identification and appointment by an administrator in a superior position, utilization of the search committee process, or election by departmental faculty.

Job Descriptions

In any efficient, smoothly operating organization, each individual knows his or her responsibilities and is also aware of the responsibilities of other individuals with whom contacts are made and working relationships developed. Job descriptions should delineate administrative positions in functional terms and with some reasonable detail. A broad description of the position might be followed by a listing of responsibilities including those requiring participation and cooperation with other offices and individuals. Consultative aspects of the position should be included as well as needed skills and educational background. The descriptions of responsibilities for deans, associate deans, and division and department chairpersons which appear in Chapter 2 would serve this purpose. Examples of the formats in which qualifications might be listed appear below. The second is preferable because of its detail and organization. The division into knowledge, ability, education, experience, and personal qualities is explicit and would be helpful to search committees in their screening and selection processes.

DEAN OF BUSINESS, CAREER, AND TECHNICAL PROGRAMS

1. Candidates should possess a Ph.D. or equivalent qualification in a field related to the Business, Career, and Technical Programs at the County College.
2. At least five (5) years teaching experience in higher education and at least three (3) years administrative experience in higher education, including significant participation in policy development, curricular planning, budgeting responsibilities, and academic decision making.
3. The ability to communicate effectively with others, together with a special sensitivity towards the needs of students and faculty.
4. Commitment to and understanding of community college concept.

DEAN OF ACADEMIC SERVICES

Knowledge and Abilities

- Knowledge of higher educational systems, laws, and regulations.
- Knowledge of curriculum construction and development.
- Knowledge of the community college concept, principles, and purposes.
- Knowledge of staff evaluative procedures.
- Knowledge of budget preparation and administration.
- Knowledge of human relations and application.
- Knowledge of community-oriented needs in course and program development.
- Knowledge of effective administrative and supervisory practices.
- Ability to assess needs, define priorities, and establish educational goals on a short- and long-range basis.
- Ability to guide division chairpersons in effective supervision and evaluation of faculty.
- Ability to develop and implement academic programs that will stimulate student participation and evoke positive responses.
- Ability to cooperate with and instill confidence and respect in superiors, peers, and subordinates.
- Ability to anticipate future needs and develop realistic budgets for the Academic Services area.
- Ability to provide the necessary administrative leadership to positively motivate personnel and enhance the academic program.

- Ability to communicate with students.
- Ability to recognize potential areas of academic concern, define solutions and recommend actions to be taken, and follow through for determined action.
- Ability to accept assigned responsibilities and to foster a sense of responsibility in others.

Education, Experience, and Personal Qualities

Doctorate or equivalent, with undergraduate and/or graduate work in educational administration and supervision desired. Preparation and experience in administration, supervision, curriculum development, and budget development and implementation. Teaching experience at the college or junior college level. Experience with governing boards, community relations, and participation in individual community activities. Experience in working with minority, disadvantaged, handicapped, and gifted students. Honesty, sincerity, vision, tact, understanding, imagination, and tolerance.

Up-to-date job descriptions are vital when selection processes begin. They are important for giving the candidate an accurate picture of the position being sought and for providing the search committee and/or administrator responsible for making the appointment with a full description of the position to be filled. Too often, search committees are assigned the inappropriate task of developing the needed job descriptions. As stated before, these should be part of an institution's permanent personnel file. One format for the description might be:

POSITION TITLE

Scope

Brief narrative description summarizing the responsibilities and identifying the administrator to whom the individual in the position reports

Detailed List of Responsibilities

Internal
External

Qualifications

Knowledge
Abilities
Experience
Education
Personal Qualities

Salary Range

Organization of the Search Committee

The use of search committees for filling administrative vacancies has been increasing as faculty have become more involved in campus decision making and students have pushed for participation in decision making that affects them. When administrators who need faculty support for functioning effectively in their positions are being sought, faculty involvement in the selection is crucial. The legalities of affirmative action and equal opportunity have been additional factors in the increasing use of search committees. These factors are discussed more fully in Chapter 4. Their implications for the selection of faculty are also applicable to the selection of administrators.

Before establishment of a search committee, the first consideration is the desirability and appropriateness of the process for filling the particular vacancy. Once it has been decided that a search process is appropriate, the composition of the committee should be determined. Before members are actually appointed, answers must be established to questions such as:

1. What is the precise charge to the committee?
2. What is its relationship to the administrator actually responsible for making the appointment?
3. How many members are needed?
4. What should be the composition of the membership, i.e., should it include faculty, students, and administrators and what proportion of each?

5. How should members be identified: appointment by an administrator(s), selection in cooperation with faculty, or election by faculty?

After potential committee members have been identified, each should receive a written invitation to serve. The letter should include the charge to the committee and as much preliminary information as possible. The chairperson, who may be appointed by an appropriate administrator or elected by the committee, should be identified at the first meeting. At the same meeting, the charge to the committee, its role, and the extent of budgetary and clerical support should be reviewed. A time table and schedule of future committee meetings should be established as well as the general procedures to be followed.

Search Committee Procedures

Before the committee is able to begin its work in earnest, a full job description for the position to be filled must be available to each committee member. The qualifications expected of candidates for the particular position must be established since these become the criteria for initial screening of the credentials. Sources of candidates must be identified and, depending upon the position to be filled, might include one or more of the following: university placement bureaus, private placement agencies, ads placed in appropriate professional publications, and recommendations solicited from individuals in the field. For some positions, an attractive printed brochure to be forwarded with an application could be appropriate. It would include information about the institution, a position description, qualifications needed, and terms of employment including salary range, fringe benefits, and terms of office. The deadline for applications alone as well as a later one for submission of all supporting credentials is needed.

Stauffer recommends that a standard format be used by each applicant in preparing his or her vita. This serves to simplify the comparison of candidates' credentials. He also suggests use of an evaluation scale on which a candidate's references may provide a rating of from 1 to 5 on specified characteristics. An opportunity to add open-ended comments should be included.[5]

Weaver and Farnham object to Stauffer's focus on the "sorting and culling function." They believe that permitting candidates to select their own format for the vita provides another element for judging. They object also to the standardization of information from references and believe the approach to be insulting. Finally, they object to some of the personal information Stauffer recommends obtaining on the basis that it is discriminatory and an invasion of privacy. The only information requested should be that related to qualifications for the position.[6] Both views have merit.

As applications are received, they should be acknowledged immediately, and a file established. The committee or subcommittee established for the purpose should conduct a preliminary screening based on the pre-established criteria and immediately inform those who are being eliminated from further consideration. Depending upon the number of applications, a second screening might be desirable to reduce the number to be invited for preliminary interviews. At this point, the total credentials for the remaining candidates should be reviewed by all members of the search committee.

The purpose of the interview should be established and a structured interview process developed. More valid comparisons will be possible if all candidates are asked the same questions. The interview should focus on those aspects that cannot be fully explored or described by means of the application and credentials. The reader will find Stauffer's suggestions about the interviewing process and his recommended questions helpful.[7] Only one candidate at a time should be scheduled with the schedule arranged so that each external candidate has an opportunity to see the institution.

At some point, telephone calls to references would be desirable to validate credentials, check on personal qualities, and obtain answers to questions. This might be prior to or after the first round of interviews.

The committee itself should conduct the first interview and include for each external candidate a briefing about the institution and the specific opening. Following another round of eliminations, the three to five who rank highest should be recalled for more extensive interviewing. Wives or husbands should also be interviewed at this point. Groups and individuals with whom the new appointee will work should participate at this time and their reactions and recommendations submitted in writing to the search committee. If feasible, visits by one or more committee members to he communities and institutions from which the top two or three candidates come are desirable.

The search committee must identify those whom it considers to be the top candidates and forward the information according to the original charge. All finalists should then be notified as soon as the appointment is made just as unsuccessful candidates should have been informed immediately following their elimination from further consideration. It is important that all candidates be left with positive feelings for as Sommerfeld and Nagely wrote: "A search committee's communications can contribute immensely to the image of an institution or they can destroy years of expensive efforts by its public relations office." [8]

The rather comprehensive statement of procedures for a Dean's Search Committee that follows was developed by the Faculty Senate of a large university. It provides an excellent model for search committees handling other positions as well. The second statement is a more simple one.

PROCEDURES FOR DEAN SEARCH COMMITTEES

The following procedures are developed in order to produce a reasonable standardization of procedures used by committees searching for deans of schools and colleges. The purpose of the procedures is to ensure thorough review of candidates and uniformity of documentation supporting the recommendations of the search committee to the president of the university who eventually makes the appointment of the dean.

I. *Composition of Search Committee*

A. The Dean's Search Committee shall consist of eleven (11) members. Composition of the Committee should be as follows:

1. Six (6) faculty on Presidential Appointment from the school or college searching for the dean; these to be elected by its Assembly.
2. One (1) full-time student (Undergraduate or Graduate) from the school or college seeking the dean, named by its Student Assembly.
3. One (1) alumnus from school or college seeking the dean, to be named by its Alumni Association; if no Alumni Association, to be named by the General Alumni Association.
4. One (1) dean or subdean from another school or college to be named by the Council of Deans.
5. Two (2) senior professors from any other school or college to be named by the Faculty Senate Committee on Administrative and Trustee Appointments (CATA).
6. Vice President and Dean of Faculties shall be an ex officio member of the Committee with no voting power.
7. The Chairperson and Vice-chairperson shall be elected from its voting members by the Search Committee.
8. In the absence of the Chairperson,

the Vice-chairperson will preside at all meetings of the Search Committee. The Vice-chairperson is responsible for day-to-day operations of the Search Committee including the setting up of meetings, schedules for interviews, dissemination of information to candidates and to members of the Search Committee, maintenance of records, and all other matters necessary for a smooth, efficient search. The Committee may wish to elect a secretary to assist the Vice-chairperson.

II. *Advertisement*

The Chairperson and Vice-chairperson will prepare the basic advertisement for the Dean.

Advertising copy must include: the announcement of the vacancy, dates, brief information about the school and the University, where to send resumes, and appropriate statements about affirmative action and equal employment opportunities.

Advertising must include internal notices in the ——— Times, ——— News, and Faculty Herald. External advertising must include the Chronicle of Higher Education, and the Affirmative Action Register and may include the New York Times, local newspapers, and appropriate professional journals.

Ads are placed through the Office of the Vice President for University Relations.

III. *Background Statement*

The first responsibility of the Search Committee is to prepare a succinct statement to describe the scope of academic efforts of the school and the responsibilities of the dean. This statement is to include such topics as the scope of the academic programs, research and training grant efforts, relationships of the school to the University and its other schools and colleges, strengths of the school, qualifications of the faculty, composition and quality of the student body, and other pertinent information in printed form or prepared especially for the search. The Search Committee will state in writing and in appropriate order the criteria it will be using for selection of the dean. This list of criteria is to be approved by the Collegial Assembly.

In addition, the statement is to include information on the role of the dean, his/her responsibilities and accountabilities, and desired professional and personal characteristics.

Every serious candidate who survives a preliminary screening of paper credentials should receive this statement.

IV. *External References*

A. The Search Committee must seek external references from persons named by the candidate and from other persons not named by the candidate. References shall be asked to comment on:
   - teaching ability and general understanding of educational goals
   - scholarship and professional capabilities
   - leadership characteristics
   - demonstrated managerial capabilities
   - other characteristics defined under Background Statement.

B. At least three (3) such references shall be solicited.

V. *Campus Visit*

A. The Vice-chairperson shall prepare a schedule for the visit of each candidate invited to the University. The schedule shall be posted at least three (3) days in advance of the visit and shall include the following activities:
   1. Meeting with Search Committee
   2. Meeting with representative chairpersons, subdeans, and the Acting Dean of the school
   3. Meeting with several Vice Presidents and Deans of other schools at the University
   4. Tour of facilities
   5. Meeting of candidate with faculty and students. The purpose of the meeting(s) is to permit faculty and students the opportunity to see and hear the candidate and provide for a demonstration of the candidate's scholarly interests and achievements, speaking abilities, and poise.

B. The campus visit is to provide optimum utilization of the candidates time, to give the candidate a representative and honest view of the University and to provide maximum exposure to faculty, students, college and central administration. A first visit is for purposes of confirming and screening of a candidate that appears attractive on paper. A second visit is to help decide on the final candidates to be submitted to the President.

VI. *Evaluation of Candidates by Search Committee*
The Vice-chairperson shall solicit and require from each member of the Search Committee and from other University personnel who interviewed the candidates written comments about the candidate. A standardized form for these evaluations will be prepared by the Office of the Vice President and Dean of Faculties. The purpose of the form is to ensure that due consideration has been given to the appropriate criteria for selection of a Dean and to develop an appropriate written record.

VII. *Recommendations of Search Committee*
After review of candidates the Search Committee shall present a recommendation for filling the deanship including no less than two (2), and preferably three (3), candidates in ranked order. Recommendations shall include resumes, a general committee statement on the strengths and weaknesses of each candidate, and information concerning salary or other special requirements stipulated by the candidates. The written evaluation by individuals shall be included with this transmittal for the benefit of the President in making the final selection of the Dean.

VIII. *Budget for Search Committee*
Wise expenditure of University funds is necessary. As much business as possible should be conducted by correspondence and telephone before candidates are invited to visit the University. Only serious and well-qualified candidates are to be invited. Normally, the University will pay for round trip transportation costs for the candidate, hotel accommodations for one night, ground transportation, and meals. For outstanding candidates who are invited to return for a second visit, payment of the expenses for a spouse may be appropriate. Good judgment and discretion in handling this matter with candidates is very important. During the campus visit, luncheon expenses for small groups are appropriate.
Secretarial costs, telephone, postage, and other miscellaneous costs are to be absorbed by appropriate object codes within the school budget.
The Vice President and Dean of Faculties will set budget guidelines for each search committee and will indicate an appropriate account number for charging expenses.

IX. *Confidentiality*
All committee deliberations, interviews with candidates, and reports of interviews are to be considered as confidential matters. Failure by committee members and others concerned to respect this policy could embarrass the committee, the University, or the candidate.

SEARCH COMMITTEES

Recommendations on the appointment of the chief administrative officers of all educational units of the university shall be made after advice from search committees.

When vacancies in administrative positions are anticipated, search committees shall be appointed sufficiently in advance of the vacancy to avoid the appointment of an acting administrator. When unanticipated vacancies occur, the search committee shall be appointed as soon as the designated procedures for appointment can be carried out.

Search committees for deans of colleges shall be appointed by the President after consultation with the appropriate vice president and the Senate Council.

Search committees for directors of schools shall be appointed by the deans of the colleges after consultation with the appropriate faculty bodies within the colleges.

Search committees for chairmen of academic departments shall be appointed by the deans of the colleges after consultation with (1) the associate dean or director of the school within the college if the department is in such a school; (2) the faculty of the department; (3) the Dean of Undergraduate Studies; and (4) the Dean of the Graduate School and Coordinator of Research if the department is involved in a graduate program.

Search committees for directors of interdisciplinary institutes shall be appointed by the Dean of the Graduate School and Coordinator of Research after consultation with the Graduate Council.

A search committee for a director of the community college shall be appointed by the Vice President for the Community College System after consultation with the faculty of the community college.

Search committees for chairmen of divisions in community colleges shall be appointed by the director of the college after consultation with at least the tenured faculty members of the concerned divisions.

Search committees shall operate under procedures prescribed by the President after consultation with the Senate Council or the Community College Council.

Recommendations of the search committees shall be transmitted to the President through the normal administrative channels along with the recommendation of the administrative officer responsible for the appointment. Recommendations on the appointment of chairmen of academic departments or divisions shall be accompanied by written statements from at least the tenured members of the department or division.

Selection and Appointment of a Dean

The final selection and appointment of a dean is the responsibility of the president with the advice of the faculty and the approval of the Board of Trustees. This advice may be in the form of recommendation of a single candidate by the search committee or it may be a ranking of the two or three top candidates for the position. An unranked list to some extent excludes faculty from the final decision making. Under any circumstances, if the president deviates from the recommendations of the search committee in any way, the president owes the committee an explanation. Maneuvers such as requesting additional names until that of a predetermined candidate appears or delaying action until an interim acting dean is "settled in" are unacceptable and inexcusable.

Division and Department Chairpersons: Selection or Election?

There is some belief that indefinite terms of office for chairpersons can lead to an authoritarian style of leadership or, if the chairperson becomes negligent, to a loss of division or department strength and effectiveness. Limitations on the terms of office ranging from two or three years to five with the possibility of succeeding oneself are not uncommon. Rotating elective chair positions are becoming more common than appointed ones. Some faculty and administrators believe that rotation of the position leads to an increase in collegiality and a consensus mode of operation and provides greater emphasis on division and department needs and concerns.

Actual selection may be accomplished through appointment by the dean in consultation with the faculty, election by fellow faculty, or rotation among senior or tenured faculty who take turns for specified terms of office. The dean's final approval is needed regardless of which of the above procedures is followed.

At times, it might be advisable to seek a chairperson from outside of the institution. In these cases, faculty involved in the search must understand and satisfy the requirements of affirmative action guidelines. A time line should be established during which the credentials of applicants are reviewed, candidates interviewed, and any other investigations felt necessary are pursued. Other department chairpersons within the college should be included in the interviewing process as well as the dean, associate and assistant deans, and chairpersons and deans of other areas within the institution where programs cut across other colleges. Search committee procedures as previously described should be followed.

As institutions have increased in size and

become more complex, it is desirable for an individual to have served in a prior administrative capacity within the division or department before assuming the top position. Also, chairpersons need to serve a substantial period of time if they are to be effective in their roles. A staff development program for chairpersons would be appropriate and would facilitate the smooth functioning of the division, department, and the college.

Whether the division or department chairperson is identified by a process of selection or election, the appointment is made by the dean subject to further approval by the appropriate individual in central administration as stipulated by institutional procedures. Basically, faculty judgment should be honored and appointments made in conformity with their wishes if the individual involved is to have the needed cooperation of staff members. Any action to the contrary must be handled most carefully or the repercussions will be disastrous to not only the division or department but also the college and possibly, the entire institution.

EVALUATION AND PROFESSIONAL DEVELOPMENT

Much discussion and progress has been taking place in the area of faculty evaluation. Consideration is being given to administrative evaluation but to a lesser extent. If teachers can be helped by student evaluation of their teaching, then administrators can be helped through evaluation by those with whom they come into contact including faculty and other administrators. The administrator should be assisted in his or her own personal growth through the process, which will be accompanied by an increase in the overall effectiveness of the educational organization.

A review system will also provide information to the administrator regarding the level of confidence he or she enjoys. For those who have a specific term of office, the review would logically take place toward the end of that term prior to the period when a decision regarding reappointment must be made. It is obvious that the review becomes particularly important when there has been any question about an administrator's performance. The following procedures for the appointment of deans and review of their performance have been adopted in one university.

APPOINTMENT AND REVIEW OF DEANS' PERFORMANCE

I. *Terms of Appointment or Reappointment*
The appointment or reappointment of the dean of a college will be for a fixed term with provisions for renewal.
Appointment or reappointment will be for a term not to exceed five years.

II. *Regular Periodic Review*
A review of the dean's performance will be initiated not later than twelve months before the expiration of the period of appointment or reappointment, and will be concluded not later than six months before the expiration of appointment or reappointment.
The President will appoint a committee to conduct the review. At least half of the committee members will be faculty from the college concerned designated by its Collegial Assembly and at least one member of the remainder of the committee will be a faculty member of another college appointed by the Faculty Senate Steering Committee.

III. *Review at Times other than Appointment or Reappointment*
At times other than those scheduled for review, the President, in his role as convenor of the review body, shall initiate a review of the dean's performance upon receipt of a resolution from the Collegial Assembly

calling for such review according to the procedures established by that assembly.*

IV. *Action after Review*

An unfavorable review by a majority of the committee shall include a prescription for corrective action. It may include a recommendation for resignation or removal from office. Such a recommendation will normally be followed by resignation of the dean, or if resignation is not forthcoming, by a decision by the President to terminate the appointment.

The administrator who encourages personal evaluation will set an example for faculty and provide additional stimulus towards their acceptance of evaluation processes.

CRITERIA

What should be the focus of the evaluation process? Should it be based on personal characteristics as proposed by Tyrus Hillway who lists qualities such as: interest in the progress of education, fairness in dealing with students and faculty, self-adjustment, tolerance of new ideas, trustworthiness, skill in securing group action, ability to organize, and ability to maintain faculty morale and faculty performance? [9] Other characteristics are listed by Skipper who conducted a study to identify the personal qualities of administrators considered "Most Effective" by their colleagues as compared to those considered "Least Effective." The "Most Effective" were judged to tend toward being more ethical, honest, calm, alert, insightful, tolerant, confident, goal oriented, inventive, and willing to make decisions. The "Least Effective" administrators were judged to tend toward being more undependable, deceitful, irritable, impulsive, defensive, stereotyped in their thinking, rigid, sarcastic, retiring, and lacking in ambition, and were more inclined to put off difficult decisions in addition to having fewer ideas.[10] Skipper also emphasized the viewpoint that greater attention should be paid to the personal qualities of leaders on the basis that

> A college or university is not a business organized to make a profit nor is it the military, but rather it is an organization where independence, intelligence, criticism, and creative thinking are valued and encouraged. In such an environment, the personal qualities of leaders have a great effect on the mood and vitality of the institution.[11]

On the other hand, increasing emphasis on goal-oriented achievement has been developing to the extent that some institutions may use a management by objectives approach to evaluation. The objectives are reviewed on a regular basis, even quarterly, by the individual(s) to whom the administrator is responsible to determine the degree of accomplishment thus reflecting to some extent the effectiveness of the individual's leadership. This approach should be combined with other evaluative measures related to the personal characteristics and mode of operation of the individual concerned. As in any evaluation process, there must be some frame of reference or base against which the individual's performance will be compared. Fisher suggests the following: (1) his or her predecessors in the position, (2) all other individuals currently in similar positions, (3) a platonic "ideal" performance, (4) one's past performance, (5) one's own performance goals, and/or (6) the performance expectations others have for him or her.[12]

Comprehensive evaluation efforts in administrative effectiveness should include personal characteristics of the specific individual as well as some goal-oriented approach to measuring

* Within one year of the adoption of these recommendations, each Collegial Assembly shall, in consultation with the President's Office, and with due consideration for the gravity of the decisions to be made, establish procedures for developing such a resolution.

accomplishment that, in turn, reflects competence. An instrument developed by Rasmussen uses this approach. It provides a means for the respondent to indicate where the "ideal" dean of the college should be on a continuum of one to seven and an estimate, on the same continuum, of the dean's "actual" performance. The "ideal behavior" ratings reflect the rater's goals for the dean. The important outcome of the system is its reflection of any discrepancy between the perceived "actual behavior" of the dean and that considered to be "ideal behavior."

Each of the twenty-two separate traits or functions has been developed into an item for the instrument. These are:

1. Administrative Management
2. Executive Judgment
3. Delegating Authority and Responsibility
4. Providing Academic Leadership
5. Acting Decisively
6. Planning Ability
7. Encouragement of Faculty Research
8. Improvement of Teaching
9. Dean's Role as Faculty Representative
10. Skill in Recruiting Faculty
11. Keeping Communication Lines Open
12. Providing Academic Freedom
13. Skill in Working with Groups
14. Communicating Ideas
15. Sensitivity to Faculty Concerns
16. Handling Conflict
17. Acceptance of New Ideas
18. Availability to Faculty
19. Listening to Faculty
20. Honesty
21. Personal/Professional Stability
22. Fairness

As Rasmussen states, there is also a possible fringe benefit from the system. He believes that administration of the instrument helps "faculty to perceive the complexity of the dean's functions and the conflicting forces that impinge upon him." [13]

Harvey has developed an administrative rating scale based on eighteen characteristics. A scale of 1 to 10 is used with 1 and 2 being outstanding, the top 10 percent, and 5 and 6 average and the middle 40 percent. The scale is simple, easy to administer, and easily handled when collating results. It appears on the following pages.

A system for assessing the administrative effectiveness of a department chairperson has been developed at the Kansas State University Center for Faculty Evaluation and Development in Higher Education. Referred to as DECA (The Departmental Evaluation of Chairperson Activities System), its emphasis in design and philosophy is administrative improvement. The Center recommends that a DECA report not be used as a sole measure of administrative effectiveness. Instead, it should be considered with other information about the department that is incorporated with information about the performance of other responsibilities of the department chairperson in addition to administration.

A copy of the survey form and a sample report follows.

Procedures

One possibility for managing the evaluation process is establishment of a college, division, or department committee. Some means must be developed to insure that input is obtained from as broad a base as possible, yet preserving the anonymity of individuals in order to acquire more valid information. While faculty in general have little competence in administration, they are affected by it and must be involved. Students, although inexperienced, must also be included on some representative basis for the same reason. Appraisal by peer administrators (other deans, or division and department chairpersons) is desirable as well as input obtained from members of central administration with whom the individual has working contact.

ADMINISTRATIVE RATING SCALE

Administrator
Being Rated __________________

Please rate the administrator named above on the characteristics below. Place the appropriate number (from 1 to 10, or X or 0) of your rating on the line preceding the characteristic.

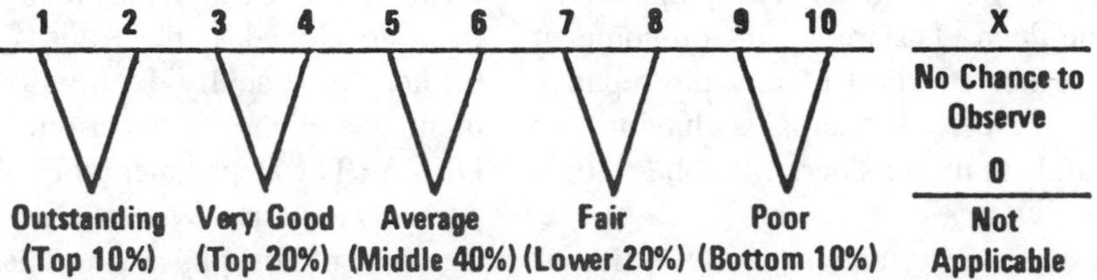

CHARACTERISTICS

______ 1. **Institutional Mission.** Knowledge of the mission, goals and objectives of the college and willingness to weigh decisions in light of the total institutional good.

______ 2. **Specific Knowledge.** Technical knowledge and skill for the area of specific responsibility assigned. Is the person competent, experienced, well informed, and keeping abreast of developments in his/her area?

______ 3. **Emotional Stability.** Does the person maintain an emotional balance, keeping his/her "cool" in difficult circumstances? Is he/she able to keep emotions from unduly affecting decisions? Is he/she emotionally healthy?

______ 4. **Human Relationships.** Does the person use tact and diplomacy in human relationships? Is he/she able to handle disagreements with finesse? Does he/she deal with others in a spirit of love and sincere concern? (Is he/she basically self-centered and seeking to further personal goals at the expense of others, or is he/she honestly concerned with those with whom he/she works?)

______ 5. **Democratic Processes.** Knowledge and skill in using democratic processes when appropriate. Does the person recognize and accept rights of others to participate in making decisions? Does he/she accept their judgements although different from his/hers? Is he/she convinced of the value of the "collective mind" vs. one man's opinion?

Reprinted by permission from L. James Harvey, *Managing Colleges and Universities by Objectives* (Littleton, Col.: Ireland Educational Corporation, 1976), pp. 79–81.

_____ 6. **Personal Integrity.** Does the person deal with others with honesty and openness? Is he/she truthful? Can he/she be trusted?

_____ 7. **Work Level.** Ability and willingness to dig in and work hard, to put in extra hours if needed, willingness to do difficult tasks, to do extra work, to take work home or come back to office on "off-hours." Thinks of work to be done and does it rather than "watches the clock."

_____ 8. **Organization.** Ability to organize area of responsibility and tasks so that work is done with a maximum of efficiency. Ability to expedite work and accomplish objectives effectively through good organizational procedures and structure.

_____ 9. **Creativeness.** Ability to perceive and use new or creative approaches in work, and willingness to try new ideas and concepts. Is the person flexible? Committed to change?

_____ 10. **Problem Solving.** Ability to use good problem solving technique. Is the person logical? Does he/she study all alternatives, collect facts thoroughly and study results of previous decisions? Does he/she use scientific methods in solving problems?

_____ 11. **Morale Maintenance.** Does the administrator work effectively to maintain a high morale among subordinates and between himself/herself, his/her staff, and others within the institution? Does he/she help avoid personality conflicts, backbiting, criticism of others on staff or in college? Is there a feeling of friendliness, sense of teamwork, feeling of importance in total picture of institutional effort?

_____ 12. **Personal Appearance.** Does the person maintain high standards of personal appearance? Does he/she dress well and appear well groomed? Are his/her clothes stylish and in good taste? Is his/her appearance in keeping with contemporary community standards for a professional person?

_____ 13. **Objectivity.** Is the person able to keep emotion from distorting his/her perspective? Can he/she look at problems with clarity, logic, and coolness and make decisions on basis of facts?

_____ 14. **Administrative Protocol.** Awareness of the administrative structure and willingness to work within it. Does the person respect lines of authority and staff relationships? Are decisions made appropriately and communicated to appropriate offices?

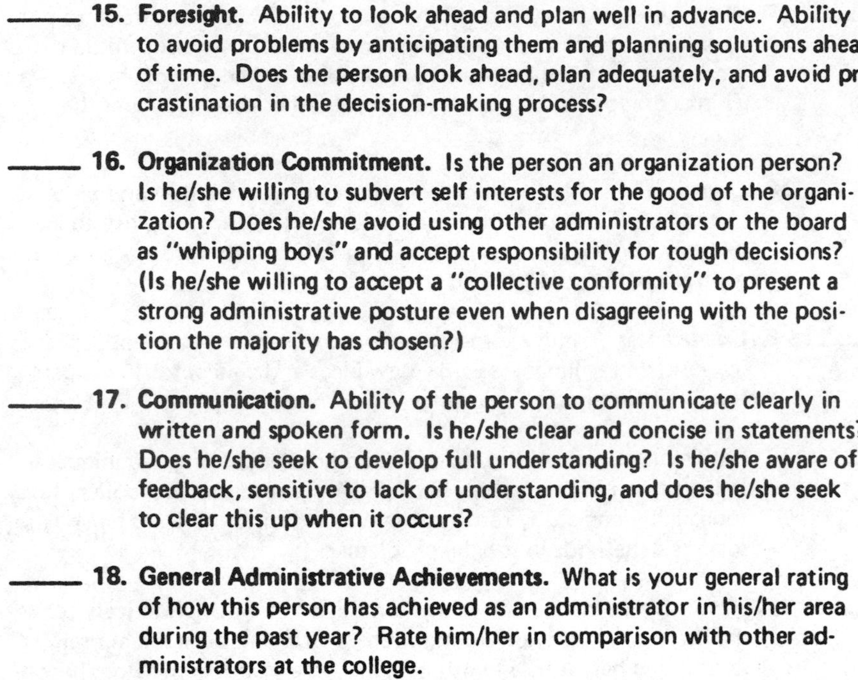

_____ 15. **Foresight.** Ability to look ahead and plan well in advance. Ability to avoid problems by anticipating them and planning solutions ahead of time. Does the person look ahead, plan adequately, and avoid procrastination in the decision-making process?

_____ 16. **Organization Commitment.** Is the person an organization person? Is he/she willing tu subvert self interests for the good of the organization? Does he/she avoid using other administrators or the board as "whipping boys" and accept responsibility for tough decisions? (Is he/she willing to accept a "collective conformity" to present a strong administrative posture even when disagreeing with the position the majority has chosen?)

_____ 17. **Communication.** Ability of the person to communicate clearly in written and spoken form. Is he/she clear and concise in statements? Does he/she seek to develop full understanding? Is he/she aware of feedback, sensitive to lack of understanding, and does he/she seek to clear this up when it occurs?

_____ 18. **General Administrative Achievements.** What is your general rating of how this person has achieved as an administrator in his/her area during the past year? Rate him/her in comparison with other administrators at the college.

A part of the process should be self-evaluation to enable the individual to compare his or her perceptions of personal performance with the perceptions of the constituencies served. Note that the Rasmussen instrument provides this kind of evaluation.

Some institutions use "outside" consultants with the idea that the process will be more objective. The decision must rest with the institution and would be dependent upon the particular circumstances at the time. Belief that outside assistance is a necessity could hamper the evaluation process since it tends to make it more of a periodic assessment rather than encouraging a continuous ongoing process. However, use of a consultant would be more appropriate for development of a process rather than the evaluation itself.

Follow-up

A comprehensive, well-planned procedure for evaluation of administrators should lead to more effective leadership. It should provide information that will assist the individual to improve in areas of weakness. Information might also be obtained that would provide a focus for one or more developmental workshops to foster the personal growth and increase the leadership effectiveness of a group of administrators including deans, associate and assistant deans, or division and department chairpersons.

For an effective evaluation process, there must also be some follow-up on an individual basis. In the case of the dean, it should be handled by the individual to whom the dean reports. Past performance and data obtained should be reviewed followed by agreement on areas to be improved and establishment or modification of goals. The dean must then become involved in the same process with associate and assistant deans and division and department chairpersons. Much hearsay and informal, probably inaccurate, information that so often circulates throughout institutions thus is replaced by systematically gathered data that provides a framework for helping the individual improve job performance and satisfaction. All involved in the process from its initiation to the follow-up reviews must reflect in their behavior a strong commitment to the improvement of professional performance. It is on this premise only that the evaluation of administrators will be fruitful and beneficial not only to the institution but also to the personal growth of each individual involved.

Professional Development

While personal characteristics, prior experiences, and educational background are important considerations in the selection of administrators, they are not sufficient to insure the continuing effectiveness of these same administrators. The evaluation procedures described are needed as well as some means for assisting in the continued development of applicable managerial skills as the knowledge continues to expand in that field. Another needed area of expertise, which is constantly changing, is the field of systems and their design.

Academicians frequently lack managerial know-how. While industrial and business organizations provide extensive in-service development for their managerial personnel, higher education institutions have not done so. Academicians who move from the classroom into administrative positions lack management skills. The instructional skills needed for the classroom are not applicable to dealing with evaluation processes, budget development, personnel administration, delegating authority, resolving conflicts, and making decisions.

In most collegial situations, the problem would be particularly severe in relation to associate and assistant deans and division and department chairpersons for these positions are frequently filled from the teaching ranks, sometimes on a rotating basis. When individuals who will assume posts as members of the dean's staff and division and department chairpersons are identified, some kind of developmental program should be immediately available—a program to prepare them for the intricacies of their new positions and provide for a smoother, more efficient, and more effective organization. A continued in-service program for administrative professional development, in which even the dean participates, would make possible additional progress toward the kind of operation needed within today's colleges.

The individual appraisal process previously described will aid professional growth and lead toward increased competence. Emphasis should always be on personal development rather than merely a critical review of strengths and weaknesses. Individual self-analysis may be followed by group analysis by the entire administrative team of its own strengths, weaknesses, and needs for improving team effectiveness. In conjunction with the evaluation and appraisal process, a formal plan should be established to provide growth opportunities for individuals and the group as a whole. Some appropriate activities for administrative devel-

CHAIRPERSON INFORMATION FORM

for use with the DECA Survey Form

Name ______________________________ (1-20)
(Last) (Initials)

Department ______________________________ (21-39)
(40-43)

Institution ______________________________

Number of faculty asked to respond ______________________________ (44-46)

Approximately what percentage of the faculty in this department is tenured?
(1) Over 80% (2) 60-79% (3) 40-59% (4) Under 40% ___ (47)

Are members of the department housed:
(1) In a single building? (2) In more than one building? ___ (48)

How many formal department faculty meetings were called in the past 12 months?
(1) None (2) 1 or 2 (3) 3-5 (4) 6-9 (5) 10 or more ___ (49)

How many years have you served as chairperson/head of this department?
(1) This is my first year. (2) 1-2 years (3) 3-5 years (4) 6 or more years ___ (50)

What are the terms of your appointment?
(1) I was appointed by the dean and serve at his/her pleasure (2) I was elected by the faculty for a specific term (3) I was elected by the faculty but not for a specific term ___ (51)

- **The list below describes responsibilities which some department chairpersons/heads pursue. Circle the number which describes your judgment of how important each of these is in your role as chairperson/head:**

1 — Not Important 2 — Only So-So 3 — Fairly Important 4 — Quite Important 5 — Essential

CHAIRPERSON/HEAD RESPONSIBILITIES

	RATING	
1. Guides the development of sound procedures for assessing faculty performance	1 2 3 4 5	(52)
2. Recognizes and rewards faculty in accordance with their contributions to the department's program	1 2 3 4 5	(53)
3. Guides development of sound organizational plan to accomplish departmental program	1 2 3 4 5	(54)
4. Arranges effective and equitable allocation of faculty responsibilities such as committee assignments, teaching loads, etc.	1 2 3 4 5	(55)
5. Takes lead in recruitment of promising faculty	1 2 3 4 5	(56)
6. Fosters good teaching in the department	1 2 3 4 5	(57)
7. Stimulates research and scholarly activity in the department	1 2 3 4 5	(58)
8. Guides curriculum development	1 2 3 4 5	(59)
9. Maintains faculty morale by reducing, resolving, or preventing conflicts	1 2 3 4 5	(60)
10. Fosters development of each faculty member's special talents or interests	1 2 3 4 5	(61)
11. Understands and communicates expectations of the campus administration to the faculty	1 2 3 4 5	(62)
12. Effectively communicates the department's needs (personnel, space, monetary) to the dean	1 2 3 4 5	(63)
13. Facilitates obtaining grants and contracts from extramural sources	1 2 3 4 5	(64)
14. Improves the department's image and reputation in the total campus community	1 2 3 4 5	(65)
15. Encourages an appropriate balance among specializations within the department	1 2 3 4 5	(66)

SURVEY FORM--FACULTY REACTIONS TO CHAIRPERSON ACTIVITIES

Department ______________________ Institution ______________________

- **The list below describes 15 responsibilities which some department chairpersons/heads pursue. In Column 1, circle the number corresponding to your judgment of how important each of these should be for your chairperson/head using the following code:**

  1 — Not Important **2 — Only So-So** **3 — Fairly Important** **4 — Quite Important** **5 — Essential**

- **Use Column 2 to describe how effectively you feel your department chairperson/head fulfilled each responsibility during the past 12 months. Omit any item if you feel you cannot make a valid judgment; otherwise circle the number best corresponding to your estimate:**

  1 — Poor **2 — Only So-So** **3 — In Between** **4 — Good** **5 — Outstanding**

	IMPORTANCE COLUMN 1	CHAIRPERSON/HEAD RESPONSIBILITIES		PERFORMANCE COLUMN 2
1.	1 2 3 4 5	Guides the development of sound procedures for assessing faculty performance	16.	1 2 3 4 5
2.	1 2 3 4 5	Recognizes and rewards faculty in accordance with their contributions to department's program	17.	1 2 3 4 5
3.	1 2 3 4 5	Guides development of sound organizational plan to accomplish departmental program	18.	1 2 3 4 5
4.	1 2 3 4 5	Arranges effective and equitable allocation of faculty responsibilities such as committee assignments, teaching loads, etc.	19.	1 2 3 4 5
5.	1 2 3 4 5	Takes lead in recruitment of promising faculty	20.	1 2 3 4 5
6.	1 2 3 4 5	Fosters good teaching in the department	21.	1 2 3 4 5
7.	1 2 3 4 5	Stimulates research and scholarly activity in the department	22.	1 2 3 4 5
8.	1 2 3 4 5	Guides curriculum development	23.	1 2 3 4 5
9.	1 2 3 4 5	Maintains faculty morale by reducing, resolving or preventing conflicts	24.	1 2 3 4 5
10.	1 2 3 4 5	Fosters development of each faculty member's special talents or interests	25.	1 2 3 4 5
11.	1 2 3 4 5	Understands and communicates expectations of the campus administration to the faculty	26.	1 2 3 4 5
12.	1 2 3 4 5	Effectively communicates the department's needs (personnel, space, monetary) to the dean	27.	1 2 3 4 5
13.	1 2 3 4 5	Facilitates obtaining grants and contracts from extramural sources	28.	1 2 3 4 5
14.	1 2 3 4 5	Improves the department's image and reputation in the total campus community	29.	1 2 3 4 5
15.	1 2 3 4 5	Encourages an appropriate balance among academic specializations within the department	30.	1 2 3 4 5

- **Indicate how frequently each of the following 30 statements is descriptive of your department chairperson/head by circling the number corresponding to your judgment:**

  1 — Hardly Ever (not at all descriptive) **2 — Less than Half the Time** **3 — About Half the Time** **4 — More than Half the Time** **5 — Almost Always (very descriptive)**

The department chairperson/head:

31. Makes own attitudes clear to the faculty	1 2 3 4 5
32. Tries out new ideas with the faculty	1 2 3 4 5
33. Works without a plan	1 2 3 4 5
34. Maintains definite standards of performance	1 2 3 4 5
35. Makes sure his/her part in the department is understood by all members	1 2 3 4 5
36. Lets faculty members know what's expected of them	1 2 3 4 5
37. Sees to it that faculty members are working up to capacity	1 2 3 4 5
38. Sees to it that the work of faculty members is coordinated	1 2 3 4 5
39. Does little things that make it pleasant to be a member of the faculty	1 2 3 4 5
40. Is easy to understand	1 2 3 4 5
41. Keeps to him/herself	1 2 3 4 5
42. Looks out for the personal welfare of individual faculty members	1 2 3 4 5
43. Refuses to explain actions	1 2 3 4 5
44. Acts without consulting the faculty	1 2 3 4 5
45. Is slow to accept new ideas	1 2 3 4 5

—OVER—

46 Treats all faculty members as his/her equal 1 2 3 4 5
47 Is willing to make changes 1 2 3 4 5
48 Makes faculty members feel at ease when talking to them 1 2 3 4 5
49. Puts faculty suggestions into action 1 2 3 4 5
50. Gets faculty approval on important matters before going ahead 1 2 3 4 5

51. Postpones decisions unnecessarily 1 2 3 4 5
52. Is more a reactor than an initiator 1 2 3 4 5
53. Makes it clear that faculty suggestions for improving the department are welcome 1 2 3 4 5
54. Is responsive to one "clique" in the faculty but largely ignores those who are not members of the clique 1 2 3 4 5
55. In expectations of faculty members, makes allowance for their personal or situational problems 1 2 3 4 5

56. Lets faculty members know when they've done a good job 1 2 3 4 5
57. Explains the basis for his/her decisions 1 2 3 4 5
58. Gains input from faculty on important matters 1 2 3 4 5
59. Acts as though visible department accomplishments were vital to him/her 1 2 3 4 5
60. Acts as though high faculty morale was vital to him/her 1 2 3 4 5

• Questions 61-70 ask about yourself or the department in general. Use this answer code:
1 — Definitely False
2 — More False than True
3 — In Between
4 — More True than False
5 — Definitely True

61. I enjoy my work in this department 1 2 3 4 5
62. I have a positive relationship with the department chairperson 1 2 3 4 5
63. I agree with the priorities and emphases which have guided recent development in the department 1 2 3 4 5
64. The department has been getting stronger in recent years (use responses 1 or 2 if it has been getting weaker; use response 3 if there has been little change) 1 2 3 4 5

During the past 12 months, the department chairperson's/head's effectiveness has been seriously impaired by:

65. Enrollment/retrenchment problems in the department 1 2 3 4 5
66. Inadequate facilities for the department 1 2 3 4 5
67. Bureaucratic requirements and regulations 1 2 3 4 5
68. Inadequate financial resources to support departmental programs 1 2 3 4 5
69. A relatively low priority given to the department by the chairperson's /head's immediate superior 1 2 3 4 5
70. Obstructionism/negativism from one or more senior members of the faculty 1 2 3 4 5

• Your responses to the following questions will be returned to your chairperson/head. If you are concerned about anonymity, you may wish to type your responses or have them typed.

Which matters need priority attention in the department during the next year or two? ____________________

____

____

Identify any departmental policies or procedures which you feel need immediate improvement ____________________

____

____

What is the most important observation you can make about the department chairperson's/head's:

a) administrative effectiveness? ____________________

____

b) administrative style? ____________________

____

Other comments: ____________________

____

____

DECA REPORT

UNIVERSITY COLLEGE

J. J. DOE
DEPARTMENT OF ADVANCED STUDIES
SPRING 1976-77

NUMBER ASKED TO REACT: 10
NUMBER RESPONDING: 10
PERCENT RESPONDING: 100%

PART I. RESPONSIBILITIES

	IMPORTANCE			PERFORMANCE							
	HEAD	FACULTY MEAN	FACULTY S.D.	NUMBER RESPONDING 1	2	3	4	5	OMIT	MEAN	COMPARISON
A. PERSONNEL MANAGEMENT											
1. GUIDES FAC EVAL PROCEDURES	4	4.2	.7	0	0	3	5	2	0	3.9	HIGH AVG
2. REWARDS FAC APPROPRIATELY	4	4.5	.7	0	1	2	6	1	0	3.7	AVERAGE
4. ALLOCATES FACULTY RESPONSIBILITY	4	4.7	.5	0	0	1	4	5	0	4.4	HIGH AVG
9. MAINTAINS MORALE	4	4.4	.8	0	1	4	4	1	0	3.5	AVERAGE
10. FOSTERS FACULTY DEVELOPMENT	3	4.4	.8	0	0	3	6	1	0	3.8	AVERAGE
11. COMMUNICATES U. EXPECTATIONS	3	4.4	.8	0	0	1	6	3	0	4.2	AVERAGE
B. DEPT. PLANNING AND DEVELOPMENT											
3. GUIDES DEVELOPMENT OF PLANS	4	4.5	.7	0	0	2	6	2	0	4.0	HIGH AVG
5. FACULTY RECRUITMENT	2	3.6	.9	1	1	3	3	2	0	3.4	LOW AVG
6. FOSTERS GOOD TEACHING	4	4.4	.8	0	3	4	1	2	0	3.2	LOW AVG
8. GUIDES CURRICULUM DEVELOPMENT	4	3.9	.7	0	0	1	3	6	0	4.5	HIGH
15. ENCOURAGES BALANCED FACULTY	4	4.0	.6	0	0	2	3	4	1	4.2	HIGH AVG
C. BUILDING DEPARTMENT REPUTATION											
7. STIM RSCH/SCHOLARLY EFFORT	3	4.3	.8	0	2	1	2	5	0	4.0	HIGH AVG
12. COMMUNICATES DEPT'S NEEDS	3	4.8	.4	0	0	2	3	5	0	4.3	AVERAGE
13. FACILITATES OUTSIDE FUNDING	2	3.7	.8	1	1	3	2	2	1	3.3	AVERAGE
14. IMPROVES DEPT'S IMAGE	3	4.3	.8	0	0	2	3	5	0	4.3	HIGH AVG

PART II. EVALUATION SUMMARY

	PERSONNEL MANAGEMENT	PLANNING & DEVELOPMENT	DEPARTMENT REPUTATION	TOTAL
A. PERFORMANCE WEIGHTED BY FACULTY IMP RATINGS	3.9 (HI AVG)	3.9 (AVG)	4.0 (HI AVG)	3.9 (AVG)
B. PERFORMANCE WEIGHTED BY HEAD'S IMP RATINGS	3.9 (HI AVG)	3.9 (AVG)	4.0 (HI AVG)	3.9 (AVG)
C. AGREEMENT AMONG FACULTY ON IMPORTANCE (INTRACLASS R)	---	---	---	.49 (AVG)
D. HEAD/FACULTY AGREEMENT ON IMPORTANCE (CORRELATION)	---	---	---	.47 (AVG)

J. J. DOE
DEPARTMENT OF ADVANCED STUDIES

UNIVERSITY COLLEGE
SPRING 1975-76

PART III. ADMINISTRATIVE METHODS

		NUMBER RESPONDING 1	2	3	4	5	OMIT	MEAN	DIFF FROM AVG	TRANSLATION
A. DEMOCRATIC PRACTICE	TOTAL SCORE = 3.9 (AVG)									
40.	EASY TO UNDERSTAND	1	0	0	3	6	0	4.3	+0.4	FAV
(43.)	REFUSES TO EXPLAIN ACTIONS	6	2	2	0	0	0	(1.6)	-0.1	-
(44.)	ACTS WITHOUT CONSULTING FACULTY	4	4	2	0	0	0	(1.8)	-0.3	FAV
(45.)	SLOW TO ACCEPT NEW IDEAS	9	0	0	1	0	0	(1.3)	-0.7	FAV
46.	TREATS FACULTY AS EQUALS	4	1	0	2	3	0	2.9	-1.0	UNFAV
47.	WILLING TO MAKE CHANGES	0	0	0	4	6	0	4.6	+0.6	FAV
49.	PUTS FACULTY SUGGESTIONS INTO ACTION	0	1	5	1	3	0	3.6	0.0	-
50.	GETS FACULTY APPROVAL BEFORE PROCEEDING	1	2	2	4	1	0	3.2	-0.8	UNFAV
53.	WELCOMES FACULTY SUGGESTIONS	0	1	1	3	4	1	4.1	0.0	-
(54.)	RESPONDS TO FACULTY CLIQUE	3	2	2	1	1	1	(2.4)	+0.4	UNFAV
57.	EXPLAINS DECISIONS	1	0	2	3	4	0	3.9	0.0	-
58.	GAINS FACULTY INPUT	1	1	1	4	3	0	3.7	-0.4	UNFAV
B. STRUCTURING	TOTAL SCORE = 4.2 (HIGH)									
31.	MAKES ATTITUDES CLEAR	0	0	0	4	6	0	4.6	+0.6	FAV
(33.)	WORKS W/O A PLAN	5	3	2	0	0	0	(1.7)	-0.2	-
34.	MAINTAINS PERFORMANCE STANDARDS	1	1	0	5	3	0	3.8	+0.1	-
35.	MAKES ROLE UNDERSTOOD	0	0	1	3	6	0	4.5	+0.8	FAV
36.	LETS FACULTY KNOW EXPECTATIONS	0	0	2	3	5	0	4.3	+0.7	FAV
37.	SEES THAT FACULTY WORK TO CAPACITY	0	0	2	5	3	0	4.1	+0.7	FAV
38.	SEES THAT FACULTY WORK IS COORDINATED	0	2	3	3	2	0	3.5	+0.2	-
C. INTERPERSONAL SENSITIVITY	TOTAL SCORE = 3.3 (LO AVG)									
39.	DOES LITTLE THINGS TO PLEASE	2	1	2	3	2	0	3.2	-0.3	UNFAV
(41.)	KEEPS TO HIM/HERSELF	1	3	1	2	2	1	(3.1)	+0.8	UNFAV
42.	LOOKS OUT FOR PERSONAL WELFARE OF FACULTY	3	1	0	3	3	0	3.2	-0.4	UNFAV
48.	PUTS FACULTY AT EASE IN CONVERSATION	1	1	4	1	3	0	3.4	-0.7	UNFAV
55.	MAKES ALLOWANCE FOR FACULTY PROBLEMS	2	0	0	3	3	2	3.6	-0.4	UNFAV
56.	ACKNOWLEDGES GOOD WORK	2	1	2	2	3	0	3.3	-0.3	UNFAV
60.	STRESSES FACULTY MORALE	2	0	2	3	3	0	3.5	-0.1	-
D. VIGOR	TOTAL SCORE = 4.7 (HIGH)									
32.	TRIES NEW IDEAS WITH FACULTY	0	0	1	2	7	0	4.6	+1.0	FAV
(51.)	POSTPONES DECISIONS UNNECESSARILY	9	1	0	0	0	0	(1.1)	-0.7	FAV
(52.)	MORE A REACTOR THAN INITIATOR	8	2	0	0	0	0	(1.2)	-1.2	FAV
59.	PLACES STRESS ON ACCOMPLISHMENT	0	0	1	3	6	0	4.5	+0.6	FAV

( ) INDICATES ITEMS WHERE LOW SCORES ARE DESIRABLE

J. J. DOE
DEPARTMENT OF ADVANCED STUDIES

UNIVERSITY COLLEGE
SPRING 1975-76

PART IV. CHARACTERIZATION OF DEPARTMENT

	NUMBER RESPONDING FALSE 1	2	? 3	4	TRUE 5	OMIT	MEAN
A. FACULTY							
61. ENJOY WORK	0	0	1	3	6	0	4.5
62. HAVE POSITIVE RELATIONSHIP WITH CHAIRPERSON/HEAD	1	0	4	4	1	0	3.4
63. AGREE WITH DEPARTMENT PRIORITIES	1	0	1	3	5	0	4.1
64. DEPARTMENT IS IMPROVING (3 = NO CHANGE)	0	0	3	6	1	0	3.8
B. CHAIRPERSON/HEAD PERFORMANCE ADVERSELY AFFECTED BY:							
65. ENROLL/RETRENCHMENT PROBLEMS	3	5	2	0	0	0	1.9
66. INADEQUATE FACILITIES	4	6	0	0	0	0	1.6
67. BUREAUCRATIC RED TAPE	0	1	4	3	2	0	3.6
68. INADEQUATE FINANCIAL RESOURCES	1	1	3	4	1	0	3.3
69. DEAN'S LOW PRIORITY FOR DEPARTMENT	0	0	1	3	6	0	4.5
70. NEGATIVISM FROM SENIOR FACULTY MEMBER(S)	4	4	0	1	1	0	2.1

PART V. DIAGNOSTIC SUMMARY

	PERF RATING	METHODS RELEVANT TO EACH RESPONSIBILITY[1] WEAKNESSES	STRENGTHS
A. PERSONNEL MANAGEMENT			
*1. GUIDES FAC EVAL PROCEDURES	HI AVG	FAVORABLE RATINGS	35,36,51,40,44
*2. REWARDS FAC APPROPRIATELY	AVERAGE	46,42,39,56	35,36,47.40
*4. ALLOCATES FAC RESPONSIBILITIES	HI AVG	FAVORABLE RATINGS	35,36,51,40
*9. MAINTAINS MORALE	AVERAGE	46,41,50,48,42,58,55,39	32,35,45,47,40,44
10. FOSTERS FACULTY DEVELOPMENT	AVERAGE	46,42,58,55,39,56	35,36,37,40
11. COMMUNICATES U. EXPECTATIONS	AVERAGE		32,35,45,36,37,51,31,40
B. DEPARTMENT PLANNING AND DEVELOPMENT			
*3. GUIDES DEVELOPMENT OF PLANS	HI AVG	FAVORABLE RATINGS	52,32,35,45,36,37,51
5. FACULTY RECRUITMENT	LO AVG	46,58,55	52,32,59
*6. FOSTERS GOOD TEACHING	LO AVG	42,39	32,35,36,37,51,40
8. GUIDES CURRICULUM DEVELOPMENT	HIGH	FAVORABLE RATINGS	52,32,51,59,44
*15. ENCOURAGES BALANCED FACULTY	HI AVG	FAVORABLE RATINGS	35,45,36,37
C. BUILDING DEPARTMENT REPUTATION			
7. STIM RSCH/SCHOL EFFORT	HI AVG	FAVORABLE RATINGS	52,32,45,59,47,44
12. COMMUNICATES DEPTS NEED	AVERAGE		52,32,35,45,37,51,47,40
13. FACILITATES OUTSIDE FUNDING	AVERAGE	55,56	52,32,47
14. IMPROVES DEPARTMENT'S IMAGE	HI AVG	FAVORABLE RATINGS	52,32,35,45,51,47,40

*RATED AT LEAST "4" IN IMPORTANCE BY BOTH FACULTY AND CHAIRPERSON/HEAD
NOTE 1: SEE PAGE 2 TO IDENTIFY CONTENT OF THE ITEMS LISTED BY NUMBER

opment might include planned reading, sessions with group dynamics specialists, visits to other institutions, participation in appropriate professional meetings, seminars on management skills, and so on.

There is an increasing recognition of the need to assist administrators in extending their views beyond the divisions, departments, and the college. Preparation for participation in the institutional planning process as well as budget development and dealing with financial statements is needed. Other possible developmental needs include student affairs, research possibilities and grantsmanship, public relations, the dynamics of leadership, and dealing with dissension. Harvey proposes the following as some topics for professional development programs:

1. The Role of the Administrator
2. Communication in Administration
3. Human Relations in Administration
4. Delegation
5. Personnel Selection
6. The Law and Higher Education
7. Coaching and Developing Subordinates
8. Working Effectively with Your Secretary
9. Management by Objectives.[14]

In fact, an administrative leave system might be just as desirable as the system for faculty leaves. It would provide an opportunity for development of a perspective from a different vantage point and professional and personal renewal. It might also be the means for making possible the intensive study of a particular problem at a Center for Higher Education.

Whatever pattern is established for the total administrative professional development program, it must be continuous and comprehensive. When combined with similar programs for faculty and supportive staff, the effect upon the institution can be only beneficial.

SUMMARY

Personal qualities are an important factor in the selection and evaluation of college administrators. In addition to integrity and numerous other desirable characteristics, the ability to obtain the cooperation of others and to make sound judgments and wise decisions is important. The caliber of an organization is dependent upon the caliber of its leadership. To be a successful leader, an administrator needs the skills of an academician, management expert, and human relations specialist.

Job or position descriptions should be a regular part of an institution's personnel files. If kept up to date, they provide a source for defining the responsibilities of particular positions as well as the interrelationships among various positions. In addition, the activity that commences when an administrator must be selected becomes simplified. Search committees should not be put in the position of needing to develop a job description before the search itself may begin.

A search committee has only recommending power. Its responsibility ends when it forwards the names of those it considers to be the top candidates to the individual specified in the charge to the committee. For maximum efficiency, a format for the selection and operation of search committees should be established.

There is greater variety in the processes for selection of division and department chairpersons than in the selection of dean's office personnel. Rotating elections are becoming more common than the permanent appointment of some scholar in the field who is named to the position for the purpose of bringing prestige to a particular department. The increased complexity of institutions has made it more desirable than ever that the chairperson have some administrative ability and, if possible, previous administrative experience.

Much has been done in the area of faculty evaluation over the past few years. It is just as important that administrators be evaluated on some systematic basis. Too often, ineffective administrators have continued in their positions without any kind of formalized review. A policy and procedural outline that calls for a periodic review can be invaluable to the effective administrator and can provide a basis for some kind of action when an administrator is perceived as ineffective.

ENDNOTES

1. John Wesley Gould, *The Academic Deanship* (New York: Bureau of Publications, Teachers College, Columbia University, 1964), p. 7.
2. Used with permission. *Changes in University Organization, 1964–1971* by Edward Gross and Paul V. Grambsch. Copyright © 1974 by The Carnegie Foundation for the Advancement of Teaching. (New York: McGraw-Hill, 1974), p. 197.
3. Elaine McIntosh and Robert Maier, "Management Skills in a Changing Academic Environment," *Educational Record* 57 (1976): 89.
4. James H. L. Roach, "The Academic Department Chairperson: Functions and Responsibilities," *Educational Record* 57 (1976): 14–15.
5. Thomas M. Stauffer, "Selecting Academic Administrators," *Educational Record* 57 (1976): 173.
6. Frederick S. Weaver and Louise J. Farnham, "On Selecting Academic Administrators," *Educational Record* 58 (1977): 322–328.
7. Stauffer, "Selecting Academic Administrators," pp. 174–175.
8. Richard Sommerfeld and Donna Nagely, "Seek and Ye Shall Find: The Organization and Conduct of a Search Committee," *Journal of Higher Education* 45 (1974): 251.
9. Tyrus Hillway, "Evaluating College and University Administrators," *Intellect* 101 (1973): 427.
10. C. E. Skipper, "Personal Characteristics of Effective and Ineffective University Leaders," *College and University* 51 (1976): 141.
11. *Ibid.*
12. Charles F. Fisher, "The Evaluation and Development of College and University Administrators," *ERIC/Higher Education Research Currents,* American Association for Higher Education, March 1977, p. 4.
13. From material supplied by Dr. Glen R. Rasmussen, President of Findlay College, Findlay, Ohio.
14. L. James Harvey, *Managing Colleges and Universities by Objectives* (Littleton, Col.: Ireland Educational Corporation, 1976), pp. 70–71.

CHAPTER 4

The Faculty

Many of the forces affecting institutions of higher education as a whole are also having a direct impact upon individual faculty members in these institutions. College professors cannot help becoming concerned when they hear discussion about elimination of tenure, staff reduction, increased workloads, increased efficiency, and demands for accountability. As a result, faculty and students as well as administrators are participating in decisions related to recruitment, tenure, and promotion all of which were previously considered the prerogative of the dean in cooperation with department chairpersons. Finally, the development of campus bargaining units and the requirements of affirmative action regulations bear implications for the college administrator when considering not only recruitment and hiring but also retrenchment procedures.

RECRUITMENT AND SELECTION

While financial belt-tightening and decreasing enrollments are having a direct effect upon faculty employment, some replacement of faculty and even the addition of faculty, in some instances, will continue to be necessary. Recruitment and selection procedures must be structured to not only obtain the best qualified person for a particular opening but also meet the requirements for federally mandated affirmative action programs.

AFFIRMATIVE ACTION

In the past, there has been a pattern of discrimination against women and blacks in higher education. Formal charges of sex discrimination have been filed against colleges and universities and upheld. When compared to the numbers of new male faculty, far fewer women have been hired, particularly in the larger, better known, higher paying institutions. In addition, their salaries have generally been lower than those of their male counterparts and their progress through the promotion ranks much slower.

As pointed out by Bernice Sandler, there were, until recently, no federal laws forbidding discrimination against women.

> Title VII of the Civil Rights Act of 1964, which forbids sex discrimination in employment, exempts faculty in educational institutions. Title VI of the same Act forbids discrimination in federally assisted programs, but it only applies to race, color, and national origin, not sex. The Equal Pay Act excludes professional, executive, and administrative employees. Even the U.S. Commis-

> sion on Civil Rights has no jurisdiction over sex discrimination; it is limited by law to matters pertaining to race, color, religion, and national origin, but not sex.
>
> The only remedy that women have is the Executive order which forbids federal contractors from discriminating in employment. It does not cover institutions which have no federal contracts, nor does it cover discrimination against students.[1]

Affirmative action requirements do not mandate the hiring of women or members of minority groups who are not qualified for the position or positions available. They do require that women and minority candidates be recruited and considered and that the same criteria be applied to these candidates as to the traditional white male. Careful and accurate records of all personnel actions must be kept and department heads and deans must be prepared to answer questions about the procedures used to recruit women and minorities if they recommend a white male for a faculty opening. Under no circumstances is it required that unqualified applicants be hired to meet affirmative action stipulations.

Goals are necessary as well as plans and timetables for achieving them in order to move institutions toward increasing the number of faculty members from the group or groups who were subject to a previous pattern of exclusion. Goals are preferable to fixed quotas because they provide much needed flexibility and are a means for preventing discrimination of another kind.

A statement by the American Association of University Professors emphasized that affirmative action guidelines do not mandate preferential or compensatory treatment of women and minorities and that

> . . . affirmative action in the improvement of professional opportunities for women and minorities must be (and readily can be) devised wholly consistent with the highest aspirations of universities and colleges for excellence and outstanding quality, and that affirmative action should in no way use the very instrument of racial or sexual discrimination which it deplores.
>
> What is sought in the idea of affirmative action is essentially the revision of standards and practices to assure that institutions are in fact drawing from the largest marketplace of human resources in staffing their faculties, and a critical review of appointment and advancement criteria to insure that they do not inadvertently foreclose consideration of the best qualified persons by untested presuppositions which operate to exclude women and minorities.[2]

In the same statement, four specific procedures are recommended:

1. Definition of the criteria of merit
2. Critical review and revision of the standards for academic appointment and advancement
3. Review and revision of academic recruitment policies
4. Development of statistical forecasts under an affirmative action plan, and the monitoring of equal protection.[3]

The last recommendation negates the establishment of quotas but, in their place, requires a predetermination of the hiring pattern likely to occur if nondiscriminatory procedures are used for recruiting and hiring. In other words, an explanation should be available if what is forecast does not occur. In order to "protect themselves," some institutions have developed specific written guidelines to be followed whenever a vacancy of any kind occurs. The following spelled-out procedures are an example.

PROCEDURE FOR IMPLEMENTING EQUAL OPPORTUNITY GOALS

1. Verify employment opportunity vacancy.
2. Prepare vacancy announcement.
3. Distribute vacancy announcement internally and review permanent employee personnel file for potential promotion.

4. Distribute vacancy announcement externally using where applicable:
   a. Advertisement in newspapers
   b. Advertisement in professional journals
   c. Notify other institutions, professional organizations, special interest groups, and agencies.
   d. Notify graduate and professional school placement offices.
5. Record:
   a. Number of applications received
   b. Number of personal interviews
   c. Responses by:
      Number of men _____
      Number of minority men _____
      Number of women _____
      Number of minority women _____
6. Prepare recommendation to hire and refer to President for review.
7. Review final decision with EEO officer.
8. Hire.
9. Announce hiring

All personnel responsible for hiring must be aware that the College assures equal opportunity to qualified individuals regardless of race, color, religion, national origin, age, or sex and that all vacancies are publicly announced to insure as broad a response as possible.

NOTE: Executive Order 11246 states that the term "minority" refers to Negroes, Spanish-surnamed, American Indians and Orientals.

Opportunities for adding women and minorities are becoming increasingly scarce as the pool of traditional students shrinks and economic pressures lead to greater student-teacher ratios. Any extensive need for new faculty will to a large extent result from the newer programs established for the nontraditional student population now being sought by many colleges and universities.

Impact of Unionization upon Recruitment

Unionized schools with faculty openings will face difficulties created by the "lockstep" fixed salary schedules that have already become the pattern in some institutions. As the demand has increased, the available supply of female and minority candidates has decreased and salary demands of these candidates may exceed those permitted by the negotiated schedule. A possible result will be that unionized schools may not be able to attract the most desirable candidates. The Equal Work, Equal Pay Act should be a deterrent to the practice of premium salaries for reasons based on race and sex but no one has yet challenged what has been common practice in the marketplace.

Of course, the same situation will make it difficult for these institutions to obtain new staff members considered to be particularly outstanding in their specialties and, therefore, able to command higher salaries. A distinct disadvantage exists because these candidates will still be able to obtain the higher salaries from colleges and universities with the necessary resources and which are not yet bound in this area by union contracts. A candidate who must decide between equally attractive academic positions may be influenced to make a final decision based upon salary considerations. It follows that the academic institutions with the greatest resources will attract the most qualified faculty.

Recruitment and Selection Processes

It is a foregone conclusion that the quality of an institution depends upon the quality of its faculty and students. Large institutions may find that their size with its inevitable bureaucratization may be a deterrent in recruitment. However, there are other factors which enhance a particular situation for some candidates. For one group, these might include the prestige factor and opportunities to work with graduate students. Because of the inherent rewards in being a member of a college faculty, other candidates will select a smaller institution with its greater opportunities for closer interpersonal relationships.

Whether an organization is a business, an industry, an educational institution, or whatever, job descriptions for each position should be on file. When the need arises for recruiting one or more faculty members, the first task should be updating an existing job description or developing one where none exists. The job description becomes the nucleus for preparation of an announcement of the vacancy; it should include: the philosophy and objectives of the institution; anything unique about its approach to teaching and learning; description of the student services; summary of academic offerings; academic calendar; description of the facilities; and information about the area in which the college is located.

It is essential that the announcement be given the widest distribution possible. It should be sent to the university and college placement offices and graduate institutions that train college personnel. A continuous attempt is needed to make the faculty one that represents various sections of the country and different backgrounds.

A simple but comprehensive application form should be designed and a process established not only for handling and acknowledging inquiries but also for screening credentials to identify the best qualified candidates. Unfortunately, some decisions are based on a subjective evaluation of the caliber of the applicant's writing and the recommendations in the credentials, which usually reflect only personal qualities and ability as a student and dissertation writer. No information is requested concerning the applicant's ability to teach even though teaching is the major area of responsibility attached to a faculty position. The new college or university teacher often begins a career with no prior teaching experience. Too many faculty members believe that one who has developed a specialty through graduate study in his or her field is qualified to teach it resulting in an emphasis in recruiting on scholarship and research rather than ability to teach.

Faculty members and students must be appropriately and actively involved throughout the process. This includes participation on an interviewing committee. Interviews are frequently rushed but, if properly conducted, could provide some insight into the strength of the applicant's interest in teaching and ideas he or she might have for use in the classroom. Letters to the applicant's former professors and/or department chairperson might reveal additional information about teaching ability or potential for becoming an effective teacher. It is highly recommended that the potential faculty member be asked to make some sort of presentation to demonstrate his or her ability to teach. This may be done in a regularly scheduled class of students or a special seminar situation involving departmental faculty. Sawyer suggests the following delimitations be provided the applicant prior to the campus visit:

1. Inform the candidate prior to the campus visit that a 30–50 minute lesson should be prepared.
2. Describe the situation in which the presentation will be made.
3. Describe the material to be covered which should be in the area he or she will be expected to teach and should not be based upon the candidate's dissertation.
4. Indicate that any method or combination may be utilized including lecture, question and answer, discussion, and audio-visual aids.[4]

Sawyer describes the advantages of the procedure as follows:

1. Enables the candidate to perform professionally
2. Enables faculty to better judge the candidate

3. Impresses upon the candidate the school's genuine concern for teaching
4. Can lead to improvement in teaching both in the candidate and at the institution.[5]

Sawyer also cites a number of disadvantages but, at the same time, has added parenthetical comments which indicate he believes the advantages outweigh the disadvantages.

1. Candidate nervous (this should wear off) Faculty make allowances
2. Single presentation not a true picture (better than nothing)
3. Too much depends upon a single presentation (actually, only a part of the selection process)
4. Faculty members may have conflicting opinions—usually some level of agreement
5. Some good candidates may withdraw rather than go through the "ordeal." [6]

As stated before, students should play an important role in the selection of faculty. If a teaching presentation is made to a class, a feedback instrument should be completed by the students involved. If a special situation is established for the presentation, students should be invited and their opinions regarding the acceptability of the candidate solicited. As a minimum, students should have an opportunity to meet the candidates in an informal situation without faculty present and then provide feedback to the appropriate department chairperson. It would be most appropriate for students to discuss with the candidate his or her conception of what constitutes good teaching, what the student's role in the institution should be, and the candidate's philosophy of the institution's role in education.

While the requirement of a presentation by the candidate for a teaching position provides one means for the general improvement of college teaching, a long-range effort launched by graduate institutions is also essential. Identification of traits indicating potential for college teaching is needed in addition to the specific preparation of doctoral candidates for college teaching where appropriate. The unsupervised and unevaluated undergraduate teaching experiences usually provided graduate assistants and teaching associates during their residency periods do not constitute adequate preparation. Continual instruction and guidance by qualified staff members is essential. Care should be exercised in the selection and assignment of graduate students for teaching experiences but, most important, adequate systematic supervision with follow-up assistance must be provided if teaching effectiveness on college campuses is to be improved.

EVALUATION

It is highly important that the purposes for evaluation of faculty be clearly defined and followed by the establishment of specific criteria. One purpose is the need for objective data to be used as a guide when making administrative decisions about promotions, salary increases, and merit considerations. Other possible administrative uses could be making teaching assignments on the basis of course and instructor evaluations and cooperating with faculty in the design of faculty development programs. Because the primary purpose of the institution is the education of students, an equally important reason for evaluation is provision of information to individual faculty members that will assist them in improving their own performance. Evaluation results are also often used by students in their selection of courses and instructors. Finally, the results will fulfill a need for much more research data on teaching and learning than is currently available.

Evaluation versus Rating

Webster defines evaluation as a careful appraisal [7] while rating implies a quantitative and/or qualitative ranking.[8] Although normative data of some kind is desirable for administrative use and for enabling an instructor to compare himself with other instructors, the improvement of teaching is the ultimate goal. Therefore, evaluation should be the primary concern.

A review of the literature reveals that much attention has been given to the development of instruments for student evaluation of teaching. However, the data obtained is only one portion, although a large and important one, of the total information needed for a comprehensive evaluation of faculty. To emphasize this, Miller lists nine areas for evaluation: classroom teaching, advising, faculty service and relations, management (administration), performing and visual arts, professional services, publications, public service, and research.[9]

Comprehensive evaluation procedures are needed in each of these areas including development of instruments that will provide feedback to the instructor as well as normative data for administrative purposes. Simple basic rating forms for each of Miller's nine areas are presented in his *Evaluating Faculty Performance.* In addition to a rather simple form identified as a Student Appraisal of Teaching, he includes forms for use in: classroom visitation and a teaching materials and procedures appraisal by colleagues; a self-appraisal of teaching; student appraisal of advising; faculty service and relations appraisal; assessment of administrative effectiveness (which could be used for gathering data from faculty and other administrators); self-evaluation in the performing and visual arts and a quantified appraisal by others; professional status and activities; evaluation of books, monographs, special reports, book chapters, and periodical articles; and assessment of public service and research.[10] Miller's forms might provide an appropriate beginning base for the development of a complete evaluation process that would be uniquely adapted to the needs and characteristics of a specific institution.

Several examples of instructor evaluation forms designed for use by students are found on pages 72 to 76. Section II of the Temple University College of Education form also provides some basic course information that could be helpful to instructors in assessing the effectiveness of their courses. By no means is it comprehensive enough to serve alone as a course evaluation instrument. The major purpose for its development was instructor evaluation.

The Faculty and Course Evaluation Instrument known as F.A.C.E. differs from the first in that it provides an opportunity for the professor to select the aspects of the course to be assessed. Provision is also made to accommodate answers to as many as forty optional questions. It should be noted that course content has not been specifically included in either of the two instruments.

Instructor and course evaluation including attention to course content are combined in the Survey Form developed at the Center for Faculty Evaluation and Development in Higher Education located at Kansas State University. The approach here is much more flexible since extensive instructions are provided for expanding the survey to meet the specific needs of an instructor. These materials are part of a total system identified as the Instructional Development and Effectiveness system or the IDEA system.

The Course Evaluation Questionnaire–Form D (page 87) has been replaced by the staff at the Measurement and Research Division, Office of Instructional Resources, University of Illinois with the more flexible Instructor and Course Evaluation System (ICES) which follows it. The new approach makes it possible for faculty to select the items they consider most appropriate for their particular courses. A description of the general operation of the system and the table of contents from the catalog are shown on pages 89 and 90. A copy of the basic form appears on pages 91 and 92 while the form on page 93 is an example of an instrument designed by one instructor for personal use. The system is both flexible and comprehensive. It also reflects the common practice of combining instructor evaluation with an evaluation of some aspects of the course itself.

A simple form designed at the departmental level appears on page 95. This form is followed by several that were developed for use in peer evaluation processes. Miller's form and the first one from Greenfield Community College were designed for use during an actual classroom observation. The second instrument from Greenfield provides for broader assessment of an individual.

The relative importance of each of the various areas of faculty activity has been a source of much controversy. Research activity has been valued because it supposedly makes the professor a better teacher but, according to Guthries [11] and Voeks,[12] there is no significant relationship between the two. Aleamoni and Yimer [13] arrived at the same conclusion in a later study. Other questions also need to be answered. If a professor is involved in research, is it essential that the results be published? What is the value of administrative duties? Are they academically respectable and to be considered within the reward system? Faculty frequently will not assume program directorship or coordination although it may be personally satisfying because such activity will not be recognized. The nature of the institution in addition to faculty interests and abilities must also be major considerations in developing a comprehensive process.

Increasing Emphasis on Teaching

Much lip service has been paid to the importance of teaching, but in the evaluation of college professors, research has often been prized more highly and prestige determined by the professor's own colleagues based on his or her publications alone. Research, publications, and delivering lectures provide visibility outside an institution but teaching ability is usually visible only within the institution. The doctorate that is the "union card' for admission to the profession assists an individual in becoming a scholar and specialized technologist; it does not prepare him or her for teaching. Deans and department chairpersons have claimed they rate teaching as being most important in evaluating individual staff members but they themselves are seldom involved in classroom observation.

During the late sixties, several trends began developing that might be attributed to the extreme activism of students on college and university campuses during that period. Among these were:

1. Decline in attention paid to research, publication, activity in professional societies, and public service
2. Increased emphasis upon classroom teaching
3. Increased emphasis upon student evaluations
4. More structured, systematic evaluations of teaching performance
5. Increased emphasis on effective student advising
6. Increased participation in campus committee work

In the total evaluation of faculty, teaching is becoming the number one factor in importance and will continue to be as the tightening budget situations lead to demands for accountability and students continue to pressure for better instruction. While it is desirable for faculty to publish, consult, and lecture, their major purpose for being is teaching.

INSTRUCTOR EVALUATION FORM
COLLEGE OF EDUCATION

COURSE NO. ____________ DATE ____________

SECTION 1 COMPARATIVE DATA (A to H – PLEASE USE A PENCIL)

DATE			COURSE NO.
MO.	DAY	YR.	
0	0	0	0
1	1	1	1
2	2	2	2
3	3	3	3
4	4	4	4
5	5	5	5
6	6	6	6
7	7	7	7
8	8	8	8
9	9	9	9

C: GLOBAL RATING: Code in overall grade you would give this instructor:

A
B
C
D
F

D: Code in the grade that you think the instructor will give you in this course:

A
B
C
D
F

E: Code in the appropriate description of how much you have learned in this course:

A. DEFINITIONS OF AREA (To be used in ratings of area below):

a. PREPARATION: has adequately planned the course and sessions; chooses content for and articulates the sessions so as to achieve the course goals; has developed meaningful and realistic course requirements which foster the attainment of course goals.

b. PRESENTATION: presents material well in classroom sessions; gets students involved through techniques other than lectures; gets students to understand the concept and ideas presented; older material is reviewed and synthesized with new materials; has a good voice, etc. and interesting manner; elicits and responds well to relevant questions; gets students to raise questions.

c. EVALUATION: uses reasonable evaluative devices (papers, group or committee self-evaluations) that are fair, reliable, and valid; gives adequate feedback to students; gets individual students to evaluate themselves in terms of the stated goals of the course.

d. PERSONALITY: relates well and is receptive to students; has a good sense of humor, etc. is flexible; generally has a good rapport with those he/she interacts.

e. INTELLECT: knows his/her subject and field; inspires intellectual confidence from his/her students; keeps up to date; is generally well read and well rounded.

B. RATINGS OF AREA:

Rate in each of the following pairs; mark the proper box beside the one area in which the instructor is better. Do this even if in your opinion, the instructor is poor or superior in both areas. You must mark one area, and only one, in all 10 pairs for your data to be valid and used. Refer to sample-coding at right. ⟶

SAMPLE CODING

1 { EVALUATION
PRESENTATION ▬

VERY LITTLE	1
RELATIVELY LITTLE	2
SOME	3
QUITE A BIT	4
CONSIDERABLE AMOUNT	5

F: Does the instructor create an interest in the subject?

ALMOST NEVER	1
NOT MUCH OF THE TIME	2
SOME OF THE TIME	3
MUCH OF THE TIME	4
ALMOST ALWAYS	5

G: Would you recommend this instructor to a friend?

WOULD NOT RECOMMEND	1
RECOMMEND WITH SEVERE RESERVATION	2
RECOMMEND WITH SLIGHT RESERVATION	3
RECOMMEND WITH NO RESERVATION	4
RECOMMEND HIGHLY	5

H: Compare, in general, this instructor to your other College of Education instructors:

ONE OF THE POOREST	1
BELOW AVERAGE	2
AVERAGE	3
ABOVE AVERAGE	4
ONE OF THE BEST	5

1 { EVALUATION / **PRESENTATION**

2 { **INTELLECT** / PERSONALITY

3 { **INTELLECT** / PREPARATION

4 { **EVALUATION** / PREPARATION

5 { **EVALUATION** / INTELLECT

6 { **PERSONALITY** / PREPARATION

7 { **PRESENTATION** / PREPARATION

8 { **PERSONALITY** / EVALUATION

9 { **PRESENTATION** / PERSONALITY

10 { **PRESENTATION** / INTELLECT

IS THIS COURSE

REQUIRED	1
ELECTIVE	2

CLASS YEAR

FRESHMAN	1
SOPHOMORE	2
JUNIOR	3
SENIOR	4
GRADUATE	5
OTHER	6

CUMULATIVE G.P.A.

3.50 - 4.00	1
3.00 - 3.49	2
2.50 - 2.99	3
2.00 - 2.49	4
1.99 & LOWER	5

SEX

MALE	1
FEMALE	2

INSTRUCTOR'S NAME

LAST													FIRST						
A	A	A	A	A	A	A	A	A	A	A	A	A	A	A	A	A	A	A	A
B	B	B	B	B	B	B	B	B	B	B	B	B	B	B	B	B	B	B	B
C	C	C	C	C	C	C	C	C	C	C	C	C	C	C	C	C	C	C	C
D	D	D	D	D	D	D	D	D	D	D	D	D	D	D	D	D	D	D	D
E	E	E	E	E	E	E	E	E	E	E	E	E	E	E	E	E	E	E	E
F	F	F	F	F	F	F	F	F	F	F	F	F	F	F	F	F	F	F	F
G	G	G	G	G	G	G	G	G	G	G	G	G	G	G	G	G	G	G	G
H	H	H	H	H	H	H	H	H	H	H	H	H	H	H	H	H	H	H	H
I	I	I	I	I	I	I	I	I	I	I	I	I	I	I	I	I	I	I	I
J	J	J	J	J	J	J	J	J	J	J	J	J	J	J	J	J	J	J	J
K	K	K	K	K	K	K	K	K	K	K	K	K	K	K	K	K	K	K	K
L	L	L	L	L	L	L	L	L	L	L	L	L	L	L	L	L	L	L	L
M	M	M	M	M	M	M	M	M	M	M	M	M	M	M	M	M	M	M	M
N	N	N	N	N	N	N	N	N	N	N	N	N	N	N	N	N	N	N	N
O	O	O	O	O	O	O	O	O	O	O	O	O	O	O	O	O	O	O	O
P	P	P	P	P	P	P	P	P	P	P	P	P	P	P	P	P	P	P	P
Q	Q	Q	Q	Q	Q	Q	Q	Q	Q	Q	Q	Q	Q	Q	Q	Q	Q	Q	Q
R	R	R	R	R	R	R	R	R	R	R	R	R	R	R	R	R	R	R	R
S	S	S	S	S	S	S	S	S	S	S	S	S	S	S	S	S	S	S	S
T	T	T	T	T	T	T	T	T	T	T	T	T	T	T	T	T	T	T	T
U	U	U	U	U	U	U	U	U	U	U	U	U	U	U	U	U	U	U	U
V	V	V	V	V	V	V	V	V	V	V	V	V	V	V	V	V	V	V	V
W	W	W	W	W	W	W	W	W	W	W	W	W	W	W	W	W	W	W	W
X	X	X	X	X	X	X	X	X	X	X	X	X	X	X	X	X	X	X	X
Y	Y	Y	Y	Y	Y	Y	Y	Y	Y	Y	Y	Y	Y	Y	Y	Y	Y	Y	Y
Z	Z	Z	Z	Z	Z	Z	Z	Z	Z	Z	Z	Z	Z	Z	Z	Z	Z	Z	Z

PLEASE TURN OVER TO OTHER SIDE AND COMPLETE SECTION II

PS 7188 / 1 TU (7235)

SECTION II (A to D)

DESCRIPTIVE USE

A. What do you feel were the strong points in the course that should be retained?

B. What do you feel were the weak points in the course that should be changed?

C. Briefly, the course has helped me in the following areas or ways:

D. Any other comments?

PS 7188/1 A TU (7235)

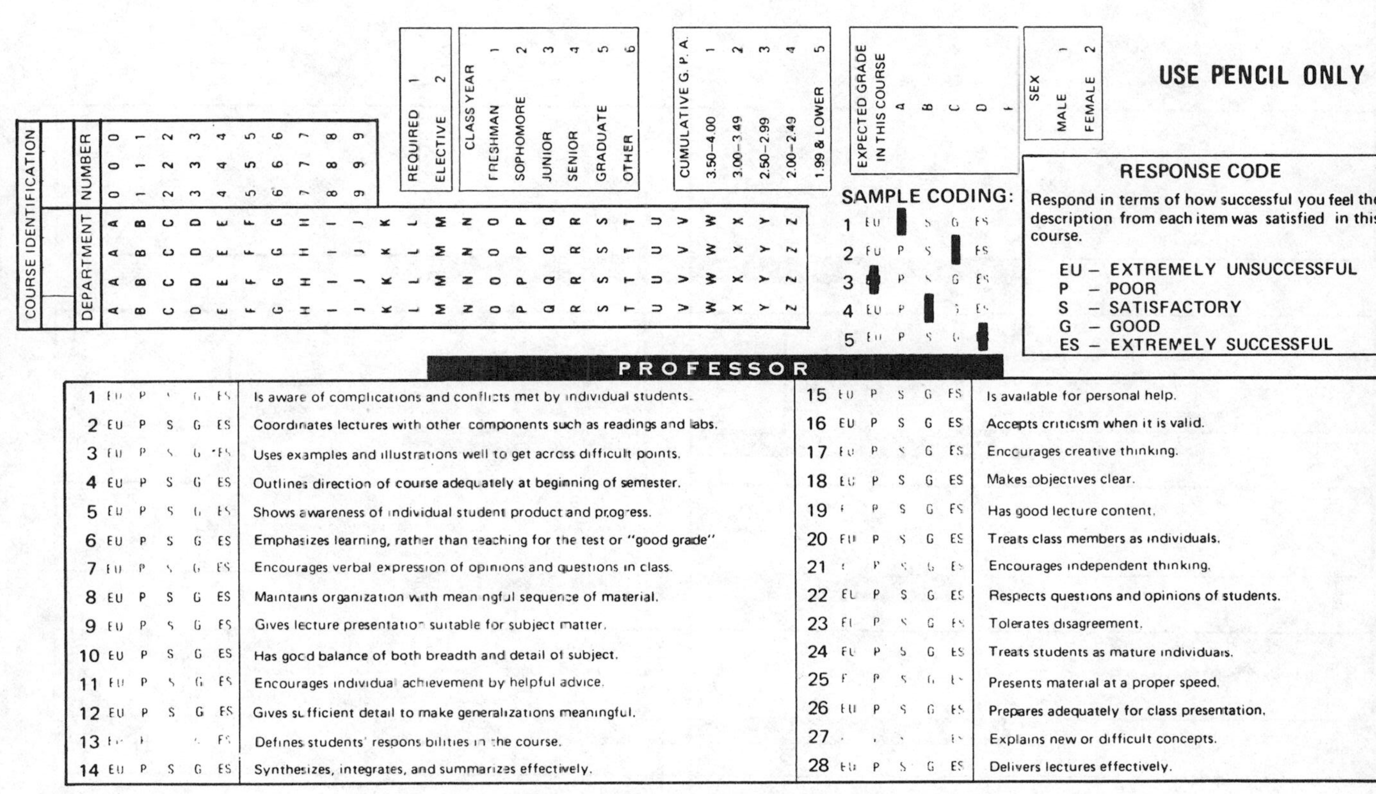

FACULTY AND COURSE EVALUATION INSTRUMENT – STUDENT SHEET

DIRECTIONS:
1. PRINT PROFESSOR'S NAME IN THIS SPACE ____________
2. CODE FIRST FOUR LETTERS OF DEPARTMENT, NAME, COURSE NUMBER, AND PERSONAL INFORMATION AT RIGHT.
3. RESPOND FRANKLY AND COMPLETELY TO THE ITEMS · ONE RESPONSE PER ITEM.
4. THIS QUESTIONNAIRE IS TO BE MACHINE SCORED · PLEASE USE FENCIL ONLY.

F. A. C. E. (FORM S2)

COURSE IDENTIFICATION

DEPARTMENT				NUMBER		
A	A	A	A	0	0	0
B	B	B	B	1	1	1
C	C	C	C	2	2	2
D	D	D	D	3	3	3
E	E	E	E	4	4	4
F	F	F	F	5	5	5
G	G	G	G	6	6	6
H	H	H	H	7	7	7
I	I	I	I	8	8	8
J	J	J	J	9	9	9
K	K	K	K			
L	L	L	L			
M	M	M	M			
N	N	N	N			
O	O	O	O			
P	P	P	P			
Q	Q	Q	Q			
R	R	R	R			
S	S	S	S			
T	T	T	T			
U	U	U	U			
V	V	V	V			
W	W	W	W			
X	X	X	X			
Y	Y	Y	Y			
Z	Z	Z	Z			

REQUIRED 1
ELECTIVE 2

CLASS YEAR
FRESHMAN 1
SOPHOMORE 2
JUNIOR 3
SENIOR 4
GRADUATE 5
OTHER 6

CUMULATIVE G. P. A.
3.50–4.00 1
3.00–3.49 2
2.50–2.99 3
2.00–2.49 4
1.99 & LOWER 5

EXPECTED GRADE IN THIS COURSE
A
B
C
D
F

SEX
MALE 1
FEMALE 2

USE PENCIL ONLY

SAMPLE CODING:
1 EU P S G ES
2 EU P S G ES
3 EU P S G ES
4 EU P S G ES
5 EU P S G ES

RESPONSE CODE

Respond in terms of how successful you feel the description from each item was satisfied in this course.

EU – EXTREMELY UNSUCCESSFUL
P – POOR
S – SATISFACTORY
G – GOOD
ES – EXTREMELY SUCCESSFUL

PROFESSOR

1	EU P S G ES	Is aware of complications and conflicts met by individual students.	15	EU P S G ES	Is available for personal help.
2	EU P S G ES	Coordinates lectures with other components such as readings and labs.	16	EU P S G ES	Accepts criticism when it is valid.
3	EU P S G ES	Uses examples and illustrations well to get across difficult points.	17	EU P S G ES	Encourages creative thinking.
4	EU P S G ES	Outlines direction of course adequately at beginning of semester.	18	EU P S G ES	Makes objectives clear.
5	EU P S G ES	Shows awareness of individual student product and progress.	19	EU P S G ES	Has good lecture content.
6	EU P S G ES	Emphasizes learning, rather than teaching for the test or "good grade"	20	EU P S G ES	Treats class members as individuals.
7	EU P S G ES	Encourages verbal expression of opinions and questions in class.	21	EU P S G ES	Encourages independent thinking.
8	EU P S G ES	Maintains organization with meaningful sequence of material.	22	EU P S G ES	Respects questions and opinions of students.
9	EU P S G ES	Gives lecture presentation suitable for subject matter.	23	EU P S G ES	Tolerates disagreement.
10	EU P S G ES	Has good balance of both breadth and detail of subject.	24	EU P S G ES	Treats students as mature individuals.
11	EU P S G ES	Encourages individual achievement by helpful advice.	25	EU P S G ES	Presents material at a proper speed.
12	EU P S G ES	Gives sufficient detail to make generalizations meaningful.	26	EU P S G ES	Prepares adequately for class presentation.
13	EU P S G ES	Defines students' responsibilities in the course.	27	EU P S G ES	Explains new or difficult concepts.
14	EU P S G ES	Synthesizes, integrates, and summarizes effectively.	28	EU P S G ES	Delivers lectures effectively.

TEXT AND READINGS

29	EU P S G ES	Text is comprehensive in explaining and describing subject matter	32	EU P S G ES	Text is related to lectures.
30	EU P S G ES	Reading assignments help to integrate facts and develop generalizations.	33	EU P S G ES	Reading assignments are worthwhile.
31	EU P S G ES	Readings are assigned in sequence with lecture material.	34	EU P S G ES	Text is essential to course.

EXAMINATIONS

35 EU P S G ES	Exams cover material on which students expect to be tested.	39 EU P S G ES	Exam questions are clear.
36 EU P S G ES	There is comprehensive coverage of the subject matter on exams.	40 EU P S G ES	Exams are graded fairly.
37 EU P S G ES	Exams reflect the material emphasized in the course.		
38 EU P S G ES	Exams are fair tests of achievement.		

PAPERS AND REPORTS (INCLUDING LAB REPORTS)

41 EU P S G ES	The professor permits enough freedom in choosing topics for papers.	44 EU P S G ES	Papers and reports stimulate development of new ideas.
42 EU P S G ES	Students are given creative freedom in writing papers and reports.	45 EU P S G ES	Papers and reports are challenging and worthwhile.
43 EU P S G ES	Papers and reports stimulate an increase of interest in subject matter.		

RECITATION

46 EU P S G ES	Student recitation classes are as informative as professor's lecture classes.
47 EU P S G ES	The number of student recitation classes is in proper ratio to regular lecture classes.
48 EU P S G ES	The professor offers helpful guidance in preparation of recitation.

LABORATORIES

49 EU P S G ES	Lab proctors have adequate knowledge of the subject matter.	53 EU P S G ES	Lab assignments parallel course material.
50 EU P S G ES	Lab proctors are well informed of class requirements.	54 EU P S G ES	Labs have adequate facilities.
51 EU P S G ES	Labs are worthwhile supplements to the course	55 EU P S G ES	Labs are interesting and stimulating.
52 EU P S G ES	Lab projects are properly prepared by professor and proctor.		

OPTIONAL QUESTIONS

1 A B C D E	2 A B C D E	3 A B C D E	4 A B C D E	5 A B C D E	6 A B C D E	7 A B C D E	8 A B C D E
9 A B C D E	10 A B C D E	11 A B C D E	12 A B C D E	13 A B C D E	14 A B C D E	15 A B C D E	16 A B C D E
17 A B C D E	18 A B C D E	19 A B C D E	20 A B C D E	21 A B C D E	22 A B C D E	23 A B C D E	24 A B C D E
25 A B C D E	26 A B C D E	27 A B C D E	28 A B C D E	29 A B C D E	30 A B C D E	31 A B C D E	32 A B C D E
33 A B C D E	34 A B C D E	35 A B C D E	36 A B C D E	37 A B C D E	38 A B C D E	39 A B C D E	40 A B C D E

PS 7519 TU (5723) PENN SCAN FORMS INC., PHILA., PA.

F.A.C.E. (FORM I2)

F.A.C.E. - FACULTY AND COURSE EVALUATION INSTRUMENT – INSTRUCTOR IDENTIFICATION SHEET

USE PENCIL ONLY

* BESIDES YOURSELF, TO WHOM DO YOU WANT YOUR RESULTS RELEASED?
OPEN FOR PUBLICATION
DEPT. CHAIRMAN AND DEAN
DEPT. CHAIRMAN
NO ONE ELSE
LEVEL OF COURSE
FRESHMAN - SOPHOMORE
JUNIOR - SENIOR
GRADUATE

ADMINISTRATION DATE					
MO.		DAY		YEAR	
0	0	0	0	0	0
1	1	1	1	1	1
	2	2	2	2	2
	3	3	3	3	3
	4		4	4	4
	5		5	5	5
	6		6	6	6
	7		7	7	7
	8		8	8	8
	9		9	9	9

CLASS ENROLL-MENT		
0	0	0
1	1	1
2	2	2
3	3	3
4	4	4
5	5	5
6	6	6
7	7	7
8	8	8
9	9	9

HOW MANY OTHER SECTIONS OF THIS COURSE ARE YOU TEACHING THIS SEMESTER?
NONE
ONE
TWO
≥ THREE

WOULD YOU LIKE TO TEACH THIS COURSE AGAIN?
YES
NO

PROFESSOR													
LAST NAME												FI	MI
A	A	A	A	A	A	A	A	A	A	A	A	A	A
B	B	B	B	B	B	B	B	B	B	B	B	B	B
C	C	C	C	C	C	C	C	C	C	C	C	C	C
D	D	D	D	D	D	D	D	D	D	D	D	D	D
E	E	E	E	E	E	E	E	E	E	E	E	E	E
F	F	F	F	F	F	F	F	F	F	F	F	F	F
G	G	G	G	G	G	G	G	G	G	G	G	G	G
H	H	H	H	H	H	H	H	H	H	H	H	H	H
I	I	I	I	I	I	I	I	I	I	I	I	I	I
J	J	J	J	J	J	J	J	J	J	J	J	J	J
K	K	K	K	K	K	K	K	K	K	K	K	K	K
L	L	L	L	L	L	L	L	L	L	L	L	L	L
M	M	M	M	M	M	M	M	M	M	M	M	M	M
N	N	N	N	N	N	N	N	N	N	N	N	N	N
O	O	O	O	O	O	O	O	O	O	O	O	O	O
P	P	P	P	P	P	P	P	P	P	P	P	P	P
Q	Q	Q	Q	Q	Q	Q	Q	Q	Q	Q	Q	Q	Q
R	R	R	R	R	R	R	R	R	R	R	R	R	R
S	S	S	S	S	S	S	S	S	S	S	S	S	S
T	T	T	T	T	T	T	T	T	T	T	T	T	T
U	U	U	U	U	U	U	U	U	U	U	U	U	U
V	V	V	V	V	V	V	V	V	V	V	V	V	V
W	W	W	W	W	W	W	W	W	W	W	W	W	W
X	X	X	X	X	X	X	X	X	X	X	X	X	X
Y	Y	Y	Y	Y	Y	Y	Y	Y	Y	Y	Y	Y	Y
Z	Z	Z	Z	Z	Z	Z	Z	Z	Z	Z	Z	Z	Z

COURSE IDENTIFICATION								
DEPARTMENT				NUMBER			SECTION	
A	A	A	A	0	0	0	0	0
B	B	B	B	1	1	1	1	1
C	C	C	C	2	2	2	2	2
D	D	D	D	3	3	3	3	3
E	E	E	E	4	4	4	4	4
F	F	F	F	5	5	5	5	5
G	G	G	G	6	6	6	6	6
H	H	H	H	7	7	7	7	7
I	I	I	I	8	8	8	8	8
J	J	J	J	9	9	9	9	9
K	K	K	K					
L	L	L	L					
M	M	M	M					
N	N	N	N					
O	O	O	O					
P	P	P	P					
Q	Q	Q	Q					
R	R	R	R					
S	S	S	S					
T	T	T	T					
U	U	U	U					
V	V	V	V					
W	W	W	W					
X	X	X	X					
Y	Y	Y	Y					
Z	Z	Z	Z					

INSTRUCTIONS

1. Please use pencil in coding your responses on this sheet.
2. For distribution purposes, it is extremely important that you code the section (*) "Besides yourself, to whom do you want your results released?"
3. Before the instrument is administered, please announce to students which sections of the evaluation (i.e. Professor, Text - Readings, Exams, Papers - Reports, Recitation, Laboratories) are applicable to you and/or the course, and therefore should be answered. These sections should correspond with what you have coded in the appropriate coding area of this sheet.
4. Directions for administration - Ask students to read the directions presented on the F.A.C.E. instrument, and code in the personal information section; then refer students to the areas marked "Response code" and "Sample coding." Students should then be prepared to begin work. The instrument should take 10 - 15 minutes to complete.

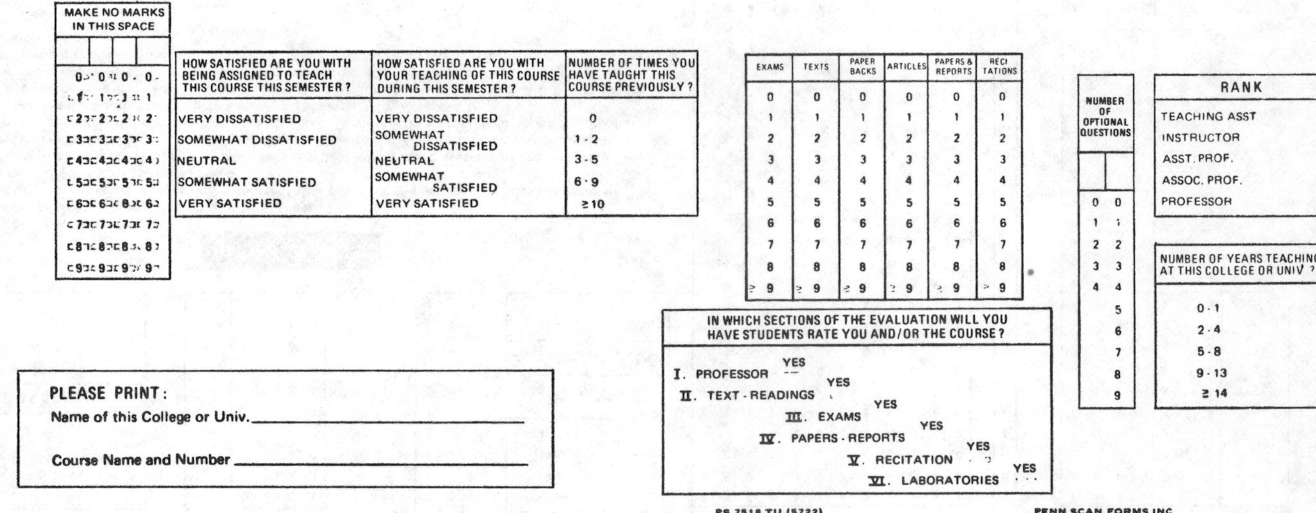

MAKE NO MARKS IN THIS SPACE

HOW SATISFIED ARE YOU WITH BEING ASSIGNED TO TEACH THIS COURSE THIS SEMESTER?	HOW SATISFIED ARE YOU WITH YOUR TEACHING OF THIS COURSE DURING THIS SEMESTER?	NUMBER OF TIMES YOU HAVE TAUGHT THIS COURSE PREVIOUSLY?
VERY DISSATISFIED	VERY DISSATISFIED	0
SOMEWHAT DISSATISFIED	SOMEWHAT DISSATISFIED	1 - 2
NEUTRAL	NEUTRAL	3 - 5
SOMEWHAT SATISFIED	SOMEWHAT SATISFIED	6 - 9
VERY SATISFIED	VERY SATISFIED	≥ 10

EXAMS	TEXTS	PAPER BACKS	ARTICLES	PAPERS & REPORTS	RECITATIONS
0	0	0	0	0	0
1	1	1	1	1	1
2	2	2	2	2	2
3	3	3	3	3	3
4	4	4	4	4	4
5	5	5	5	5	5
6	6	6	6	6	6
7	7	7	7	7	7
8	8	8	8	8	8
≥ 9	≥ 9	≥ 9	≥ 9	≥ 9	≥ 9

NUMBER OF OPTIONAL QUESTIONS

0	0
1	1
2	2
3	3
4	4
	5
	6
	7
	8
	9

RANK
TEACHING ASST
INSTRUCTOR
ASST. PROF.
ASSOC. PROF.
PROFESSOR

NUMBER OF YEARS TEACHING AT THIS COLLEGE OR UNIV?
0 - 1
2 - 4
5 - 8
9 - 13
≥ 14

PLEASE PRINT:

Name of this College or Univ. ____________________

Course Name and Number ____________________

IN WHICH SECTIONS OF THE EVALUATION WILL YOU HAVE STUDENTS RATE YOU AND/OR THE COURSE?

I. PROFESSOR YES
II. TEXT - READINGS YES
III. EXAMS YES
IV. PAPERS - REPORTS YES
V. RECITATION YES
VI. LABORATORIES YES

PS 7518 TU (5722)

PENN SCAN FORMS INC.

INTERPRETATION OF F.A.C.E. PROFILES

An example of the report (Profile) produced by the Faculty and Course Evaluation processing is attached. The following comments will aid in the interpretation and understanding of this Profile. Please note that the circled numbers on the Profile correspond to the numbers in parentheses below.

A. If the class enrollment section of the Instructor Identification Sheet was left blank, the NO. ENROLLED (1) will be 999. The only effect of this omission is to shrink the PERC. RESPONDENTS (2).

B. The sections of the Student Sheet which are evaluated for each class are those that were indicated on the Instructor Identification Sheet in the box labeled "In which sections of the evaluation will you have students rate you and/or the course?" Each section is represented by one scale (3) on the Profile except for the Professor section which is divided into two scales, LECTURE-PRESENTATION EFFECTIVENESS and PROFESSOR-STUDENT RELATIONSHIP.

Under each scale are the mean and the standard deviation for that scale. In order for a student's responses to be included in the calculation of a scale mean, the student must answer the minimum number of items for that scale as listed below.

Lecture-Presentation	10
Professor-Student	9
Text and Readings	4
Examinations	4
Papers and Reports	4
Recitation	2
Laboratories	5

If five or more students answered the minimum number of items for a scale, the scale mean will range in value from 1.00 to 5.00 (Extremely Unsuccessful to Extremely Successful). If less than five students answered the minimum number of items for a scale, the scale mean will be 0.00.

C. Stanines (Standard Nine Scores) provide a comparison of the instructor with all instructors who have returned F.A.C.E. forms for processing to date (4). Stanines are calculated with respect to the following normative groups: Temple University; the College in which the course is offered; the Department in which the course is offered; and all Temple University courses of the same level, i.e., Freshman-Sophomore, Junior-Senior, or Graduate-Professional. NOTE: The level is indicated on the top left corner of the Profile (5).

Stanines are based on the normal curve of probability and range in value from one to nine. Stanines 2 through 8 are each one half standard deviation in width with stanine 5 being centered on the mean of the distribution. Stanines 1 and 9 are open-ended and encompass, respectively, the extreme low and high ends of the distribution (see Figure 1).

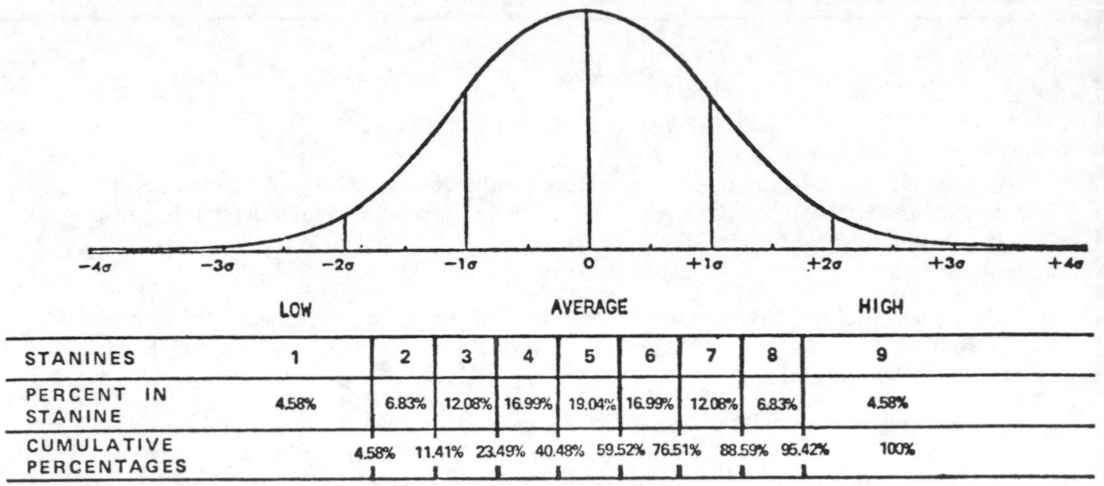

STANINES	1	2	3	4	5	6	7	8	9
PERCENT IN STANINE	4.58%	6.83%	12.08%	16.99%	19.04%	16.99%	12.08%	6.83%	4.58%
CUMULATIVE PERCENTAGES	4.58%	11.41%	23.49%	40.48%	59.52%	76.51%	88.59%	95.42%	100%

FIGURE 1

Figure 1 illustrates the relationship of stanines to the normal probability curve, the percentages expected to fall within each stanine, and the cumulative percentages expected to fall below the upper limit of each stanine.

For example, on the attached sample Profile, the instructor received a stan of 6 on the Professor-Student Relationship scale with respect to College. From Figure 1, we see that, in a normal distribution, 16.99% of the instructors receive ratings which fall in the same stanine and 59.52% receive ratings which fall in a lower stanine (5 or below). By adding the percentages in the 7th, 8th, and 9th stanines, we find that 23.49% receive ratings which fall in a higher stanine.

D. Stanines are not calculated for those scales with a mean of 0.00 (6).

E. Stanines are not given in relation to a normative group if that normative group does not contain at least five classes (7).

F. The Profile labeled "SELF" (8) lists the ten highest and the ten lowest rated items and their means (9). NOTE: The item lists do not appear on additional copies of the Profile.

****

Please call Susan Overlander at 787-8611 if you have any questions regarding F.A.C.E.

MEASUREMENT AND RESEARCH CENTER FACULTY AND COURSE EVALUATION INSTRUMENT

PROFESSOR
COLLEGE
DEPARTMENT
COURSE NO.
(5) COURSE LEVEL FRSH-SOPH

ADMIN. DATE 12/10/76

(8) COPY SELF

(1) NO. ENROLLED 10
NO. RESPONDENTS 8
(2) PERC. RESPONDENTS 80

FREQUENCY OF USAGE	
EXAMS	1
TEXTS	2
PAPERBACKS	0
ARTICLES	0
PAPERS-REPORTS	4
RECITATIONS	0

(4) STANINES WITH RESPECT TO

SCALES (3)

	UNIVERSITY LO AVE HI	COLLEGE LO AVE HI	DEPARTMENT LO AVE HI	LEVEL LO AVE HI
LECTURE-PRESENTATION EFFECTIVENESS MEAN= 4.06 S.D.= .36	****5	*****6	****5	****5
PROFESSOR-STUDENT RELATIONSHIP MEAN= 4.12 S.D.= .44	****5	*****6	*****6	****5
TEXT AND READINGS EFFECTIVENESS MEAN= 4.19 S.D.= .58	******7	******7	******7	******7
EXAMINATION EFFECTIVENESS MEAN= 3.98 S.D.= .72	****5	****5	***4	****5
PAPERS AND REPORTS EFFECTIVENESS MEAN= 3.97 S.D.= .77	***4	****5	****5	***4
RECITATION EFFECTIVENESS (6)→ MEAN= 0.00 S.D.= 0.00				
LABORATORY EFFECTIVENESS MEAN= 4.64 S.D.= .44	*******8	*******8	(7)	*******8

---

(9) HIGHEST RATED ITEMS

MEAN	ITEM
4.75	LABS--ASSIGNMENTS PARALLEL COURSE MATERIAL
4.71	LABS--PROCTORS HAVE ADEQUATE KNOWLEDGE OF SUBJECT
4.63	LABS--WORTHWHILE SUPPLEMENTS TO COURSE
4.63	LABS--PROJECTS PREPARED BY PROFESSOR AND PROCTOR
4.63	LABS--HAVE ADEQUATE FACILITIES
4.57	LABS--PROCTORS WELL INFORMED OF CLASS REQUIREMENTS
4.50	USE OF EXAMPLES-ILLUSTRATIONS TO CLARIFY DIFFICULT POINTS
4.50	EMPHASIS OF LEARNING, NOT TEACHING FOR TEST GRADES
4.50	BALANCE OF BREADTH AND DETAIL OF SUBJECT
4.50	TEXT--RELATED TO LECTURES

(9) LOWEST RATED ITEMS

MEAN	ITEM
3.86	EXAMS--QUESTIONS ARE CLEAR
3.86	EXAMS--COVER MATERIAL ON WHICH STUDENTS EXPECT TESTS
3.86	MAINTAINING ORGANIZATION WITH MEANINGFUL SEQUENCE
3.83	PAPERS-REPORTS—CREATIVE FREEDOM GIVEN IN WRITING
3.83	PAPERS-REPORTS—FREEDOM PERMITTED IN CHOOSING TOPICS
3.83	EXAMS--GRADED FAIRLY
3.75	READINGS—ASSIGNED IN SEQUENCE WITH LECTURE MATERIAL
3.75	PRESENTATION OF MATERIAL AT A PROPER SPEED
3.75	USE OF EFFECTIVE SYNTHESIS, INTEGRATION AND SUMMARIZATION
3.75	SUFFICIENT DETAIL GIVEN TO MAKE GENERALIZATIONS MEANINGFU

IDEA USING ADDITIONAL QUESTIONS

with the IDEA system

No single survey form can anticipate all the needs of all teachers. The IDEA system, which asks students a) to rate their progress on ten different course objectives, and b) to rate the frequency with which their instructor employs each of twenty teaching "methods," offers the instructor the option of asking twenty additional questions. The teacher may wish to ask questions which pertain to the special characteristics of his/her course which were not asked by any of the standard items Or students may be asked to give their weighting of the relative importance of the ten course objectives

The following guidelines and suggestions are written for the teacher who wants to ask additional questions. The IDEA Report for this teacher will provide the distribution of student responses and the average (mean) for each additional question

PREPARING ADDITIONAL QUESTIONS

When you are preparing additional questions it is important that you follow these directions.

1. You must prepare the questions on a separate sheet.
2. The questions should be numbered consecutively, beginning with "40."
3. You may use from two to five response options for each question; these responses should be numbered (1), (2), (3), (4), (5) rather than lettered.
4. You must duplicate the questions on separate sheets to be distributed with the IDEA Survey Forms at the time of administration. *(Please do not staple the additional sheets to the Survey Forms.)*

OR

You may prefer to make a transparency of the additional questions and use an overhead projector. It is also possible to put the questions on the chalkboard when class size and room facilities permit.

You may also use an open-ended approach by asking students to respond on the back of the IDEA Response Card

ITEMS USING UNIQUE RESPONSE OPTIONS

You may wish to supplement the Survey Form with questions using response options specifically designed to fit each question. Feel free to create your own as long as they meet the format requirements outlined above. Two examples are given below:

The present prerequisite for this course is (1) General Chemistry, (2) Chemistry I, or (3) a "B" or higher in high school chemistry:

1—This prerequisite is satisfactory.
2—More chemistry should be required.
3—There is no need for a chemistry prerequisite.

Homework problems were given to help students formulate concepts through problem solving. What was your reaction:

1—Always worked problems and appreciated the opportunity.
2—Worked problems if I felt I needed the help
3—Seldom worked problems because I understood concepts.
4—Seldom worked the problems because the instructor explained them anyway.

ITEMS USING UNIFORM RESPONSE OPTIONS

You may wish to use the same set of response options for all of your additional items.

On the following pages are lists of items designed to fit special teaching situations. The last section contains items designed to be generally applicable.

Although the items are categorized by instructional setting or approach, you should not feel restricted by these Several items are appropriate to more than one teaching situation; you are encouraged to use any which you feel would help you You may wish to rewrite some of them, or you may want to devise entirely different questions.

For the items in these lists you might use one of the following sets of response options; response options which are most appropriate are shown in ( ):

OPTION A

1 = Hardly Ever
2 = Occasionally
3 = Sometimes
4 = Frequently
5 = Almost Always

OPTION B

1 = Strongly Disagree
2 = Disagree
3 = Neither Agree or Disagree
4 = Agree
5 = Strongly Agree

OPTION C

1 = Definitely False
2 = More False than True
3 = In Between
4 = More True than False
5 = Definitely True

LABORATORY (A, C)

I. The Instructor:

Was available for assistance throughout the lab sessions.
Clearly explained the lab procedures.
Moved about the lab rather than staying in one place.
Returned graded lab reports promptly.
Strictly enforced safety regulations.
Clearly explained how to use lab equipment.
Graded in line with the lecture instructor.

II. The lab sessions were well-coordinated with the lectures.

The lab sessions were well-organized.
I could usually finish the experiments (exercises, assignments) during the scheduled lab time (by the due date).
I had sufficient access to equipment and supplies needed for experiments.
The lab experience added to my understanding of the course material.
The concepts underlying the experimental procedures were covered.
Laboratory discussions of methodology were related to the lecture assignments.

CLINICAL and PRACTICUM (A, C)

I The Instructor:

Identified specific problems with my clinical technique.
Demonstrated the clinical techniques I was expected to develop.
Clearly identified appropriate clinical behavior.
Embarrassed me in front of clients.
Provided feedback on my performance which made me feel more (less) self-confident.
Stated in advance the criteria to be used in evaluating my performance.
Arranged for clinical experiences which were realistic, given client availability.

II. I developed skills for communicating professionally with clients or laypersons.

I developed skills for communicating professionally with colleagues.
I developed diagnostic skills and sensitivities.
I developed skills in applying therapeutic techniques.
I gained an understanding of professional ethics and attitudes.
I gained an understanding of the problems of prevention, diagnosis and treatment.
I worked harder in this course than in most courses I have taken in my (professional school) studies.

SELF-PACED (A, C)

I. The Instructor:

Permitted students to set and work toward some of their own goals.
Showed a sensitivity to individual interests and abilities.
Allowed me to study and learn at my own pace.

II. The programmed learning materials were effective.

Many methods were used to involve me in learning.
I had easy access to course materials.
I was able to keep up with the work load in this course.
My background was sufficient to enable me to use the course material.
This process was too time-consuming for the knowledge gained.

SEMINAR and DISCUSSION (A, C)

I The Instructor:

Developed classroom discussion skillfully.
Encouraged students to debate conflicting views.
Respected divergent viewpoints.
Allowed student discussion to proceed uninterrupted.
Allowed sufficient time for questions and discussion.
Helped me feel confident in expressing new ideas.
Encouraged students to participate in class discussion.
Discussed points of view other than his/her own.

II. This course provided an opportunity to learn from other students.

Challenging questions were raised for discussion.
Student presentations were interesting and stimulating.
Group work contributed significantly to this course.
Discussions raised interesting new ideas.
Discussion was helpful to my learning.
I was stimulated to discuss new ideas in or out of class.
I was free to express and explain my own views in class.

TEAM TEACHING (A, C)

I. The Instructors:

Graded in proportion to their contributions
Worked together as a well-coordinated team to provide instruction

II. Team teaching was effectively used in this course

Team teaching provided insights a single instructor could not
Having more than one instructor confused the issues
Team teaching approach adequately met my needs and interests
I liked the variety and change of pace team teaching provided

STUDIO and CREATIVE ARTS (A, C)

I. The Instructor.

Was readily available for consultation
Was patient with students.
Personally demonstrated artistic effects which students were expected to achieve
Encouraged students to develop their own styles
Was tactful in criticizing students' work.
Permitted students to pursue some of their personal interests
Encouraged students to seek their own solutions to "artistic" questions or problems
Asssigned projects which helped students develop needed competencies and skills.

II. I gained a broader and more critical understanding of creative work.

I developed capacities for creative thinking and problem-solving
I developed insights into issues upon which professionals in the field disagree
I had easy access to the equipment/tools required in the course
My technical skills were improved as a result of this course

RECITATION (Help Sessions) (A, C)

I. The Instructor:

Gave a short summary of the previous lecture, emphasizing important points
Explained the problems in a clear, concise manner.
Explained topics not entirely clear from lectures
Seemed aware of what material had been covered in lectures (the information portion of the course)
Encouraged questions over related material that wasn't covered in lecture.
Was well-prepared to answer questions

II. Tests in recitation helped prepare for lecture exams

Work (attendance) in recitation helped prepare for exams
Discussions in recitation added to my understanding of the subject
Recitations are most helpful when the Instructor works the problems
Recitations are most helpful when fellow students are assigned to give solutions to problems

GENERAL QUESTIONS

Self-Rating: (B, C)
I skipped this class more than three times (not counting absences due to illness)
I took an active part in class discussions and related activities.
To date, I have completed all required assignments in this class.
I have learned to value new viewpoints.

Options for #37 on Survey Form: (B, C)
Overall, this instructor is among the best teachers I have known
Compared to others I have had, this instructor has been one of the most effective
If I were in a position to do it again, in taking this course I would like the same instructor
I would recommend this instructor to a friend planning to take this course

Objectives: (A, B, C)
The course objectives helped me to know when I was making progress
I was able to set and achieve some of my own goals
I had an opportunity to help determine course objectives
There was considerable agreement between the announced objectives and what was taught

Exams: (A, B, C)
Were used to help me find my strengths and weaknesses
Accurately assessed what I learned in this course
Had instructional value
Were coordinated with major course objectives
Required more than recall of factual information.
Reflected the emphases of class presentations.
Covered material on which I expected to be tested.
Required creative, original thinking.
Gave balanced coverage to major topics.

Assignments: (A, B, C)
Length and difficulty of assigned readings were reasonable.
Assigned readings were interesting and held my attention.
Assignments were of definite instructional value.
Assignments were related to the course goals.
Directions for assignments were clear and specific.
The number of course assignments was reasonable.
Class projects were related to course objectives.
I knew what improvement was needed from feedback on assignments.
Assigned readings were clear and understandable.
I usually had no difficulty in obtaining outside reading materials.
Reading materials seemed up-to-date.

Grades: (A, B, C)
I believe my final grade will accurately reflect my overall performance (learning) in this course.
The grading was objective and unbiased.

Miscellaneous: (B, C)
Bibliographies for this course were current and extensive.
Handouts were valuable supplements to this course.
Guest speakers contributed significantly to this course.
An appropriate number of outside lecturers was used.
Field trips offered insights that lectures or readings could not.
This course made excellent use of (TV, films, transparencies, etc.)
The media used in this course were well chosen to aid learning.
The physical condition of the classroom facilitated learning.
The classroom was a comfortable size for the number of students enrolled.

The Instructor: (A, C)
Seemed to have a well developed plan for each class session.
Seemed to lack energy.
Answered student questions as completely as reasonable.
Adjusted his/her pace to the needs of the class.
Wasted class time.
Was incoherent and/or vague in what he/she was saying.
Received student comments without asking for them.
Monopolized class discussions.
Presented examples of what he/she wanted by way of homework, papers, etc.
Presented material in a humorous way
Lectured in a low monotone.
Attempted to induce silent students to participate.
Lectured in a rambling fashion.
Understood student comments and questions even when not clearly expressed.
Differentiated between significant and non-significant material.
Repeated material to the point of monotony.
Told the class when they had done a particularly good job.
Made good use of teaching aids (list those used in the class).
Spoke too rapidly.
Requested and obtained students' questions and reactions.
Clearly stated the course requirements and deadlines.
Became angry or sarcastic when corrected or challenged by a student.
Displayed favoritism.
Was available for individual help.
Spoke clearly and distinctly.
Gave ample notice for lengthy assignments.

IDEA SURVEY FORM -- STUDENT REACTIONS TO INSTRUCTION AND COURSES

Your thoughtful answers to these questions will provide helpful information to your instructor.

• Describe the frequency of your instructor's teaching procedures, using the following code:
1 — Hardly Ever 3 — Sometimes
2 — Occasionally 4 — Frequently 5 — Almost Always

The Instructor:

1. Promoted teacher-student discussion (as opposed to mere responses to questions).
2. Found ways to help students answer their own questions.
3. Encouraged students to express themselves freely and openly.
4. Seemed enthusiastic about the subject matter.
5. Changed approaches to meet new situations.
6. Gave examinations which stressed unnecessary memorization.
7. Spoke with expressiveness and variety in tone of voice.
8. Demonstrated the importance and significance of the subject matter.
9. Made presentations which were dry and dull.
10. Made it clear how each topic fit into the course.
11. Explained the reasons for criticisms of students' academic performance.
12. Gave examination questions which were unclear.
13. Encouraged student comments even when they turned out to be incorrect or irrelevant.
14. Summarized material in a manner which aided retention.
15. Stimulated students to intellectual effort beyond that required by most courses.
16. Clearly stated the objectives of the course.
17. Explained course material clearly, and explanations were to the point.
18. Related course material to real life situations.
19. Gave examination questions which were unreasonably detailed (picky).
20. Introduced stimulating ideas about the subject.

• On each of the objectives listed below, rate the progress you have made in this course compared with that made in other courses you have taken at this college or university. In this course my progress was:
1 — Low (lowest 10 per cent of courses I have taken here)
2 — Low Average (next 20 per cent of courses)
3 — Average (middle 40 per cent of courses)
4 — High Average (next 20 percent of courses)
5 — High (highest 10 per cent of courses)

Progress on:

21. Gaining factual knowledge (terminology, classifications, methods, trends).
22. Learning fundamental principles, generalizations, or theories.
23. Learning to apply course material to improve rational thinking, problem-solving and decision making.
24. Developing specific skills, competencies and points of view needed by professionals in the field most closely related to this course.
25. Learning how professionals in this field go about the process of gaining new knowledge.
26. Developing creative capacities.
27. Developing a sense of personal responsibility (self-reliance, self-discipline).
28. Gaining a broader understanding and appreciation of intellectual-cultural activity (music, science, literature, etc.).
29. Developing skill in expressing myself orally or in writing.
30. Discovering the implications of the course material for understanding myself (interests, talents, values, etc.).

• On the next four questions, compare this course with others you have taken at this institution, using the following code:
1 — Much Less than Most Courses
2 — Less than Most
3 — About Average
4 — More than Most
5 — Much More than Most

The Course:

31. Amount of reading
32. Amount of work in other (non-reading) assignments
33. Difficulty of subject matter
34. Degree to which the course hung together (various topics and class activities were related to each other)

• Describe your attitudes toward and behavior in this course, using the following code:
1 — Definitely False
2 — More False than True 4 — More True than False
3 — In Between 5 — Definitely True

Self-rating:

35. I worked harder on this course than on most courses I have taken.
36. I had a strong desire to take this course.
37. I would like to take another course from this instructor.
38. As a result of taking this course, I have more positive feelings toward this field of study.
39. I have given thoughtful consideration to the questions on this form.

• Describe your status on the following by blackening the appropriate space on the Response Card.

A. To which sex-age group do you belong?
1 — Female, under 25 3 — Female, 25 or over
2 — Male, under 25 4 — Male, 25 or over

B. Do you consider yourself to be a full-time or a part-time student?
1 — Full-time
2 — Part-time

C. Counting the present term, for how many terms have you attended this college or university?
1 — 1 term 3 — 4 or 5
2 — 2 or 3 4 — 6 or more

D. What grade do you expect to receive in this course?
1 — A 3 — C
2 — B 4 — D or F 5 — Other

E. What is your classification?
1 — Freshman 3 — Junior or Senior
2 — Sophomore 4 — Graduate 5 — Other

F. For how many courses have you filled out this form during the present term?
1 — This is the first course
2 — 2 or 3 courses 3 — 4 or more courses

G. How well did the questions on this form permit you to describe your impressions of this instructor and course?
1 — Very well 3 — Not very well
2 — Quite well 4 — Poorly

If your instructor has extra questions, answer them in the space designated on the Response Card.

Your comments are invited on how the instructor might improve this course or teaching procedures. Use the back of the Response Card (unless otherwise directed).

Measurement and Research Division
Office of Instructional Resources
UNIVERSITY OF ILLINOIS

COURSE EVALUATION QUESTIONNAIRE — Form D

PART I
ITEMS 1-50

DIRECTIONS:
1. Write and mark subject code in box #1.
2. Write and mark course number in box #2.
3. Write and mark section code in box #3.
4. Write and mark student number in box #4 - start in space #1.
5. Respond to statements in questionnaire as indicated by your instructor.

BOX #1 SUBJECT CODE — BOX #2 COURSE NUMBER — BOX #3 SECTION CODE

BOX #4 STUDENT NUMBER 1 2 3 4 5 6 7 8 9

	STRONGLY AGREE	AGREE	DISAGREE	STRONGLY DISAGREE	
1	SA	A	D	SD	I learn more when other teaching methods are used.
2	SA	A	D	SD	It was a waste of time.
3	SA	A	D	SD	Overall, the course was good.
4	SA	A	D	SD	The textbook was very good.
5	SA	A	D	SD	The instructor seemed to be interested in students as persons.
6	SA	A	D	SD	More courses should be taught this way.
7	SA	A	D	SD	The course held my interest.
8	SA	A	D	SD	I would have preferred another method of teaching in this course.
9	SA	A	D	SD	It was easy to remain attentive.
10	SA	A	D	SD	The instructor did not synthesize, integrate or summarize effectively.
11	SA	A	D	SD	Not much was gained by taking this course.
12	SA	A	D	SD	The instructor encouraged the development of new viewpoints and appreciations.
13	SA	A	D	SD	The course material seemed worthwhile.
14	SA	A	D	SD	It was difficult to remain attentive.
15	SA	A	D	SD	Instructor did not review promptly and in such a way that students could understand their weaknesses.
16	SA	A	D	SD	Homework assignments were helpful in understanding the course.
17	SA	A	D	SD	There was not enough student participation for this type of course.
18	SA	A	D	SD	The instructor had a thorough knowledge of his subject matter.
19	SA	A	D	SD	The content of the course was good.

O M C IA IN SP L

OPTIONAL PART II ITEMS 51-75

No.	SA	A	D	SD	Statement
20	SA	A	D	SD	The course increased my general knowledge.
21	SA	A	D	SD	The types of test questions used were good.
22	SA	A	D	SD	Held my attention throughout the course.
23	SA	A	D	SD	The demands of the students were not considered by the instructor.
24	SA	A	D	SD	Uninteresting course.
25	SA	A	D	SD	It was a very worthwhile course.
26	SA	A	D	SD	Some things were not explained very well.
27	SA	A	D	SD	The way in which this course was taught results in better student learning.
28	SA	A	D	SD	The course material was too difficult.
29	SA	A	D	SD	One of my poorest courses.
30	SA	A	D	SD	Material in the course was easy to follow.
31	SA	A	D	SD	The instructor seemed to consider teaching as a chore or routine activity.
32	SA	A	D	SD	More outside reading is necessary.
33	SA	A	D	SD	Course material was poorly organized.
34	SA	A	D	SD	Course was not very helpful.
35	SA	A	D	SD	It was quite interesting.
36	SA	A	D	SD	I think that the course was taught quite well.
37	SA	A	D	SD	I would prefer a different method of instruction.
38	SA	A	D	SD	The pace of the course was too slow.
39	SA	A	D	SD	At times I was confused.
40	SA	A	D	SD	Excellent course content.
41	SA	A	D	SD	The examinations were too difficult.
42	SA	A	D	SD	Generally, the course was well organized.
43	SA	A	D	SD	Ideas and concepts were developed too rapidly.
44	SA	A	D	SD	The content of the course was too elementary.
45	SA	A	D	SD	Some days I was not very interested in this course.
46	SA	A	D	SD	It was quite boring.
47	SA	A	D	SD	The instructor exhibited professional dignity and bearing in the classroom.
48	SA	A	D	SD	Another method of instruction should have been employed.
49	SA	A	D	SD	The course was quite useful.
50	SA	A	D	SD	I would take another course that was taught this way.

No.	SA	AGREE	D	STRONGLY DISAGREE
51	SA	A	D	SD
52	SA	A	D	SD
53	SA	A	D	SD
54	SA	A	D	SD
55	SA	A	D	SD
56	SA	A	D	SD
57	SA	A	D	SD
58	SA	A	D	SD
59	SA	A	D	SD
60	SA	A	D	SD
61	SA	A	D	SD
62	SA	A	D	SD
63	SA	A	D	SD
64	SA	A	D	SD
65	SA	A	D	SD
66	SA	A	D	SD
67	SA	A	D	SD
68	SA	A	D	SD
69	SA	A	D	SD
70	SA	A	D	SD
71	SA	A	D	SD
72	SA	A	D	SD
73	SA	A	D	SD
74	SA	A	D	SD
75	SA	A	D	SD

P

N

T

DC 1354

Instructor and Course Evaluation System
Office of Instructional Resources
Measurement and Research Division
University of Illinois at Urbana-Champaign

NEWSLETTER NUMBER 1

NEWSLETTER NEWSLETTER NEWSLETTER NEWSLETTER NEWSLETTER

ICES ITEM CATALOG

The Instructor and Course Evaluation System (ICES) is a computer-based system for obtaining student ratings of instructors and courses. With this system you can select items or complete rating forms which you consider to be the most appropriate for evaluating your course. This catalog contains over 400 items and 10 complete forms for your use.

GENERAL OPERATION OF ICES

Each ICES questionnaire contains space for 26 items. The first three items are preprinted on each questionnaire. They are:

1. Rate the Course Content — Excellent - Very Poor
2. Rate the Instructor — Excellent - Very Poor
3. Rate the Course in General — Excellent - Very Poor

These global items were selected to permit comparisons of ratings from nearly all teaching situations. The other 23 item spaces may be filled according to one of the three options described below. The three Global items above contain 6 response positions; all other items contain 5 response positions.

Option 1: Departmental Core Plus Instructor-Selected Items

Each department has the option to designate a set of items (not necessarily contained in the catalog) to use as its departmental core. Once a core has been established, all instructors in that department will automatically have the department core items included as part of the 23 items printed by the computer on the ICES questionnaire. The number of items contained in a given core thus limits the number of instructor-selected items that may be chosen. The total number of core plus instructor-selected may not exceed 23.

Option 2: Instructor-Selected Items Only (No Departmental Core)

If your department does not have a core set of items, then you have the option of choosing up to 23 items from the catalog. Since you must request an ICES questionnaire for each class section, you can select a different set of items for each section to be evaluated.

Option 3: Complete Forms

If your department does not have a set of core items and you do not wish to use the catalog of Instructor-Selected Items, then you may select one of the available complete forms. Complete forms are ready-made questionnaires that either have been used at UIUC or were designed for a special purpose. Short descriptions of each form are given on page 23 of this catalog. If you choose this complete form option you cannot also use the Instructor-Selected Items.

NEWSLETTER NEWSLETTER NEWSLETTER NEWSLETTER NEWSLETTER

TABLE OF CONTENTS

SIDE 1

SPECIAL CODE

INSTRUCTOR AND COURSE EVALUATION SYSTEM

For:

A	B	C	D	E
0	0	0	0	0
1	1	1	1	1
2	2	2	2	2
3	3	3	3	3
4	4	4	4	4
5	5	5	5	5
6	6	6	6	6
7	7	7	7	7
8	8	8	8	8
9	9	9	9	9

See Side 2 for directions. Use pencil only on this side.

1. When registering, what was your opinion about the

Positive / No opinion / Negative

Instructor ○○○

Course ○○○

2. Course in
○ Major
○ Minor
○ Other

3. Sex
○ Male
○ Female

4. This course was
○ Specifically required
○ Required but a choice among several
○ An elective

5. Class
○ Fresh
○ Soph
○ Junior
○ Senior
○ Grad
○ Other

6. Expected Grade
Ⓐ
Ⓑ
Ⓒ
Ⓓ
Ⓔ

SPECIAL INSTRUCTIONS

A) For Items | Respond
I
J
K
L
M

B) For items | Respond
I
J
K
L
M

TM

1. RATE THE COURSE CONTENT — EXCELLENT ○○○○○○ VERY POOR
2. RATE THE INSTRUCTOR — EXCELLENT ○○○○○○ VERY POOR
3. RATE THE COURSE IN GENERAL — EXCELLENT ○○○○○○ VERY POOR
4. Ⓘ Ⓙ Ⓚ Ⓛ Ⓜ
5. Ⓘ Ⓙ Ⓚ Ⓛ Ⓜ
6. Ⓘ Ⓙ Ⓚ Ⓛ Ⓜ
7. Ⓘ Ⓙ Ⓚ Ⓛ Ⓜ
8. Ⓘ Ⓙ Ⓚ Ⓛ Ⓜ
9. Ⓘ Ⓙ Ⓚ Ⓛ Ⓜ
10. Ⓘ Ⓙ Ⓚ Ⓛ Ⓜ
11. Ⓘ Ⓙ Ⓚ Ⓛ Ⓜ
12. Ⓘ Ⓙ Ⓚ Ⓛ Ⓜ
13. Ⓘ Ⓙ Ⓚ Ⓛ Ⓜ
14. Ⓘ Ⓙ Ⓚ Ⓛ Ⓜ
15. Ⓘ Ⓙ Ⓚ Ⓛ Ⓜ
16. Ⓘ Ⓙ Ⓚ Ⓛ Ⓜ
17. Ⓘ Ⓙ Ⓚ Ⓛ Ⓜ
18. Ⓘ Ⓙ Ⓚ Ⓛ Ⓜ
19. Ⓘ Ⓙ Ⓚ Ⓛ Ⓜ
20. Ⓘ Ⓙ Ⓚ Ⓛ Ⓜ
21. Ⓘ Ⓙ Ⓚ Ⓛ Ⓜ
22. Ⓘ Ⓙ Ⓚ Ⓛ Ⓜ
23. Ⓘ Ⓙ Ⓚ Ⓛ Ⓜ
24. Ⓘ Ⓙ Ⓚ Ⓛ Ⓜ
25. Ⓘ Ⓙ Ⓚ Ⓛ Ⓜ
26. Ⓘ Ⓙ Ⓚ Ⓛ Ⓜ

Ⓘ Ⓙ Ⓚ Ⓛ Ⓜ

DO NOT WRITE IN THE SHADED AREA	**DIRECTIONS FOR ICES** **SIDE 2** Please use this side of the form for your personal comments on teacher effectiveness and other aspects of the course. Use <u>pencil only</u> in responding to the objective questions on the reverse side. Objective items 1 - 3 will be used to compare this course and instructor to others in the department and institution. Data from other items after item 3 would be useful to the instructor for course improvements. Your instructor will not see your completed evaluation until final grades are in for your course. NOTE: Someone other than your instructor should collect and mail these forms. PLEASE WRITE COMMENTS BELOW
A What are the major strengths and weaknesses of the instructor?	
B What aspects of this course were most beneficial to you?	
C What do you suggest to improve this course?	
D Comment on the grading procedures and exams.	
E Instructor option question	
F Instructor option question	

SIDE 1 **INSTRUCTOR AND COURSE EVALUATION SYSTEM**

SPECIAL CODE **For:**

See Side 2 for directions. Use pencil only on this side.

A	B	C	D	E
0	0	0	0	0
1	1	1	1	1
2	2	2	2	2
3	3	3	3	3
4	4	4	4	4
5	5	5	5	5
6	6	6	6	6
7	7	7	7	7
8	8	8	8	8
9	9	9	9	9

1. When registering, what was your opinion about the

	Positive	No opinion	Negative
Instructor	○	○	○
Course	○	○	○

2. Course in
○ Major
○ Minor
○ Other

3. Sex
○ Male
○ Female

01- 14935

4. This course was
○ Specifically required
○ Required but a choice among several
○ An elective

5. Class
○ Fresh
○ Soph
○ Junior
○ Senior
○ Grad
○ Other

6 Expected Grade
Ⓐ
Ⓑ
Ⓒ
Ⓓ
Ⓔ

SPECIAL INSTRUCTIONS

A) For Items 04-24 Respond
I STRONGLY AGREE
J AGREE
K NEUTRAL
L DISAGREE
M STRONGLY DISAGREE

B) For Items Respond
I
J
K
L
M

1. RATE THE COURSE CONTENT — EXCELLENT ○○○○○○ VERY POOR
2. RATE THE INSTRUCTOR — EXCELLENT ○○○○○○ VERY POOR
3. RATE THE COURSE IN GENERAL — EXCELLENT ○○○○○○ VERY POOR
4. I WOULD TAKE ANOTHER COURSE THAT WAS TAUGHT THIS WAY. — STRONGLY AGREE Ⓘ Ⓙ Ⓚ Ⓛ Ⓜ STRONGLY DISAGREE
5. THE INSTRUCTOR SEEMED TO BE INTERESTED IN STUDENTS AS PERSONS. — STRONGLY AGREE Ⓘ Ⓙ Ⓚ Ⓛ Ⓜ STRONGLY DISAGREE
6. I WOULD HAVE PREFERRED ANOTHER METHOD OF TEACHING IN THIS COURSE. — STRONGLY AGREE Ⓘ Ⓙ Ⓚ Ⓛ Ⓜ STRONGLY DISAGREE
7. IT WAS EASY TO REMAIN ATTENTIVE. — STRONGLY AGREE Ⓘ Ⓙ Ⓚ Ⓛ Ⓜ STRONGLY DISAGREE
8. THE INSTRUCTOR DID NOT SYNTHESIZE, INTEGRATE, OR SUMMARIZE EFFECTIVELY. — STRONGLY AGREE Ⓘ Ⓙ Ⓚ Ⓛ Ⓜ STRONGLY DISAGREE
9. NOT MUCH WAS GAINED BY TAKING THIS COURSE. — STRONGLY AGREE Ⓘ Ⓙ Ⓚ Ⓛ Ⓜ STRONGLY DISAGREE
10. THE INSTRUCTOR ENCOURAGED DEVELOPMENT OF NEW VIEWPOINTS AND APPRECIATIONS. — STRONGLY AGREE Ⓘ Ⓙ Ⓚ Ⓛ Ⓜ STRONGLY DISAGREE
11. I LEARN MORE WHEN OTHER TEACHING METHODS ARE USED. — STRONGLY AGREE Ⓘ Ⓙ Ⓚ Ⓛ Ⓜ STRONGLY DISAGREE
12. THE COURSE MATERIAL SEEMED WORTHWHILE. — STRONGLY AGREE Ⓘ Ⓙ Ⓚ Ⓛ Ⓜ STRONGLY DISAGREE
13. THE INSTRUCTOR DEMONSTRATED A THOROUGH KNOWLEDGE OF THE SUBJECT MATTER. — STRONGLY AGREE Ⓘ Ⓙ Ⓚ Ⓛ Ⓜ STRONGLY DISAGREE
14. IT WAS A VERY WORTHWHILE COURSE. — STRONGLY AGREE Ⓘ Ⓙ Ⓚ Ⓛ Ⓜ STRONGLY DISAGREE
15. SOME THINGS WERE NOT EXPLAINED VERY WELL. — STRONGLY AGREE Ⓘ Ⓙ Ⓚ Ⓛ Ⓜ STRONGLY DISAGREE
16. THE COURSE MATERIAL WAS TOO DIFFICULT. — STRONGLY AGREE Ⓘ Ⓙ Ⓚ Ⓛ Ⓜ STRONGLY DISAGREE
17. THIS WAS ONE OF MY POOREST COURSES. — STRONGLY AGREE Ⓘ Ⓙ Ⓚ Ⓛ Ⓜ STRONGLY DISAGREE
18. THE INSTRUCTOR SEEMED TO CONSIDER TEACHING AS A CHORE OR ROUTINE ACTIVITY. — STRONGLY AGREE Ⓘ Ⓙ Ⓚ Ⓛ Ⓜ STRONGLY DISAGREE
19. IT WAS QUITE INTERESTING. — STRONGLY AGREE Ⓘ Ⓙ Ⓚ Ⓛ Ⓜ STRONGLY DISAGREE
20. I THINK THE COURSE WAS TAUGHT QUITE WELL. — STRONGLY AGREE Ⓘ Ⓙ Ⓚ Ⓛ Ⓜ STRONGLY DISAGREE
21. THE COURSE CONTENT WAS EXCELLENT. — STRONGLY AGREE Ⓘ Ⓙ Ⓚ Ⓛ Ⓜ STRONGLY DISAGREE
22. SOME DAYS I WAS NOT VERY INTERESTED IN THIS COURSE. — STRONGLY AGREE Ⓘ Ⓙ Ⓚ Ⓛ Ⓜ STRONGLY DISAGREE
23. IT WAS QUITE BORING. — STRONGLY AGREE Ⓘ Ⓙ Ⓚ Ⓛ Ⓜ STRONGLY DISAGREE
24. OVERALL, THE COURSE WAS GOOD. — STRONGLY AGREE Ⓘ Ⓙ Ⓚ Ⓛ Ⓜ STRONGLY DISAGREE
25. Ⓘ Ⓙ Ⓚ Ⓛ Ⓜ
26. Ⓘ Ⓙ Ⓚ Ⓛ Ⓜ

DEPARTMENT OF MANAGEMENT
COURSE AND FACULTY EVALUATION

Instructor____________________________ Course__________________________ Date________

Instructions: After filling in the information above, please circle the number under each item below which best indicates your impressions of the instructor and course.

You are asked to rate the instructor and the course on each of those aspects of performance on a seven-point scale as shown below:

(unsatisfactory) 1 2 3 4 5 6 7 (outstanding)

It is very important that you do not omit any scale.

1. The assistance given by this instructor's teaching methods to my personal growth and development was:
   (unsatisfactory) 1 2 3 4 5 6 7 (outstanding)
2. The instructor's preparation and organization of the course was:
   (unsatisfactory) 1 2 3 4 5 6 7 (outstanding)
3. The value of the classroom sessions in aiding my understanding of the course material was:
   (unsatisfactory) 1 2 3 4 5 6 7 (outstanding)
4. The extent to which the course assignments, readings, papers or projects, complemented the instructor's classroom activity was:
   (unsatisfactory) 1 2 3 4 5 6 7 (outstanding)
5. My overall evaluation of the instructor would be:
   (unsatisfactory) 1 2 3 4 5 6 7 (outstanding)

Please rate the three items below on a seven-point scale shown as follows:

(low) 1 2 3 4 5 6 7 (high)

6. The extent to which the workload given to students in this course was:
   (low) 1 2 3 4 5 6 7 (high)
7. The extent to which performance standards expected from students in this course were:
   (low) 1 2 3 4 5 6 7 (high)
8. My overall evaluation of the course would be:
   (unsatisfactory) 1 2 3 4 5 6 7 (outstanding)

CLASSROOM VISITATION APPRAISAL

Teacher____________________ Course____________________

Term____________________ Academic Year____________________

Visitor(s)____________________ Title____________________

The following appraisal form contains 12 questions, many of which are found on the student appraisal of teaching form. In addition, you may want to develop a narrative description of your visitation.

Directions: Rate teaching on each item, giving the highest scores for unusually effective performances.

Highest			Average			Lowest	Don't Know
7	6	5	4	3	2	1	X

______ 1. Were the major objectives of the course made clear to you?

______ 2. How well was the class presentation planned and organized?

______ 3. Were important ideas clearly explained?

______ 4. How would you judge the professor's mastery of the course content?

______ 5. Was class time well used?

______ 6. Did the professor encourage critical thinking and analysis?

______ 7. Do you believe the professor encouraged relevant student involvement in the class?

______ 8. How did the professor react to student viewpoints different from his own?

______ 9. How would you describe the attitude of students in the class toward the professor?

______10. Do you believe that your visitation was at a time when you were able to fairly judge the nature and tenor of the teaching-learning process?

______11. Considering the previous 10 items, how would you rate this teacher in comparison to others in the department?

______12. As compared with others in the institution?

______13.

______14.

________ Composite rating.

Yes____ No____ Did you have a preliminary conference with the teacher before the visitation?
Yes____ No____ Did you have a follow-up conference?

Comments after class visitation:______________________________

____

Comments after follow-up conference:______________________________

____

Richard I. Miller, *Evaluating Faculty Performance* (San Francisco: Jossey-Bass, 1972), p. 33.

Class Observation Report For The File Of ____________________

Instructor ____________________ Observer ____________________

Subject __________ Topic of the Day __________ No. in class ____

Approach(es) Used: Lecture __ Exposition__ Demonstration__ Discussion __

Other ____

To the Observer: Please respond specifically to every part of the following questions. Where the question is not appropriate to the particular class, please so indicate.

1. Comment on the instructor's clarity in a) exposition b) questioning of students and c) responding to questions.

2. Did the students seem involved in the learning process? How was this involvement manifested?

3. What, if any, teaching devices were used? Could this particular class have been more effective if others were used?

Used with permission. Developed by Greenfield Community College, Greenfield, Mass. 01301. Form 2. Cited in William J. Genova et al., *Mutual Benefit Evaluation of Faculty and Administrators in Higher Education* (Cambridge, Mass.: Ballinger Publishing Co., 1976), pp. 96–97.

4. What impressed you most about this class?

5. Every instructor has a characteristic manner toward his students. Try to describe this attitude as you perceived it.

6. Offer comments or suggestions for improvement; please try to offer at least one specific suggestion.

Peer Evaluation Form For The File Of ______________________

One part of the Faculty Professional Improvement Program at Greenfield Community College involves the professional judgment and insight of one's peers. You are among those who have been selected as one whose experience and close association with the individual named above may provide a useful source of first-hand information regarding professional performance.

Please answer the questions as candidly as possible, responding only to those areas wherein you feel especially knowledgeable. Your thoughtful assistance is appreciated.

1. From your particular point of view, and observation, what is/are this individual's greatest asset(s) as a community college instructor?

2. What areas of professional activity or responsibility, if any, do you see as needing attention, evaluation, improvement, change?

3. In your judgment, what are this individual's shortcomings?

4. Additional insights or comments. (Use reverse side if necessary).

(Signature of Respondent) Date

Used with permission. Developed by Greenfield Community College, Greenfield, Mass. 01301. Form 3. Cited in J. Genova et al., *Mutual Benefit Evaluation of Faculty and Administrators in Higher Education* (Cambridge, Mass.: Ballinger Publishing Co., 1976), pp. 94-95.

Evaluation by Students

The state of the art in course and faculty evaluation is by no means a highly developed one. In fact, one might say that "only the surface has been scratched." An accurate and complete description of good teaching has not yet been defined. Results of evaluative efforts are being questioned because of their ambiguous and sometimes contradictory results. Sheehan identifies the following potential areas of invalidity:

1. The affective is not included so existing measures are only a partial measure of teacher effectiveness.
2. The relationship between student ratings and achievement measures of instructional effectiveness are still not clear cut.
3. Instructor rating scales are predominantly composed of general evaluative items and do not uniformly tap all dimensions of teaching.
4. Student differences in learning styles influence perceptions of effective teaching.
5. The way in which directions are given and tactics of the instructor negate uniformity in administration of the instrument used.[14]

The last point above was investigated in a study to measure the effect of several variables influencing TRF (Teacher Rating Form) scores at the time of their administration. Factors included identity of the sponsor (in this case, the Faculty Association or the Student Association), attitude of the sponsor toward student evaluations, and whether or not the respondent remained anonymous. As a result of the study, users of TRFs in university settings were cautioned that situational factors may influence student evaluation of teaching effectiveness. While there is some advocacy for each instructor to handle his or her own administration of evaluation instruments, two contrary recommendations resulted from this particular study. The first was that an attempt should be made to make the "testing" conditions as uniform as possible with the instrument administered simultaneously for all instructors. The other recommendation was for use of a group of trained evaluators representing the same sponsor so as to maintain similar testing conditions and eliminate sponsor variability.[15]

Research in the field shows that numerous other factors have caused variations in student ratings including student sex, expected cumulative grade point average, and whether the course is required or elective for the particular student rater. The general character of a course may also have a definite influence upon evaluation results. In this instance, Ebel and Berg found that within a physical education program, instructors of lecture courses in theory were viewed as having greater mastery of subject matter and being fairer in methods of evaluation than instructors of activity courses for particular skills. The latter instructors were viewed as superior in their ability to explain and clarify their subject matter (i.e., in skill courses). In the same study, it was also found that the grade expectations of the students affected the instructor ratings.[16]

Because all teaching situations are not the same, a particular evaluation instrument or rating scale may not be valid for all instructors or courses. McKeachie suggests a core of test items that might form a base for comparative purposes in addition to which instructors might develop relevant items for their own courses.[17] It is also possible to have a "bank" of questions from which instructors may select those items they consider most relevant. The F.A.C.E. instrument and the ICES and IDEA systems mentioned earlier in this chapter provide this kind of flexibility.

Hill cautions that any student rating form must cover only those aspects of teaching that students are competent to judge and lists the following criteria for using student evaluation forms:

1. Administration—The instrument should be administered by the instructor himself during the regular class or examination period. (Some researchers believe that administration during the final examination period tends to intimidate students.)
2. Time—The period of time needed to administer the instrument should be short enough to be acceptable to faculty yet long enough to insure reliability and an adequate measurement of a wide sample of attitudes.
3. Content—Opinions and attitudes that have been developed about the total instructional program and not just a single element should be measured. Invalid items such as dress and room temperature are not to be included.
4. Scoring—The instrument should be objective and machine scorable. It should be designed so as to standardize scoring and make prompt feedback possible.
5. Reliability—Scores should be reproducable upon subsequent rating by the same students of the same instructor and course.
6. Interpretation—The instrument should yield scores which differentiate among instructional programs and can be interpreted so that instructional effectiveness can be improved. Results should be of assistance in diagnosing strengths and weaknesses of the instructional program.
7. Realism—The instrument should include critical elements which comprise opinions the student has and wishes to express. It should be capable of eliciting "real" feelings and not careless or merely socially acceptable or expected responses.[18]

The evaluation of instructors reflects not only the instructor's behavior but also the expectations and perceptions of their students. It is entirely possible that students may weigh certain teaching characteristics in a way different from an instructor's peers and administrators. A situation where high student ratings are accepted as an absolute indication of excellent teaching must be avoided.

A number of factors may have an effect upon the classroom situation and the student evaluations reflecting their perceptions. If a class is scheduled during the dinner hour, students who have worked all day at a full time job may be tired and hungry. The student who works a night shift or late evening hours and must attend a class beginning at 8:00 A.M. or thereabouts may be immediately biased about the offering.

Some courses by virtue of their content may be less likely to stimulate student interest just as whether a course is required or elective may be a factor. Students also frequently have difficulty in making a distinction between evaluation of teaching and requirements for the course and program.

While extensive research in the area is still developing, one other limitation should be mentioned. Some relationship has been found between a student's expected grade and the rating given. Students who expect higher grades rate instructors higher. The reverse is also true. Whether this bias can ever be eliminated is doubtful.

Evaluation by Colleagues

Rating by one's colleagues is not always reliable and particularly not if it is based only upon "scholarly reputation." Colleague ratings may be influenced by academic rank indicating that an instructor's reputation has a definite bearing upon his rating according to Aleomani and Yimer.[19]

The most accurate measure of teaching ability will be obtained only by careful observation over a period of time. To accomplish this, there must be a commitment to investing large amounts of time and effort if the observations are to be reliable.

In moving toward actual classroom observation, guidelines must be established which include: who will observe, number of times per semester observations will take place, what the observer or observers will be looking for, form that feedback to the instructor will take, and other uses, if any, to be made of the data obtained. Training sessions for the evaluative efforts must be devised. However, students who spend a full semester with a particular instructor will get to know that professor as a teacher better than another professor or the department chairperson who might observe one class during the semester. Multiple observations appear to be necessary. However, Blackburn and Clark did find in their study of faculty (limited to a "typical" liberal arts college) a reasonably high agreement between faculty peers and students on their assessment of professors and to a lesser extent between administrators and the above mentioned two role sets.[20]

In addition to classroom observation, another vehicle for evaluation might be colleague review of the instructor's knowledge in his subject area; examination of the course syllabus, objectives, and reading list; materials used; and assignments and examinations. In fact, this might be a first step in moving toward classroom observation since it would be less threatening to the instructor and could begin to establish a collegial atmosphere for instructional improvement.

Ideally, a measure of each student's learning should be a basis for evaluation but we are still far from this level of sophistication. In the same direction, however, activities just described might be supplemented by examining evidence of student achievement such as term papers, course projects, and examinations.

Finally, complete objectivity in assessment of one another by department members will be difficult to achieve because of the very close relationship among them.

Evaluation by Administrators

In many instances, evaluations by administrators are not acceptable in themselves because they are based mainly upon hearsay. The documentation of comments, either positive or negative, which might come from students, alumni, and peers, may provide a source of information about an individual's accomplishments in numerous areas, but caution must be taken so that gossip and hearsay do not become mixed with valid information.

Administrators are in a difficult situation because of the prevailing notion that college professors are and should be completely autonomous in their classrooms and these classrooms should never be "invaded" by department heads or deans. The trend appears to be more toward faculty committee evaluation than administrative in order to increase the reliability and range of information gathered. Miller recommends that, in addition to the usual resume or yearly accounting of professional activities, there be an annual performance review in the form of individual conferences scheduled by department chairpersons with their faculty.[21]

If, for some reason, evaluations by the department chairperson and/or dean differ from peer evaluations, immediate discussion between the administrator and faculty members should be scheduled. Department heads are "caught in the middle." They must be responsive to the administration yet remain popular with their faculty colleagues. As a result, they may find that they must decide whether or not it is wise to disagree with a department committee or to take a stand different from that of the administrators above them. In the evaluation of faculty, the major function of administrators is to collect as much data from as many sources as possible, summarize it, and forward it to the next level of administration as needed.

Whatever mechanism is established for evaluating faculty performance, it must be developed by the faculty if it is to be implemented. Otherwise, faculty resistance will prevent the process from ever beginning. The following statement from the American Association of University Professors emphasizes the need for written policies and procedures. It is clearly an important responsibility of college and department administrators to see that these are not only developed but also periodically reviewed as indicated.

> At the college or department level, the expectations as to teaching, the weighting of teaching in relation to other expectations, and the criteria and procedures by which the fulfillment of these expectations is to be judged should be put in writing and periodically reviewed by all members of the college or department. This policy statement should specify the type of information which is to be gathered for all faculty members, the basic procedures to be followed in gathering it, and the time schedule for various aspects of the review process.[22]

FACULTY DEVELOPMENT

Faculty development programs are a natural follow-up to faculty evaluation efforts, but caution must be exercised so that the programs are viewed as positive forces rather than remedial efforts. Ideally, a comprehensive program is needed, one in which evaluation is viewed as an integral component of continuous ongoing activities. If institutions are to be responsive to new demands being made upon them, ways must be found to also help faculty members adjust their beliefs and behaviors. Note that instructional development is one part, although a major part, of the total development process as defined in the comprehensive definition below:

> Faculty development may be described as an institutional process which seeks to modify the attitudes, skills, and behavior of faculty members toward greater competence and effectiveness in meeting student needs, their own needs, and the needs of the institution. Successful programs change the way faculty feel about their professional roles, increase their knowledge and skills in those roles, and alter the way they carry them out in practice. Instructional development increases faculty awareness of the importance of teaching, provides specific and intensive training in classroom skills, and established institutional policies and practices which support instructional improvement as a continuing objective.[23]

NEED FOR FACULTY DEVELOPMENT PROGRAMS

Faculty development is the chief means for improving education. During a period of rapid growth in higher education, the mechanisms for change generally result from establishment of new programs and facilities with an accompanying growth in staff. When growth is replaced by steady-state staffing and declining faculty mobility, decreasing enrollments, adjustment to inflation accompanied by fiscal retrenchment, and demands for accountability and greater productivity, faculty must recognize the need for and be willing to embark upon comprehensive programs for examining what they are doing, how well they are doing it, and what can be done toward improvement. Many believe that if faculty do not embark upon such a program, legislators and trustees will with the risk of an application of inappropriate criteria.

While retrenchment, changing enrollment figures, and accountability demands dominate the scene, a number of related influences cannot be ignored. Appropriate responses to changing student populations are needed. The traditional undergraduate and graduate students will continue to provide a major portion of the enrollment, but a new body of students has appeared on the scene including increased numbers of minority students, older students, and part-time and off-campus registrants. The concept of lifelong learning and an accompanying emphasis on continuing education are providing challenges that must lead to a broadening concept of student populations serving not only their needs but also the needs of society.

Another factor leading to recognition of the need for faculty development is the number and kinds of attempts to experiment with innovative ideas. Exploration is needed to find ways to more effectively utilize new instructional technologies including mediated learning and the somewhat unexplored and unevaluated potential of the computer. Cluster colleges, living–learning centers, increased use of independent study, field-study projects and cooperative education programs, interdisciplinary courses and programs, mini-courses, and competency-based approaches are some of the new structures requiring development of programs for stimulating faculty growth.

Finally, comprehensive examination of the role of a faculty member is essential. Effectiveness as a teacher is one part of the expectation. A faculty member is also expected to be a researcher, a writer, an adviser, a consultant, and a committee member. Ways must be developed to improve effectiveness in these areas in addition to instructional effectiveness.

Educators have long advocated more education for everyone but themselves. They must begin to recognize that in-service activities are essential for providing the institution with a means for developing personnel flexibility and helping faculty meet the challenges of rapid change.

Program Development

The major focus of faculty development programs has been the examination and improvement of teaching. As mentioned before, the other roles of a faculty member cannot be ignored. However, to provide direction the first consideration in program development must be that of institutional mission. The purpose of the particular college and/or university is then made operational by means of the teaching and learning activities. Throughout, there is a need for examination of values, attitudes, and behaviors of faculty whose view of any change program will depend upon how anticipated changes relate to their value systems. Evaluation procedures can lead to defensive behaviors since faculty members will be fearful about revealing inadequacies and might even be philosophically opposed to new methods and new curricular proposals. For some, teaching and learning rank low in priority while research and writing will take precedence. An effective program will cause faculty members to reexamine their own goals and values without becoming a personal development or therapeutic program, which such programs were never meant to be.

Development programs must be nonthreatening and reflect concepts of academic freedom, individual autonomy, and the competencies it is assumed faculty already possess particularly in their own areas of discipline. Planning must take into consideration the prevailing climate in the institution if it is to be successful. In fact, it might be wise to begin with a small, carefully organized program designed for those who express a desire to participate and take advantage of it. Any program, whether on a large or small scale, must be developed with the faculty, not for the faculty.

To begin, clearly stated institutional policies emphasizing support are needed. Purposes of the program and its content must be defined. Adequate funding is essential. From 1 to 3 percent of the instructional budget is recommended; that amount would cover the program and related situations including sabbaticals and reduced load time for related special purposes. Funds are needed to cover secretarial support, supplies, special equipment needs, travel, and competent outside participants serving as speakers, workshop leaders, and consultants. Adequate facilities are also necessary for success of the program.

One of the greatest problems will be time. Time is needed for planning, coordination, evaluation, and participation. Released time in some form for a semester might be considered to enable professors to participate fully. While it might not be feasible to lighten class load, release from committee membership for a specified period of time could be an acceptable alternative. In larger institutions, it would probably be feasible and appropriate to either release a faculty member from all other responsibilities to serve as director of the development program or to employ someone specifically to direct the total effort.

Centra found that over 405 of the more than 700 institutions in his study had some kind of development unit. As can be seen in Table 4–1, the prevalence of such units is greater in universities (65 percent) than in two- and four-year colleges (49 percent and 34 percent, respectively). Staffing ranged from a program director or coordinator working alone to more comprehensive organizations including specialists in instructional development, evaluation, technology, and media.

The success of the effort will depend upon related and concurrent processes including committee activity, faculty senate participation and support, and existing staff evaluation measures. The total environment of the institution is crucial as is the understanding, attitudes, and behavior of those in leadership positions.

Centra also explored the funding aspect of development programs in the previously cited study and found that the cost of development programs was a concern. Estimates provided by the 700 institutions in the sample showed that an average of 70 percent of the total budget for development activities came from institutional general funds. An average of 20 percent was supplied by grants from foundations or the federal government, while an additional 7 percent came from state funds. "Other" sources such as alumni or special funds accounted for the remaining 3 percent. Funding sources for two-year colleges and doctorate-granting universities were virtually the same. However, four-year colleges differed in that they received a higher proportion from founda-

TABLE 4–1 **Organization of Faculty Development Programs**

	All Institutions N = 756	*Two-Year Colleges N = 326*	*Four-Year Colleges N = 315*	*Universities N = 93*
A. Proportion with unit(s) or person for development or instructional improvement	44%	49%	34%	65%
B. Median number of years unit has existed	2.3	2.5	1.4	4.0
C. Number of people involved (percentage based on number from A above)	less than 1—15%	12%	19%	13%
	1—48%	56%	46%	27%
	2 or 3—16%	14%	11%	31%
	4 or more—21%	18%	24%	29%

John A. Centra, "Types of Faculty Development Programs," *Journal of Higher Education* 49 (1978): 160.

tions or federal sources, 27 percent, as compared to 15 or 16 percent for two-year colleges and universities. Four-year colleges, as a group, received only 3 percent directly from their states. This might be explained by the fact that many of these institutions were private colleges.[24]

As can be seen, a number of colleges have had success in obtaining outside funding for faculty development. With the support of the federal government and philanthropic foundations including the Carnegie Corporation and the Danforth, Kellogg, Lilly, and Mellon Foundations, they have established projects, programs, and centers for the improvement of teaching.

Objectives

Professors have individual beliefs and values of their own which must be considered when planning development programs and particularly when formulating objectives. The value system of the institution itself is another consideration including its impact on the roles of the professor and relationships between professors and students. The nature and purpose of teaching and learning situations as well as the need for higher education to be responsive to the demands of a changing society cannot be ignored. Above all, the objectives must reflect that the faculty development program is to be a long-term positive effort rather than a short-term remedial activity.

Faculty need to assess what they are doing, why they are doing it, how well they are doing it, and the problems facing them. From this information, specific objectives both long and short range can be developed. First and foremost among the objectives should be those concerned with the improvement of instruction. Development of improved instructional skills and a knowledge of alternative modes for teaching and learning as well as keeping instructors current on their subject matter is important. Helping instructors to define the competencies that should be acquired by students with an accompanying emphasis upon learning rather than upon teaching behaviors alone is important.

Many instructors have need for a broader knowledge about higher education in general. What should be its mission not only now but also in the decades to come? Knowledge about institutional policies, procedures, and campus politics is essential if faculty members are expected to participate in the governance structure. A development program should assist them in becoming effective, contributing members of the organization.

The areas of research and writing provide another challenge. Why shouldn't workshops be organized to help faculty develop skills such as identifying appropriate research topics, proposal writing, and appropriate use of the computer? Another component in this area should be development of workshops for improving skills for writing that hopefully will be published. Experience has shown that different kinds of journals require different styles of writing. What are the steps toward having a book published? Many faculty members have no knowledge at all about the development of a prospectus, required style, or contract provisions. In such instances, appropriate objectives might include developing:

1. Understanding of the kinds of topics in which specific journals might be interested
2. Knowledge of the format for preparing journal articles for publication
3. Familiarity with publishing firms and their specializations
4. Knowledge of procedures for obtaining a contract for publication of a book including preparation of a table of contents and a prospectus
5. Knowledge of the basic minimal provisions to be included in a publication contract
6. Skill in manuscript preparation

Another activity in which many faculty members participate is that of consulting. Definite capabilities are again needed and appropriate objectives might include the development of skills such as:

1. Defining the area of coverage
2. Negotiating for a contract
3. Working with large and small groups
4. Interviewing techniques
5. Data gathering
6. Preparing the report

A comprehensive objective particularly appropriate during a period of retrenchment might be to extend the range of knowledge possessed by faculty members to include not only other disciplines but also the community and its needs.

COMPONENTS

The environment of the institution is an important factor in determining both the structure of a staff development program and how to best expedite the growth process for staff members. Leaders must be identified who understand the processes of development, how programs relate to one another, and institutional objectives. Awareness of the context in which programs are to be implemented is crucial to their success.

The various components of a faculty development program must be introduced when most appropriate and in a logical order. Different approaches are needed at different stages. Initially, faculty interest and concern must be aroused. Global statements from administrators expressing their concerns are needed. To get the program started, consultants might be brought in who, after talking with faculty and students and possibly observing faculty, would bring faculty together to discuss what actually exists rather than the abstract.

Specific activities in the area of professional development might include:

1. Attendance at professional meetings and subsequent sharing of information in structured seminars
2. Visits to other institutions
3. Discussions of the latest ideas gleaned from professional literature both of a generalized nature and that related to specific academic disciplines
4. Lectures and campus conferences analyzing contemporary educational issues
5. Development of a library representing current thought
6. Presentations by doctoral students on the results of their research
7. Seminars on the various aspects of teaching/learning situations including a sharing by faculty members of descriptions of what they are doing
8. Workshops for the development and reinforcement of specific skills such as preparation of lectures and other presentations, evaluation of student achievement, academic advising, credit for prior learning and relevant life experiences, and use of media including computers
9. Consultative services to individual faculty members upon request
10. Projects for the evaluation of teaching and subsequent use of diagnostic feedback
11. Establishment of a center for the study of teaching
12. Workshops for the development of proposal writing and improvement of research skills
13. Workshops for the improvement of skills in preparation of manuscripts for publication and techniques for enhancing the possibility of their acceptance

In the area of curriculum development, activities might include:

1. Seminars on student development and, in particular, meeting the needs of new types of students
2. Workshops on the evaluation of life experiences and the subsequent awarding of appropriate credit
3. Workshops exploring new approaches such

as computer assisted instruction, contract learning systems, self-paced courses, and personalized systems of instruction
4. Workshops on production of learning materials for classes
5. Seminars and workshops on development and implementation of new and/or revised courses and curricula
6. Workshops on team teaching, interdisciplinary teaching, and development of interdisciplinary offerings
7. Exploration of alternatives to the traditional classroom including nonclassroom learning situations, use of community resources, blocks of time other than the traditional fifty-minute periods
8. Visits to other institutions to review programs and possibly identify appropriate models

Faculty development programs will most often begin with activities directed toward the professional development of individuals followed by curriculum development. A natural outgrowth would be movement toward more effective institutional involvement and organizational development. Activities might progress from those preparing individuals for effective participation in college and university efforts to an evaluation and revision of institutional structures. In this area, possible activities might include:

1. Training in interpersonal skills for working in large and small group settings
2. Workshops including role playing for the development of leadership personnel
3. Encounter groups for improving administrative relationships
4. Seminars for discussion of pertinent legislation and its impact upon the institution
5. Seminars on current issues in American colleges and universities
6. Seminars on institutional policies, procedures, and politics
7. Task forces for establishing goals and priorities for the institution and its subunits
8. Task forces focusing on the institution as a whole and on appropriate subunits for the purpose of analyzing the administrative and governance structures followed by (a) recommendations for developing a more cohesive entity and the direction to be taken (b) definition of the tasks for moving in that direction and identification and agreement on priorities for the tasks
9. Structures for continuous evaluation and feedback to assess the effectiveness of changes, monitor the maintenance of those found effective, and identify ineffective changes for further study and possible alternate recommendations

An interesting approach is the educational planning and development program at the Medical College of Virginia (Virginia Commonwealth University) which was established to assist educational units in defining their goals more precisely and assist in goal accomplishment. Assistance was provided in grant preparation, educational policy formulation, and evaluation research, but the bulk of the effort described was in the area of faculty development. The thrust was toward helping "faculty members function more comfortably and effectively in the university setting." Eight specific activities were conducted: (1) workshops on simulations and self-instructional packages; (2) a workshop and extensive activity toward conversion of a departmental curriculum to self-instruction; (3) a one day workshop on subject matter objectives; (4) a school faculty retreat; (5) a follow-up retreat; (6) a nine session faculty in-service series; (7) a seminar in human interaction skills; and (8) a curriculum development retreat. Each of the eight activities was evaluated and a model for faculty development practices was designed. The model covers the complete process from planning through evaluation. Various roles of the consultant from "the expert" to "collaborative" are included as well as strategies for assessment, planning and intervention, and evaluation.[25]

As shown in Table 4–2, Centra's factor analysis of the use of twenty-eight specific development practices identifies four groups and provides numerous examples of the kinds of

TABLE 4–2 **Factor Analysis of the Approximate Use of the Faculty Development Practices**

Group 1 (Factor 1): High Faculty Involvement	*Factor Loading*
Workshops, seminars, or programs to acquaint faculty with goals of the institution and types of students enrolled	.65
"Master teachers" or senior faculty work closely with new or apprentice teachers	.61
Faculty with expertise consult with other faculty on teaching or course improvement	.60
Workshops or program to help faculty improve their academic advising and counseling skills	.57
Personal counseling provided individual faculty members on career goals, and other personal development areas	.53
Workshops or presentations that explore general issues or trends in education	.51
Informal assessments by colleagues for teaching or course improvement	.48
System for faculty to assess their own strengths and areas needing improvement	.46
Group 2 (Factor 2): Instructional Assistance Practices	
Specialists to assist individual faculty in instructional or course development by consulting on course objectives and course design	.75
Specialists to help faculty develop teaching skills such as lecturing or leading discussions, or to encourage use of different teaching-learning strategies such as individualized instruction	.70
Specialists to assist faculty in constructing tests or evaluating student performance	.69
Assistance to faculty in use of instructional technology as a teaching aid (e.g., programmed learning or computer-assisted instruction)	.65
Specialists on campus to assist faculty in use of audiovisual aids in instruction, including closed-circuit television	.56
Workshops or presentations that explore various methods or techniques of instruction	.42
Group 3 (Factor 3): Traditional Practices	
Visiting scholars program that brings people to the campus for short or long periods	.58
Annual awards for excellence in teaching	.52
Sabbatical leaves with at least half salary	.43
Workshops or seminars to help faculty improve their research and scholarship skills	.43
Summer grants for projects to improve instruction or courses	.43
Temporary teaching load reductions to work on a new course, major course revision, or research area	.39
Use of grants by faculty members for developing new or different approaches to courses or teaching	.37
Travel grants to refresh or update knowledge in a particular field	.33
Group 4 (Factor 4): Emphasis on Assessment	
There is a periodic review of the performance of all faculty members, whether tenured or not	.55
Travel funds available to attend professional conferences	.47
Systematic ratings of instruction by students used to help faculty improve	.41
Formal assessments by colleagues for teaching or course improvement (i.e., visitations or use of assessment form)	.40
A policy of unpaid leaves that covers educational or development purposes	.40
Systematic teaching or course evaluations by an administrator for improvement purposes	.40

John A. Centra, "Types of Faculty Development Programs," *Journal of Higher Education* 49 (1978): 155.

development programs employed by different types of institutions. In reality, the possibilities for relevant development programs are endless.

Orientation for New Faculty

While it will be appropriate for newly appointed faculty members to participate in selected staff development activities, a specifically designed separate program is needed. Prior to actually entering the classroom as an instructor, the new professor should have ample opportunity to become familiar with the courses assigned to him or her including content, their place in the total curricular structure, and possible methodology. Provision should be made for practice in preparation of resource materials, the construction and evaluation of written assignments and examinations, videotaped practice sessions, and observation of experienced instructors.

Assistance should also be provided in the areas of planning class sessions from specific course outlines and selecting methods of presentation. Inexperienced instructors should be supervised in the classroom by an experienced master instructor who would serve as a guide, consultant, and tutor. This same master instructor would assist the new staff member in becoming an effective academic adviser.

Other orientation activities might include seminars on the formal and informal processes of the specific institution in addition to a discussion of institutional problems. Attempts should be made to develop collegiality and prepare new staff for full participation in the on-going development program.

Preparation of Future Professors

Frequently, the only preparation for college level teaching available to graduate students is observation of their own instructors who, unfortunately, do not always provide the best models. Systematic training should be available as an integral part of the student's graduate program.

Participating in some of the orientation and staff development activities just described would be profitable for future college instructors. It is essential, also, that teaching associates and graduate students be involved in some kind of teaching practicum with opportunities to experiment with various modes of teaching, monitor their own performance on videotape, study the learning styles of students, and collaborate with professors on planning and implementing new courses. An internship at some college off campus would be another approach. In some instances, a junior college experience would be most appropriate because it would provide a wider range of student needs and differences. The experience would be supervised and provide adequate critical feedback to the neophyte instructor. From these experiences, reports on teaching competence could be prepared for the dossiers of the students involved.

In addition to the structured teaching experience, graduate students are entitled to being treated with professional respect. They should be provided with adequate physical facilities not only for teaching but for their own professional studies and needs. Work assignments should be appropritae rather than the menial duties too often delegated by ranked staff. The entire experience should be looked upon as a developmental one.

Extensive involvement in potential instructional development activities will eventually lead to long-range improvement in the caliber of instruction and, hopefully, remove the separation between faculty and administrators.

Benefits

If institutions are to be responsive to the concerns of the future, ways must be found to change the attitudes and behaviors of staff members. Much depends upon the process established including senates, committees and task forces, evaluation procedures, and, most important of all, the attitudes, encouragement, and cooperation of administrators. Staff members must establish their own individual goals and relate them to the larger institutional goals. A truly effective development program will reap benefits for faculty, students, and the institution as a whole. Gaff summarizes these possible consequences as

> Benefits for faculty members: acquire additional knowledge about teaching–learning issues, develop and use new or improved teaching skills, develop and use new techniques or methods of instruction, clarify attitudes and values about teaching–learning issues and problems more frequently and with greater sophistication, develop more stimulating and supportive relationships with colleagues, obtain more accurate and favorable feedback from students.
> Benefits for students: acquire more knowledge about subject matter, improve thinking skills and cognitive abilities, increase interest in the subject, gain a desire to learn more about the topic, develop more enlightened or sophisticated attitudes or values concerning the subject matter, find learning more enjoyable or satisfactory, increase speed or ease of learning, acquire greater self-consciousness about teaching–learning matters, increase the amount and sophistication of discussion of subject matter, develop closer and more productive relationhsips with teachers.
> Benefits for the institution: increase the number of courses, substantially revised or new courses added, increase the range of learning opportunities for students, plan and implement new educational programs, develop more or more effective learning materials, improve relationships between faculty members, students, and administrators, devise and implement policies supportive of teaching effectiveness and improvement, reduce student dropout rate, improve group problem-solving skills, improve leadership abilities of key faculty and administrators, enhance morale and improve the organization.[26]

RETRENCHMENT AND RETRAINING

As described in Chapter 2, a number of influences have been exerting severe pressures upon colleges and universities creating situations that are completely opposite to those existing during the earlier period of tremendous growth; for example, decreasing enrollments resulting from a decreased birth rate, skepticism about the advantages of a college degree on the labor market, and a shift in attitudes toward priorities for expenditure of the tax dollar. As a result, some institutions are finding it necessary to implement procedures for staff reduction. This might take the form of not filling positions vacated by those who retire or move to other jobs. A more serious and more difficult situation exists when positions must be eliminated and decisions made regarding which staff members will stay and which will be released from among those considered competent and who have been awarded tenure.

Faculty Work Load

In the past, fiscal flexibility made it possible to cover miscalculations, overexpenditures in some areas, and indulgences in establishing faculty work loads. Phrases which include input-output, cost-benefit analysis, operational analysis, credit generation, and faculty work load reports tend to create a feeling of resentment among faculty. Counter arguments that mirror the values of faculty members include:

1. Many outcomes of educational activity cannot be measured on paper.
2. Certain practices are valued as ends in themselves.
3. "Training" is being emphasized more than education.
4. Unique characteristics of one faculty member's contributions make it difficult to compare them with another's contributions
5. Attempts to equate the number of hours

spent with the level of contribution denies the concept of faculty professionalism.
6. Load reports inadequately reflect all the expectations concerning faculty activity.
7. Operational analysis and requirements for work load reports are politically initiated.

Load should include all the activities in which faculty are expected to participate in their roles as teachers, scholars, institutional employees on campus, and institutional representatives off campus. Faculty activity data should be gathered for informational purposes, not evaluative, and should be viewed as such by faculty. Faculty should also be provided with information regarding who is gathering the data, to whom it will be reported, the purposes for obtaining the information, and feedback on the consequences.

Ideally, faculty should be involved in developing the instruments and procedures for data gathering plus analysis of the results so that they will be more likely to be receptive to the inevitable establishment of priorities and reallocation of limited resources.

Procedures

A self-analysis process must be instituted at each level and within each subunit including the dean's office. Questions to be answered include: (1) What should be the role of the dean's office? (2) What is the role of each of the various departments? (3) Which departments should be strengthened, put in a service role, restructured, or, perhaps, even eliminated? and, (4) What should be the balance between programs that are specialized in nature and those that are broad based?

Goals describing the mission of each unit or subunit must first be established in qualitative and quantitative terms including a definition of the relationship to the mission of the total institution. Different approaches to accomplish the goals must then be devised to accommodate changing circumstances, particularly in the area of available funding, which requires the establishment of priorities among goals. Continual reassessment on an annual basis is essential to determine progress towards the established goals and to reevaluate the practicality and desirability of future goals. This annual assessment may lead to decisions related to the elimination of some programs so that others may be strengthened. It may also be recognized that a reduction in resources dictates that some program areas be substantially reduced or eliminated, and that while the majority of the established goals are practical, some portion cannot be implemented because a substantial increase in costs would be required.

Institutions should be prepared for possible reduction and elimination of programs by establishing policies and procedures prior to the actual need for them. Faculty consultation is essential in both the development and implementation of these policies and procedures. Alternatives to termination of faculty should be explored including early retirement, joint appointments and transfer to other departments (both of which necessitate retraining), and layoff and recall in place of termination. Academic due process procedures must be considered along with adequate notice and, where possible, assistance in finding new positions. It is ultimately an administrative reponsibility to maintain the best possible overall program of education, which in times of financial exigency dictates maintaining the most necessary programs and deciding which faculty members are needed to maintain those particular programs.

Allshouse points out that:

> . . . recent court decisions, contrary to the AAUP's guidelines, make it clear that: (1) tenured faculty members can be terminated independent of the discontinuance of an entire program or department; (2) it is not

> necessary for faculty to be involved in the determination of which programs or departments, if any, will be eliminated; and (3) faculty need not be part of the initial decision to terminate a specific tenured faculty member.[27]

Under any circumstances, care should be taken to avoid involvement of the courts, which might prove to be costly and would also dispel the healthy climate needed for accomplishing change and preserving the integrity of the institution. The five principles below provide some appropriate and timely advice.

1. The first principle deals with the determination of bona fide financial exigency. This principle, briefly stated, might be, "Take time to do your homework carefully."
2. The second principle deals with the federal, state, and local statutes, rules, regulations, constitutions, and other legal or quasi-legal documents bearing upon the operation of your institution. This principle, briefly stated, might be, "See your lawyer before, during, and after."
3. The third principle deals with the necessity of mounting a broadly participatory process. This principle suggests, "Find ways to get *everyone* involved."
4. The fourth principle deals with the anxieties and hostilities that inevitably will be developed. This principle advises, "Learn to live with the result."
5. A final principle is to look within the institution for solutions. Plan for the solutions to lie within more effective utilization of present resources.[28]

Retraining

Layoff and recall are preferable to termination. In some instances, another alternative involves retraining of faculty. While two departments may not each require a full-time person to cover a particular assignment, a shared faculty member might be desirable. This requires a retraining program for the faculty member in preparation for the new assignment. Faculty should be encouraged to develop their competencies beyond those required by the more rigid departmental assignments and allegiances so common in most institutions.

Another possibility is the recommendation for institutionalizing the public service mission in higher education made by James L. Bess who says that institutions should

> take on a more direct stance in addressing the practical needs of the society and in enriching its culture. By making institutions more valuable to the surrounding social system, higher education should become more visibly productive, increasing the possibility of greater financial and moral support.[29]

Bess advocates separate and well-funded public service units that meet the needs of the institution by making it more valuable to the constituencies that support it.

Whether faculty become involved in broadening their capabilities and making possible a wider range of assignments or in the various kinds of service activities recommended by Bess, Gollattscheck, and others,[30] they cannot help becoming more effective staff members capable of making greater contributions to their profession, their institutions, and society as a whole. Most important of all, students should profit as instructors broaden their base of activity.

TENURE AND PROMOTION

In the not too distant past, tenure and promotion decisions were often the province of administrators and it was common for department chairpersons to make recommendations to the dean which were then forwarded to the appropriate individuals for final sanction by the Board of Trustees. In some instances, approval by a body of administrators at the collegial level and/or university level provided additional steps in the process. With increasing faculty demands for involvement in decision making, particularly in the academic area, peer evaluation has become an important part of the process. Students also clamored for a part; it is not unusual to find them providing input for decision making and participating in committee procedures as voting members.

During periods of rapidly increasing enrollments and institutional expansion, decisions related to tenure and promotion are made more easily. Constant turnover resulting from instructors leaving for "greener pastures" tends to keep the proportions among tenured and nontenured professors and the distributions across the ranks more fluid than occurs when institutions enter periods of no growth or decreasing enrollments and cutbacks. At times like these, new factors creep into the decision-making process in addition to consideration of the merits of the individual involved. The introduction of collective bargaining and affirmative action requirements has provided additional dimension. As a result, it is not unusual to find that standards for tenure and promotion are higher than they were in the past. Expectations of younger staff members today are similar to those of senior professors five to ten years ago.

Essential to decision making in tenure and promotion cases is the concept of academic due process—a series of steps established by an institution and published in its regulations for determining how faculty members are appointed, tenured, and dismissed. To be avoided is the unfortunate connotation that academic due process is a disciplinary procedure only.

Tenure

Some individuals mistakenly believe that tenure guarantees lifetime employment. It does not. Tenure does provide that a person continuously employed as a full-time faculty member beyond a lengthy probationary period may not be dismissed without adequate cause as defined by institutional standards and without the observance of academic due process. Generally, the standards are without restriction with the exception that the academic freedom or the ordinary civil liberties of the individual may not be violated.

Concern has developed that institutions will become stagnant as the tenured proportion of the faculty grows. Institutional inflexibility is not inevitable. Mature, professionally oriented faculty are interested in self-renewal and desirable institutional change. Some reformists have advocated the abolishment of tenure to provide administrative flexibility in planning. Tenure provides no security when programs and particular faculty members must be eliminated due to an authentic financial emergency. It does guarantee that such elimination be conducted in a nonarbitrary and reasonable manner. The abolishment of tenure is, therefore, unnecessary. Instead, institutions might explore alternatives such as establishing a policy for avoiding tenure contracts, establishing nontenure classifications, and establishing more rigorous standards for awarding tenure.

Challenges to tenure are also coming from another direction. It is possible that union grievance procedures and civil court rulings may make the concept obsolete. Faculty members have already sought redress from outside arbitrators under collective bargaining contracts, human rights commissions, and the courts. In the converse, it is possible that there may be a demand through negotiating efforts to award tenure at an earlier stage than now exists. (Tenure at the beginning of the seventh year is a common pattern, although variations beginning with the fourth year on up are not uncommon.) Tenure at too early a stage is questionable since there might not be sufficient opportunity to observe the capabilities of individuals in the expected areas of performance.

A number of questions about tenure must be resolved as institutions face a period of steady-state staffing and retrenchment. Among these are: Is tenure related to a specific department, an institution, or a system of institutions? Does it apply to a particular rank or a particular salary? Can rank or salary be reduced without recourse to the due-process procedures appropriate to dismissal?

Quotas or Guidelines?

Quotas provide limitations within which an institution may determine whether or not to pursue tenure and promotion actions. If, for example, a policy stipulates that no more than 75 percent of the faculty should be tenured and that level has been reached, no consideration may be given to placing individuals under tenure until some attrition has taken place in the tenured ranks. Quotas become a time-saving device and provide a firm base on which to stand when stating that no one will be considered for tenure or promotion at a particular point in time. Individuals who are unable to be considered for tenure or promotion because of a quota system may decide to look for another position thus creating room for bringing in "new blood." Unfortunately, some of those who decide to leave might be the very ones who would enhance an institution the most.

Quotas for either tenure or promotion can be stifling and establish tensions. It is difficult to support a situation where individuals are informed that tenure and promotion are unattainable despite their personal industriousness, scholarly capabilities and productivity, and excellence in teaching. Academic personnel policies are needed rather than quotas. Besides, the smaller the institution, the greater the difficulty in establishing a quota system or even developing guidelines for a proportional distribution of tenured and nontenured staff members and the numbers desirable in each of the academic ranks from instructor to full professor.

A comprehensive faculty profile is a useful tool for analysis of trends, patterns, ratios, and probabilities. The next step involves development of some mathematical or computerized model such as "The Twelve College Faculty Appointment and Development Study" developed by the Institute for Educational Development and Educational Testing Service in 1973. The profile makes it possible to project results in terms of current policies, allows manipulation of variables, and identification of options and alternatives. In some instances, it will lead to changes in institutional policies. In any event, it should replace the rigid quota system for both tenure and promotion with some kind of flexible approach involving ratios and proportions.

Some of the areas in which policy changes might occur include: length of probationary period for tenure, minimum length of time in rank prior to promotion, appointment policy for new faculty, retirement age and policy, use of part-time faculty, and salary and benefit policies.

It would also be advisable for an institution to examine its personnel policies and practices followed during a previous no-growth period. The years of the 1940s and 1950s could provide valuable information regarding staffing procedures that would be useful in making the adjustments demanded by the more recent changing circumstances.

Affirmative Action and the Impact of Collective Bargaining

Affirmative action and collective bargaining are directly related to tenure and promotion practices. Because a larger percentage of faculty are tenured and the proportions are becoming greater, little flexibility exists for affirmative action appointments. There is just not enough turnover to provide opportunities for more blacks, chicanos, and women; because of the scarcity of positions, little statistical difference in the proportions of women and minorities on college faculties can be anticipated for a long time.

Chait and Ford clearly identify the conflict developing between affirmative action, unions, and tenure which emphasizes the need for examination and revision of current policies and practices:

> Whereas affirmative action challenges the criteria and procedures used to award tenure, unions challenge tenure by addressing its traditional purposes: Employment security and the protection of academic freedom. As an alternative route to job security, unionization is likely to supplant tenure only because it is more effective. Unions aim to protect everyone within the bargaining unit; tenure protects only the tenured. Unions seek to provide immediate job security; tenure requires a probationary period and affords little protection to probationary personnel. Unions shift the burden of proof onto management—employees are presumed competent unless proven otherwise. Under a traditional tenure system, the employee must demonstrate worthiness for tenure during the probationary period. Not unexpectedly, therefore, unions concentrate on developing elaborate criteria and procedures the institution must use to prove an individual does not deserve to be retained; tenure systems, on the other hand, focus principally upon criteria the candidate must satisfy to merit tenure, and only secondarily upon general criteria that should be applied to detenure someone.[31]

Chait and Ford conclude by predicting that "affirmative action and unionization are likely to force an end to current tenure practices. And where affirmative action conflicts with unionization, federal and state agencies will hold for affirmative action."[32] Thus, affirmative action and unionization are having and will continue to have a direct impact upon promotion and tenure practices.

Procedures for Promotion and Tenure Decisions

Precise standards and definitions of tenure are acceptable for inclusion in the bargaining process along with standards for promotion. Meaningful, concrete, and nondiscriminatory standards are essential and not only should cover the usual areas of teaching, scholarly activity, and service but also should precisely define the acceptable levels of performance. Existing performance standards for both tenure and promotion may have to be raised to reduce the number who can meet them so that along with possible policy changes, the chances for promotion and tenure may diminish, but the possibilities will still exist. It is possible that promotion may be warranted in some cases but delayed. Regardless, procedures must be established to provide for equitable and objective decisions.

Separate administrative and faculty mechanisms for assessing the relative achievement of the candidates are needed with communication between the two throughout the process. Assessment should begin at the departmental level and then move to a college level body with a broad view of the overall college situation. Independent assessments should be made by the department chairperson and dean although the dean has ultimate responsibility for final recommendations to the appropriate body beyond collegial limits.

Student input cannot be ignored. Because the process and files should be confidential, students were originally excluded from participation in deliberations to protect the faculty members under judgment. As students continued their efforts for representative involvement in the actual process and also demonstrated their ability to be intelligent, contributing participants in college and university governance structures, it has become common to find one or more students serving as voting members of tenure and promotion committees at both the departmental and college levels.

To add to the objectivity of the process, a standard format for presentation of the candidate's vita should be used. The comprehensive format on the following pages was developed to meet the needs of a college within a university structure. It could be adapted to meet specific circumstances within other kinds of institutions where less comprehensive information would be sufficient. Whatever the format is, it should reflect the established standards upon which tenure and promotion decisions will be made and provide a basis for objective assessment. In some instances, an interview of the candidate might also be desirable.

In addition to the full vita, other materials submitted for examination should include summaries of teaching evaluations, copies of all scholarly writing, both published and unpublished, documentation of other professional activities, and evaluations of college and university service. Letters from peers including faculty outside the candidate's department and college can also be helpful.

The Candidate Presentation Form on page 124 is used when forwarding a department's recommendation for tenure, promotion, or contract renewal of a specific candidate. Each recommendation should be accompanied by the same material used in the departmental deliberations. Ordinarily, members of the college level personnel committee would not examine all the supporting materials accompanying the vita, but the materials should be easily available if the need arises for more detailed and exact information.

In summary, each institution must develop procedures appropriate to its structure that will enable the fairest possible evaluation of candidates for tenure and promotion. The entire process must be consistent with the established policies, procedures, and guidelines that are becoming increasingly important.

SUMMARY

Administrative leadership is needed whether faculty must be recruited or whether an institution is overstaffed. Despite decreasing enrollments and financial problems, some replacement and addition of faculty will be required from time to time in one or more areas. For this reason, job descriptions and well-defined procedures for recruitment and selection should be part of the records and ready for use when needed. Faculty and students should be involved in the process of faculty selection. Affirmative action guidelines with procedures for their implementation are necessary.

Increasing interest in the evaluation of faculty has been developing, but the state of the art still leaves much to be desired. The nature of good teaching has not yet been accurately and completely defined. Variations in student ratings are created by numerous factors including student sex, expected grade point average, whether the course is elective or required, type of course, course content, and even the time of day a course is offered. A number of the evaluative procedures combine instructor and course ratings.

Faculty development programs are an important follow-up to the evaluation efforts. There is a need for faculty to examine what they are doing, how well they are doing it, and how they might improve. In addition, changing student populations and the changing needs of society require that faculty explore new offerings and innovative delivery systems for

SAMPLE VITA

Instructions to the candidate:

All faculty are requested to follow the format of the attached sample vita closely.

Note: It is *not* necessary to include categories for which you have no listing.

The following are possible attachments to this vita:

1. Colleague evaluations of teaching
2. Peer evaluations of scholarly work
3. Letters of recommendation
4. Candidate's statement

The following types of materials should be included with the supporting materials, *not* with this vita:

1. Reprints of all entries listed in the personal bibliography
2. Teaching materials (course outlines, examinations, handouts, etc.)
3. Raw data, teaching evaluation forms
4. Letters of commendation for service

REQUIRED VITA FORMAT September, 1977

VITA

Bertha Q. Quimby, Associate Professor
Department of Early Childhood and
Elementary Education

Professional Preparation

1960 *B.A.*, Temple University, Philadelphia, Pa., Mathematics Education

1963 Permanent Certification in Elementary Education, State of Missouri

1965 *M.Ed.*, Washington University, St. Louis, Mo., Elementary Education

1969 *Ed.D.*, State University of New York at Albany, Albany, New York, Elementary Education

1969 Postdoctoral Research Fellow in Education, University of Kansas, Lawrence, Kansas

Professional Experience

1960–1967 Teacher, Elementary Education, School District of St. Louis, Missouri

1967–1969 Teaching Associate, State University of New York at Albany, Albany, New York, Elementary Education

1970–1973 Assistant Professor, Temple University, Philadelphia, Pa., Elementary Education

1973–present Associate Professor, Temple University, Philadelphia, Pa., Elementary Education

1974–1975 Visiting Professor, University of California, Berkeley, California, Department of Mathematics Education

Professional Memberships

Society for Research in Child Development
Association for the Advancement of Behavior Therapy
National Council of Teachers of Mathematics
National Association for the Education of Young Children
American Educational Research Association

Professional Recognition

Who's Who in the East
Who's Who in American Women

TEACHING

Courses Taught (LIST EACH COURSE ONLY ONCE. USE NAME AND NUMBER. INDICATE COURSES YOU PRIMARILY OR TOTALLY DEVELOPED. INDICATE THE SPECIAL NATURE, IF ANY, OF TEACHING ASSIGNMENTS, AND SPECIAL CREDENTIALS OR PREPARATION.)

At Temple

Math Ed. 140 Teaching Mathematics in the Elementary School
Math Ed. 312 The Metric System (Developed the course)
Math Ed. 460 Basic Concepts of Modern Mathematics

Outside Temple

Math Ed. 469 Mathematics Curricula, State University College at Albany, N.Y.
Math Ed. 761 Mathematics in the Elementary School, University of California, Berkeley, California

Teaching Philosophy (OPTIONAL: see pg. 12, para. d)

Advisees

Current number of academic advisees

Undergraduate: 15
Masters: 4
Doctoral: 2

Masters theses or projects (DO NOT INCLUDE ORAL EXAMS)

Completed

Student	*Department*	*Chm*	*Title*	*Year Completed*
Richard Darley	ECEEd (Math Ed.)	X	Training teachers to teach the metric system	1975

In Progress

Student	*Department*	*Chm*	*Title*
John Slavic	ECEEd (Math Ed.)	X	Elementary teacher's attitudes toward the metric system

Doctoral Dissertations (DO NOT INCLUDE ORAL EXAMS)

Completed

Student	*Department*	*Chm*	*Title*	*Year Completed*
Sandra Smith	SecEd (Math Ed.)		The development of negative negative attitudes toward statistics	1973
David Danley	SecEd (Math Ed.)		Sex differences in algebra achievement	1974
Robert Reine	ECEEd (Math Ed.)	X	A comparison of individ-ualized and group instruction on number concepts	1975
John Jones	ECEEd (Math Ed.)	X	The prediction of success in geometry	1976

In Progress (PROPOSAL ON FILE IN GRADUATE SCHOOL OFFICE)

Student	*Department*	*Chm*	*Title*
Harriet Brody	ECEEd (Math Ed.)	X	An experimental study of the relative effectiveness of three methods of teaching the metric system to elementary school students
Thomas Hart	Ed Psych		The development of a diagnostic mathematics test for use in the elementary school

At the Proposal Stage (INCLUDE ONLY IF A COMMITMENT TO SERVE HAS BEEN MADE)

Student	*Department*	*Chm*	*Title*
John Schwartz	Voc Ed.		A study of the mathematics needed in automotive mechanics
Susan Smart	ECEEd (Math Ed.)		A survey of the use of electronic calculators in the elementary school

Student Evaluations of Teaching

(*SUMMARIZE* THE DATA FROM THE SPECIFIC EVALUATION FORM(S) YOU USED HERE. INDICATE WHICH FORMS WERE USED, AND ATTACH A COPY OF EACH TO THIS DOCUMENT. BE CERTAIN THE DATA ARE READILY INTERPRETABLE BY THOSE WHO ARE NOT FAMILIAR WITH THE FORM(S) YOU USED. INCLUDE THE RAW DATA IN YOUR SUPPORTING MATERIALS.)

Colleague Evaluations of Teaching (OPTIONAL: see pg. 12, para. c) IF INCLUDED ATTACH TO THIS VITA.

Teaching Awards

Lindback Award, 1972

SCHOLARSHIP

(LIST ALL AUTHORS IN THE ORDER IN WHICH THEY APPEARED IN JOURNAL OR BOOK. INCLUDE THE PAGE NOS. INCLUDE *PUBLISHED* WORK, WORK *IN PRESS*, AND WORK *SUBMITTED FOR PUBLICATION.* DO *NOT* INCLUDE IN THIS LIST *WORK IN PROGRESS.* INCLUDE COPIES OF ALL LISTED WORKS IN YOUR SUPPORTING MATERIALS.)

PUBLICATIONS

1. *Books* (DISTINGUISH BETWEEN EDITED AND AUTHORED BOOKS.)

Quimby, B. (Ed.). *Collected readings in teaching mathematics.* Springfield, Ill: C.C Thomas, 1973, 250 pp.

Sano, J.P., & Quimby, B. *For the mathematics teacher.* New York: McGraw-Hill, in press, 122 pp.

2. *Books contracted for* (A STATEMENT OF PROGRESS AND PROJECTED PUBLICATION DATA SHOULD BE INCLUDED FOR BOOKS FOR WHICH THERE IS A FORMAL CONTRACT)

3. *Monographs* (DISTINGUISH BETWEEN EDITED AND AUTHORED MONOGRAPHS.)

Quimby, B. (Ed.) *When the new mathematics gets old. Monograph of National Council of Teachers of Mathematics,* 1973, *27* (5, whole No. 115) 30 pp.

4. *Chapters in Books* (DO NOT REPEAT HERE REPRINTED ARTICLES THAT HAVE ALREADY BEEN LISTED ABOVE.)

Cohen, P., & Quimby, B. Teaching mathematics in grades K-3. In P. Coleman (Ed.) *Mathematics instruction at all levels.* Springfield, Ill: C.C. Thomas, 1971, pp. 50–98

5. *Articles in Referred Journals and in Edited Books*

Quimby, B., Smith, J.O., & Segal, R.P. A field tested mathematics curriculum for inner-city children. *Journal of Mathematics Education,* 1972, *37*, 4-12. Reprinted in: A.R. Brown (Ed.) *Mathematics for today's child.* Boston: Houghton Mifflin, 1973, pp. 127–135

Kurtz, B.O., & Quimby, B. One and one are not always two. In T.Z. Prince (Ed.) *Misconceptions about the teaching of mathematics.* New York: McGraw-Hill, 1973, pp. 14–27

Quimby, B. An expanded mathematics curriculum. *Mathematics Today,* 1976, *4* in press

6. *Articles in Nonreferred Journals, Newspapers, Newsletters,* etc.

Evans, P., & Quimby, B. Teaching your child to multiply. *New Jersey Teacher,* 1974, *4*, 1–16

7. *Reviews of Books and of Non-Print Media*

Levin, E.R. Mathematics for the slow learner.
(Review of Mathematics for the slow learner by B. Quimby). *Mathematics Today,* 1974, *3,* 117

8. *Government and Technical Reports*

Quimby, B. *Progress report on an investigation of factors leading to success in learning number concepts* (N I H D S Progress Report No. 3, U.S. Public Health Service Publication No. 1217). Washington, D.C.: U.S.

OTHER SCHOLARLY ACTIVITIES

1. *Presentations at Professional Meetings*

Quimby, B. *Subtraction with borrowing.* Paper presented at the meeting of the Council for Exceptional Children, Miami Beach, April, 1971

Quimby, B. *The cognitive aspects of multiplication.* Colloquium presented at Brandeis University, Waltham, Mass., February, 1974

2. *Funded Research*

HEW Research Project No. 1221
Title: The concept of number in young children
Principal Investigator: Bertha Q. Quimby
Funding Period: September 1973 to August 1975
Amount Funded: $83,000

3. *Audiovisual Productions*

Quimby, B. (writer) *How to get your child interested in mathematics.* Slide-tape; 51 slides, color, 6 min. (Distribution from writer)

Quimby, B., & Johnson, L. (consultants) *New Math Techniques for Teachers.* Videotape, color, sound, 22 min. (available from Temple University Instructional Materials Center)

Randall, L., & Quimby, B. (producers). *Teaching Mathematics with Tokens.* Film; 16 mm, sound, color, 12 min. New York: Time-Life Films; 1973

4. *Art Exhibits*

*2*s & *3*s. In Boston Printmakers Show, Waltham, Mass., April 1974

5. *Presentations at Public Meetings and in/on Mass Media.*

Interview on Channel 10, "Problems in Changing to the Metric System," June 10, 1977

6. *Editorial responsibilities*

Board of Editors — Journal of Mathematics Education — 1973–present
Review Editor — Allyn & Bacon — 1973–1974

7. *Proposals submitted for funded research* (INDICATE STATUS)

8. *Awards, Research/Study Leaves, and Other Special Recognition for Scholarship*

SERVICE

Service within Temple University

University (INCLUDE INTER-COLLEGE SERVICE)

1973 to present Representative Faculty Senator
1974 Search Committee for Associate Dean, School of Business Administration

College (INCLUDE INTERDEPARTMENT SERVICE)

1970–1972 Student Experiences Committee
1973–1974 Task Force on Temple's Role in the Open University

Department

1972 Department Personnel Committee (Chairman)
1973 Department Committee to Evaluate Certification Program
1974 Department Program Committee

Other Professional Services

International

1973 Chairperson, session on teaching mathematics with tokens at 5th Annual Convention of African Teachers of Mathematics. Lagos, Nigeria, August 1973

National

1973 Secretary of National Teachers of Mathematics Society
1974 Program Chairman for National Convention of Association for Research in Science Teaching, Detroit, Michigan, March 1973

Regional and State

1975 Served on State Curriculum Committee for Mathematics Education at the request of the State Department of Education

Local

1970–present Inservice workshop (2 all-day demonstrations and seminar periods) each year for Marple-Newton School District
1971–present Mathematics consultant to Cherry Hill (N.J.) School District

Community Service

1976–present Committee of Seventy (Philadelphia)

Service Awards

COLLEGE OF EDUCATION

CANDIDATE PRESENTATION RECORD

Form 1

Candidate ______________________

Action under consideration

Tenure_____; Mandated (if promoted): Yes__No___

Promotion______________ to ______________

Contract renewal for ____________________years

Years at ______________ including present year______

Tenured: Yes__No__Date ______________

Years in Rank, including present year______________

Years in rank at other institutions______________

Department Faculty by Rank:

P	AP	aP	I	Other	Total

Personnel Committee by Rank:

P	AP	aP	I	Other	Total

How was the Department Personnel Committee constituted?______________________________

As a member of the Department Personnel Committee, I have reviewed this sheet and the 500 word summary *after* its completion:

____

____

____

____

____

____

____

____

____

____

____

____

____

The 500 word summary is to be prepared by the Department Personnel Committee. It should be an appraisal of both the strengths and weaknesses of the candidate and should be consistent with the Department Personnel Committee's ratings.

Department Personnel Committee's Evaluations
(tally marks only)

	Unsatis.	Satis.	Excellent
Teaching			
Scholarship			
Service			

Departmental Personnel Committee's Recommendations
(ballot totals)

Grant tenure: Yes_______ No._______

Promote: Yes_______ No._______

Renew Contract: Yes_______ No _______

Department Chairperson's Evaluations (check marks)

	Unsatis.	Satis.	Excellent
Teaching			
Scholarship			
Service			

Department Chairperson's Recommendations
(check marks)

Grant tenure: Yes_______ No_______

Promote: Yes_______ No_______

Renew Contract: Yes_______ No_______

The contents of this record were discussed with the candidate and a copy given to him/her on______________

/S/ Dept. Rep. to Col. Pers. Com. ______________ /S/ Dept. Chairperson ______________ making these offerings available most effectively.

While there may be a need to recruit faculty for some areas, it may be necessary to reduce staff in others. Faculty work loads are being carefully scrutinized. An appropriate policy and some kind of self-analysis procedure is needed in preparation for possible reduction and elimination of programs. Procedures for rctraining and reassignment of faculty are a necessary part of the total process.

It is becoming increasingly apparent that tenure does not provide a faculty member with lifetime job security. More stringent criteria and procedures for awarding tenure are appearing while collective bargaining and affirmative action have an impact upon promotion and tenure practices. It is obvious that policies, procedures, and guidelines are becoming increasingly important in all areas affecting faculty, including recruitment, hiring, evaluation, in-service development, promotion, tenure, and retrenchment.

ENDNOTES

1. Bernice Sandler, "Equity for Women in Higher Education," in *The Expanded Campus,* edited by Dyckman W. Vermilye, (San Francisco: Jossey-Bass, 1972), pp. 82–83.
2. American Association of University Professors, "Affirmative Action in Higher Education: A Report by the Council Commission on Discrimination," *Bulletin* 59 (1973): 178.
3. *Ibid.,* pp. 178–182.
4. Paul Sawyer, "The Presentation: Testing Potential New Faculty's Ability to Teach," American Association of University Professors *Bulletin* 60 (1974): 379–380.
5. *Ibid.,* p. 381.
6. *Ibid.,* pp. 381–382.
7. *Webster's New International Dictionary of the English Language,* 2nd., s.v. "evaluation."
8. *Ibid.,* s.v. "rating."
9. Richard I. Miller, *Evaluating Faculty Performance* (San Francisco: Jossey-Bass, 1972), p. 21.
10. *Ibid.*
11. E. R. Guthries, "The Evaluation of Teaching," *Educational Record* 30 (1949): 109–115.
12. V. W. Voeks, "Publications and Teaching Effectiveness," *Journal of Higher Education* 33 (1962): 212–218.
13. Laurence M. Aleamoni and Makonnen Yimer, "Investigation of the Relationship between Colleague Rating, Student Rating, Research Productivity, and Academic Rank in Rating Instructional Effectiveness," *Journal of Educational Psychology* 64 (1973): 277.
14. Daniel S. Sheehan, "On the Invalidity of Student Ratings for Administrative Personnel Decisions," *Journal of Higher Education* 46 (1975): 696.
15. Philip C. Abrami, Les Leventhal, Raymond P. Perry, and Laurence J. Breen, "Course Evaluation: How?" *Journal of Educational Psychology* 68 (1976): 300–304.
16. H. C. Ebel and Howard Berg, "Student Evaluations in Physical Education: Role of Course Type and Grade Expectation," *The Physical Educator* 33 (1976): 13–17.
17. Wilbert J. McKeachie, "Student Ratings of Faculty," American Association of University Professors *Bulletin* 55 (1969): 441.
18. Charles I. Hill, "Limitations of Student Evaluation of College Instruction," *Physical Educator* 33 (1976): 10–12.
19. Aleamoni and Yimer, "Investigation of the Relationship," p. 277.
20. Robert T. Blackburn and Mary Jo Clark, "An Assessment of Faculty Performance: Some Correlates Between Administrator, Colleague, Student and Self-Ratings," *Sociology of Education* 48 (1975): 249–250.

21. Miller, *Evaluating Faculty Performance,* p. 75.
22. American Association of University Professors, "Statement on Teaching Evaluation: Committee on College and University Teaching, Research, and Publication," *Bulletin* 60 (1974): 168.
23. John Bruce Francis, "How Do We Get There from Here? Program Design for Faculty Development," *Journal of Higher Education* 46 (1975): 720.
24. Reprinted by permission. John A. Centra, "Types of Faculty Development Programs," *Journal of Higher Education* 49 (March/April 1978), pp. 151–162. Copyright © 1978 by the Ohio State University Press.
25. Jon F. Wergin, Elizabeth J. Mason, and Paul J. Munson, "The Practice of Faculty Development: An Experience-derived Model," *Journal of Higher Education* (1976): 289–308.
26. Jerry G. Gaff, *Toward Faculty Renewal* (San Francisco: Jossey-Bass, 1970), pp. 165–166.
27. Merle F. Allshouse, "The New Academic Slalom: Mission—Personnel, Planning—Financial Exigiency—Due Process," *Liberal Education* 61 (1975): 354.
28. Kent G. Alm, Elwood B. Ehrle, and Bill R. Webster, "Managing Faculty Reductions," *Journal of Higher Education* 48 (1977): 161–162.
29. James L. Bess, "New Life for Faculty and Institutions," In *Lifelong Learners—A New Clientele for Higher Education,* edited by Dyckman W. Vermilye (San Francisco: Jossey-Bass, 1974), p. 147–148.
30. James F. Gollattscheck, Ervin L. Harlacher, Eleanor Roberts, and Benjamin R. Wygal, *College Leadership for Community Renewal* (San Francisco: Jossey-Bass, 1976).
31. Richard Cheit and Andrew Ford, "Affirmative Action, Tenure, and Unionization," in *Lifelong Learners—A New Clientele for Higher Education,* p. 127.
32. *Ibid.,* p. 130.

CHAPTER 5

Support Staff

Colleges and universities could not function without the assistance of a support staff who see to the day-to-day operations. As with faculty and administrators, recruitment and selection of these vital human resources are important. Staff development programs should be established for the purpose of insuring continued growth. Personnel policies and practices must be continually assessed, revised, and, where needed, new ones established. In this way, administrators and faculty both will receive the necessary support which will enable them to provide the optimum educational experience for students.

KINDS OF SUPPORT PERSONNEL

Numerous staff resources are required at both the institutional and collegial levels. Some positions may be categorized as nonacademic or nonprofessional while others are filled by academic professionals and technicians whose responsibilities require specific training including, in some cases, at least a baccalaureate degree. Custodial, maintenance, food service, security personnel, and computer specialists as well as various student affairs personnel, and financial officers are a few of the resources found at the central level. Only those positions pertaining to instructional, technical, and clerical staff at the collegial level will be discussed here.

Instructional and Technical Support

While instructional and technical support services are frequently supplied by some central operation, it is not unusual to find complementary or specialized services within individual colleges. Media services is an area in which specialized materials, both print and nonprint, may be handled within a college, division, or department. Where only print materials are held, the traditionally prepared librarian with appropriate clerical support may be sufficient. A small resource center that includes print and nonprint materials plus appropriate equipment will require an individual with the more comprehensive background of a media specialist. Regardless of the background, the director of a resource center is responsible for preparation and implementation of the center's budget as well as the evaluation, selection, acquisition, cataloging, and maintenance of the resources. A cooperative relationship with faculty members is important so that materials and services meet the needs of the instructional program. The preparation and distribution of bibliographies is part of this service.

A comprehensive media operation includes technicians with appropriate training in the preparation and production of materials from simple transparencies to elaborate television productions. Individuals who have a broad background and experience in not only the design and production of specific instructional materials but also the design and development of instructional systems are particularly needed.

Another group of specialists are those associated with the computer operation. Computers may be used for instructional, research, and administrative purposes depending upon the nature of the institution and its programs. Large institutions maintain a central computer center with numerous terminals installed in appropriate areas and offices throughout the institution. Lack of qualified personnel and poor administration can result in an operation of such poor quality and so plagued with misinformation that it is useless for enhancing the academic program. In such cases, it would be preferable to have none at all. A computer operation of high caliber is indispensable for enhancing the administrative and educational functions of the institution. Where a central system exists, it is not inappropriate to include one or more qualified individuals on the staff of the college administrator to meet the specific needs of administrators and faculty of that college by serving as resource personnel and as liaison with the central operation.

Classification

Some of the positions above fit into the classifications defined in a proposal for the University of Hawaii described by Hohenstein and Williams.

> Professional—Those employees engaged in occupations which normally require specialized academic training at least equivalent to graduation from a professional college or from a master's program.
>
> Technical—Those engaged in unique or unusual jobs which require the application of knowledge and skill to a specialized field of endeavor in the performance of complicated tasks.[1]

The classification also divides the two categories into five classes each of which is subdivided into four or five ranks.

Another descriptive classification is that of the Academic Professional at Temple University.

> An Academic Professional is a full-time employee of the University whose work is necessary or adjunct to the teaching of students. The work shall:
>
> A. 1. be predominantly intellectual and varied in character; and
>
> 2. require consistent exercise of discretion and judgment; and
>
> 3. require knowledge of an advanced nature customarily acquired by specialized study in an institution of higher learning or its equivalent; and
>
> 4. be of such character that the output or result accomplished cannot be standardized in relation to a given period of time; and/or
>
> B. be original and creative in character in a recognized field of artistic endeavor and the result of which depends primarily on the invention, imagination, or talent of the employee.[2]

Each institution must develop for itself some classification scheme to cover the numerous kinds of positions which often are unique to that particular college or university.

Business Manager

Business management in its total sense includes a multitude of responsibilities among which are: receiving all monies, paying all bills, accounting, purchasing, managing student accounts, preparing financial reports of various kinds, administering the payroll and maintaining buildings and grounds. A number of business oriented positions are needed to accomplish the functions. Appropriate policies and procedures are needed at the central, college, division, and department levels.

In universities, many functions are handled at the central level only while others must be supported within the individual colleges. Someone is needed to monitor, approve, and process information and requisitions, as well as to administer the college budget. The internal communication system including accountability for the telephone and mail systems may be an additional assignment for that individual as well as the responsibility for the handling and inventory of materials, equipment ,and supplies. There are numerous possibilities for assigning the responsibility including establishment of a position for an appropriately credentialed business manager who becomes a member of the administrative staff. Assignment of the responsibility to an associate or assistant dean or an administrative assistant are other possibilities.

In a two year college, most of the responsibility will be placed at the central level and assigned to a controller, dean for administrative services, vice president for financial affairs, or some variation of these. A job description for this comprehensive position in a two-year college follows:

JOB DESCRIPTION—CONTROLLER

Scope

Under administrative supervision of the President, is responsible for the fiscal, business administration, auxiliary and plant operation of the College.

Responsibilities

- Responsible for administrative supervision and management of College fiscal, general business, and auxiliary service functions.
- Responsible for recommendation for employment assignment and retention of professional, quasi-professional and nonprofessional personnel under his jurisdiction.
- Responsible for budget development, analysis, interpretation, and control.
- Responsible for audit control of State and Federal restricted educational funds.
- Responsible for development of data systems and computer center operations.
- Responsible for development, improvement and expansion of the physical plant and its environs.
- Responsible for College Store and service development.
- Responsible for development of Cost Analysis and Distribution Program.
- Responsible for recommending ways and means for most effective investment of college funds.
- Responsible for devising and recommending changes and procedures for most efficient and economical operation of plant and facilities.

Qualifications

- Knowledge of modern principles, methods and techniques of institutional business management.
- Knowledge of public administration as it applies to purchasing, budget preparation, personnel administration, payroll and accounting procedures, merchandising.
- Knowledge of plant operations, security functions, and buildings and grounds maintenance.
- Knowledge of computer operations and data processing procedures.
- Ability to plan, direct and administer business activities of the College; to estimate needs and requirements accurately in advance, and to coordinate supporting services.
- Ability to evaluate building and facilities and to determine needs in terms of present and future growth.
- Ability to exercise initiative and judgment in interpreting and applying policies and regulations; in delegating responsibility; in systematizing procedures; in promoting favorable public relations; and in planning and analyzing administrative activities.
- Ability to plan, assign, and direct the work of subordinates.

- Ability to devise, design, and establish new procedures for more efficient and effective operation of the accounting and administrative areas.

Education, Experience, Personal

- Education and training equivalent to an advanced degree in Business Administration.
- Experience in supervision of technical and/or administrative personnel.
- Practical experience as an accountant, purchasing agent, budget analyst, personnel or management supervisor.
- Integrity, courtesy, understanding.
- Sensitivity, patience, courage and vision.

Clerical Staff

Numerous kinds of clerical staffing are required to keep an organization functioning at optimum level. Positions range from file clerks to administrative secretaries who function as administrative assistants. Some institutions have found the centralization of a number of secretarial tasks under the aegis of one or more word processing centers to be efficient and economical while others believe totally decentralized services to be more appropriate. Each must decide for itself which approach will best meet the needs of faculty, administrators, and other staff.

Many aspects of clerical personnel management are central level responsibilities but need to be coordinated and supplemented at various levels below. At the college level, this would be an appropriate assignment for the business manager or an administrative assistant. Regardless of where the responsibility is placed, no institution can function without the support of an efficient and capable clerical staff.

ADMINISTRATION OF SUPPORT PERSONNEL

The overall objective of personnel administration must be facilitating the accomplishment of the goals of the institution. Colleges and universities have tended to relegate the personnel function to a level of minor importance, but the areas of expertise defined by Bernard Ingster make it apparent that the personnel function is an important one both at the central level and within the individual colleges that comprise a university. Ingster's areas for "know-how" are: personnel selection; organizational effectiveness; institutional research and human resource planning; human resources development; employee safety and health; communications; compensation and classification; labor relations; and human resources records management.[3]

Centralization of the personnel function is essential to the consistent application of policies, laws, and governmental regulations particularly in the light of the increasing impact of federal and state legislation. The central office must provide leadership and college level administrators must utilize the specialized assistance available to them for structuring necessary and appropriate activities at the college and department levels.

Objectives

The National Association of College and University Business Officers has identified a number of activities which a well-developed personnel program should provide. Those most pertinent to the college level administrator are listed below:

- Assist administrators in clarifying the organization of the staff and workload in their departments.
- Assist employees in understanding the organization and in identifying with it.
- Encourage and assist department heads and supervisors in initiating and maintaining orientation, training, and development programs that will make it possible for employees to understand what is expected of them, to perform their work efficiently, to

develop their skills and abilities, and to achieve their full potential.

- Help employees motivate themselves to work productively.
- Facilitate communication among administrators, supervisors, and employees about personnel matters.
- Assist administrators in interpreting and reacting to concerns of employee organizations, unions, and special-interest groups.[4]

Central Office Relationships

Concerns of a central personnel office include: recruitment, selection, and training of new employees; responsibility for compliance with federal and state laws; data for federal, state, and local audits and reports; procedures for resolving grievances; record keeping; and administration of compensation and benefits programs. Among the latter are salaries, length of service increments, insurance, health plans, leaves of absence, pension plans, and tuition benefit programs.

An important function of the central operation is position analysis and classification. The analysis should lead to development of a description of the major duties and responsibilities attached to a particular position. Thus, a clear understanding for both the employee and the supervisor of what is expected and required will be provided. The analysis also provides the basis for determining accountabilities and assessing performance as well as serving as a tool for recruitment and selection. The tasks for each position and the needed qualifications must be clearly delineated. Actually, the same principles apply here as previously outlined in relationship to position descriptions for administrators (Chapter 3). Examples of descriptions for supporting staff are found in the following pages. These include several varieties such as clerical team coordinator, clerk-typist, duplicating–mailroom clerk, and a clerk with a very highly specialized function. The last example differs somewhat in format. It was prepared for a management consulting firm hired by the institution to develop position analyses and a clerical classification system. An examination of the various descriptions will lead to a recognition of the importance of each position for accomplishing institutional and organizational goals.

The results of the position analysis process serve as a basis for determining the appropriate compensation level for each of the positions. Salary should be dependent upon the responsibilities attached to the position, the difficulty of the position, and the level of skills and experience required.

TEAM COORDINATOR

Definition

Under direction, performs responsible typing and clerical work varied in nature but requiring a considerable knowledge of office procedures and functions and the exercise of independent judgment; coordinates and supervises the work of an assigned group of clerical employees; may be a stenographer. Acts as Secretary to Chairmen. Does related work as well.

Responsibilities

- Organizes assigned stenographic, typing, and other related clerical work and develops effective work methods.
- Takes dictation, including correspondence, minutes, reports, agendas, orally and from dictating equipment and transcribes notes on typewriter.
- Types a wide variety of materials from pencil copy, rough notes, or dictating equipment, such as correspondence, forms, memoranda, reports, lists, contracts, manuscripts.
- Prepares materials for duplication; checks and compares finished copy.
- Reviews and checks reports and other documents for correctness.
- Prepares requisitions, fills in and completes forms.
- When necessary, will perform or assist with duties of other team members.
- Answers routine and nonroutine inquiries of

nontechnical nature in accordance with established procedure.

- Composes and types replies to routine correspondence.
- Operates various types of office machines.
- Files correspondence, papers, and records; pulls classified papers and folders as required.
- Assists with training of new clerical employees and student workers.
- Makes appointments and/or reservations.
- Maintains essential files and records.
- Insures that Team Station is manned at all times.
- Delivers or picks up materials.
- Maintains records of work done and charges out individual slips for billing purposes.
- Coordinates vacation schedules and assigns deputy responsibilities as feasible.
- Performs other related duties as required.
- When so required, gives suitable assignments and instructions to members of other Teams and directs the performance of their work.

Requirements

Education High school graduation with business curriculum background and/or business course completion.

Experience Minimum of two years' experience in varied office routines.

Knowledge and Abilities

- Considerable knowledge of modern office methods, practices, routines, machines, and equipment.
- Knowledge of the problems encountered in organizing assigned stenographic, typing, and related clerical work, in taking dictation manually and/or from dictating equipment and transcribing notes.
- Knowledge of approved English usage and of correct spelling, punctuation, sentence structure, and paragraphing.
- Knowledge of commonly used office machines and their use and care.
- Knowledge of telephone procedures and manners.
- Ability to organize assigned workloads, comprehend established office routines and College regulations, and develop effective work methods.
- Ability to work cooperatively and harmoniously with other people.
- Ability to take dictation manually and/or from dictating equipment and transcribe accurately on a typewriter.
- Ability to type neatly and accurately at 50 WPM.
- Ability to use approved English, spell correctly, to use correct punctuation and sentence and paragraph structure, and to compose routine replies to nontechnical correspondence.
- Ability to use and care for office machines and equipment.
- Ability to locate and assemble various materials and statistical data as needed.
- Ability to maintain essential files and records.

Good health and freedom from disabling and mental defects which would impair the proper performance of the required duties or which might endanger the health and safety of oneself and others.

CLERK-TYPIST

Definition

Under direction, types and performs other routine clerical work of a varied nature. Does related work as required.

Responsibilities

- Types a wide variety of materials from pencil copy, rough notes, dictating equipment, and detailed instructions, such as correspondence, forms, memoranda, lists, reports, statements—technical, scientific, financial, statistical, agendas, purchase orders, bills, charts.
- Opens, sorts, and distributes mail to proper personnel as directed.
- Addresses envelopes and prepares material for mailing.
- Types requisitions, fills in and completes forms as directed.
- Answers the telephone and takes messages accurately; directs calls to the proper persons.
- Prepares and keeps records of various types.

- Makes outgoing calls as requested.
- Types material for duplication.
- Checks and compares finished copy.
- Collates and staples materials.
- Looks up needed information and assists in compiling data.
- Tabulates data and prepares lists as directed.
- Sorts, classifies, and files correspondence and other papers; pulls papers from files and folders as requested.
- Maintains established files and records.
- Maintains prepared mailing lists.
- Delivers and picks up materials.
- Answers routine inquiries in accordance with established policies.
- Operates various types of office machines.
- Performs other related duties as required.
- Maintains records of work done and charges out individual slips for billing purposes.
- Assists in training student workers.

Requirements

Education High school graduation with business course background.

Knowledge and Abilities

- Basic knowledge of office methods, practices, procedures, routines, and equipment.
- Knowledge of use of telephone and telephone manners.
- Ability to read, write, speak, and understand English sufficiently to perform the duties of the position.
- Ability to understand, remember, and carry out oral and written directions and to learn quickly from oral and written explanations and from demonstrations.
- Ability to type from varied forms of copy at 40 WPM.
- Ability to use good English and grammar and to spell.
- Ability to use and care for various office machines and equipment.
- Ability to maintain essential records and files.
- Ability to work cooperatively with others.

Good health and freedom from disabling and mental defects which would impair the proper performance of the required duties or which might endanger the health and safety of oneself and others.

DUPLICATING–MAILROOM CLERK

Definition

Under direction, operates duplicating machines and equipment and performs routine clerical tasks of a varied nature. Does related work as required.

Responsibilities

- Operates effectively varied duplicating machines including spirit, offset, mimeograph, photocopy, and master makers.
- Maintains machines and equipment for maximum efficiency, and advises proper persons of need for repairs.
- Determines duplicating method to be used and makes appropriate master.
- Advises originator of exceptions or inability to complete work as presented.
- Maintains records of work done and charges out individual slips for billing purposes.
- Prepares lists of charges for distribution.
- Collates, staples, and cuts materials as required.
- Uses other equipment such as paper drill, folder, as needed.
- Keeps work area and shelves neat and clean.
- Maintains inventory of supplies and materials on hand and advises superior of need to reorder.
- Keeps superior informed of work load and backlog.
- Assists in operation of switchboard when needed.
- Assists in training student workers.
- Does simple clerical tasks including sorting, distributing, and metering mail, filing, preparing bills and lists.
- Maintains control and respects confidential material and tests.
- Advises superior of irregularities.
- Maintains essential records and files.
- Delivers completed jobs when necessary.

Requirements

Education High school graduation with office routine background.

Knowledge and Abilities

- Basic knowledge of methods and procedures used in routine clerical and general office work.
- Basic knowledge of problems encountered in operation of various machines and equipment.
- Ability to operate varied duplicating machines and equipment properly and efficiently.
- Ability to understand, remember, and carry out oral and written directions.
- Ability to learn quickly from oral and written instructions and demonstrations.
- Ability to meet deadlines and observe work schedules.
- Ability to make judgments on best medium to be used for individual duplicating jobs.
- Ability to use varied office machines and equipment including paper cutter, paper drill, folder, postage meter.
- Ability to operate telephone switchboard accurately and courteously.
- Ability to work cooperatively and harmoniously with others.
- Ability to prepare bills and make simple reports.
- Ability to maintain established files and records.

Good health and freedom from disabling physical and mental defects which would impair the proper performance of the required duties or which might endanger the health and safety of oneself and others.

JOB DESCRIPTION

Position Title: Records–Statistics Clerk

Department: Dean's Office, College of Education

1. *Major Function:*
   Primary responsibility for maintaining all undergraduate student records. This includes but is not limited to keeping accurate statistics on: transfers from Liberal Arts, other intra-university transfers, intra-college transfers, new admissions to the university and college, and special (visiting) students.
2. *Specific Duties:*
   Responsible for:
   a. Updating all undergraduate files and statistics.
   b. Keeping accurate records of all incoming undergraduate students including preparation of appropriate charts, tables, and lists to show entrance and egress and making copies available to other departments.
   c. Quickly and accurately notifying departments and advisers of changes in student status such as probation, drop, change of program, withdrawal from the university, and readmission.
   d. Identifying students who have left and transferring their credentials to the morgue.
   e. Reading transfer credits, adding to internal credits, and translating into student classification status.
   f. Identifying the various programs and screening incoming credentials for completeness of program and recording of program.
   g. Checking incoming transcripts against registration cards and against files for missing parts and errors and reporting needed corrections to the Records Office.
   h. Identifying students with averages below 2.0 for probation or exclusion.
   i. In emergency situations, answering telephone, acting as receptionist, filing, handling routine correspondence, processing and routing reports, dispensing forms, letters, etc. and other tasks as assigned by the Senior or Head Secretary, also covering for the Senior Secretary on student problems dealing with records when she is out.
   j. Preparing input for updating semi-annually the internal computerized student data print-out.
   k. Checking current college statistical run against files each semester.
   l. Distributing copies of necessary advising credentials for new students to departments. This includes copies of any transfer credit statements as well as transcripts.
   m. Updating files as students "pass out of"

ELECT (a special program for students needing remediation in writing skills).

3. *Assignment, Review, and Approval of Work:*
Senior Secretary instructs and assigns work. Work should be reviewed as part of the total office assignment by the Senior Secretary unless there are specific problems which must be discussed by the Records–Statistics Clerk with the Assistant Dean.
4. *Responsibilities and Decision-making Authority:*
Responsible for meeting all distribution deadlines. Make decisions on most routine matters coming across the desk as part of the job except for academic matters that must be referred to the Assistant Dean.
5. *Report Preparation*
See specific duties. This particular job deals with lists averaging three per week. It includes correction of lists from SIRS (Student Information Retrieval System), keeping lists of incoming students and outgoing students, and maintaining the total undergraduate student list for the College. Preparation of the enrollment report used as official statistics is also a responsibility. Lists from departments are checked upon request.
6. *Equipment Operation:*
Xerox, mimeo, and spirit duplicator, paper sorter and folder, adding machine and calculator. Time spent is minimal, only where needed for maintenance of records and no other help is available.
7. *Relations with Others:*
Must relate well to faculty advisers and department chairpersons and satisfy their needs. Work around and with the Graduation process in the office. Direct and supervise student workers assigned to help with maintaining records. Contact is also maintained with the University Director of Academic Records and high level secretarial personnel in other colleges with the same responsibility.
8. *Hardest Part of Job:*
Dealing with the up and down changes caused by conflicting deadlines and overlapping periods of transfer in and out.
9. *Experience:*
High school graduation and, preferably, some knowledge of college transcripts. Typing must be good. Ability in shorthand or dictaphone desirable. Adding machine and calculator operation are also desirable but could be learned quickly on the job.
10. *Learning Period:*
Two to three months as most of the tasks must be done at least once before the complete process is understood.
11. *Additional Information:*
The employee must possess the skills and potential for eventually reaching a level of independent judgment, management, and competence.

Another necessary position is that of the personnel specialist who maintains files such as payroll and recruitment, layoff, and recall information in addition to data concerning employee turnover. Responsibility for managing these records adequately requires a knowledge of various systems of record keeping, both manual and automated.

The central personnel operation should also maintain appropriate records for faculty and administrators that enable it to not only administer the various benefit plans but also provide a total record of the individual's employment status. This places all personnel information in one location, which expedites the gathering of information and statistics for institutional studies and budget development, for example.

Some supplemental coordinated activity is necessary within each of the institution's operating units, which includes the establishment of files containing basic information and evaluations for each employee, time sheets, and payroll information. In addition, deans and chairpersons should utilize the expertise and resources of the central personnel operation to avoid confusion and overlap. Assistance should be obtained in the development of job descriptions, recruitment, selection, orientation and training programs, evaluation, and labor relations. Regardless of the level, central or college, consideration for the dignity, morale, and general well being of each individual is essential.

Human Relations

One of the challenges in working with support staff is creation of an environment that will draw out the best in each individual and motivate people to perform at a high level in order to strengthen the organization and make it effective in achieving its objectives. A clear delineation of expectations including duties and hours is an essential first step in this direction. Because the success of the total academic operation depends upon their attitude, support staff members must have a feeling of belonging and feel that they are making a valuable contribution toward achievement of institutional goals both as members of a team and as individuals. Each must be made to feel that he or she is essential to the effectiveness of the organization. Administrators must find time to consult with individuals and, while appearing to be really interested in each one, emphasize that each is essential to the organization. Information should be shared, and suggestions should be solicited. Regular meetings with support staff to share information on recent developments, plans, and problems should be scheduled for effective communication. In fact, the use of the term support staff instead of nonacademic staff could be one step in the right direction.

Ways must be found to eliminate excessive absenteeism, tardiness, turnover, and low productivity. Every effort is also needed to draw out the best in each individual from induction to termination through salary benefits, promotion, staff development programs, and objective disciplinary and grievance procedures.

Recruitment and Selection

Central office personnel should be experts in the recruitment, screening, and hiring of individuals.

> Personnel selection requires expertise in organizing recruitment efforts, screening and interviewing, verifying previous employment information, setting up testing programs, and validating those testing programs against job requirements to meet EEO guidelines. Selection also includes a strong familiarity with the market sources from which new employees might come, and familiarity with the means for communicating with persons in these markets.[5]

Qualifications for any position must include not only the particular skills and abilities for that position, but the individual selected should possess the traits and qualities needed for strengthening the unit and providing balance in the staffing pattern.

Munsterman and Masters provide a unique viewpoint in the recommendation of a systems approach.

> Systems analysis is one method of looking at employment practices; this includes identifying objectives and available resources, determining alternatives, and selecting the alternative which is economically feasible and assists in achieving the goals of the organization. The systems approach involves the total employment package, that is, recruitment and application, interview and selection, orientation and training, placement, and post-placement training.[6]

Maner and Cosby describe an empirical approach which might have potential for personnel selection. They believe that by utilizing biographical data from pre-employment application forms, it is possible to select personnel with greater staying power. At the same time, the image of the organization as an equal opportunity employer may be improved. In their study, Maner and Cosby were able to identify factors positively correlated with tenure in a specific employee category by the use of multivariate analysis of biographical data. An institution might want to apply this same approach to a particular category to determine its applicability.[7]

UNIONIZATION

Unionization of nonfaculty employees had been in existence prior to organization for collective bargaining by faculty. It is possible that a large university might find itself involved with between fifteen and twenty different unions. There is no longer a question of willingness to deal with a union; instead, provisions must be made for negotiating with numerous groups and administering the various contracts that result. In state systems of education, a single contract that is applicable to all institutions in the system may be negotiated and finalized. Regardless, wages, hours, and conditions of employment are a legitimate and understandable concern of all staff members. The need for resolving disputes between employees and employers has become increasingly obvious and has provided impetus for the growing number of bargaining units found on college and university campuses. While public institutions were the first to be affected, increasing numbers of private ones will find themselves involved in collective bargaining whether they are agreeable to the process or not.

Positive Results of Unionization

Unionization is not all bad. Appropriately handled, crises should be kept to a minimum and, with experience, contract agreements are leading to development of the reasonable and clearly stated policies needed for good employer/employee relations. Some conflict is inevitable because administration needs maximum flexibility to meet changing conditions and requirements, while unions want fixed rules and limitations on all working conditions.

The National Association of College and University Business Officers cites the following positive results from collective bargaining:

1. More internal consistency in the interpretation and application of personnel policies
2. More equitable treatment of employees with less favoritism shown by certain supervisors
3. Earlier consideration of the employee relations impact on institutional planning[8]

Thus, the results of collective bargaining do not necessarily have to be adverse ones. In fact, the contract could be a means for more effective utilization of resources and, if properly administered, an instrument for control of routine institutional operations in areas such as regulation of working hours.

The Contract: Provisions and Implementation

The bargainable issues for support staff are usually conventional. However, as faculty bargaining continues to spread and deal with broader concepts, some of these concepts may become applicable to support staff. In some instances, they already have as in cases where librarians and library technicians have been taken in as members of faculty bargaining units.

While wages are the most important aspect of a contract settlement to some, many other items are of equal and perhaps of greater importance. Benefit plans have become increasingly important and may include tuition, medical, dental, eye care, and prescription plans. Other negotiable items may include job classifications with related work assignments, definition of personal days and holidays, overtime compensation, physical conditions for a safe and healthy work environment, personnel files and access to them, procedures for discharge from employment, promotion and transfer, reduction in force, and, of course, provisions for negotiating the succeeding contract and for the handling of grievances.

The college level administrator has an obligation to be completely familiar with all provisions of the contracts and to insure their implementation within the organization whether it be at the college, division, or department levels. Filing of grievances by support personnel can be only disruptive to the smooth functioning of the organization and, in the end, will be a serious deterrent to the achievement of the objectives of the institution.

An administrative calendar is an important aid to the implementation of the contract as well as to the effective functioning of the office concerned. It should be in monthly format and include dates for notification of particular tasks with deadlines for their completion. The periodic evaluation of clerical personnel is an example. The administrative calendar of the college level administrator would include entries indicating when all college administrators should be reminded of the due date for evaluations, dates all evaluations are due in the dean's office, and the dates they are due in the central personnel office of the institution. The division and department administrator would include the due date for evaluations on his or her calendar.

Planning for Strikes

Regardless of the level of operation, every administrator must have emergency plans ready for implementation in the event of slowdowns, mass call-ins of sickness, picketing, and strikes. An institution may find itself able to cope with the situation for an indefinite period of time with the loss of the services of instructional and technical support staff. It is quite feasible for instructors to adjust their classroom procedures to accommodate the loss of services. Loss of the services of clerical staff becomes another matter. Telephones must be answered, students and visitors served, and the most crucial functions continued. A plan for the deployment of administrative assistants and the assumption of some routine operations by administrative personnel in the event of an employee action should be prepared and ready for implementation if and when necessary. The same kind of plan is needed to cover essential services in the event of a breakdown in support services supplied by the central administrative offices. This might include the areas of maintenance, security, and computer services.

STAFF DEVELOPMENT PROGRAMS

Development programs for faculty have always been desirable and, in recent years, there seems to be an increasing emphasis upon them. Development programs for support personnel are also desirable. These should be implemented on the institutional level and supplemented by appropriate activities at the college, division, and department levels. Design of such programs should focus upon the improvement of staff morale, human relations, and job efficiency.

Orientation

An important aspect of development programs is orientation. Every effort is needed to ensure that new employees "get off to a good start."

A comprehensive orientation requires more than the one-half day briefing sessions provided by some central personnel offices that involve nothing more than a presentation of personnel policies and the completion of numerous forms for establishing the employee's personnel file and implementing the fringe benefits program.

An important aspect of a centralized orientation program should be provision of assistance to new employees in identifying with the institution as well as assisting them in developing an understanding of the concepts and philosophies of higher education. An introduction to the institution the employee is entering should include its specific philosophy and organization.

Business and academic policies should be discussed in addition to either distributing them in printed form or announcing the most immediate locations where they are available for frequent reference. Appropriate office techniques peculiar to the institution must be presented. Of course, the role of the personnel office should also be included.

At the college and department levels, business and academic policies specific to the level of organization should be part of the supplemental orientation activities. The immediate supervisor of the area to which the new employee has been assigned will provide more detailed knowledge of the functions performed in that area and how they relate with functions performed in other areas. An important task of the central personnel office is provision of assistance to college and department supervisors in the development of these activities for assisting employees in becoming acquainted with the department and its work methods.

Another area frequently omitted in orientation sessions is public relations. Each employee should be briefed in the need for promoting good public relations and enhancing the image of the institution. Appropriate relationships with faculty, students, and other staff members are also needed, as well as what constitutes professional and ethical behavior.

In short, the orientation sessions should provide new employees with information about all aspects of their jobs, build confidence in them as they begin their new positions, and help them feel that they belong.

Needs Assessment

Staff development needs must be identified in order to implement a meaningful and complete program. A representative committee could be one means for not only defining needs but also assisting in planning an appropriate and ongoing program for meeting these needs as well as those that may continue to emerge. Committee members should meet and discuss the question with their colleagues, draw upon their own experiences, and review appropriate literature. A comprehensive assessment effort will focus upon intra- and inter-departmental and institutional relationships as well as the continued enhancement of existing skills and the development of new ones.

Follow-up interviews with new employees at thirty- and sixty-day intervals not only will provide assistance in appraising the effectiveness of the orientation program but also may indicate special needs for coverage in the development program.

Development Activities

A variety of activities is possible as shown by Meyerson who identified four categories applied to a student affairs office at the University of Nebraska. These same types of activities may be readily applied to staff development programs in other areas as well. Their general coverage includes:

1. Colleague Interaction: opportunity for all levels of staff and from all departments to personalize their relationships in order to maximize individual professional and social growth
2. Informational Emphasis: opportunity for each staff member to learn as much as possible of the philosophy, organization and services existent in each of the departments
3. Skill Training: opportunity for staff to develop more effectively those actual skills that are necessary in everyday work performance
4. Thinking Time: opportunity for staff to critically examine and study current issues and emerging philosophies in higher education [9]

Employees should be encouraged to enroll in developmental courses within the institution. A tuition waiver policy provides additional incentive to staff for doing so. Where appropriate courses are not available "in house," financial support should be provided to encourage staff members to enroll in programs offered by other colleges and universities as well as vocational schools and the numerous varieties of programs in continuing education. Attendance at appropriate professional meetings and workshops must also be encouraged and supported by resources including released time and some travel funds. Institutionally sponsored workshops and presentations must not be overlooked. Outside consultants are another valuable resource who can assist not only in planning development activities but also by participating in them.

Finally, leaves of absence similar to academic sabbaticals should be available. A leave for up to six months with pay for a developmental activity can bring an institution twice the value. Of course, employees granted such leaves should provide a detailed plan of their activities when applying and must also make some kind of commitment regarding an obligation to return to the former position for a specified length of time.

EVALUATION

The quality of services provided by support personnel is too often measured by unsolicited user feedback that is negative and critical. Criticism can be demoralizing but, if it is totally ignored, the staff and its individual members lose an opportunity for constructive change and individual growth. To overcome this, there should be an evaluation program that is a continuous process interspersed with periodic formal reviews. Several approaches recommended by the National Association of of College and University Business Officers include: employee characteristics analysis, task performance analysis, and a management by objectives approach.[10]

Purposes of Performance Evaluation

Besides determining who will get a pay raise, a number of purposes have been identified that support more than ever the need for an evaluation program. Those identified by the National Association of College and University Business Officers are:

1. Help employees see how their work appears to supervisors.
2. Assist employers in improving their performance.
3. Assist supervisors and management in analyzing the effectiveness of the organization and its operations.
4. Help supervisors and management in identification of employees who should be considered for development, promotion, transfer, or dismissal.
5. Increase employee morale by providing a means of communication with management.
6. Assist in attainment of departmental and institutional goals.[11]

Some Approaches to Evaluation

Employees are constantly being observed by their employers in a casual and unsystematic manner. Earlier methods of evaluation were frequently subjective ratings of personal characteristics which might include initiative, cooperation, relationships with coworkers, tactfulness, work habits, appearance, and absenteeism. This kind of approach is not sufficient in itself but can be useful as a supplement to either of two others described below.

Robustelli and Ericsson describe the development of an appraisal form at the University of Tennessee. The appraisal form serves as a stimulus to supervisor–employee discussions of the employee's performance at regular intervals. They used the critical incident approach for development of two instruments, one for jobs of a technical nature and one that focused on semiskilled and unskilled positions. This approach involved identifying, classifying, and recording critical incidents in employee behavior which became the basis for appraisal and follow-up evaluation interviews.[12] Critical incidents are defined as follows:

> Briefly, an incident is "critical" when it illustrates that the employee has done, or failed to do, something that results in unusual success or unusual failure on some part of his job.
>
> Critical incidents are facts (not opinions or generalizations), but not all facts are critical . . .
>
> Critical facts are the employee actions that really make performance outstandingly effective or ineffective.[13]

Using the critical incident approach, one can record strengths and weaknesses as portrayed through specific incidents and obtain concrete information for supervisor/employee conferences. Another use of critical incidents is to provide behavioral descriptions that may become items or scales for another type of rating form.[14]

In a management by objectives approach to employee evaluation, goals and objectives based upon the job description for the specific position are established. These become targets for the employee to work toward but should have the approval of his or her superior. In some instances, these targets are developed cooperatively by the employee and the supervisor.

At the end of a specified period of time, the employee does a self-appraisal of progress attained toward accomplishment of the previously established objectives and then an evaluation of his or her job performance takes place with the immediate supervisor. A new set of targets is established and the cycle is repeated.

As the need grows for better planning and more effective organizations, improved communications, greater cooperation within institutions, and less mediocrity, a higher level of competence must develop not only in faculty and administrators but should also be expected of those in supporting positions. Orientation and staff development programs along with related well-developed ongoing evaluation efforts will provide a means for attaining optimum productivity.

SUMMARY

A support staff of the highest caliber available is required for successful day-to-day operation of an institution. There is no single classification scheme that covers the numerous kinds of positions since these depend upon the organization of a particular college or university. Nonacademic or nonprofessional positions are needed as well as those for individuals classified as academic professionals or technicians. At the college level, the various support services are more apt to be specialized and complement those supplied by the central administrative organization.

A well-developed personnel program reflecting expertise in recruitment, selection, pre- and in-service training, and evaluation can provide invaluable service to the college administrator. A centralized operation provides needed consistency at the college level.

For each type of position, there should be a complete description of the major duties and responsibilities attached to the position and the needed qualifications. This description becomes a tool for recruitment as well as evaluation of an individual in a specific position.

One of the most important aspects of working with support staff is creating an environment that will motivate people to perform at the highest level possible. Support staff need to feel that they are an important part of a team effort. The collective bargaining movement with its possibilities for creating adversarial relationships makes this team approach more important than ever. It is essential, also, that administrators be completely familiar with all contractual provisions and see that they are appropriately implemented within the units for which they are responsible.

Finally, a comprehensive, systematic evaluation system is necessary both from an organizational point of view and for the well being of the individual employee.

ENDNOTES

1. Walter V. Hohenstein and Bernard Jay Williams, "The Forgotten Man—The Non-Faculty Non-Classified University Employee," *College and University Personnel Association Journal* 25 (1974): 26–27.
2. Agreement between Temple University of the Commonwealth System of Higher Education and the American Association of University Professors, Temple University Chapter, July 1, 1976–June 30, 1980, pp. 37–38.
3. Bernard Ingster, "Challenge of Staff Resources Development," *College and University Personnel Association Journal* 27 (1976): 2.
4. National Association of College and University Business Officers, *College and University Business Administration,* Third Edition (Washington, D.C., 1974), p. 67.
5. Ingster, "Challenge of Staff Resources Development," p. 2.
6. Richard E. Munsterman and Robert J. Masters, "Business Office Employment and Training—A Systems Approach," *Journal of College and University Personnel Association* 26 (1975): 15.
7. Arnold H. Maner and Arthur Q. Cosby, "Personnel Selection: An Empirical Approach," *Journal of College and University Personnel Association* 24 (1973): 96–98.
8. National Association of College and University Business Officers, "Labor Relations and Collective Bargaining," *College and University Business Administration,* Third Edition (Washington, D.C., 1974), p. 92.
9. Ely Meyerson, "Mini University Provides Training for a Big University," *College and University Business* 56 (1974): 31.
10. National Association of College and University Business Officers, *College and University Business Administration,* Third Edition (Washington, D.C., 1974), p. 70.
11. *Ibid.*
12. Joseph A. Robustelli and Carl W. Ericsson, "Developing a Performance Appraisal Form for University Support Personnel," *Journal of College and University Personnel Association* 16 (1975): 3–9.
13. Herbert J. Chruden and Arthur W. Sherman, Jr., *Personnel Management* (Cincinnati: South-Western Publishing Co., 1968), p. 260 citing John C. Flanagan and Robert B. Miller, *The Performance Record Handbook for Supervisors* (Chicago: Science Research Associates, 1955), p. 6.
14. *Ibid.,* p. 261.

CHAPTER 6

Faculty Collective Bargaining

Collective bargaining is being increasingly viewed as a desirable means for resolving disputes between employers and employees in a peaceable way. Some see it as a sensible, rational means for improving salaries and fringe benefits. Others see it as a means for getting faculty to accept new work patterns and the concept of accountability as these are forced upon them by outside pressures.

Garbarino and Aussieker rather simply define bargaining as "decision making by negotiation between interest groups with more-or-less formal representative roles."[1] The National Association of College and University Business Officers precedes its definition with one of labor relations which is "the relationship between the administration of an institution (management) and organized faculty and staff (employees) together with organizations to which faculty and staff belong." Then, collective bargaining is defined as "an important facet of labor relations (and) refers to negotiations between representatives of organized employees and the institution to determine such matters as salaries and wages, hours, work rules, and working conditions."[2] In the long run, collective bargaining should be viewed as a mutual effort by both parties involved to find a middle ground as favorable as possible to each of their interests, yet acceptable to the other party—it is based upon the fine art of compromise.

FACTORS LEADING TO THE COLLECTIVE BARGAINING MOVEMENT

Traditionally, the employer/employee relationship in education differed substantially from that found in industry. Several influences have led to a recent drastic alteration of this relationship among which are the legislative actions taken by individual states that are affecting public employees. Other influences are related to internal conditions involving stress and changing relationships within institutions. Finally, the fact of diminishing resources and the understandable concern of faculty that their needs are recognized cannot be ignored. The fast changing circumstances in which higher education finds itself have led to a totally new set of relationships.

Legislative Influences

The unionization movement, in general, was given greatest legitimacy by the Wagner Act (also known as the National Labor Relations Act) passed by Congress in 1935. While it applied to the private sector only, it granted employees the right to organize, select their own representatives, and to bargain collectively. The Taft-Hartley Act (Labor-Management Relations Act) of 1947 served to strengthen the national legislative foundation for collective bargaining, but the process was still confined to the private sector and even more specifically only where interstate commerce was involved.

Bargaining in the public employment area was given its beginning by President Kennedy's Federal Executive Order 10988 established in 1962 requiring that certain employee rights be extended to those employed by the federal government. The rights included:

1. The right of employees to join organizations of their choice.
2. Organizations could be granted informal, formal, or exclusive recognition.
3. The executive of the agency is required to meet and confer with respect to personnel policies and working conditions.
4. Advisory arbitration of grievances arising under the operation of agreements resulting from such meet-and-confer sessions must be provided for.[3]

Note that the right to strike was denied.

A major impetus to collective bargaining by public employees and particularly in higher education was passage of the Taylor Act in New York State in 1967. By 1969, there were sixteen negotiated contracts among thirty community colleges outside New York City.[4] Today, over ninety percent of the faculty in public institutions of higher education in New York State are organized. The character of the laws explains the patterns of unionization. Thus, policies and procedures affecting faculty are becoming more similar to those affecting other public employees.

Bargaining in the public sector has grown tremendously. The first legislative act was passed in 1959 by the Wisconsin legislature. Municipalities were required to bargain with their employees and in 1965, this requirement was extended to cover state employees. In 1965, public negotiation laws were also enacted by California, Connecticut, Massachusetts, Michigan, Oregon, and Washington.[5] The movement spread to include public school teachers. By the beginning of the 1974–1975 school year, thirty-eight of the fifty states had provided some form of legal sanction for collective bargaining by teachers. Thirty of these had passed statutes authorizing collective bargaining by teachers. Attorney generals' opinion in six states permitted bargaining while in another, state legal recognition was in the form of an opinion by the attorney general that prohibited teacher strikes. In one state, a court decision provided for bargaining.[6]

Major activity in higher education has taken place in Michigan, Pennsylvania, New Jersey, and New York. It is in these states that a large number of organized public colleges and universities are located. Approximately half the states, however, have passed legislation specifically providing for collective bargaining by professors.

Legislative influence over the collective bargaining process does not end with enactment of enabling laws but

> . . . is manifested in at least four additional ways: the force of legislative expectations that faculty will unionize once enabling legislation is passed; legislative involvement in the contract ratification process; legislative control over the funds needed to finance collective bargaining agreements; and legislative pressures for the standardization of public employee personnel policies and procedures.[7]

In addition, much legislative interest in what faculty are doing has developed in the name of accountability. There is increasing concern that pressure from legislators will result in a

TABLE 6–1 **Summary of Faculty Bargaining Decisions**

	4-Year Campuses			*2-Year Campuses*			*Grand Total*
	Public	*Private*	*Total*	*Public*	*Private*	*Total*	
American Association of University Professors	24	25	49	5	1	6	55
American Federation of Teachers	70	18	88	119	6	125	213
National Education Association	46	13	59	183	2	185	244
A.A.U.P.—N.E.A.	4	0	4	7	0	7	11
Independent and Other	19	11	30	46	1	47	77
Total	163	67	230	360	10	370	600
Bargaining Rejected	22	38	60	14	3	17	77

Chronicle of Higher Education, 26 June 1978, p. 8. Reprinted with permission. Copyright 1978 by Editorial Projects for Education, Inc.

push to require greater work loads and the relinquishing of some faculty prerogatives.

The movement among elementary and secondary teachers spread to higher education to such an extent that by late 1974, the faculties of more than 330 institutions of higher education had chosen exclusive bargaining agents and more than one-fifth of the full-time teaching faculty in higher education were represented by recognized bargaining agents.[8] Ladd and Lipset determined that by the end of 1977, about 500 campuses throughout the nation had organized and a quarter of the entire professoriate was unionized. However, a leveling-off of general faculty support for the unionization of professors at about 75 percent was indicated by the same survey.[9] As of May 15, 1978, there were 600 campuses where faculty had chosen agents and 77 where unionization had been rejected. Table 6–1 contains a summary of these decisions.

INSTITUTIONAL INFLUENCES

Once the legal impetus was felt, a variety of institutional situations affected the growth of the bargaining movement. Not all of those to be described apply to every single institution but any one or any combination of several might be associated with a specific institution.

As public institutions grew rapidly (and their growth far surpassed that of private institutions), structural changes took place. In some cases, multiple campuses were developed which were then brought together into larger administrative units. Larger institutions meant that decision making on major issues was moved farther from individual faculty members and their colleagues with common interests. A number of colleges changed character not only through growth but through the addition of new programs. As an example, many state teachers' colleges broadened their offerings to include degree programs in liberal arts and business administration. This led to two problems. In some instances, the more diverse faculty with more diverse viewpoints led to a decrease in consensus creating internal conflicts. In other instances, the administrators of these colleges did not adapt to the different and more academic atmosphere.

While some administrators failed to adjust administrative patterns to changing circumstances, others became more aggressive and even repressive. Some faculty began to look at unionization as a means for protection against both capricious or unfair management and administrative pressure to increase work load. Some also see collective bargaining as a means for making administrators accountable for some of their actions. Another factor in changing faculty and administrative relationships is the more militant younger faculty who believe adversarial relationships in the patterns of relationship within the institution are necessary.

Other influences include faculty who have become dissatisfied with the effectiveness of the faculty senate and the governance structure and nonteaching professionals who have become involved in the movement because of their desire to share in the governance authority. All are concerned about the question of priorities in assigning continually decreasing resources as the budget pressures and effects of inflation make their impact upon salaries, sabbaticals, and travel. Despite the prevalence of tenure, threats to employment security are very real to faculty and academic professionals as they observe retrenchment activity.

Finally, there are external influences that have provided impetus to the bargaining movement. In addition to intruding upon institutional autonomy, outside forces such as state coordinating agencies, legislators, and governors appear to be eroding faculty power in some areas where it had previously been quite strong.

Faculty cannot help being impressed by the gains made by elementary and secondary teachers followed by a desire to do the same toward improving their own circumstances. Community colleges are a natural for organization since so many of the faculty had previously been secondary school teachers. Some community colleges are part of K–14 school systems where collective bargaining has been "a way of life" for some time, which explains the greater prevalence of collective bargaining organization and activity in two-year colleges than in four-year institutions.

Collegiality vs Collective Bargaining

The concept of collegiality is an idealistic one that has been implemented with varying degrees of success. It is based upon a belief that faculty have commonalities that make it possible for them to act as a body in managing their own affairs. Decision making is accomplished through accommodation and adaptation leading to consensus rather than conflict. Under these circumstances, professors enjoy great autonomy in defining their responsibilities and determining how they will accomplish them. Administrators are seen as expediters and managers for executing policy, handling business and management problems, and generally providing and preserving a situation that makes it possible for faculty to carry out their self-determined responsibilities.

A bureaucratic approach emphasizes efficiency and order while

> On the other hand, the collegial emphasis (the community of scholars) largely ignores efficiency or would measure it in quite different terms than the bureaucratic approach. The collegial emphasis gives precedence to scholarly values; autonomy for the individual; attention to quality rather than quantity; the existence of a scholarly, intellectually challenging environment; and flexibility in adapting faculty assignments and responsibilities to personal needs (and whims).[10]

Unionism challenges the collegial nature of "shared authority" which, in the past, was the basis or rationale for faculty participation in college and university government. Unfortunately, authority did not always accompany the process and faculty bodies were only recommending or advisory in nature. Their recommendations could be ignored or neglected by the governing board and/or administration. "As accountability became the watchword, the classic management principle required that the scope of responsibility be matched by the scope of authority." [11] It is becoming increasingly obvious that the management structure of institutions is becoming more emphasized and aggressive. It is also becoming apparent that the real authority and power are money based and lie where fundamental budgetary decisions are finalized. At the same time, faculty are becoming more and more concerned over how the limited resources will be allocated.

Conflict within colleges and universities is not new. It has always existed and will continue to exist. Past conflicts have not always been resolved. However, recent years have witnessed the development of more mechanisms for settling disputes than have existed in the past. There is increased recognition that conflict cannot be totally eliminated and means are being devised to manage it.

Many problems are people problems, which are often more difficult to deal with than some others. Faculty are concerned that administrative authority not become too extensive and believe that the more restricted it is, the better it will be for faculty and students. Who holds the power and how to get some of it has become increasingly important. Institutional loyalty and faith in people seem to have been decreasing while faith in rules and procedures has been increasing. The situation becomes more severe as hard decisions with considerable impact have to be made regarding the elimination of programs, reduction of costs, and reduction of staff. These are not decisions that faculty are likely to make. It is possible that more concern will be directed toward resolving conflict than working within a framework of collegiality. Collective bargaining provides a mechanism for doing so.

Special Problems of Private Institutions

As previously stated, public institutions are regulated by state law. Private colleges and universities are not. Instead, they fall within the guidelines of the National Labor Relations Board and are subject to the provisions of the National Labor Relations Act. In 1970, the National Labor Relations Board decided to take jurisdiction over private institutions of higher education which receive an annual gross revenue of more than one million dollars. Faculty of some private institutions may be reluctant to become involved in collective bargaining because of the possibility of federal intervention and influence that many consider undesirable. These same faculty also tend to be more highly involved in decision making, which may also explain why the growth of collective bargaining in private colleges and universities has not been anywhere near that in the public ones.

Public colleges and universities will most likely withstand the special problems created by collective bargaining. On the other hand, private colleges are finding it increasingly difficult to keep a balanced budget and economic difficulties are forcing a number of them to close. If faculty demands for collective bargaining increase in the private sector, they may push budgetary demands to a point that exceeds the income and resources of some institutions.

THE BARGAINING UNIT

Several decisions must be made as soon as it has been determined that faculty will engage in collective bargaining. Among these are selection of the group or bargaining association that will represent the faculty and determination of the composition of the unit. In addition, both the administration and faculty must identify their teams and chief negotiators prior to meeting at the bargaining table.

Selection of the Agent

An election process is used to identify the bargaining agent that will represent the faculty.

Any combination of the following might be presented as possible choices: AFT, NEA, AAUP, AAHE, NFA, a faculty senate, or some general faculty organization. Of those listed, the first three are most active. It is also possible for no existing organization to be identified and, in its place, an ad hoc group established for the specific purpose each time a contract is to be negotiated. When a union has been certified as the exclusive bargaining agent according to the dictates of the law, no other organization of any kind may represent the employees, in this case—faculty, in dealing with the employer.

The previously cited Ladd-Lipset survey indicated that 19 percent of the faculty members belong to an NEA affiliate; 11 percent to the AFT; 14 percent to a state, county, or municipal employee's association not confined to college teachers; and 46 percent belong to none of the above organizations. It was also pointed out that 22 percent claimed membership in AAUP but apparently were not all paid-up members. The AAUP itself reports a membership of 19 percent of all professors.[12]

The above figures suggest that some faculty retain membership in more than one organization. It is obvious, too, that since the survey indicated about 25 percent of the professors are actually represented by bargaining agents, many others who retain membership in the same organizations are not involved in collective bargaining.

Administrative Representation

The administration must also identify its representative "team." One or more representatives from central administration such as a Vice President for Personnel, an academic vice president, an assistant to the president, and possibly one or more academic deans may comprise the group. It is rare and inadvisable for the president to be involved because the inordinate amount of time required would make it necessary for him to neglect the already overburdensome duties of the position. More important, it would place the president in an adversarial position, a situation to be avoided. It is also possible for an "outsider" to be appointed chief negotiator for the institution. Faculty may find this approach objectionable on the basis that the chief negotiator is not a member of the academic community and would not be aware of the academic ramifications of various bargaining positions. Those who argue for the "outside" negotiator stress increased objectivity and a decrease in the adversarial relationships between faculty and administrators.

In a state system, institutions belonging to the system bargain as one unit with the representatives of the governor. In this instance, all institutions are treated equally and the outcome is applicable to all in exactly the same fashion. An important issue at the state level is the ability to meet a financial commitment particularly if it spreads over a period of time when the legislative membership changes. State legislatures are limited in their power to commit their successors to multiyear contracts. To offset this, a contingency clause indicating that ultimate implementation of the agreement is contingent upon action by other executive or legislative bodies is not uncommon.

Composition of the Unit

Determination must be made of the group of employees to be represented by the specified union or organization in collective bargaining and resolution of grievances. There seems to be a tendency toward bargaining units defined along comprehensive geographical and occupational lines. An example of the former would be the state colleges in New Jersey that are represented as a whole by the American Federation of Teachers. The employer's "representatives" are the State Board of Higher Education and the Executive Office of Employee

Relations. Faculty of the State University of New York system bargain with a state Office of Employee Relations. As for occupational limitations, the membership (in this case, faculty) determines which other groups, if any, may participate. This situation is illustrated by the inclusion of librarians and so-called academic professionals (who have nonteaching responsibilities) by some faculty unions. Ladd and Lipset found that members were not limited to teachers in 25 percent of the universities; 52 percent of four-year colleges; 24 percent of two-year colleges; 92 percent of public institutions; and 9 percent of private institutions.[13]

Too much variance in the types of institutions and professions in the same unit can lead to internal bickering. If two- and four-year schools are in the same unit with law and medical schools or research assistants, media technicians, librarians, advisers, counselors, full- and part-time faculty are all in the same unit, it is obvious that agreement within the unit will be difficult to achieve because of the diversity of interests.

Ordinarily, labor relations laws designate the state level labor relations agencies that may determine appropriate units on a case-by-case basis following union admission of a petition describing the unit. This is done according to legislative intent or administrative guidelines. The same agency may also resolve disputes over inclusion or exclusion of particular groups of employees.

Problems have developed, in some instances, over the inclusion of part-time faculty. Where the two parties involved have been unable to agree on the status of part-time faculty, the National Labor Relations Board has been called upon for a decision. The Board's position has been a varied one dependent upon the circumstances of each particular situation. In general, it has favored inclusion in the unit of those who regularly teach more than a minimum amount.

The question about inclusion of department chairpersons in the unit continually appears. Each decision must be an independent one. The major issue revolves around the extent of the supervisory role of the chairperson. The extent of control over personnel decisions is one means for definition. A chairperson who is elected and serves on a rotating basis is generally included in the bargaining unit.

Garbarino and Aussieker point out that the institutional administration generally prefers that chairpersons represent management and the administration's interests in the conduct of departmental affairs. In this case, the chairperson becomes a first-line manager and would be excluded from the bargaining unit since the role becomes that of a member within the administrative hierarchy. On the other hand, "unions see the inclusion of chairpersons in bargaining units as a way of moving the chairperson closer to the role of 'shop steward'—the protector of the interests of the faculty in the implementation of contract provisions."[14] Whatever decision is made regarding inclusion of the chairperson in the unit, it cannot help having an impact upon the total governance system of the institution. Where the various parties are unable to agree, the issue is decided by the appropriate labor board. In summary, the traditional decision-making policy and practices at a particular institution will probably determine the composition of the collective bargaining unit.

THE SCOPE OF BARGAINING AND ITS IMPLICATIONS

As discussed in Chapter 5, collective bargaining usually centers about the issues of wages, hours, and conditions of employment. However, faculty complaints and issues that have been bargained and spelled out in written agreements are very different from those covering service and support personnel. Despite their longer experience with the process, the interpretation and scope of conditions of employment has still not been stabilized in the K–12 educational organizations. The problem is even greater in the higher education sector because of the unique nature of faculty responsibilities that tend to be somewhat nebulously defined. It is possible that conditions of employment will take on greater importance than monetary rewards as job security tends to become weakened in the near future.

The scope of negotiations beyond the areas mandated by law can be controlled by the administration. A common management reaction is to attempt to limit the scope as much as possible which, in turn, limits the extent of faculty power. Once an item has been negotiated and becomes part of a contract, it becomes virtually impossible to bargain its removal as a negotiable item. When the long process is extended to an area previously not included, some concession from the faculty is usually required in return.

Contracts have become increasingly comprehensive in nature but the topics for bargaining will vary. Some are strictly defined by law; others are permitted by law; and still others are considered nonnegotiable. Grievance procedures are an important part of every contract. Once a contract has been agreed upon by the administration and ratified by the faculty, it becomes legally binding on both parties and takes precedence over any previous contracts as well as superseding past practices.

Mandatory and Permissible Topics for Bargaining

George Angell presents several categories of bargaining topics. Those generally agreed upon as mandatory are:

> grievance procedures, including arbitration
> work hours
> work loads
> hours and work schedules
> pensions, unless established by state law
> insurance benefits
> sick leave and other types of leaves of absence
> holidays and vacations
> parking space and other perquisites related to employment
> procedures for evaluation, retention, promotion of unit employees
> procedures for discipline and discharge
> union security, except where specifically prohibited by law
> wages and salaries, merit increases
> safety rules and policies
> savings clause
> management rights clause
> impact of management decisions on work conditions [15]

The last item can be clarified by understanding that while certain decisions are in the domain of management rights to exclusively determine, the effects of these decisions on terms and conditions of employment become bargainable issues. This is but one example of the difficulty involved in trying to draw a line between bargainable and nonbargainable areas.

The same writer defines permissible in the bargaining context as

> one that either party can refuse to bargain without being guilty of an unfair labor practice. Unions, of course, may refuse to bargain a management right even when the employer permits it. However, a union spokesman usually demands that certain management rights be bargained, and it is the employer who either refuses to bargain or bargains at a "price." [16]

He then cites the following subjects that have been identified by the Academic Collective Bargaining Information Service in its Special Report No. 25 as management rights and subjects of bargaining only if permitted by management:

mission and purpose of the institution
hiring and discharging employees
assignment and transfer of employees
supervision and direction of employees' work performance
employment of substitutes
size of work force, number of employees
retrenchment of funds, programs, number of employees
distribution of resources (funds and employees) to departments
type of organization, reorganization of departments and divisions
emergency executive powers in all matters
overall budget, level of funding, allocation of funds within units
selection and composition of programs
evaluation of programs
changes in programs
evaluation of employee performance
establishment of performance standards
promotion of employees
wages, hours and work conditions for employees not in the bargaining unit
nonjob related prerequisites for employees
discipline of employees
employer's business procedures [17]

Angell also points out that some states reserve to the public employer such rights as:

class size
college calendar
teacher evaluation procedures
code of ethics
academic freedom
preparation time for teachers
selection of texts
procedures for granting tenure
right to bargain in public [18]

Wages, Hours, and Conditions of Employment

As previously stated, wages, hours, and conditions of employment are mandatory subjects for collective bargaining. The area includes not only salary and pay for summer teaching assignments but also fringe benefits such as hospital, dental, and prescription plans, insurance, sick leave, study leaves, travel funds, family tuition benefits, and retirement contributions. There is almost no limit.

Negotiation of hours of employment is more difficult to define in higher education than in other sectors. Unions prefer to negotiate in definable terms while the academic image is that of the professional who earns a salary for his or her services and does not work for an hourly, daily, or weekly wage. Traditionally, unions would tend to think about the area of hours only as teaching load defined by credits. This would be expressed in terms such as a twelve-hour teaching load which may easily be translated into four courses meeting three hours per week or three courses meeting four hours per week. Professors resent such specificity because they feel it limits their academic freedom.

It is even more difficult to determine the definition of working conditions. Unions tend to view everything not covered by wages or hours as a term or condition of employment. On the other hand, management views only what cannot be defended as a management right as negotiable. There is no consensus regarding what constitutes terms or conditions of employment that would be applicable to all cases. A neutral third party such as the national or state labor relations board is often called upon to clarify what must be negotiated.

Through academic governance structures of various kinds, faculty have traditionally had a greater voice in their conditions of employment than labor unions. They want to include academic and institutional policy matters as conditions of employment. This has resulted in some contracts that specify how faculty will share authority and participate in the formulation of policies that delineate or affect the performance of their duties in some way. Faculty want to be assured that they are consulted. They want opportunities to present their opinions and ideas to the governing boards or similar authorities on matters of curriculum, academic standards, and other academic concerns so as not to lose academic freedom.

Job security is becoming an increasingly important issue. Untenured faculty perceive the union as a means for negotiating some kind of job security. Due process procedures for the discharge of untenured faculty are becoming issues for bargaining. The most common grievance being processed under negotiated contract agreements is failure to reappoint.

For tenured faculty, retrenchment procedures are becoming more and more important. An example is the dissatisfaction and turmoil surrounding the contract approved at the State University of New York that expired in 1979. While union members did ratify the contract, there is still concern about provisions for layoff which some faculty feel virtually abolishes tenure. The new contract continues a provision from the old that the SUNY chancellor could lay off faculty members "after such consultation as may, in his judgment, be appropriate." However, a new section requires the administration to determine whether a laid-off faculty member could teach some other course or courses being taught by less-senior faculty members in that department. Union leaders believe the change makes it more difficult for the administration to lay off faculty members. Some faculty believe that the change was not a significant improvement.[19]

Grievance Procedures

A grievance procedure is a judicial mechanism for resolving disputes and misunderstandings. Many contracts limit grievances to violations of the contract, a practice that is considered desirable. The other extreme would be to make it possible for faculty to grieve any administrative action they believe to be unfair or inequitable. In any case, administration of the contract becomes extremely important and uniformity is essential.

The area of grievance procedures has given deans and college chairpersons new responsibilities. Grievances must be processed and the first step is most frequently the department chairperson. The logical next step is the dean although where divisions exist, the division chairperson would be involved before the dean. In order to avoid grievances as far as possible, deans and chairpersons must know and understand the various provisions of the contract and the reasons behind them. Ideally, representatives of the administration and the union should meet with administrators and faculty to explain the contract and interpret its provisions in terms of the daily operations of the institution.

Administrators should make every attempt to settle grievances quickly. This is an area where real leadership can be demonstrated. Specific training for administrators is recommended in areas such as laws and legal processes affecting collective bargaining, labor, management relations, grievance processing, and conflict management. Daniel McLaughlin lists numerous recommended training aids which should be of assistance in improving management skills and could provide a base for some administrative staff development sessions.[20]

The exact nature of the grievance procedure will depend upon the circumstances and conditions of each particular institutional setting. The kinds of grievances filed by faculty will vary, but are most likely to be related to their peers and based on promotion and tenure rather than related to administrative actions. Precise statements of the prerogatives and responsibilities of both parties are needed as well as the definition of a grievance. The step-by-step process must be defined as well as the procedures for resolving a grievance through arbitration, a commonly accepted approach. Every effort should be made to avoid the final resort to arbitration, which becomes a time-consuming and expensive process. An agreement reached within the institutional framework is more acceptable than one arrived at by a third party from outside.

Memoranda of Understanding

As the various provisions of a contract are implemented, deficiencies as well as ambiguous language may be uncovered. Where a serious deficiency is identified, negotiations may have to be reopened in order to correct them by amending the contract. Where the problem is one of ambiguous language, so-called meet and discuss sessions might be scheduled for preparation of an interpretation. When the language and its implications have been clarified, the results should be distributed in what has become known as a memorandum of understanding. In fact it is advisable to provide for meet and discuss sessions within the contract framework with the understanding that such sessions could result in memoranda of agreement or understanding. These codicils or memoranda serve to make the contract more specific and workable.

OTHER EFFECTS OF COLLECTIVE BARGAINING

While unionism among faculty in higher education was seen as inevitable by many, it will probably not become universal particularly in private institutions. Its spread in public institutions has been given impetus by state legislation, which will continue to be the major factor in its growth.

Since unionism with the accompanying collective bargaining activity first appeared on the higher education level in the mid 1960s, conflicting opinions have been heard about its effects. Where unionism itself may not penetrate all institutions, the concept of collective bargaining may still become more prevalent as some sort of faculty association or representative group of faculty become involved on a more formal and aggressive level than in the past.

Where strikes have been used as a coercive measure by faculty, an adversarial relationship develops not only with the administration but also with students whose lives are very much affected by a strike. While faculty may enjoy benefits they might not have had without unionism and collective bargaining, their status as professionals may very well be greatly altered.

Are Adversarial Relationships Inevitable?

The industrial model of collective bargaining with its management versus labor orientation is conflict oriented. Unfortunately, where faculty assume that the collective bargaining process requires adversarial relationships, educational leadership gives way to labor-oriented leadership. Confrontation between faculty and institutional administration tends to broaden conflict between faculty and the governing boards or coordinating boards. Faculty concerns and the concessions they obtain will, in the long run, determine what the college or university will be.

Ideally, there should be a cooperative effort directed toward problem solving instead of a relationship based on confrontation. Conflict should be limited as far as possible through the established process for negotiation. Colleges and universities have traditionally reflected a philosophy of collegiality and shared decision making. Faculty have perceived themselves to be partners in a professional organization. Situations that lead to "us versus them" attitudes run contrary to that philosophy and will serve only to weaken the educational structure.

It should be remembered, too, that the pressures of declining resources and increasing external control are affecting administrators as well as faculty. The contract itself just might be an instrument to protect institutions from the increasing external pressures.

Positive Aspects of Collective Bargaining

Collective bargaining has resulted in economic benefits for the faculty. It has brought the salaries of community and state college teachers closer to university levels. Lower-paid faculty and nonteaching professionals have benefited particularly.

Faculty have always had the advantages of fringe benefits. Freedom in establishing work patterns outside of assigned class loads, allowances for sabbaticals, group insurance, and travel funds for professional meetings have been common. To these are being added medical, dental, and prescription plans. What other benefits might be sought in the future is not clear, although subsidized eye care and legal assistance are additional possibilities that have been included in some agreements. The greatest benefits have been improved salaries and the establishment of definitive grievance procedures.

As professionals, college and university faculty have enjoyed job security emanating from the tenure system. A number of contracts spell out the procedure for awarding tenure. Evaluation criteria and procedures for their application have been adopted. The faculty member has been given an opportunity to provide more input into the process, in addition to having access to the information used in making the decision. As the need for staff reduction becomes increasingly obvious, tenure will be coming under attack. A number of foresighted bargaining units have already included in their contracts a procedure for staff reduction revolving about the tenure and nontenure status of faculty as well as seniority.

The adversarial aspect of collective negotiations, while involving fewer people, could lead to more rapid change than the processes involving large numbers of people which reflect congeniality and consensus. Collective negotiations make is possible to "package" a number of separate issues in a single settlement which has to be approved by only a majority of those voting in the ratification process. This differs substantially from a consensus approach to governance that implies veto power by minorities on specific issues.

Faculty: Professional or Employees?

Collective bargaining is a process designed for resolving disputes between employer and employee through compromise. Economic issues involved were previously handled by salary and welfare committees established by faculty senates or similar faculty associations. These committees "negotiated" with the governing bodies or administration on a somewhat informal basis. Collective bargaining tends to emphasize a competitive employer and employee relationship. It also emphasizes the dual role of the faculty member who, although technically an employee, determines the nature of his work load and other responsibilities, his working hours, etc. The process can be instrumental in preventing an administrative unilateral imposition of demands.

On the other hand, there are possible benefits to the institution with which faculty may not be too happy. These would be in the form of productivity agreements which require that both sides make major concessions but which also hold promise of making the educational process more efficient. Such agreements have already appeared in industry. Garbarino described a possible academic equivalent that involves trading of a "multi-year wage and fringe package and more flexible calendar scheduling for an agreed-on definition of work load, flexibility in assignments, and more detailed conduct guidelines."

> Academic management initiative in designing proposals of this kind for faculty consideration would not only offer the possibility of making the educational process more efficient, but would hold out the possibility of influencing the pattern of organizational response of the faculty. The resort to formal adversary collective bargaining relationships and the inevitable organizational politics will have high personal costs to individual faculty members and will not be undertaken lightly. Whatever organizational form evolves, the prospects of preserving the tradition of shared authority and the working assumption that a community of interest exists will be enhanced if administration response to the present situation is more flexible, more positive, and not least, more realistic and practical.[21]

Monetary recognition for merit has become an accepted pattern in higher education. A distinct possibility exists that merit pay will be abolished in favor of a salary scale for which salaries will be negotiated by degree, rank, and the number of years of service. Since merit recognition is initiated at the departmental level, its abolishment will not only curtail departmental autonomy but remove the incentive for a faculty member to perform beyond the minimal expectations. Faculty members are accustomed to receiving selective rewards in recognition for professional productivity above and beyond the minimal level of effort. Collective bargaining could thus lead to a leveling in the character and quality of faculty performance as faculty assume more characteristics of employees and fewer characteristics of professionals.

As economic concessions are made, a larger number of noneconomic issues will be placed upon the bargaining table. The result will be increased formalization and structure with accompanying rules. Faculty will probably lose more and more of their "professional" autonomy as their status becomes more like that in any other employer—employee relationship.

STRIKES

A question related to professionalism is the use of the strike. How professional is it to strike? For what reasons are faculty willing to strike? What about faculty members who believe that a strike is unprofessional and should not be used?

Strikes do threaten cooperative decision making with its concept of a "community of scholars" and the ideal of service. They emphasize the self-interests of employees rather than professional commitment. Strikes violate the accepted academic processes of reason and argument. They negate the freedom for individualized judgment since they require political solidarity for effectiveness. Use of the strike as a power play must be avoided. The use of compromise supported by reason is far more desirable.

The after effects of strikes are sometimes more serious and long reaching than the effects from the strike itself. As a result, students and faculty find themselves in adversarial relationships because of a strike just as faculty and administrators do. This serves only to heighten conflict by establishing a second adversarial relationship beyond that between faculty and administrators.

The major reason for the existence of any college or university is to provide the best possible education for its students. This gives rise to several questions. Do students belong at the faculty–administration bargaining table as some students believe? What means can be found to prevent students from becoming a third adversarial party? What means exist for them to express their interests? Students represent the consumer. Little or no mention of their rights appears in faculty contracts. Alan Shark mentions three areas identified by concerned students in which negotiations can affect the student:

1. Increases in salaries and fringe benefits won by faculty unions will come out of the students' pockets in the form of higher tuition or fees. Resources may be curtailed, such as certain course offerings which can no longer be offered.
2. Faculty strikes will interrupt the students' education. The very threat of job actions or strikes can cause much anxiety among students who are planning to complete a specific course of study.
3. Faculty collective bargaining will diminish the expanded student role in campus decision making won during the turmoil of the 1960s.[22]

Where extended strikes have occurred, students have turned to the courts for assistance in having the strikes terminated. Students will be seeking ways to protect their own interests and it is anticipated that if they succeed, they could be observers, a third party at the bargaining table, or they may even become involved themselves in bargaining for a contract with the administration or faculty.

Effect Upon Governance Structures

It had been believed that the spread of collective bargaining would result in the demise of traditional governing bodies such as faculty senates. James Begin concluded from his study funded by the Carnegie Corporation that while changes in senate structure and changes in senate decision making have been taking place, there is no evidence to support any conclusion that collective bargaining has led thus far to a significant dismantling of the traditional institution-wide or system-wide governance procedures such as senates or faculty councils.[23]

Currently, there is no evidence that traditional procedures for faculty involvement in governance will, even in the future, give way totally to the bargaining process. It appears more likely that governance procedures may be recognized and protected by inclusion in the contract. If so, there will be two separate vehicles for faculty participation, one for those economic and personnel matters that are negotiable and the other for educational policy matters. In this way, the union and the faculty senate or another similar body are more likely to complement one another rather than overlap in their activities, or become competitive. Union intrusion into academic matters is undesirable. Instead, union activity should focus upon economic matters and working conditions. The following statement by Caesar Naples, a negotiator for the State University of New York system, reflects the opposite view.

> When the union feels that management is able to circumvent it by dealing with the senate over issues for which the union has firm faculty support, the union will be in a position to mount an effective bargaining table attack on collegial governance. Conversely, when management perceives the senate as a vehicle through which the union may achieve advances it was unable to achieve at the bargaining table, I believe the time for collegial governance will be past. In the meantime, however, both parties will have much to gain from the senates' continued existence.[24]

Only time will tell which situation will prevail.

Administrative Implications

Administrators involved in bargaining must be knowledgeable about which subjects are mandatory, permissible, or prohibited. They must also have the foresight to perceive the potential impact of the negotiated outcomes and compromises upon the institution as both sides work toward some mutual agreement. Just as faculty make demands of management, management has the same right to make demands of the faculty. As mentioned earlier, it is not out of the realm of possibility that some increase in teaching loads may be obtained in return for increased salaries and broader fringe benefits.

Whether they agree with it or not, administrators are often restricted in their actions by provisions in the contract. Negotiated grievance procedures emphasize the need for formalized policies, attention to procedural detail, and consistency by administrators in their treatment of individuals. Well-spelled-out contracts provide a vehicle for achieving the required consistency but, as a result, administrative decision making may become even more centralized as well as routine. Unfortunately, the situation may also lead to greater impersonality between faculty members and administrators. The able dean and chairperson will develop a thorough knowledge of all contract provisions, be most careful in all actions so as not to violate any of the provisions, interpret the provisions to subordinate administrators and faculty where needed, and, at the same time, develop and maintain an open free-flowing relationship with faculty.

Finally, it appears that administrators may have made accommodations resulting in increased faculty participation in institutional decision making. There have been some gains in institutions where faculty voted not to elect an agent or no election at all had been held. Whether this was the result of an attempt to reduce pressure by faculty for election of a bargaining agent or an indirect impact of collective bargaining activity in general is a matter for speculation. This reflection is based upon Adler's 1977 repetition of the American Association of University Professors 1970 survey of faculty participation in institutional decision making. Adler observed in a general comparison of the study groups and their response patterns, that, with few exceptions, no one group tended consistently to surpass the improved (1977) performance of the others. Instead, there appeared to be a "leveling" or "catch up" effect which brought the three groups into roughly equivalent, but higher, levels of governance participation in the period under study.[25]

SUMMARY

The changing circumstances in education have led to changing employer/employee relationships. A number of factors, external and internal, have provided impetus for these changes, which is particularly true of the collective bargaining movement. The collegial nature of "shared authority" as the rationale for faculty participation in college and university governance is being challenged by unionism.

When the decision to organize for bargaining has been made by faculty in an institution, several steps must be taken prior to actual involvement in the process. These include selection of the bargaining agent to represent the faculty, identification of the administrative "team," and determination of the group of employees to be represented by the bargaining unit.

Collective bargaining usually centers about the issue of wages, hours, and conditions of employment. The interpretation and scope of conditions of employment have not yet been stabilized. The problem is particularly complicated because of the unique nature of faculty responsibilities, some of which are nebulously defined. Some topics for bargaining are defined by law; others are permitted by law; and still others are considered nonnegotiable. Job security and retrenchment procedures are becoming increasingly important. A well-spelled-out grievance procedure is also a vital part of any contract.

Unionism with its accompanying collective bargaining activity does not automatically lead to adversarial relationships and strikes. It should be looked upon as a cooperative effort directed toward problem solving and constructive change. It is possible that the traditional governance structures will continue in existence as a vehicle for dealing with academic matters while union activity will focus upon economic matters and working conditions. Faculty and administrators should view the two structures as complementary and as instruments for strengthening the institution.

ENDNOTES

1. Used with permission. *Faculty Bargaining: Change and Conflict* by Joseph W. Garbarino in association with Bill Aussieker. Copyright © 1975 by The Carnegie Foundation for the Advancement of Teaching. (New York: McGraw-Hill, 1975), p. 23.
2. National Association of College and University Business Officers, *College and University Business Administration,* Third Edition (Washington, D.C., 1974), p. 81.
3. Robert L. Walter, *The Teacher and Collective Bargaining* (Lincoln, Neb.: Professional Educators Publications, 1975), p. 13.
4. William F. McHugh, "Collective Bargaining and the College Student," *Journal of Higher Education* 42 (1971): 176.
5. "Growth of Teacher Contracts: 1966–1973," *Negotiation Research Digest* 7 (Jan., 1974): 16. Cited in Ralph B. Kimbrough and Michael Y. Nunnery, *Educational Administration: An Introduction* (New York: Macmillan, 1976), p. 412.
6. William R. Hazard, "Courts in the Saddle: School Boards Out," *Phi Delta Kappan* 56 (1974): 260.
7. Kenneth P. Mortimer and Mark D. Johnson, "Faculty Collective Bargaining in Public Higher Education," *Educational Record* 57 (1976): 36.
8. Used with permission. Garbarino and Aussieker, *Faculty Bargaining: Change and Conflict,* p. 1.
9. Everett Carll Ladd, Jr. and Seymour Martin Lipset, "Faculty Support for Unionization: Leveling Off at About 75 Per Cent," *The Chronicle of Higher Education* 16 (February 13, 1978): 8.
10. Paul L. Dressel and William H. Faricy, *Return to Responsibility: Constraints on Autonomy in Higher Education* (San Francisco: Jossey-Bass, 1972), p. 126.
11. Used with permission. Garbarino and Aussieker, *Faculty Bargaining: Change and Conflict,* p. 24.
12. Ladd and Lipset, "Faculty Support for Unionization," p. 14.
13. *Ibid.*
14. Used with permission. Garbarino and Aussieker, *Faculty Bargaining: Change and Conflict,* p. 110.
15. George W. Angell, Edward P. Kelley, Jr., and Associates, *Handbook of Faculty Bargaining: Asserting Administrative Leadership for Institutional Progress by Preparing for Bargaining, Negotiating, and Administering Contracts, and Improving the Bargaining Process* (San Francisco: Jossey-Bass, 1977), pp. 136–137.
16. *Ibid.,* p. 134.
17. *Ibid.,* p. 134–135.
18. *Ibid.,* p. 135.
19. "Contract Ratified by SUNY Union," *Chronicle of Higher Education* 14 (March 21, 1977), p. 14.
20. Daniel R. McLaughlin, "Training Admin-

istrative Personnel for Collective Bargaining," in Angell, Kelley, and Associates, *Handbook of Faculty Bargaining,* pp. 115–125.

21. Joseph W. Garbarino, "Precarious Professors: New Patterns of Representation," *Industrial Relations* 10 (1971): 20.
22. Alan R. Shark, "The Educational Consumer and Academic Collective Bargaining," *Liberal Education* 61 (1975): 263.
23. James P. Begin, "Faculty Governance and Collective Bargaining: An Early Appraisal," *Journal of Higher Education* 45 (1974): 584.
24. Caesar Naples, "Collective Bargaining," in *Encountering the Unionized University,* edited by Jack H. Schuster (San Francisco: Jossey-Bass, 1974), p. 58.
25. Dan L. Adler, *Governance and Collective Bargaining in Four-Year Institutions 1970–1977,* Monograph No. 3 (Washington, D.C.: Academic Collective Bargaining Information Service, 1977), p. 17.

CHAPTER 7

Governance, Decision Making, and the Administrator

As discussed in Chapter 2, an institutional structure of some kind is needed to determine what shall be done, how it is to be accomplished, and when. Colleges and universities are free to establish an individual structure within the limitations defined by law. The resulting organization defines the roles for those involved in management and governance. Most important, it establishes a framework within which those in leadership roles may assist others in making decisions and accomplishing institutional objectives.

With the addition of bargaining units to faculty senates on some campuses, several basic questions have arisen regarding the establishment of college and university goals and the role of governance structures. Should there be dual organizations? If so, what is or what should be the relationship between two structures one of which is related to academic concerns and the other to bargaining? Are the basic concerns really different? Can their areas of activity be completely separated or does one overlap the other? Will the increasing activity of bargaining units put an end to traditional faculty governing processes?

There is no clear pattern that enables one to clearly define what the future will bring. If institutions of higher education are to continue being viable and effective, it will be necessary for each to develop an organization that will enable all constituencies to work together toward identifying problems, establishing priorities, developing solutions, and allocating effort and resources. Administrators, faculty senates and similar organizations, and unions must develop complementary relationships rather than adversarial.

RECENT DEVELOPMENTS IN GOVERNANCE

The growth in enrollments and institutional size in the 1960s led to more complicated university and college organizations. With this growth came an increasing number of problems requiring both administrative attention and the attention of faculty academic structures. Meanwhile, students clamored for "a piece of the action." While student involvement did develop full scale in some institutions, faculty became more and more involved in managerial matters and the development of institutional policies. The scene has been complicated by the advent of collective bargaining. While some see an adversarial relationship as inevitable, every effort is needed to utilize the process and its outcomes toward achieving the institution's major mission—the education of students.

PRESSURES AFFECTING INSTITUTIONAL GOVERNANCE

Universities and colleges are experiencing increasing intrusion upon their autonomy. This is particularly true of those classified as public or state related by virtue of varying levels of financial support from state funds. Private institutions are also affected but to a lesser extent. Challenges are coming from parents of students, citizens as a group, members of state legislatures, and various public officials. Judicial rulings are eroding the decision-making authority of campus officials. Multicampus systems and an increase in statewide coordination and planning by state level boards are exerting additional constraints. These same pressures have been discussed before but they are also critical in governance issues. The question has become one of how individual institutions can retain the power needed for effective governance rather than who has the power on campus: students, faculty, administrators, or trustees.

The problems of the 1960s with an unprecedented number of students enrolled in higher education institutions accompanied by the visible displays of student discontent attracted the attention of the mass media. This public attention has not diminished. If anything, it has increased, but with a different emphasis, an economic one.

Internally, the modern college and university is becoming increasingly fragmented by the independence of faculty and students. Institutional unity based on common ideals and values is most often nonexistent. Structures for grievance procedures for both faculty and students are developing. More and more procedural regulation is found leading to a need for more precise definition of jurisdictional authority. A means to define faculty rights and responsibilities as well as enforce professional ethics and deal with faculty irresponsibility is needed.

Faculty are pressing for involvement in institutional operation as the economic crunch increases. Decentralization due to size has tended to encourage this press for greater faculty authority. As a result, academic departments have emerged not only as administrative subunits but as basic units for faculty authority. The power of the senior professoriate is exerted at the departmental level through initiation and monitoring of academic policies, as well as involvement in personnel matters.

On the other hand, some of the authority previously held by senates is being revoked. As budgets are cut, advisory recommendations by faculty bodies that were formerly ratified routinely are now being reviewed and even reversed. Policies are being established without faculty consultation or sometimes unilaterally despite faculty objections. Some institutional governing boards are strengthening their control by becoming more involved in internal governance matters and through their use of veto power.

Previously, administrative influence over academic affairs was of a most general nature resulting from financial control. Now, "pressures for more aggressive and more comprehensive management" are appearing. This is in contrast to what had been an accepted state of affairs where management involving actions related to administrative direction and control of business and external affairs taken primarily at the initiative of the administrators and governance, defined as the structure and processes of decision making primarily but not exclusively concerned with academic matters, were able to coexist.[1]

Another change has been the addition of nonprofessional personnel to governance structures previously the exclusive province of professors. Librarians, administrative staff employees, professional research assistants, other types of academic support staff, and students are often included. The variety and multiplicity of concerns representative of such a varied group might lead to the necessity for some separate faculty mechanism for the handling of purely academic matters.

Elizabeth Sutherland conducted a survey of the attitudes and opinions of staff personnel (nonfaculty) on the Bloomington campus of Indiana University regarding the possibility of their participation in the governance of the university. She arrived at a number of conclusions among which were:

1. Staff members are interested in participating in University governance. However, at the time that their interest was revealed an accompanying unexpectedly large amount of lack of opinion or concern was also recorded.
2. Staff want to be represented by other staff members in University governance. They do not want to be represented by faculty members.
3. Sex (men more than women), university-relatedness, and higher levels of formal education are significant in relation to willingness to serve as representatives in University governance structures.
4. Staff members are concerned about university goals and purposes and are strongly aware of a lack of communication on these and other matters.[2]

While the study was limited to a single campus, there are some interesting implications for others. Based upon her conclusions, Sutherland made a pertinent recommendation supporting the inclusion of nonfaculty staff members in the governance structure in some way. In light of her second conclusion, the faculty organization may not be the most desirable vehicle, but strong leaders among the staff personnel should be identified and prepared for their eventual acceptance as voting members in university governance. Strong leadership in all segments has the potential to bring higher education back into public favor and support and to unite, in understanding and common goals, all the constituencies of the unit.[3]

Administrative and Faculty Relationships

Because so much depends upon the relationships between faculty and administrators, clarification of the roles of each is essential. A weakened administrative staff can lead only to inefficient management. Administrative control to some extent is essential. Dressel and Faricy emphasize that administrators must have the authority to enforce policy and cannot afford to have their effectiveness diluted by a faculty sharing of their powers. Policy controls are essential for fundamentally efficient and effective university operation. If the governance structure cannot provide management controls or if the faculty will neither impose nor permit such controls to be imposed by boards and administrators, faculty members may expect increasing external control.[4]

Faculty values and viewpoints do not always agree with those of members of the administrative structure but faculty and administrators cannot operate in isolation. In fact, faculty tend to believe that administrators possess more power and authority than they actually do. It is necessary to recognize that the roles of each at any point in time will depend upon the particular issue involved. Policy decisions by faculty are possible only when authority has been delegated by the appropriate administrators empowered to do so by the institution's governing board. Unfortunately, problems sometimes develop because faculty are traditionally academically oriented and when action is needed they tend to talk instead. Combining this tendency with the complexity of interlocking committees involving faculty, students, deans, department chairpersons, and central administrators, the result is sometimes too much discussion and not enough action.

Administration in higher education has generally reflected a dual nature with an administrative hierarchy accompanied by a faculty structure for educational matters. Faculty should be involved in definition of the aims and purposes of the institution and in control of academic matters (subject, of course, to the ultimate approval of the governing board) while administrators are responsible for the management aspects of the complex operations our institutions have become. To illustrate, the need for expertise was recognized early in the 1970s by faculty included in a study by Gross and Grambsch. They found that faculty members who had been forced into unfamiliar roles through increased involvement in administration and policy making found the tasks time consuming and highly complex, demanding an expertise of their own.[5]

Faculty need not be involved in purely administrative tasks nor should committees. Administration itself should be left to administrators and the governance involvement of faculty and administrators should be complementary.

FACULTY AND GOVERNANCE

Faculty may express several reasons for desiring participation in institutional governance. Some are committed to change. They have ideas about how things should be and are willing to help carry the burden in accomplishing them. Unfortunately, other faculty tend to think the institution exists for them and are too shortsighted to see that their interests and those of the institution are compatible. Philosophically, many faculty perceive participation in institutional decision making to be a right and a duty in addition to being a means for upholding academic objectives and preserving professional autonomy. Faculty effectiveness may be reduced if there is any substantial number who are indifferent and unwilling to devote the time and effort needed for effective collegial decision making.

Policy and Program Decisions

Faculty involvement in decision making has traditionally been in the academic area with primary responsibility (and even autonomy) with respect to curriculum, degree requirements and how they may be met, research efforts, and policies related to the educational aspects of student life. Physical plant and detailed financial matters have not generated great faculty interest in the past. Policy and program decisions do have financial impact so that in a period of economic belt-tightening, faculty will also want to be involved in financial policy decisions. With the advent of collective bargaining, the trend has been toward an increased faculty role in financial decision making.

Faculty sometimes find it difficult to achieve a high level of agreement in opinion, so that discussions become dominated by power blocs and strong personalities. The process or structure and participation in the process may become more important than the outcome. In other words, exercising the right to participate in making a decision becomes more important than the decision itself. Faculty authority could be taken back by the source of its original delegation which may be the trustees and/or the president. A major question is whether university-wide, college, or departmental faculties should be given final authority in educational policy decisions or whether their role should be advisory to presidents, deans, and chairpersons. Many faculty did and still do see administrators playing the role of clerks who administer only what the faculty dictates. Another basic issue involved is the extent of faculty participation in policy making and implementation.

It is possible that as faculty increasingly clamor for more authority and reject administrative ideas, a major source of innovation and organizational improvement will be destroyed. Contributing to this possibility is the lack of information evident among faculty. Many know only what goes on in their institutions or previous experiences they had at others and nothing of research being done and current related literature. So much is happening that it is difficult to keep abreast of matters in one's own department and college much less at the university level and on the national scene.

Advantages and Disadvantages of Faculty Participation

An advantage of faculty involvement in college and university affairs is that it provides a source for a wide variety of ideas and alternatives. It is commonly believed that participation will strengthen the feeling of allegiance toward the institution. A third advantage is the previously mentioned concept of democratic administration holding that involvement in making a decision will lead to greater willingness on the part of faculty to have the decision implemented and abide by it.

As for disadvantages, Corson raised a number of questions some years ago that are still pertinent today.

> Against the advantages of involving faculty members in collaborative effort—and it is clear that the process of consultation strengthens their allegiance to the institution and their individual zeal and satisfaction—stand some reservations. Do faculties have time for participation in decision making on issues of physical development and finance? Do faculty members have a sufficiently broad understanding of the total operation to participate intelligently in making such decisions? How and to what degree can such views and time as they have be incorporated in the decision-making process? These and similar questions which relate to the increasing size and complexity of modern higher education institutions need to be given careful consideration.[6]

As the processes become more complex, the time and energy required for effective participation can be enormous. Many faculty are not willing to spend the time, nor do they wish to give the right to others. The individualized schedules of faculty members pose difficulties when establishing times for meetings. Sometimes the ones who become involved in the processes are those who are available, but are not necessarily the best qualified.

Finally, academicians are known for embarking upon lengthy oral dissertations on minuscule matters. Faculty haggle over trivial details while the larger issues remain unresolved. As a result, other faculty are reluctant to participate in decision-making processes because they view it as a waste of their valuable time.

Implementation

The ultimate authority for implementation of a decision must rest at some administrative level. Within a college structure, this would most likely be a chairperson or dean. The administrator is generally more organization oriented and may find it necessary to delay implementing a faculty decision or to return the matter to the group as unacceptable or impractical to implement. The latter action must be accompanied by reasons for the administrative decision, which is certainly preferable to no communication of the negative reaction. Faculty with any astuteness at all will consider the administrative implications of their decisions so as to enhance the possibilities for implementation. An unrealistic view is that expressed by a faculty member who made a statement to the effect that, "It is our job to decide what should be done; it is the administration's job to find out how to do it." In this case, the faculty decision involved a change in the undergraduate grading system requiring a revamping of the computerized transcript system. The problem was complicated by the fact that no change was being made in the graduate grading system.

While faculty may control curriculum, a decision that would require expenditure of funds where none are available may require a negative action on the part of a chairperson or dean. A strong, able administrator who has demonstrated responsible leadership would alert the faculty to the financial difficulty making implementation unfeasible. If the warning is disregarded, the same administrator must be able to make a negative decision while retaining the respect of the faculty. Strong leadership is needed if the collective efforts of faculty and administrators are to be effective in defining and attaining institutional goals.

THE STUDENT ROLE IN GOVERNANCE

The concept of collegiality implies an equal voice in governance for students as well as faculty and administrators. It is obvious that as a result of student activity in the 1960s, changes have taken place in student-college and student-university relationships. While students are represented on many governing bodies, there is variation in the extent and character of their influence and participation. Basically, students have three areas of concern which involve: campus behavior and the accompanying regulatory procedures, student residential life related to housing and the use of campus facilities, and involvement in the instructional process.

Events Leading to Increased Participation

During the 1960s, students were vocal in their demands for representation in decision making and, in many instances, demanded it on a 50–50 basis. They expressed their grievances and concerns about programs, regulations affecting them, and administrative managerial decisions. The protest movement also reflected their reactions to the social and political climate of the time with the expectation that colleges and universities would respond along lines similar to student ideas and demands. Their demands for participation in decision making were based upon the same supposition as that of faculty—all those affected by a policy should participate in the formulation of that policy.

Despite the extremely vocal and sometimes violent demonstrations by students, their participation and influence in governance structures is still limited and may decrease even more as collective bargaining plays a more extensive part in campus decisions. While faculty have the power to share some aspects of decision making with students, they have been and will continue to be reluctant to do so.

Possible Student Roles

It has been found that when colleges have involved students, their contributions can be responsible and worthwhile if they are provided with full and necessary information. It is more feasible for students to play an active role at the department level because they are closer to the institutional structure at this level, will have similar concerns, and are fewer in number. It is appropriate for them to be involved at this point since the department is the most active working level in the area of instructional concerns. The student role should be one of active involvement in the regular policy making structure and not as members of a separate student structure.

No real answer has yet been found to the representation question. Contrived opportunities for student participation tend to "turn students off" and do not really make possible a true reflection of student opinion. The representatives may be the most vocal students, but are not always the best informed, nor do they always accurately reflect the opinions and concerns of the total student body.

Earl McGrath emphasizes the problem of student representation when he writes:

> There is then no single conclusive response to the question, "What proportion of the members of academic bodies should be students?" The only practically useful answer now seems to be that the membership should include students and non-students, the numbers of each varying with the types of issues which come before a particular committee and with the special knowledge and expertise required for their solution. It does seem reasonable, however, that the very decision with respect to proportionate membership itself should be reached through joint consideration by representatives of the constituent groups.[7]

Ideally, some way should be found to include students interested in playing an active role in the policy formulation process and, at the same time, making it possible for the student body whom they represent to monitor their activity and provide the necessary information reflecting student opinion as a whole. Although faculty and students may disagree upon academic policy, curricular matters, evaluation standards, and personnel decisions, student opinion must be gathered through some regularized procedures. Where students have participated in committee activity, it has been a "token" representation. Even where they have voting privileges, their voice has been so limited by minimal representation that, to all effects, their participation is still token. It is far better to gather information from many students which is given serious and thoughtful consideration by faculty members in their deliberation than to provide for token representation with voting privileges.

Some appropriate areas for student participation include: curriculum planning and evaluation; course and teacher evaluation; academic policies such as attendance requirements, grading systems, examination methods, and degree requirements; new student orientation; and planning for special events. The functions of a student steering committee as instituted in the Department of Health and Physical Education at Trenton State College in New Jersey are an excellent example of the possible breadth of the student role.

1. To be a communications channel between faculty and students.
2. To serve as a catalyst for student ideas and recommendations.
3. To work in close cooperation with the faculty of the Health and Physical Education Department during periods of campus crisis.
4. To appoint students to department committees.
5. To initiate opportunities for professional growth through workshops, part-time employment, conferences, and conventions.
6. To assist in department freshman and transfer student orientations.
7. To provide opportunities for faculty-student social interaction.[8]

The student steering committee meets twice a month with the department chairperson and twice a semester in a joint meeting with the faculty steering committee. The students have also sponsored workshops, served as a sounding board for curricular proposals, assisted in developing a faculty evaluation instrument, established a student grievance procedure, been active in preparing a five year plan, provided input for personnel decisions, and participated in public relations activities.

It is more important to obtain the best judgment possible that is representative of student thinking than to be concerned over the concept of majority decision. It has become a fact of life that students are represented on commissions, task forces, and committees covering a variety of areas, but one word of caution is needed. Students are learners not administrators and because of their transient status do not have the right to alter the institution.

Faculty are divided over the role students should play. Some see them as a threat to their security and do not want their own influence weakened. However, unless students have an opportunity to be active in their own self-interests, it is not unlikely that faculty interests will take precedence over student interests.

Advantages and Disadvantages

Students are the consumers in education and, as such, should have some basis for evaluating the objectives for a program, the program itself, and the classroom methods for achieving the program objectives. While student participation may serve to enhance program evaluation efforts, it may also serve to provide students with an understanding of the objectives behind the program and particular instructional methods. Their participation can provide a new dimension as they contribute information about their needs and opinions about the good and bad features of the total education process.

Faculty and students tend to change their opinions of one another after working together. More often than not, they develop a mutual respect, tolerance, and understanding of each other as individuals and of their expressed views as the channels of communication between students and other institutional bodies are opened. Their joint efforts enable them to understand one another better.

Participation in the governance process provides students with learning experiences that are unavailable in a classroom. It provides training in group processes leading to the development of leadership skills and participation in democratic methods. Learning by doing replaces theoretical learning. Finally, the process should produce graduates who have learned about the policy-making process and how to participate in the process effectively in addition to learning how change in bureaucratic organizations (which most higher education institutions are) may be brought about.

Just as there are advantages to the student and the institution, there are disadvantages to both. It may be found that students

1. often are more concerned with their immediate short-range interests rather than the long-range objectives of the programs and the institution
2. want fast action and quick responses since their time perspective is different from that of faculty and administrators
3. are not as informed as they might be or should be for effective participation, which increases the time needed for deliberation
4. because of their transient status, lack training and experience due to rapid turnover in committee membership
5. must spend hours in preparation for their duties, which may detract from their studies and employment
6. suffer from the same time constraints and often, even more so, as faculty leading to irregular attendance patterns
7. if politicized, may use their participation for further developing adversarial relationships and increasing the incidence of conflict situations within the deliberating body
8. are not as unanimous in their thinking as often assumed.
9. do not have an adequate mechanism for discussing proposals with other students
10. who are most articulate and volatile may not necessarily be the leaders of student opinion and thus may not represent the

best interests of the majority of the student body

Student input is needed if higher education is to advance as well as portray the concept of an academic community. Their interests and efforts can be particularly effective at the department and division levels where the constituency is likely to be more homogeneous. Different modes of participation, accompanied by varying representation patterns and relationships between students, faculty, and administrators should be utilized according to circumstances at the time. It is in this way only that the advantages, and there are advantages, of student participation in decision making may be accrued.

DECISION MAKING

Who should share in what decisions has become a question of increasing importance. Occasionally, this question appears to become more important than the decision itself. No one can deny that ways are needed to enlist and coordinate the enthusiasm, energies, and expertise of as many individuals as feasible to produce the best possible decisions. How decisions are made as well as by whom provides the framework for administrative and governance structures.

Decision making requires negotiation and compromise, which some individuals are unwilling to accept. Those with strong personalities requiring ego satisfaction find it even more difficult to accept current processes because of the submersion of the individual. The good administrator is a good persuader. If he or she exercises leadership appropriately, others will cooperate and abide by the decisions more often than not. A high level of morale and productivity should result. Decisions and the process by which they are accomplished must be made on the highest level of integrity and preserve cohesion.

The Process

The process of decision making is related to the governance and administrative structures. Wide variation is found in the ways in which faculty are involved, as well as the range and kinds of matters in which faculty are involved. The more people involved in decision making, the more complex and slower the process becomes so that the end product is quite often delayed extensively. Institutional size has an additional impact upon the process by making it more difficult to achieve a collaborative effort leading to consensus.

Where feasible, those who will be affected by a decision should be consulted as well as informed about what is going on. (Remember, however, that not everyone is an expert about everything.) Those consulted should be helped to understand the way in which their ideas, advice, or recommendations will be utilized as well as the limitations upon their own roles in the process. People who participate in making a decision that affects them are more apt to be committed to abiding by or executing the decision than if the decision were mandated. People believe their opinions are important. Many decisions that must be made are related to people. Therefore, it seems logical that people should be involved in these decisions.

At all times, institutional purposes and goals must be kept in mind so that decisions are related to an underlying philosophy. Those administrators, faculty, and students involved in the decision-making process must understand and accept these goals if there is to be full commitment to the task at hand.

Every one participating in the process must have the same basic information. Timely and adequate data are needed. The administrator, whether a dean, chairperson, or other, may initially specify the kind of data needed and how it should be summarized. If those involved in the process believe additional information is essential, that too should be provided by the administrator. Efforts should be made to keep the data from being too voluminous and unmanageable so that anything not needed for the immediate decision is eliminated. In this day of the computer, it does not take long to literally "drown in paper."

Once the problem or issue at hand has been clearly delineated and sufficient appropriate data available, the next step is the generation of alternatives. At this stage, the tendency of academics to talk and rationalize instead of acting might hinder the process. When it appears that everything has been said that needs to be said, the committee chairperson might speed the process by requesting that a small subcommittee come to the next meeting with a rough draft of one or more proposals for solving the problem, establishing a policy, or whatever is needed to meet the mission of the committee. The process may be slow and effort may be needed to keep it orderly. It is at this point that a few gentle procedural suggestions by an administrator might be helpful.

Finally, some mechanism is needed to obtain feedback at appropriate points. Feedback from administrators, faculty, or students not actively involved in the process can be helpful in making the final decision.

It is common knowledge that the decision-making process in many colleges and universities needs improvement. Each must determine its own, within the general framework just described, based upon local structure, needs, and specific circumstances at the time. Finally, faculty and administrative time and effort are expensive. The process must be as expeditious as possible to avoid a situation where it costs $1200 to decide upon the color of a set of brochures. Ultimate approval of the committee recommendation by the administrator whose area of responsibility is involved is needed. Follow-up feedback and revision, if necessary, make the process a circular, continuous one.

Duality of the Process

While much of the decision making in colleges and universities has been dispersed, there is a pattern of areas in which faculty contributions are more extensive. These include curriculum, admission and degree requirements, academic standards, and, to some extent, personnel matters.

Where there are financial implications, institutional administrators, and possibly the governing board, reserve authority for the final decision. For example, implementation of a faculty-approved change in the grading system is delayed or not accomplished at all because the administrative decision-making body has determined that it is not financially possible to do so within available resources.

It is apparent that on one hand, there is a structure involving department and division chairpersons, deans, vice presidents, the president, and the governing board with its final authority. At the same time, there exists an organization involving faculty bodies ranging from department committees to institution-wide committees, faculty senates, faculty senate committees, etc. that focus on academic matters. If these two are to be productive and the institution is to thrive, their responsibilities must be clearly delineated.

Role of Deans and Chairpersons

The role of the dean in the overall process of decision making requires two-way communication and consultation as well as constant follow-up on what has been accomplished and what is in process. The role of the dean in decision making is enhanced by responsibility for the financial resources allocated to the college. The deanship may be looked upon as senior or middle level management depending upon the importance of the decisions for which he or she is responsible, the amount of autonomy vested in the position, and the authority and influence exerted. As central controls increase and the dean becomes responsible for implementation of higher level decisions, planning and determination of strategies must take place as well as decision making.

At the same time, departments traditionally enjoy a certain level of administrative autonomy. A basic reason is the high degree of specialization in an academic discipline possessed by the chairperson and faculty. The initiation of education policy and making personnel decisions at that level thus becomes appropriate. An examination of the roles played by chairpersons will show a wide range of patterns of decision making. Chairpersons may be autocratic, encourage wide participation in decision making, or exert little or no administrative leadership. The chairperson's role can be an influential one and when chairpersons possess a great deal of power and status, the dean's may be diminished proportionately.

Division and department heads and deans should demonstrate leadership in appropriate ways throughout the process. Their own decisions should be in light of what is best for the college or institution as a whole. Administration is not a popularity contest. The long-range goals of the institution must take precedence over the short-range interests of various subgroups. Final decisions are generally not made by committees, but by the responsible person nearest the situation. If the administrative responsibility is carried out correctly, it is inevitable that some criticism will occur from time to time. Administrative powers of persuasion become most important when unpopular decisions are deemed necessary. Personal style becomes important if the individual is to hold the trust and confidence of faculty, students, and other administrators.

Leadership, Governance, and Management

Because of the numerous formal and informal pressures upon educational institutions, leadership is essential for reconciling differences and acquiring support for the mission, programs, and procedures for the particular institution. Distinctions between leadership, governance, and management are sharply emphasized by Millett who sees leadership as being concerned with decisions about both purpose and performance, whereas the major concern of governance is purpose, and that of management is the performance of services. He goes on to define leadership more explicitly as

> . . . the process of encouraging and persuading those involved in governance to decide and those involved in management to perform. Ideally, leadership seeks objectives that embody purpose and seeks effective performance to achieve these objectives. Thus academic leadership seeks positive, definite, desirable, and timely decisions in the best interest of those who are served by higher education as well as of those who serve.[9]

The true leader is both responsible and accountable for his actions. The concepts of responsibility and accountability require not only providing leadership in direction but also motivating individuals to cooperate, support, and generally work together toward common goals. Formal authority is not enough. Knowledge and wisdom must back up efforts to create decision-making mechanisms and situations that will inspire mutual respect and trust. Situations of financial stringency tend to require an even more forceful role in initiating and guiding change. There is no universal all-purpose leadership style that will fit all situations, or even a single situation at all times. The age, experience, stage of growth, organizational structure and relations, organization climate, and organization culture all comprise the context in which action must take place. To achieve results, a leader must study the context or frame of reference within which an action is to take place, which becomes the basis for a choice of leadership style from a range of available behaviors and skills in their application.[10]

When a decision is under discussion, the administrator must carefully select the most appropriate behavior. If too forward in espousing a particular resolution, the administrator becomes open to criticism for trying to influence the committee and control the decision. If an administrator is "wishy-washy" or takes no stand, the accusation may be one of lack of leadership. At times, a stand must be taken if the decision begins to go in a direction that may be irreversible or unfeasible. An effective administrator must exert sufficient control so that the decisions made and the changes implemented are beneficial and warranted in terms of the institution's viability and success.

Succinctly summarized, "Leadership is an organized arrangement for linking governance and management—for linking decision making and work performance." [11]

Emergency Decision Making

Group processes for decision making will work well for many situations, but there are occasions when time does not permit implementation of the process. Some problems may need immediate resolution so that the group process may not be a viable mechanism. Guidelines are needed along with procedures for handling emergency situations. Appropriate individuals should be identified and assigned the authority for particular kinds of action. In other instances, time might make it feasible to consult with a small group of faculty members. A policy undergirded by appropriate procedural guidelines will assist in avoiding possible chaos in the event of the need for a vital decision in an emergency.

GOVERNANCE STRUCTURES

The administrative organization and governance structure of a college or university should be determined by its goals and purposes. Those involved in governance must see themselves as responsible for their own behavior as well as responsible to the institution, instead of acting to protect special interests. Relationships between individuals and groups must be trusting, open and honest, and reflect respect for one another's opinions.

The degree to which faculty enjoy freedom of speech as individuals and as a group will not be found in any other organization nor will the responsibility placed upon faculty in many higher education governance structures be as great. The major portion of this responsibility, as already mentioned, is in the academic areas. Traditional faculty organizations have served as vehicles for carrying out the responsibilities and, to some extent, continue to do so particularly where collective bargaining has not been introduced. Where collective bargaining and unions exist, governance mechanisms are being restructured to accommodate the new influence.

Definition and Functions of Governance

Governance might be described as the process by which trustees, administrators, faculty, certain other staff, and students make decisions and monitor their implementation. Millett includes the concept of power in his description of the process.

> Governance is the process of decision making by which basic policies are determined concerning objectives, programs, benefits, standards, and resources. Governance is a procedure for relating power to purpose, and for exercising power responsibility. It should seek the general welfare through expression of the general will.[12]

Governance provides a means for faculty to participate with their colleagues in making academic policy decisions and providing professional direction for themselves. In its larger sense, the term may be used to include the total structure through which the various constituencies of the institution collaborate in the development and refinement of specific policies and programs that enable the institution to move closer to achievement of its goals.

The legitimacy of governance structures as perceived by faculty and administrators has much to do with their effectiveness. David Leslie's investigation of the parameters of faculty perceptions of the legitimacy of governance led to a conclusion that perceived legitimacy may vary from one institution to another or with the issue in question. His study was based on a sample of fifty full-time faculty selected randomly from three community colleges, three state-owned "state" colleges, and three state-related universities all located in Pennsylvania. He found that formal authority may be conferred upon the body by the governing board or the board's designated administrator or the faculty may assume authority based on its self-perceived expertise in the area under scrutiny. A related conclusion supports the notion that faculty expertise in academic matters legitimizes their decision-making role in academic matters. Leslie found that although the issue's effects differed from type to type, and within some types from institution to institution, it appeared that faculty tended to perceive the governance processes in which they expected to have relatively greater influence as being more legitimate. An example cited was governance related to the introduction of new courses.[13]

Shared Authority

The term "shared authority" describes a middle ground between administrative dominance and faculty dominance. Faculty and students see it as a means for increased involvement in campus governance while administrators might view it as an attempt to usurp some of their authority. Shared authority may mean shared participation in decision making on one hand and, on the other, an agreement that different parties will make decisions alone. The latter may be illustrated by the common practice of delegating academic decisions to faculty and financial decisions to administrators. The dichotomy may not always be possible because academic decisions do sometimes have financial implications.

The concept of shared authority should ideally negate an adversarial role for all those involved. Tolerance and mutual respect are essential, along with a shared sense of responsibility for the ultimate outcome. The major characteristics of the concept of shared authority may be summarized as follows:

1. Campus structure should reflect a genuine desire to share power among the various constituencies.
2. The structure must provide each constituency with the opportunity to pursue its legitimate interests within a cooperative framework while at the same time minimizing the possibility that the special interests of a specific group will exercise a controlling influence within the decision-making process.
3. Each constituency must have the opportunity of influencing action at each level where decisions are made affecting their interests.
4. Constituents of a multi-institutional system must be provided with appropriate procedures to influence decisions at the system level as well as in their local unit.

5. Procedures must exist to resolve differences of opinion among constituencies without creating the necessity for coercion or conflict.
6. The structure of governance must be flexible in order to accommodate rapidly changing conditions.[14]

Kinds of Models

Because institutions vary, numerous patterns for governance structures will be found. A particular university, college, or even a department will need to experiment with different ones to determine which best enables the organizational unit to function at the optimum level. The groups involved in college governance include trustees, administrators, faculty, and students. While each of the groups has its own structure, all are interrelated and some means is needed to enable them to function within this relationship.

Lines of responsibility and authority must be clarified so that all may see where answers can be obtained as well as the policies to be followed. The kinds of decisions to be made along with the responsibility of each unit in the organization must be specified. The structure must make it possible for decision-making processes to be explicit and visible, as well as providing means for expression of opinion.

Increasing size leads to increasing complexity and formality. If, at the same time, there is too strong a centralization of authority, decision making can be delayed and will often be less responsive to specific problems. On the other hand, direct democracy with all individuals involved in the process is neither feasible nor desirable, in most instances, because of its cumbersome nature. As a result, a shift to some form of representative government is taking place. If this is not done to expedite the decision-making process, administrators may have to assume additional executive power to enable the institution to function efficiently with speedy decisions and continuity in the handling of critical problems.

As one views the events of past years, three governance models emerge: bureaucratic, collegial, and political. The bureaucratic model with its pyramid structure is most applicable to the administrative structure of institutions. There is a delegation of authority and responsibility down the line to various levels of administrators, each of whom is responsible to his or her immediate supervisor. While this model may be looked upon as authoritarian in character, it is also likely to be the most efficient. Because it is not geared to individual needs, it can lead to frustration and conflict, a frustration often voiced by faculty and students in institutions with strong bureaucratic structures and the accompanying emphasis on predetermined procedures, rules, and regulations.

Dressel and Faricy define the bureaucratic style

> . . . as an impersonal pattern with (1) a well-defined chain of command, rules, practices, or procedures covering practically all contingencies that may occur; (2) an assignment or assumption of tasks based upon special competencies; (3) promotion and selection based upon these technical competencies; and, as a result of all of these characteristics; (4) a strong tendency toward impersonality in human relations.[15]

Although the bureaucratic approach most nearly describes the way in which the administrative organization of an institution actually functions, the same writers do not view the university as a true bureaucracy. They believe that the second and third conditions are not completely satisfied in addition to which there is "concern for democracy, cooperation and humanistic values rather than a mechanistic, coercive approach." [16]

A second model is that identified as collegial and is based on the concept of a community of scholars managing its own affairs. The faculty see their right to govern as coming from professional and technical competence and expertise rather than some formal or official authority. It is based on a human relations approach to organization that views conflict as abnormal and is not suited to the resolution of serious conflict. In addition, the model tends to ignore efficiency.

Another collegial model is Henderson and Henderson's participative plan based on a strong tradition of collegiality. It is established on the role of the professor in research and instruction, and the student as a learner, and the belief that both will do a better job if they participate in determining goals, methods, and evaluation procedures. Students are directly involved. Henderson and Henderson believe the group participation plan best accounts for individual and group needs and describe it as

> an orderly pattern for the involvement of people in relation to their interests and their abilities to contribute, with all efforts coordinated by the administration and the final power appropriately vested in the governing board.

They point out that the current trend is toward more complete utilization of business philosophy and methodology and express a strong concern that this will produce inferior education.[17] The group participative approach should counteract this trend.

While the collegial model is opposed to hierarchy and structure, neither is really exclusively practical. The collegial model is just as idealistic as a total bureaucracy is impractical. Some formal structure or some form of hierarchical management structure with official authority for decision making is needed if an institution is to function properly.

A third model is the political that views competition and conflict as normal and the institution as a political system. It takes into account interest groups and power blocs and views decision making as negotiation and political. While a bureaucratic organization emphasizes execution of goal setting and policy, the collegial and political models tend to emphasize their formulation and not deal with the management process in any way. The advent and fast rise of collective bargaining which is based on the political model is lending support to the model.

No one model can be designated as the best for all institutions or for all situations. A variety of models and variations of the three basic ones just described may be effective and uesful just as elements of each may be compatible and serve to complement one another. It is apparent that much still needs to be accomplished in the development of organizational and management theories for higher education.

Due to changing circumstances, governance systems must be revised from time to time as they outlive their effectiveness. Whatever form a structure takes, it must provide for consultation and even negotiation to make possible peaceful resolutions to any conflicts that may arise.

Faculty Senates, Unionization, and Collective Bargaining

A traditional governance mechanism has been the faculty senate supported by the institutional budget. This particular governance structure was originally conceived as a kind of town meeting body to which all faculty members automatically belonged. The authority or legal powers of a senate are usually delegated to it by the administration and governing board and are spelled out in its constitution and the faculty handbook. While the body is often an advisory one for academic matters, its recommendations have frequently been routinely ratified although the extent of its influence will vary greatly among institutions. It may possess some delegated decision-making power in the academic area in which the final decision is achieved through faculty vote since the faculty senate does provide an arena for debate through which faculty may come to some agreement. Where there is a university senate, there are usually comparable bodies at the college level with some sort of organization at the division and department levels also. Whichever level, it is inappropriate for any administrator to chair such groups but exofficio membership is often desirable.

As many institutions grew in size, the all-faculty senate was no longer feasible. Another difficulty arose because faculty became lax about their participation in such bodies. Instead, some took advantage of the many opportunities available outside of the institution and spent their time on financially rewarding consulting activities which were plentiful during the 1960s. These two factors led to a representative type of faculty senate in place of the all-inclusive. In addition, the recommendations of the senate are no longer routinely implemented in many institutions. They are subject to the scrutiny of an administrator or administrative body who analyze the implications of adoption before finally approving them.

Unions represent the most formal and structured approach to faculty participation in governance. Their appearance on the scene is a response to faculty concern over economic issues. In two-year colleges, the faculty senate or faculty association often serves as bargaining agent and negotiates contracts. Four-year institutions usually have two separate bodies, one for academic issues and the other for economic ones.

Where there may have been little faculty participation in institutional decision making, the introduction of collective bargaining appears to have increased the level of participation. It is possible, too, that a faculty senate may achieve its legal status or derive its power through a collective bargaining agreement which spells out its role in clearly defined terms. Under these circumstances, the identities of both bodies and their specific functions must be kept separate. In other instances, a contract may shift so much responsibility to the bargaining unit that the senate becomes totally ineffective as a governance instrument. In the long run, faculty might find that collective bargaining will decrease their involvement in governance decisions because of the adversarial relationships it may create between faculty and administration.

Garbarino and Aussieker describe three possible relationships between unions and senates. The first of these is a cooperative model or one of coexistence. This model is the most common. Both maintain their own identities and each concentrates on its own area of activity. Another, the competitive model, pits one organization against the other in trying to gain control of the decision-making process and for the right to choose the objectives of the group, to pursue their achievement, and to gain credit for the result. The third model is the cooptative model described as bargained collegiality or collegiality by contract. In the purest form of the model, the senate, as a formal organization with separate facilities and its own officers, might not even exist on a unionized campus. Conversely, on a campus where a union is not a formally recognized exclusive bargaining agent, the senate may dominate administrator-faculty-union relationships, including the determination of bargaining policy.[18]

In the cooptative model, it is possible for a union, as the recognized bargaining agent, to assume some of the areas of concern previously the responsibility of the senate. The result could be either elimination of the senate as a governance body or removal of its power to the point of ineffectiveness.

The desirable approach is a cooperative one

in which the union and the senate work together in an informal relationship, instead of either a competitive one or a situation where the union becomes the dominant participant in governance. The senate and, where applicable, its corresponding bodies within the units of a university must be aware of the issues that are bargainable and omit them from the agenda for senate consideration.

College and university administrators would do well to heed the words of John Millett:

> Some faculty members and representatives want to combine collective bargaining with participatory governance and shared management. Institutional management will probably be recreant in its trust if it accepts this position. Collective bargaining embodies an obligation to achieve an agreement on compensation and working conditions within the framework of the purposes and intended work outputs of the enterprise. In collective bargaining agreements in business, management retains its basic authority and responsibility to plan and direct the enterprise. In collective bargaining agreements in a university, dual management authority and responsibility in an adversary relationship may well be impossible and undesirable.
>
> When university management perceives the changed role forced upon it by faculty collective bargaining, then university management may indeed come to resemble more fully the authority and responsibility of business management.[19]

COMMUNICATION

A major problem in college and university governance structures is communication. Too often, faculty spend enormous amounts of time in expressing their views loudly and rhetorically. Hour upon hour is spent in academic debate, but the accomplishments are minimal compared to the time and effort spent. Opportunity for individual faculty members to communicate their views is needed, but care should be exercised to avoid a situation where a few more vociferous individuals see it as an opportunity for "public display of oratorical proficiency."

There must also be an atmosphere of openness making it possible for every member to be aware of what is happening, so as to avoid feelings of alienation. For this reason, communication must be horizontal as well as vertical. Most important of all, those involved in the decision-making process must possess adequate information to guide them in their deliberations. A weakness in the process has been that the increased participation by faculty in establishing educational policy has not been accompanied by a corresponding increase in their information about higher education. James Soles recommends twelve specific ways for developing informational programs.

1. Provide subscriptions to the *Chronicle of Higher Education* for those engaged in university governance (central administrators, deans, department chairmen, committee chairmen, faculty senate, and major student government officers) or for the library, each major administrative office, each university committee chairman, faculty senate chairman, and student body president.
2. Designate an information officer.
3. Prepare a brief guide to reference works, research aids, and sources of information on higher education, including reports prepared regularly by the individual institution.
4. Order multiple subscriptions to leading periodicals. Have the information officer distribute the periodicals or clipped articles to appropriate individuals or committees.
5. Get more mileage from present information sources. Institutional copies of publications should be passed on by administrators.
6. Purchase and distribute large quantities of inexpensive publications concerned with higher education.
7. Purchase several copies of important works

on higher education for the library and put them on two-week reserve.

8. Get on the mailing list of organizations and agencies producing free documents significant to higher education. The information office can do this.
9. Break the strangle hold of administrators on attendance at meetings and conferences on higher education. Subsidize at least travel and send a faculty member or student.
10. Subsidize subscriptions to the leading periodicals in higher education (25% for the first 100 people).
11. Conduct one-meeting workshops. Distribute inexpensive materials, provide brief annotated bibliographies. Topics such as: grading practices, evaluation of teaching, tenure, collective bargaining, external degrees, University Year for Action, credit by examination, and other concerns in higher education.
12. Conduct an all day workshop for new members of governance groups.[20]

Soles sees the "fallout" from such a program as:

1. a less parochial approach to issues and an increase in data-based discussion.
2. an increase in faculty awareness of their role as educators and a strengthening of their concern for that role.
3. use of the additional information as a measuring stick, however imperfect, to evaluate institutional efforts, concerns, and performance in the context of movements and developments in higher education.
4. serving to alert governance groups to activities at other institutions and provide something akin to an "early warning system" by calling attention to issues and problems.
5. a more efficient governance process. The ready availability of information, knowledge of information sources, and use of research and studies conducted elsewhere should conserve both time and energy.
6. the breaking of an administrative monopoly on information leading to faculty leadership in calling for new approaches which will bring proposals forward for consideration without the "stigma" of administrative sponsorship.[21]

COMMITTEES

Committees play a central role in governance since faculty and student governance functions in most institutions of higher education in the United States are accomplished through committees. The committee has become a recognized vehicle for sanctioning or officially recognizing the importance of some issue or activity. A benefit derived from the committee process is that the collective input based on the experience and expertise of its members is a valuable contribution toward making an appropriate and worthwhile decision.

As the forum-consensus model no longer appears to be a viable vehicle for faculty participation in governance, committees have become more important than ever as a means for participation in governance by faculty, students, and other personnel. By having been part of the decision making, even though on only a representative basis, the various factions involved may be more willing to accept the outcome. Committees must be used properly if the process is to result in increased administrative efficiency and the most effective use of faculty time.

Committee Functions

A committee, if it is to be productive, must know its purpose. Committees may be used to make decisions, assist in research projects, conduct long range studies, establish goals, formulate policy, seek or communicate information, or generate and coordinate ideas. A committee may also be nothing more than an advisory body. Committees should never play an administrative role by becoming involved in day-to-day control.

The committee approach is most effective for topics or problems requiring careful deliberation rather than problems needing immediate resolution. The result of a committee effort should be a thoughtful report reflecting serious and thorough consideration of the issue at hand. Committees should not be used to camouflage ineffective management. They should be established when a decision cannot be properly made by an individual, or when a diversity of opinion is desirable before a decision is made.[22]

Along these same lines, McKeachie makes the following suggestions:

> 1. Don't demand that everyone decide everything or that all committee decisions be referred to the total department staff before they are implemented.
> 2. . . . committee work can be reduced if committee jobs are limited to decision making rather than administration.
> 3. Don't use committees to duck responsibility. One of the most irritating ploys of administrators is the speech beginning "the Executive Committee has received your request and. . . ."[23]

A committee might be a viable vehicle for handling complaints. If an agreement is made in advance to abide by a committee decision, a critical, explosive situation might be averted. This approach should be used rarely and carefully. Deliberate referral of an issue to a committee might be a tactic for delaying decision making. This too should be done seldom if at all.

Dressel found a number of patterns for faculty committees in department and university matters.

> In some, the entire faculty raised issues, discussed them thoroughly, voted on what should be done, and then outlined the tasks for a sub-group to carry out. Other departments depended on committees to do the work or to develop policies for the approval of the faculty. Committees were organized around other sub-disciplinary interest groups or administrative functions . . . Committees on curriculum, admission, tenure, and promotions, which are basically administrative functions, represented another pattern of organization, alternative or supplemental to the interest groupings. In some departments, a single administrative, executive, or advisory committee assisted the chairman on almost every phase of departmental operations.[24]

Committees should not be involved in day-to-day administrative matters. An administrator cannot abdicate final responsibility. To establish a system of collective decision making without leadership can lead to mediocrity.

Standing Committees versus Ad Hoc

Governance organizations usually include standing committees that are responsible for some specific function or activity such as new course and program approval. Care must be exercised to avoid a multiplicity of such committees and particularly to avoid a situation where the agendas of standing committees begin to include administrative detail. Problems may arise also when standing committees become self-perpetuating and then eventually lose their usefulness and effectiveness.

Ad hoc committees may be established to deal with a particular issue or issues. Consideration might be given to the elimination of standing committees in favor of ad hoc committees established as the need arises. These would consist of members concerned enough about the issue at hand to be willing to work toward its solution. Upon completion of its task, the ad hoc committee would disband. This procedure clearly has some advantages.

A judicious combination of standing and ad hoc committees would probably be most effective. Both types should be kept to a minimum to prevent overlap, slow ineffective decision making, and inappropriate use of the committee mechanism.

Selection and Role of Committee Chairpersons

The caliber of its chairperson is crucial to the effectiveness and success of any committee. Should the chairperson be appointed by an administrator or the presiding officer of the particular organization to which the committee is responsible or be elected by the committee? The answer may depend upon circumstances. Executive and administrative appointments may lead to criticism for attempting to influence the committee, while election may lead to politicking. Either process does not necessarily lead to the most capable candidate becoming chairperson. There is no one answer to the problem.

A weak chairperson can alienate administrators and committee members alike. A strong chairperson can obtain results even though the committee members are themselves weak. The first quality needed by a committee chairperson is leadership. Can the individual bring together the thinking of the diverse membership? Is he or she able to obtain support from the administration when needed or find support where administrative leadership is lacking?

The chairperson must be committed to the accomplishment of the task at hand and the goals of the institution. He or she must also be secure in a personal sense and within the context of the institution. Most important, the chairperson must possess the special knowledge or skills needed to deal with the problem area in addition to being interested in the issue at hand. The chairperson must be able to organize the activities of the committee so as to utilize the strengths, skills, and expertise of the members to the best advantage.

Where the role of the committee makes it appropriate, the committee chairperson should be appointed on the basis of possessing the qualities above as well as having some knowledge and preferably some experience related to the task at hand. Whether chairpersons are elected or appointed, some time limitation should be placed upon the term of office if the committee is a standing committee.

Qualifications and Selection of Committee Members

To be effective, committee members as well as the committee chairperson should be personally and professionally secure. They should have the respect of both administrators and faculty peers, be looked upon by others as leaders, and have some knowledge of the area of concern. They should be more action oriented than philosophical. Too much time is frequently lost because each member of a committee feels it imperative to present a long involved statement of position and justification for the stance taken.

Alexander Astin describes several problem types of committee members who should be avoided. Among these are the methodologist or critic who sidetracks into highly technical critiques of alleged defects; the substantive critic who cannot accept any of the data as being relevant; the member who is antidata; the pro-data member who enthusiastically accepts the empirical data without recognizing ambiguities and discrepancies; the passive resistor who just does not become involved, lacks enthusiasm for even the best ideas, and believes committee membership is an imposition; the opportunist who sees the committee as a vehicle to promote some favorite cause and looks for data to support preconceived notions; and the exhibitionist who likes to talk and show off knowledge, erudition, or verbal skills.[25]

As with the chairperson, there may be instances when the task at hand makes it preferable for committee members to be identified by executive or administrative appointment. Ad hoc committees fall into this category because appointment expedites the beginning of committee activity. Standing committees with membership rotating on a one, two, or more year basis might be better established through an election process once the representative composition of the committee has been determined by appropriate constituencies.

Unfortunately, many administrators tend to view committee appointments in light of political implications rather than the task at hand. Attempts are made to keep everyone satisfied (which is never really possible) rather than to select individuals on the basis of their competencies. Selection of members for curricular committees might be most appropriately the responsibility of faculty since faculty view curriculum as their exclusive responsibility. Committees dealing with administrative matters might be formed best through appointment following previously developed patterns of representation from various constituencies.

Students should be included as committee members only when the issue at hand is related to their concerns. As previously stated, student committee members pose a special problem because they frequently lack the relevant specific knowledge and expertise needed to deal with the issue at hand. Those who are selected for committee membership should be identified on the basis of the appropriateness of their skills to the committee's project. They cannot be considered as representing student opinion if they are the only sources consulted. Under no circumstances should students be included only because pressure was placed upon the administration.

It is advisable to include the administrator as an ad hoc member to assure constant availability as a resource person. Under any circumstances, it must be clear that the responsible administrative officer has authority to override a committee report but is also morally responsible for making known the specific reasons.

Committee membership must not be too large. Five to nine is advisable since it is sufficient to provide stimulation and a variety of ideas, yet small enough to encourage individual contributions and full participation. Small subcommittees involving "outsiders" can be utilized for supplementation.

Committee Procedures

At the very beginning of the committee activity, the selection of a chairperson should take place if one has not been administratively identified. The usual process is election. The administrator to whom the particular committee is responsible must determine whether it would expedite the committee's accomplishment of its task to appoint the chairperson or whether the situation is such that an election would be preferable. Political implications cannot be totally discounted, but neither can they be an overriding factor. When a chairperson is not appointed, it is necessary to request that a member of the committee serve as convenor for the first meeting.

The administrator to whom the committee is responsible should make it known that the committee's work is of high priority and that its recommendation or recommendations will be seriously considered. The purpose, function, and scope of the committee's activities should be delineated in writing to its chairperson and members. Is its purpose policy formation, policy implementation, facilitation of communication, or advisory? How should it interact with other committees, bodies, and administrators within the institution? These are some of the questions to be considered.

The chairperson is responsible for effective management of each meeting. A maximum time for the length of each meeting should be established and adhered to except under unusual circumstances or when there is consensus among the members to extend the time limit. The chairperson plays a vital role in making each meeting efficient by preventing individuals from monopolizing discussions often resulting in a denial of opportunity to others. Some means for limiting individual discussion might be appropriately established at the beginning of each meeting. This may be done by definite time limitation or limiting individuals to one presentation of an idea and one rebuttal statement. When discussion becomes too extensive or argumentative, tabling an item might be effective. Availability of additional information and discussion by members prior to the next meeting often result in resolving problems expeditiously when the tabled item is removed from the table at a subsequent meeting. Another possible approach is the presentation of ideas or possible solutions to problems by the chairperson or the administrator involved. These are then used for discussion purposes.

The first meeting should be devoted to a discussion of the general background for the committee and its objectives. A broad agenda of its total activities should be developed along with a timetable and specific deadlines for completing each of the various items on the broad agenda. Where appropriate and available, reports from other sources should be used when gathering data to avoid duplication of effort and to save time.

The agenda for each meeting should be carefully planned by the chairperson with working statements and supporting documents distributed beforehand to committee members. When possible, recommended solutions to problems, policy drafts, etc. should be included to provide a starting base for committee discussion. It is best to place the most important items for consideration at the beginning of the agenda with the least important at the very end. This enables the committee to deal with the most vital items while members are most "fresh." An estimated amount of time should be established for each agenda item and adhered to as far as possible. Many times, discussion becomes circular, wheel spinning develops, and the time of highly paid administrators and faculty members is wasted.

When a meeting has been concluded, the appointed secretary should carefully and immediately prepare the minutes. When possible, the minutes should be distributed within twenty-four hours of the meeting, which enables committee members to review them while events of the meeting are still fresh in their minds. Corrections and additions may then be forwarded to the secretary prior to the next meeting. If immediate preparation and distribution of minutes is not feasible, it must be done before the next meeting. Last minute distribution of minutes at the subsequent meeting with a request for immediate approval may lead to an inaccurate record of the committee's deliberations.

Continuous appraisal of the committee's accomplishments in moving toward completion of its task and achievement of the established goals is an essential part of the committee process. The chairperson may handle this by asking the group at the end of the meeting whether or not its purpose was accomplished and what percentage of time was actually used productively. Such appraisal is also the responsibility of the administrator in whose area of responsibility the committee is functioning.

A draft of the final report might be best prepared by an individual or small subcommittee for review and revision where needed by the full committee. This is another instance where a concrete proposal as a starting point will expedite the work of the group.

Disadvantages of the Committee Process

While committees are advantageous in that they bring into play the ideas of a number of individuals which, theoretically, should result in a better decision than one made by an individual, the decision may not always be the best. In addition, there are a number of accompanying disadvantages to the process.

Some administrators find it easier to appoint committees to make decisions than to make a decision and find that others are furious at them. Unpopular decisions are left to committees by "passing the buck." Committees appointed by administrators are often viewed with suspicion. Yet, there is a disadvantage in using the election process since it does not guarantee that those elected possess the greatest expertise and appropriate skills for dealing with the matter at hand. Excessive use of committees also reduces the opportunity for personal interaction between individuals. Constant referral of problems to committees eliminates the contacts between administrators, faculty, and students on the one-to-one basis that tends to personalize an institution.

Too often, the committee process consumes much valuable time that is out of proportion with the importance of what is accomplished. Inefficient and ineffective committees are expensive and wasteful. This may be illustrated by computing the cost per hour of a meeting by figuring the total salary cost per hour of those involved to which 30 to 35 percent is added for fringe benefits. It might be easier to compute the total man-hours spent that could be applied more appropriately to teaching and research. Committee management training for administrators followed by involvement of faculty who are going to serve on committees in training for their roles may be the answer.

Another disadvantage is the tendency to overload the faithful and most competent people while others do not participate at all. The unfairness is apparent when committee participation is accomplished above and beyond one's assigned responsibilities for which load time is allocated.

The committee process may also be viewed as inefficient when there is rapid turnover in membership resulting in the need for new members to acquire enough background to be effective. Often, the individual's term is ended at the peak of effectiveness and a replacement is seated.

Finally, the usually cumbersome committee process must be adjusted if committees are to survive. Institutions are operating in a new, more dynamic, and more complex setting. Quicker responses are often needed, and the old governance mechanisms may not be equal to the task.

IMPLEMENTATION OF DECISIONS

In some instances, it may be advisable for recommendations to be submitted to all faculty for approval. Occasionally, all students might be involved where the issue is pertinent to their concerns. This is more apt to be the case in a division or a department since representative groups are often given full responsibility in the context of the larger units.

The lag time between initiation of committee activity and completion of its task may lead to an impression of inaction on the part of the committee and the administrator to whom it is responsible. Since committees generally serve only a recommending function, time spent is sometimes seen as nonproductive and useless. Procrastination in decision making can be a factor in faculty indifference. If there is an "in-between" relationship of an administrator to one who makes the ultimate decision, committee members may be unsure about how their views will be forwarded.

The major responsibility of the administrator is an immediate decision on whether or not committee recommendations shall be accepted and implemented. Once accepted, implementation should follow as soon as feasible following an announcement of the decision and a timetable for implementation. If administrators and members of governance groups maintain open communication and are willing to negotiate and compromise, institutions should benefit from improved morale and understanding among their constituencies. Energy, sensitivity, and determination on the part of all are necessary. Under these circumstances, it should be a rare occasion when the recommendations of a committee must be rejected.

SUMMARY

The increasing involvement of a multiplicity of constituencies and numerous external governmental and legal pressures are resulting in changes in governance structures. The framework within which administrators play a leadership role in decision making is determined by this structure. The governance involvement of faculty and others must be complementary to the activities of the administrator. All decision-making activities should take place in accord with institutional purposes and goals.

While faculty contributions are generally more extensive in academic areas such as curriculum, admission and degree requirements, and academic standards, the ultimate authority is in the hands of institutional administrators and, in some instances, the governing board. This is particularly true when there are financial implications. The result is a dual process and the role of division and department heads as well as deans is an important one. Their role is concerned with decisions about purpose and performance and requires leadership ability as well as managerial.

On campuses where collective bargaining and unions have been instituted, governance mechanisms are being restructured to accommodate them. The new structures provide a means for trustees, administrators, faculty, certain other staff, and students to participate in making decisions and in monitoring their implications.

Governance models may be characterized as bureaucratic, collegial, or political but, in actuality, none of the three is exclusively practical. The administrative hierarchy of an institution reflects the bureaucratic approach, and while it may be viewed as authoritarian, it is also likely to be the most efficient. The collegial model is based on the concept of a community of scholars managing its own affairs. It is a means for accounting for individual and group needs and involving people in relation to their interests and abilities. The third or political model views competition and conflict as normal and decision making as negotiation and political. This model is supported by the advent of collective bargaining.

Until recently, the traditional governance mechanism had been a faculty senate of some form that provided an arena for debate through which faculty might arrive at agreement. Its role was advisory, its activity concentrated in academic areas, and its recommendations frequently routinely ratified by administrators and the governing board. The senate which previously involved all faculty members in its deliberations has been replaced by a representative group in institutions where increased size made the original form unwieldy. In addition, its recommendations and their implications are now being carefully scrutinized before final approval.

The advent of unions with their collective

bargaining activity appears to have increased the level of faculty participation in decision making. While differing patterns of relationships are possible, the most desirable and most common is a cooperative one. This increased involvement of faculty in the establishment of educational policy must be accompanied by an increase in their information about higher education.

While faculty participation in institutional governance has been common, student involvement has not. There has been no real answer yet to the problem of student representation. It does appear that participation at the department level is most feasible and most appropriate with emphasis on academic matters involving curriculum, course and teacher evaluation, academic policies, new student orientation, and special events.

Involvement of faculty, other personnel, and students in governance is accomplished through committees. Committees should not be involved in day-to-day administrative matters. A major factor in their effectiveness is the caliber of their chairpersons and members. A judicious combination of ad hoc and standing committees can be an asset to administrators as well as a benefit to the institution.

ENDNOTES

1. Used with permission. *Faculty Bargaining: Change and Conflict* by Joseph W. Garbarino in association with Bill Aussieker. Copyright © 1975 by The Carnegie Foundation for the Advancement of Teaching (New York: McGraw-Hill, 1975), p. 24.
2. Elizabeth Sutherland, "Nonacademic Personnel and University Governance," *The Journal of the College and University Personnel Association* 24 (1973): 80–81.
3. *Ibid.,* p. 82.
4. Paul L. Dressel and William H. Faricy, *Return to Responsibility: Constraints on Autonomy in Higher Education* (San Francisco: Jossey-Bass, 1972), p. 134.
5. Used with permission. *Changes in University Organization, 1964–1971* by Edward Gross and Paul V. Grambsch. Copyright © 1974 by The Carnegie Foundation for the Advancement of Teaching (New York: McGraw-Hill, 1974), p. 206.
6. John J. Corson, *Governance of Colleges and Universities* (New York: McGraw-Hill, 1960), p. 109.
7. Earl J. McGrath, *Should Students Share the Power?* (Philadelphia: Temple University Press, 1970), p. 79.
8. Kenneth G. Tillman, "Student Participation in Departmental Responsibilities," *Journal of Health, Physical Education and Recreation* 45 (1974): 59.
9. John D. Millett, *Strengthening Community in Higher Education* (Management Division, Academy for Educational Development, Inc., 1974), p. 2–3.
10. George S. Odiorne, *Management Decisions by Objectives* (Englewood Cliffs, N.J.: Prentice-Hall, 1969), p. 105.
11. Millett, *Strengthening Community,* p. 48.
12. Millett, *Strengthening Community,* p. 3.
13. David W. Leslie, "Legitimacy of Governance Higher Education: A Comparative Study," *Educational Administration Quarterly* 9 (1973): 112.
14. Richard C. Richardson, Jr., Clyde E. Blocker, and Louis W. Bender, *Governance for the Two Year College* (Englewood Cliffs, N.J.: Prentice-Hall, 1972), pp. 185–186.
15. Dressel and Faricy, *Return to Responsibility,* p. 119.
16. *Ibid.,* p. 119.
17. Algo D. Henderson and Jean Glidden Henderson, *Higher Education in America: Problems, Priorities, and Prospects* (San Francisco: Jossey-Bass, 1974), pp. 214–217.
18. Used with permission. Garbarino and Aussieker, *Faculty Bargaining,* p. 147.
19. John D. Millett, "Higher Education Man-

agement Versus Business Management," *Educational Record* 56 (1976): 225.

20. James R. Soles, "Information: Missing Ingredient in University Governance," *Educational Record* 54 (1973): 53–55.
21. *Ibid.*, p. 55.
22. C. Richard Decker and Alan D. Fletcher, "Campus Committees: Values and Hazards," *Educational Record* 54 (1973): 229.
23. Wilbert J. McKeachie, "Memo to New Department Chairmen," *Educational Record* 49 (1968): 225–226.
24. Paul L. Dressel, F. Craig Johnson, and Philip M. Marcus, *The Confidence Crisis: An Analysis of University Departments* (San Francisco: Jossey-Bass, 1970), p. 84.
25. Alexander W. Astin, *Academic Gamesmanship* (New York: Praeger, 1976), pp. 93–95.

CHAPTER 8

Curriculum Development

Colleges and universities have sometimes appeared to concentrate more on personnel situations and institutional procedures than on the educational purposes which should be of primary importance. Professors have contributed to retaining an educational status quo by protecting their personal domain of course offerings. As a result, old programs that have outlived their attraction and effectiveness are retained.

If educational programs are to be dynamic and vital, educational objectives and the means for achieving them must be scrutinized. Policies providing flexibility in structuring curriculum components and expediting implementation of new courses and programs are needed. Faculty and administrators must recognize the need to broaden their activity from routine policies regarding credit hours, titles, and course numbering systems to exploring new patterns of offerings, scheduling, and use of institutional resources. The role of the administrator in providing the necessary leadership and support is essential to the success of any curriculum development effort.

FACTORS AFFECTING CURRICULUM CHANGE

Organizations, especially long standing ones, tend to be passive and serve as a means for accomplishing certain defined tasks. Their members are often self-selected since individuals generally affiliate with an organization because they agree with its purposes and activities. Institutional vitality, in turn, requires continuous activity in the direction of adaptability for meeting new demands and new needs rather than sporadic fits and spurts of action. Too often change has been a periodic reaction to some crisis as was illustrated by institutional response to the student activism of the 1960s.

A variety of positive and negative factors impact upon decisions related to curriculum change. Among these is the misconception that adding and deleting a course or two is the means to revision. Rather than radical transformation, change takes place through gradual accretion and attrition. While this is the simplest means for accomplishing academic change, it does not constitute real reform because it does not involve reorganization and synthesis of the knowledge, skills, and attitudes that are desirable for acquisition by students.

Another misconception is that new ideas are always desirable. New ideas may generate enthusiasm among some faculty because they present a measure of uniqueness. Others will react negatively immediately because the status quo is threatened. Change only for the sake of change must be avoided.

External Influences

Patterns of federal and foundation support for specific projects will continue to affect institutional decisions. A shifting of research support to nonacademic agencies is having an impact upon curriculum (particularly at the graduate level). The same is true of an increasing emphasis on the natural and social sciences accompanied by decreasing emphasis on the humanities. Another effect of external funding is found in the area of program evaluation. Much of the formal program evaluation has revolved around special projects rather than the regular curriculum because funding agencies have required it. Accrediting agencies have an effect in this area too since their approval of an institution is often one of the requirements for eligibility for financial assistance. As described more fully in the last chapter, direct impact of the accrediting agencies is felt when institutions must satisfy their established criteria in order to acquire approval for eligibility.

At the state level, coordinating agencies and boards are becoming more prevalent and increasingly active. Some require that they review and approve all new programs in public institutions, which places increasing constraints upon decisions about courses and curricula in general. This is in addition to the special attention being given to policies, performance, and costs of the institutions. Curriculum changes may become even more difficult as a result of state "interference" that may lead to a custodial role for faculty, students, and administrators. Some states are moving toward uniformity of procedures and rules for all state campuses. There are indications that this may soon include academic matters as well, such as the proposed "common-course-numbering" system for the state institutions in Florida.[1]

Internal Influences

One factor mitigating against curriculum change is institutional size. As colleges and universities increased their enrollments and faculty increased in numbers, the emphasis on specialization increased and divisions and departments grew in size and power. This led to narrow viewpoints and self-serving which, in turn, have become a block to curriculum innovation, particularly in attempts to develop interdisciplinary offerings.

The vested interests of colleges, divisions, and departments pose a formidable roadblock to curriculum change. Strong division and department organizations with their accompanying autonomy become deterrents to needed comprehensive integrated programs. Too often, these organizational units are concerned only with themselves which leads to a lack of unity and coherence in their programs and an unwillingness to work with others to achieve better integrated and coherent educational experiences for students. Programmatic changes become conservative compromises which encroach upon vested interests with minimal effect, thus avoiding confrontation and alienation. To be most effective, continuous curriculum review is needed, accompanied by continuous reexamination of organizational structures to determine their appropriateness as disciplines are reorganized and new fields of study open. A coherent set of objectives and a viable means for achieving them is much more important than a curriculum reflecting departmental priorities.

When higher education is experiencing a period of rapid growth, curriculum change occurs as new faculty members join the staff and bring new ideas. In fact, recruitment of faculty often involves a search for those who are creative and exciting with the expectation that they will add to the stature of the department and institution. To illustrate: Hefferlin, in a study based on 234 interviews of administrators, department heads, and professors at 110 institutions, found that the amount of change in course descriptions and offerings was significantly related to changes in faculty.[2] As faculty turnover decreases and virtually disappears, a major problem will develop if curriculum reform also disappears.

As previously mentioned, the effectiveness of change processes may be reduced by the allegiance of faculty to their divisions or departments and to their disciplines rather than to the institution. Faculty are relatively autonomous and frequently resist program changes that affect them. Many concentrate on their own disciplines with little or no concern for the broader educational problems. Others do not want to relinquish old and traditional ideas and values. Some see the purpose of higher education as providing a broadly based liberal education for students, while still others believe equipping students to earn a living should be foremost. The effects of these faculty attitudes on students and learning outcomes of the curriculum cannot be ignored.

A comparatively new factor affecting curriculum change is the increasing number of lower ability students. Emphasis upon nontraditional populations is bringing in students who are not equipped to handle their learning needs. These students are more vocationally oriented and often find it difficult to participate in the traditional academic setting. In addition, they show particular strengths and interests in the emerging specialties dealing with human problems and those involved with keeping the machinery of the technological age in running condition.[3] Changes in institutional attitudes and objectives are needed to accommodate these students. Development programs focusing on preparing faculty to work with the nontraditional students and to develop appropriate new programs are more important than ever.

A major problem in curriculum improvement is the relatively slow adoption of change. Governance mechanisms may require review and approval at several levels from department to college to the university level and, in some instances, the governing board of trustees. The involvement of numerous subcommittees and committees makes the process lengthy and cumbersome. A full year or more may elapse between the time a proposal is submitted at the first level and its ultimate approval for implementation. While a review procedure is desirable since it should result in a less capricious undertaking, it can also be discouraging to the initiator and detrimental to the change process. Hefferlin provides a rather picturesque description of this process.

> Changing the curriculum, it has been said, is like moving a graveyard. In both cases, for better or worse, the content is generally lifeless. Moreover, the physical problems pall before the issues of sanctity and sacrilege. A multitude of deep-seated and traditional values are threatened. The emotions of everyone even remotedly related with the enterprise need to be respected. And the onerous task is most typically referred to a committee—one that is respected, honorable, and judicious.[4]

The image an institution presents to its members also has an effect. Is it exciting, active, and vital or static and passive, even stagnant? What is traditional? Is there tradition for the sake of tradition or a tradition of flexibility and change? Is the climate trusting and personalized, and does it encourage and reward participation, or is there an atmosphere of insecurity, impersonality, and reward for conformity? Are ideas circulated? Newsletters, seminars, faculty workshops, and encouragement of attendance at professional and inter-institutional meetings are important.

Finally, a capacity and mechanism for reorganizing programs and organizational structures as well as redistributing resources must exist so as to encourage promising change and innovation. These mechanisms and structures must make it possible for change to take place quickly.

THE PROCESS

Administrators, faculty, and students should be involved in a continuous process of curriculum improvement. The process itself is a major factor in the success of any change since a curriculum imposed upon faculty and students by the administration is unlikely to be effective regardless of quality. A coherent overall philosophy that is known and understood by students, faculty, alumni, and trustees is needed as a starting point. From the philosophy, basic underlying objectives are developed, desired student outcomes clearly delineated, and a comprehensive evaluation process established.

Curriculum: Courses or Programs?

One of the first efforts in curriculum change should be toward development of a common understanding of the definition of curriculum. Is the curriculum a series of courses, each standing on its own with no relationship to any others? Is it only the courses offered in a specific discipline? Is it the total academic experience of the student? Or, should it be defined even more broadly as a total college experience?

Curriculum must be viewed as more than an array of independent courses. Single courses with no meaning or which have become obsolete in light of changing conditions must be examined carefully to determine their relationship to the program as a whole. A decision must be made whether they should be revised and retained or eliminated completely. The academic as well as the so-called extracurricular components of the students' total experience must present some coherent whole reflecting an underlying overall philosophy based on institutional values. Noncurricular aspects of the student's experience make an institution's educational program even broader. In addition to the courses of study and what goes on in the classrooms, laboratories, studios, and the library, the effects of counseling, student activities, athletics, lounges, cafeterias and dining rooms, dormitories, lectures and exhibitions, and informal student and faculty contacts must be included.[5]

It is not feasible within the focus of this work to examine all the above mentioned influences. The remaining discussion will emphasize the academic experiences provided within the framework of courses and academic programs.

Institutional Philosophy: Mission, Goals, and Objectives

Many existing programs, undergraduate and graduate, were literally developed overnight to satisfy the hordes of students descending upon institutions. The time has come to examine them rationally and retain, revise, or delete them based on the relevance of their underlying philosophy to current situations. Future needs must also be considered.

A comprehensive statement of educational philosophy includes statements of mission and goals. While the terms may appear to be used interchangeably at times, they are not the same. Mission statements are the broadest followed by goals which are still quite general. Objectives developed at the program and course level are the most specific and include criteria that make it possible to evaluate institutional progress toward the stated goals. John Bolin established the following six criteria which he believes will lead toward better goals. The comments and related questions have been summarized from his detailed discussion of each of the criteria.

1. Compatibility—Goals must be consistent with the central mission of the institution and mutually supporting or complementary. They must also be internally consistent.
2. Attainability—How realistic are the goals and can they actually be achieved? On the other hand, they should not be too easily attained or some resources would not be tapped.
3. Intelligibility—Does each goal clearly identify a particular expected behavior or level of achievement?
4. Acceptability—How well will the goals be received by faculty, staff, and students? Their support and cooperation are essential.
5. Measurability—Evaluation criteria must be included in goal statements if we are to know when we have arrived and how well we did what we were supposed to do.
6. Accountability—Someone must follow up on the achievement of the goals and stimulate and encourage their achievement. Goals must also be reevaluated on a systematic basis.[6]

Goals of society as well as those concerned with the personal development of students need to be considered. These are not incompatible, as some might believe, since students are a part of society. Instead, they are complementary. The broad needs of the individual and society cannot be ignored. The focus of education is not preparation of a student for a specific career and membership in a well-defined group, but for a full life as a responsible, informed, contributing member of society as a whole.

Sinclair Goodlad discusses the problems of defining goals that are created by the conflicts in higher education. He sees these conflicts as

1. Conflict of goals for education
2. Conflict between different disciplines for comprehensive power
3. Conflict between "objective" knowledge with which all disciplines claim to deal and "subjectivity"
4. Potential conflict between personal commitment and institutional detachment as it appears in the curriculum and in the methods by which the curriculum is taught.[7]

When developing mission and goal statements, some time and effort may be saved by examination of standard lists from which some goals may be modified for use or even used as is while others are added. Prepared lists are helpful, too, by providing a model for specificity and wording. Lawrence and Service recommend the following sources for lists:

1. E. Gross and Grambsch, P. V., Survey of Educational Goals in *University Goals and Academic Power*. Washington, D.C.: American Council on Education, 1968.
2. ETS's Institutional Goals Inventory (R. E. Peterson, *Institutional Goals Inventory Manual*. Princeton, N.J.: Educational Testing Service, 1973).
3. Micek, S. S. and Arney, W. R. (*The Higher Education Outcome Measures Identification Study) A Descriptive Summary*. Boulder, Col.: National Center for Higher Education Management Systems at Western Interstate Commission for Higher Education, 1974.
4. NCHEMS Inventory of Higher Education Outcome Variables and Measures in Micek, S. S. and Wallhaus, R. A. *An Introduction to the Identification and Uses of Higher Education Outcome Information,* Technical Report No. 40. Boulder, Col.: NCHEMS at WICHE, 1973.[8]

Mission and goal statements for various kinds of institutions appear on pages 192 to 198. The first is taken from the catalog for a women's college.

Even though Women's College embodies traditions which are among the oldest in the education of women, it still faces, with its students, the new issues and major readjustments of the 1980s. Perhaps never before in American society has there been such need

> of truly liberal education. As society changes in the subtle and powerful ways which now face us, clear thought, generous judgment, and tenacious purpose are crucial. Acquisition and development of just these qualities are the aim of a Women's College education.
>
> As each student comes to the college, she comes both to discover her own talents and to explore the ways in which such talents have been exercised in the past. Her thinking is refined as she is introduced to problems in science and in the humanities. At the same time, as she explores the context of these problems, some of them as old as civilization, her judgment grows with her powers of analysis. It is this dual talent for thought and judgment which enables Women's College students to move powerfully into the larger community and into the world. They are capable of reasoning to a solution, and capable of the far more difficult task of evaluating that solution dispassionately.
>
> Women's College liberal tradition is strengthened by its special commitment to women. This is a time of great testing for women; opportunities for work and experience are vastly increased, but real restraints, whether of attitude or of conflicting responsibilities, remain. In a sense, every Women's College woman is a pioneer today, for each is charting new directions in circumstances radically altered from past expectations. As a community dedicated to the education of women, Women's College creates a sense of continuity and comradeship which adds immeasurably to confidence and the resolve of its students.

A specific statement of goals does not accompany the mission statement in the above case. Instead, a rather lengthy discussion of liberal arts education and the role of the liberal arts college appears under the title of *Principles of the College.*

The second is a statement of goals developed by a private four-year coeducational liberal arts college. The college's mission that is presented as its "one central commitment" is "to provide a balanced, comprehensive liberal arts education fulfilling the highest standards of intellectual excellence." The goals which follow amplify the basic statement.

> The goal of the College is to provide an education in the liberal arts and sciences with emphasis on the highest intellectual and scholarly standards.
>
> The education pays particular attention to a balance between a broad study in the various major areas of human knowledge and a close, in-depth study in a recognized academic discipline.
>
> The general program is designed to provide a background of humanistic and scientific study which will give an understanding of cultural phenomena as they relate to each other and modes of thought as they bear on the problem of man's various attempts to understand himself and his world.
>
> The advanced program provides opportunity for intensive examination of the subject matter and techniques of a more narrowly defined academic discipline.
>
> The balance of a general and more specialized education is best achieved where students and faculty work closely together in an atmosphere of shared intellectual and scholarly concern, and where individual interests and disciplines must be pursued, not in isolation, but with a sense of the larger intellectual life of which they are a part.

The mission statement for a large urban university is presented below followed by broad general mission statements for the three largest colleges within that university. The relationship between the university statement and the college statement is more obvious in those from the School of Business Administration and the College of Education than in the College of Liberal Arts statement. All three college statements reflect the college specialization more than the university mission.

URBAN UNIVERSITY STATEMENT OF MISSION

As an urban university in an increasingly urban society, Urban University sees its role as being similar to that fulfilled by the land-grant institution for an earlier agricultural economy.

Urban University has an obligation to use its knowledge resources to explore and investigate the complex array of urban problems—education, employment, housing, health, transportation, crime, pollution, and other obstacles to the full achievement of individual potential.

In striving to meet its responsibility to provide higher education for disadvantaged urban youngsters who show academic promise, the University does not neglect its commitment as a Commonwealth University to serve the entire eastern portion of the state.

COLLEGE OF LIBERAL ARTS

Programs for the undergraduate are dedicated to the student's fulfillment as an individual, his education for responsible citizenship, and his preparation in an area of special interest or professional competence.

SCHOOL OF BUSINESS ADMINISTRATION

Today's business community is an integral part of a highly complex and changing society, arising not only from changes in technology but also from the changing roles of labor, management and government. Members of that community must be prepared to participate in the affairs of that society as well as being technically and professionally competent and knowledgeable in their special spheres of activity. It is the goal of the School of Business Administration to provide to its students high quality educational opportunities which are responsive to these needs.

COLLEGE OF EDUCATION

The College of Education owes its origin to a desire to satisfy the present demand for the best possible professional training for teachers in prospect and teachers in service.

The fourth example is a precise presentation of mission and goals developed for a two-year community college.

THE PHILOSOPHY OF THE COLLEGE

County College was founded to help meet the varied educational, cultural, and social needs and interests of the community. To do so, the programs, policies, and procedures of the College are designed to serve career, transfer, continuing education, and community service needs and interests.

It is the intent of County College to provide for each of its students that program or experience most appropriate for him in accordance with his determined ability and interest. Because it believes strongly in the "one-college concept," the college acknowledges the equal status of each student, and considers its entire enrollment as one student body.

The College seeks to develop in each student the ability to think clearly and critically, to communicate effectively, and to assess and reconcile his concerns. Above all, a premium is placed upon uplifting student self-concepts and upon total student growth through the primary vehicle of teaching excellence and the support of all of the necessary service functions.

It is the aim of the College to give full consideration to each student's level of development, his aspirations for the future, and the needs of his community.

OUR DECALOGUE OF OBJECTIVES THE GOALS OF COUNTY COLLEGE

1. To provide an educational opportunity to any interested high school graduate or holder of a high school equivalency diploma, and to any individual whose age, background, military service and experience make probable the successful completion of study leading to the associate degree.
2. To provide programs, courses, and services in career, transfer, remediation, and continuing education areas, as needs appear, with or without formal matriculation for a degree.
3. To provide a faculty dedicated to teaching excellence and the concept that personal and group interchange between students and instructor is of foremost importance.

4. To seek to instill in each student the ability to think clearly and critically, to communicate effectively, and to assess and reconcile the concerns he faces.
5. To provide counseling and academic advisement and various other needed student services to assist the student in developing a healthful self-concept and in becoming a fully functioning individual.
6. To create a "one-college" atmosphere in which there exist no status distinctions between students, whether they are enrolled as day, evening, Saturday, Summer, full-time, part-time, on-campus, or off-campus students.
7. To provide a broad and constantly enlarging spectrum of cultural, social, and recreational opportunities, and to make the facilities and services of the College available to the entire community.
8. To seize every opportunity, through courses, services, counseling, and activities, to help every student develop a guiding set of personal values, standards, and behavioral criteria.
9. To develop a climate which encourages the continuous examination, improvement, and implementation of college programs and services, together with the instructional processes and practices designed to further them.
10. To promote, in every way possible, an atmosphere of cooperation, partnership, and trust among faculty, students, administration, and Board of Trustees in implementing the philosophy and objectives of the College.

MISSION, FUNCTIONS, AND GOALS

UNIVERSITY MISSION

The State University, the Commonwealth's principal university, exists to provide opportunities for the education, personal growth, and development of individuals, and to contribute to the improvement of the society in and for which it exists. Stated in general terms, the State University's mission is the betterment of human welfare.

This statement of mission is concerned with the ultimate end which the State University was created to attain. It provides the basis for integration of the University's present and future activities into a coherent whole; it gives direction to institutional effort; it underscores institutional identity and validity; and it lays claim to the support due the State University as an agency of society. As a public institution, all undertakings of the State University are supportive of this mission in the interests of the Commonwealth, as well as the larger society of which the Commonwealth is a part.

UNIVERSITY FUNCTIONS

In accomplishing its mission, the State University's efforts and program activities are directed toward performing three primary functions which are highly interwoven and represent different aspects of the same thing—knowledge: TEACHING—the dissemination of knowledge; RESEARCH—the creation of knowledge; and SERVICE—the application of knowledge to human problems.

The primary functions performed by the State University and the scope of programs conducted in each functional area are defined by statute. Revised Statute 164.125 in particular authorizes State University to offer baccalaureate, professional, masters, specialist, doctoral, and postdoctoral programs and to conduct joint doctoral programs in cooperation with other institutions; it designates State University as the Commonwealth's principal institution to conduct statewide research and service programs, and it additionally stipulates that the University is authorized to provide the state community with programs of a community college nature. KRS 164.575–164.600 creates the Community College System as a part of the State University and authorizes the community colleges to offer two-year transfer programs, two-year technical and semiprofessional programs, and courses in general education.

The primary functions performed by State University are further defined by state and federal statutes (KRS 164.100, State Land Grant Act; the Hatch Act of 1887 and KRS 164.110, acts supporting research and extension; KRS 164.120, supporting instruction; and the Smith Lever Act, KRS 164.605, and KRS

164.675, supporting extension) as necessary and appropriate for the Commonwealth's land-grant institution in accordance with the Morrill Act of 1862.

UNIVERSITY GOALS

To be useful in the management and planning of primary programs, which are the means through which State University achieves its mission, the general statement of University mission must be translated into more specific goal statements which provide focus and direction for current and future program activities in each of the functional areas.

State University's goals in the three primary program areas are stated generally as follows:

- *Instruction:* To provide high quality, progressive programs of instruction which are both responsive to the needs of the Commonwealth and compatible with the needs and interests of students and the community.
- *Research:* To conduct programs of basic and applied research which are vital to graduate and professional programs, advance the frontiers of knowledge in areas of concern to modern society, and enhance and facilitate the well-being of the nation and the Commonwealth by seeking solutions to acute societal problems whether these are economic, scientific, technological, social, cultural, or philosophical.
- *Service:* To sustain and develop public service programs which serve the needs and interests of the community and Commonwealth by application of those measures which are unique to the University and which facilitate economic and social improvement within the Commonwealth.

Goals of the Three Academic Sectors

From organizational and operational viewpoints, the mission of State University is best expressed by describing groups of program goals which apply to each of the University's three academic sectors: the Community College System, the Division of Colleges, and the Medical Center. Primary programs conducted in the three sectors are so unique that separate groups of goals are justified and desirable for instruction, research, and service activities in each organizational area. These goals are as follows:

Goals of the Community College System

1. To provide easily accessible educational opportunities through a statewide Community College System offering comprehensive programs designed to meet the needs of students, communities, and the Commonwealth.
   a. To provide progessive, high-quality, two-year lower division programs applicable to baccalaureate degrees.
   b. To provide progressive, high-quality, two-year nonbaccalaureate programs leading to the granting of associate degrees or appropriate certificates in occupational areas to meet the needs of students, communities, and the Commonwealth.
   c. To provide progressive, high-quality programs of adult education oriented toward community interests and needs.
2. To provide progressive, high-quality programs of service directed toward community interests and needs.

Goals of the Division of Colleges

1. To sustain and develop graduate, undergraduate, professional, adult, and continuing education programs of the highest quality, compatible with the needs and interests of the students, and responsive to the needs of the Commonwealth.
2. To sustain and develop programs of research which are of the excellence characteristic of a major university and which support graduate programs as well as enhance and facilitate the progress of the Commonwealth.
3. To use the competencies and specialized talents within the University to offer public service programs that will enhance and facilitate the well-being and progress of the Commonwealth.
4. To sustain and enlarge the archival function of the University by creating outstanding collections of books and other media material, artifacts, geological and biological samples, and works of art, all

of which are made freely available to individuals and groups within the Commonwealth who can benefit from access to these resources.

Goals of the Medical Center

1. To prepare health workers to meet the state's health manpower requirements.
2. To conduct basic and applied research in the health sciences, including research which focuses on the delivery of health care with emphasis on research programs needed for effectiveness and quality of educational programs focusing on problems within the Commonwealth.
3. To maintain public service as a major and significant objective of the Medical Center, with particular emphases on health care services to citizens of the Commonwealth within the context of educational and research objectives.
4. To expand and extend the Medical Center's leadership role in the area of continuing education programs, with increasing emphasis upon continuing professional education, coordinated with other institutions, formalized, and made available to more health professionals in the Commonwealth.

DIVISION OF COLLEGES GOAL STATEMENT FOR INSTRUCTION

To sustain and develop graduate, undergraduate, professional, adult, and continuing education programs of the highest quality, compatible with the needs and interests of the students, and most responsive to the needs of the Commonwealth.

DIVISION OF COLLEGES PROGRAM OBJECTIVES

Baccalaureate Programs

1. To offer baccalaureate programs which provide the opportunity for citizens of the Commonwealth and surrounding region to further develop their human potential through a general or liberal education.
2. To provide baccalaureate programs which are central or essential to the fulfillment of the statutorily defined functions of State University.
3. To help meet the manpower requirements for highly trained, highly educated personnel in the Commonwealth and surrounding region, including manpower requirements in those fields requiring licensure and/or certification.
4. To prepare students for further studies in graduate and professional programs.
5. To meet the needs of graduates of typical two-year college programs and of students enrolled in cooperative programs by providing them with the opportunity to complete upper division course work in baccalaureate programs.

Masters Programs

1. To offer masters programs which enable individuals to acquire an educational foundation contributing to their long-range development for professional employment.
2. To offer masters programs which are central or essential to the fulfillment of the statutorily defined functions of State University.
3. To offer masters programs which prepare graduates who are highly qualified for positions related to specific manpower needs in the Commonwealth and surrounding region or, more generally, for careers in industry, government agencies, health care organizations, and educational institutions.
4. To prepare individuals to understand relationships between fields and to develop techniques in the transfer of knowledge.
5. To prepare students for further advanced graduate and/or professional studies.
6. To contribute to new knowledge through research and publication.

Doctoral Programs

1. To offer programs at the graduate level which provide opportunities for citizens of the Commonwealth and elsewhere to fulfill their potential in intellectual and cultural leadership and which provide technical and professional training enabling them to cope with problems of a highly complex society.
2. To offer programs of advanced graduate training and education which prepare grad-

uates who are highly qualified for positions related to specific manpower needs in the Commonwealth and elsewhere or, more generally, for careers in teaching, research, and public service in universities, government agencies, industry, health care organizations, or other types of agencies.
3. To expand the boundaries of knowledge through basic research and study.
4. To provide doctoral programs which are central to or necessarily supportive of the statutorily defined functions of State University.

Postdoctoral Programs

1. To provide postdoctoral programs which are central to the mission of the University.
2. To provide expert assistance in ongoing research programs being conducted by University professors and researchers.
3. To provide doctoral graduates with opportunities for extended research and/or teaching experience through activities of direct benefit to the University's teaching and research programs.
4. To help meet the specialized manpower requirements of the Commonwealth and surrounding region.

Professional Programs

1. To help meet the manpower requirements for highly specialized, highly educated personnel in the Commonwealth and surrounding region.

Certificate Programs

1. To help meet the highly specialized manpower requirements of the Commonwealth and surrounding region by providing specialized training and course work necessary for the fulfillment of specialty certification in several fields of education.

Community Education Programs

1. To offer programs of continuing education which permit citizens of the Commonwealth and surrounding region to upgrade skills; become familiar with changing technology, techniques, and concepts in their career fields; learn new skills; and acquire the background necessary to maintain professional competency, gain certification, and/or retain licensure.
2. To offer programs of general adult education which provide citizens of the Commonwealth with information and culture, provide opportunities designed to help individuals discover their potential, or help individuals to discover and develop their ability to do a vocation.
3. To offer programs of community education with an avocational or recreational focus.
4. To provide continuing education programs which will facilitate and enhance the quality of services provided to the citizens of the Commonwealth by several important professions.
5. To provide community education programs which indirectly contribute to a flourishing state economy.
6. To provide community education programs which will indirectly assist communities and local governments in their search for solutions to their problems.

Adult and Preparatory Programs

1. To offer educational programs that (a) arm academically and socioeconomically disadvantaged students with the basic knowledge and skills which they need in preparation for formal course work leading to a postsecondary degree or certificate and/or (b) provide individuals with the opportunity to fulfill standard requirements which must be met before beginning work on a postsecondary degree or certificate.

The various statements demonstrate clearly the differences that are found in institutional mission and the ways in which goals are presented.

Several program statements follow. The reader should note the use of the terms *objectives* and *aim*. These statements actually qualify as goal statements. They are not specific enough to serve as statements of objectives.

1. The objectives of the Department of Economics are threefold: to offer a liberal arts

approach to economics as a social science; to equip the prospective professional economist with some of the basic analytical techniques; and to provide nonspecialists with the understanding necessary for their effectiveness as citizens and judges of economic policies.

2. The aim of the curriculum is twofold: to introduce students to the three major religious traditions of the West—Jewish, Christian, and Greco-Roman—and to introduce students to the variety of approaches employed in the study of religion—existential, phenomenological, theological, philosophical, scientific, historical, and literary.
3. The Department of Physical Education aims to develop in the student an awareness and an intelligent understanding of the need for physical activity.
4. The purposes of the Marketing curriculum are: (1) to enable students who choose Marketing as a major field to develop occupationally viable skills; and (2) to enable students who plan careers in fields other than Marketing to understand its role in relation to other business activities and social institutions.

When measuring achievement, major questions become what level of quality should be required to meet the objective? and how will it be measured? Written examinations have been universally utilized for this purpose. It is a rather simple matter to define acceptable achievement as solving a series of mathematical problems at the 80 percent level of accuracy. The definition of an acceptable level of achievement becomes much more difficult when dealing with less precise objectives like those for the following Master's Degree Program.

COMPETENCY OBJECTIVES FOR A MASTER'S DEGREE PROGRAM IN SECONDARY EDUCATION

Teachers will describe and demonstrate curricular needs assessment and assessment of learning needs of students.

Teachers will describe and evaluate a variety of organizing principles for curriculum development.

Teachers will identify and evaluate various existing curricula and approaches.

Teachers will identify cross-disciplinary and interdisciplinary linkages between curriculum areas, including thematic and problem-centered approaches.

Teachers will describe and demonstrate procedures in adjusting curriculum for students with special needs.

Teachers will demonstrate diagnostic-prescriptive approaches to student acquisition of skills and concepts in their fields.

Teachers will describe and demonstrate approaches to instructional planning, including:

- identification of the assumptions and premises basic to curriculum choice
- identification of curricular scope and sequence
- demonstration of a content and task analysis
- writing performance objectives
- identification of instructional techniques, materials and equipment appropriate to the instructional objectives
- planning with a variety of approaches to instructional unit development
- lesson planning
- describing and demonstrating curricular evaluation approaches

Teachers will describe and demonstrate formative and summative evaluation regarding their curriculum and instruction approaches.

Program and instructional objectives and the accompanying criteria for measuring achievement are the most difficult to develop. Evaluation of the achievement of the objectives listed for the Master's Degree Program is the responsibility of the individual instructors within the framework of a traditional course structure followed by a culminating project through which the student will be evaluated by a committee of faculty members.

A more specific example of instructional objectives is the material developed for preparation of vocational education teachers. In this

UNIT 2

TITLE: Instruction Sheets

General Objective: After you have completed this unit of instruction you should be able to: (1) name and explain the use, advantages and disadvantages of 9 different instruction sheets and (2) design and construct an example of each type of instruction sheet.

Specific Objectives	Recommended Learning Experiences	Method of Evaluation
After you participate in the learning experiences of this unit you must be able to: 1. State the advantages and disadvantages of written instruction sheets for teaching trade and industrial education. 2. Define "Instruction Sheets." 3. Specify at least 5 considerations concerning the form of instruction sheets. 4. Name and explain the purpose of at least 7 different kinds of instruction sheets (as described in handouts). 5. Name the factors to consider in selecting jobs for training. 6. Name the teaching factors to consider in selecting jobs for training. 7. Name the management responsibilities to consider in selecting jobs for training. 8. Using the form presented in your hand-outs, design and construct: (All for one unit of work) A. One Job Sheet (A Task) B. One Operation Sheet (one or more steps) C. One Information Sheet (Concepts and Principles) D. One Experiment Sheet of Problem Sheet E. One Assignment Sheet F. One Job-Plan Sheet G. One Performance Test (unit) H. One Written Test (unit)	The following experiences are recommended for your use: 1. Attend class meetings. 2. Read all Hand-outs given to you (make sure you can meet Objectives 1–7). 3. Take written test which asks you to perform the behaviors in Objectives 1–7. 4. Hand in the instruction sheets designed and constructed for Objective 8.	The following method of evaluation will be used: *Objectives 1–7* will be evaluated on a written test to be given on the 4th class meeting. You must pass this test at a minimum level of 70% or retake it until you do. *Objective 8* will be evaluated on your ability to design and construct the 9 different instruction sheets named. **Note:** All sheets must be related to the same unit of work, be typed, and have no spelling or grammatical errors. These sheets must prove your ability to apply what has been learned in this unit of instruction. They will be graded: Acceptable (A, B or C) Not Acceptable (D or F). You must submit them until acceptable. *All Submitted First Time Together*

case, the example represents a unit of work. Note the comparative specificity of the criteria for measuring achievement as well as the statement of a general objective supplemented by eight specific ones.

Review Process

While departmental review of existing programs is essential, it alone may be too objective. Some mechanism at the college level must exist to provide the necessary objectivity. One approach might be a departmental review and, if deemed necessary, development of a course of action followed by submission of the results to a college committee whose function is program evaluation. If the latter disagrees with results of the department review, consultation with the department followed by some resolution of the disagreements would take place.

Another procedure might involve a single review initiated at the college level followed by the consultation/resolution process involving the department. The advantage to this approach is that the single review rather than two should reduce the length of time that elapses between initiation of the program review and its ultimate effect upon the curriculum. The first approach, however, would be more desirable to most since it tends to be in line with the concept that curriculum development is a departmental responsibility.

Among the elements to be examined in a curriculum review are the underlying philosophy and its relevance. Some questions that might be considered are:

1. What students should be educated?
2. Does the existing philosophy reflect the nature of the students being served or should it be revised?
3. Do the stated goals and objectives adequately reflect the philosophy?
4. How much diversity in program and goals should there be?
5. What should be the balance between general education and so-called vocational education?
6. Are the learning experiences and instructional methods appropriate and related to the objectives?
7. Are the programs up to date, future oriented, and flexible enough to meet changing circumstances?
8. Are they attractive and appropriate for the student population they serve?

A thorough, systematic curriculum review requires the collection of data, involvement of many individuals and a somewhat lengthy period of time for the review itself and development of any needed proposals. To expedite the process, routine revisions may be covered by formal policy. These revisions might include changes in: course titles, hours of credit, course numbering, prerequisites, and number of credits required for majors. Major changes in course content and programs fall into the category of new proposals and should be handled as such.

New Curriculum Proposals

New curriculum proposals should generally emanate from the division or department level. In the case of interdisciplinary offerings, they may be the product of several cooperating organizations. The thoroughly prepared proposal should be critically examined at the level where it was developed and at the college level. Review committees should take as much time as necessary (but, at the same time, avoid unnecessary delay) and demand as much information as needed. There should be no qualms about denying proposals not in accord with existing policies. A well-conceived, detailed, and rigorous process will be a limiting factor in the actual number of proposals submitted. Knowing that approval at the previous levels was not automatic, deans and chairpersons who eventually screen the proposals will view them differently and be extremely careful about taking any negative action.

Several examples of proposal forms for new courses and programs appear on the following pages. The second form which is for course revision is a much simpler procedure than that called for by the fourth document where the same outline is used for new and revised courses and programs.

PROCEDURES AND FORMAT FOR SUBMITTING PROPOSALS FOR NEW GRADUATE AND PROFESSIONAL PROGRAMS

Recommendation

That the Council approve the following procedures and format for submitting proposals for new graduate and professional programs.

Procedures

A. The Council will consider new program proposals at two regularly scheduled meetings each year—in January and July. Proposals must be received by the Council at least sixty (60) days prior to the Council meeting at which they will be considered. Programs which are expected to be initiated in the fall semester will be considered no later than the January meeting of the Council. Programs which are planned to begin in the spring or summer semesters will be considered no later than the previous July meeting of the Council.

B. A new program proposal will be viewed as a comprehensive institutional plan which has the approval of the institution's board and president.

C. New program proposals will be developed according to the format which follows. Thirty (30) copies of each proposal will be submitted to the Council.

FORMAT FOR PROPOSAL

A. Program description and objectives
   1. Describe the curriculum, including clinical, internship or other experimental components.
   2. Discuss the overall objectives of the program.

B. Program justification
   1. Indicate the projected enrollment in the program, the probable source of students, and the projected number of graduates of the program for the remainder of the present biennium and for the next biennium.
   2. Discuss the evidence available concerning the current and future needs of the state and nation for graduates of the program.
   3. Justify the program in terms of its uniqueness or distinctiveness.
   4. Describe how the proposed program relates to other graduate or professional programs in the state and to the total educational system of the state. Justify any duplication.
   5. Indicate what contributions the program may make toward meeting service and research needs of the state, region, and nation.
   6. List similar programs which are offered in contiguous states.

C. Program integrity
   1. Describe the admission and degree requirements, including options for majors and minors, of the proposed new program. List courses presently being offered which will be used to meet requirements of the proposed program and list new courses to be added, indicating which new courses will be service courses for other graduate or professional programs.
   2. Provide a list of faculty members associated with the program and include pertinent information as to their qualifications. If anticipated growth during the remainder of the current biennium and for the next biennium require additional faculty, indicate the number and general qualifications of such new faculty.
   3. Describe the physical facilities available to support the proposed new program, including the adequacy of classrooms, laboratories, teaching and research equipment and offices.
   4. Describe the library support which is

PROPOSAL FOR A NEW COURSE

Return to the Academic Policy Committee, Office of the Dean of the Faculty.

COURSE ____

(Dept., No., semester (f or s), title)

DEPARTMENT ENDORSEMENT ____________________ PROPOSER ____________________

(Person to whom questions should be directed)

DATE ____________________

This course will replace ____

(If "none," please explain on page 2 how the increased course load will be handled.)

CATALOGUE DESCRIPTION OF PROPOSED COURSE

Include Department, number and title of course, number of meetings, laboratory hours, prerequisites, and credits, exactly as they will appear in the catalogue.

PROPOSED INSTRUCTORS ____

____

If the course requires new or different skills or specialties, please describe the relevant qualifications.

PLANNED PATTERN OF OFFERING

Fall ____________________ Spring ____________________ Alternate years ____________

Other (please explain) ____

____

ANTICIPATED ENROLLMENT ____

SPECIAL NEEDS

A. Staff

B. Space

C. Equipment (estimate costs insofar as possible)

D. Library

Are present library resources adequate to support the proposal? ____________ If not, please consult with the Librarian and specify proposed additions (with anticipated costs) under "Bibliography" below.

OUTLINE AND BIBLIOGRAPHY

Please attach a brief summary which includes POSSIBLE required texts and supplementary readings (see LIBRARY entry above).

RELATION OF COURSE TO *OTHER* WORK WITHIN THE DEPARTMENT

A. If this course REPLACES an old course, please explain the rationale of the proposal (its position in the context of other department offerings, the circumstances that brought about the proposal, specific reasons for prerequisites, etc.).

B. If this course is an ADDITION to current department offerings, please respond to items in A. above and add, in some detail, an explanation of the intellectual necessity for the increased offering and how, within present academic and budgetary restrictions, that increase will be handled. Use separate sheet, if necessary.

C. To what extent and with what result have students been consulted in planning this proposal?

D. Given the College commitment to the education of women in a multi-racial community have you considered including, where appropriate, topics that will make the curriculum better reflect the experiences of women and minority groups in society?

RELATION OF COURSE TO WORK IN *OTHER* DEPARTMENTS AT COLLEGE

A. What other departments offer courses similar in interest and/or subject matter?

B. Have these departments been consulted?______________ If yes, with what results? Specific comments and written responses from consultants would be helpful here.

RELATION OF COURSE TO FIVE-COLLEGE OFFERINGS

A. Are similar courses offered at the other colleges?________ If so, why should this course also be offered at

B. What use, if any, will this course make of resources at the other colleges?

PROPOSAL FOR REVISION OF A COURSE

Return to the Academic Policy Committee, Office of the Dean of the Faculty.

COURSE ____________________

(Dept., No., semester (f or s), title)

DEPARTMENT ENDORSEMENT ____________________ PROPOSER ____________________

(Person to whom questions should be directed)

DATE ____________

This is a revision of course ____________________

CATALOGUE DESCRIPTION OF PROPOSED COURSE

Include Department, number and title of course, number of meetings, laboratory hours, prerequisites, and credits, exactly as they will appear in the catalogue.

PROPOSED INSTRUCTORS ____________________

____

____

NATURE OF REVISION AND RATIONALE

Add extra pages as needed. Additional space, staff, equipment, or library requirement should be stated. (Consult with the Librarian if additional library resources are needed.) If modification of the course content is substantial, please attach a course outline and reading list. If the basic nature of the course is being changed, please use a NEW COURSE PROPOSAL FORM.

SUGGESTED OUTLINE FOR THE PROPOSAL

The proposal should be prepared in acceptable manuscript form and duplicated so that 30 copies can be presented to the Program and Course Subcommittee. It should contain the data in clear, yet concise form. The following steps should be followed where they pertain:

a. Title page which indicates that the contents provide: "A Proposal for the Establishment of a Program or Course(s) in ______________________________
Leading to the Degree of ________________ in the College of ________________."

At the bottom should be a statement that: "This proposal was approved by the department of the College(s) of ____________________ on ________________ 19___. This proposal is being submitted by ______________________________."

b. Signature of involved department chairmen.

c. Introductory statements which include an explanation of the need for the program or course change and its relationship, if any, to existing programs.

d. Objectives of course or program: Specified in ways appropriate to content (e.g. student competencies, behavioral objectives, etc.)

e. Content outline.

f. Class hour requirement for course, or program.

g. Catalogue description.

h. Suggested bibliography.

i. Description of student population.

j. Qualifications of the faculty to be involved.

k. Admission requirements or prerequisites for the proposed course, or program.

l. Financial aid programs for graduate students; i.e., fellowships, graduate assistantships, research assistantships, and others.

m. Present courses, program and comments on facilities, laboratories, library collection, space, and equipment.

n. New faculty needed.

o. New courses needed.

p. New library and other special acquisitions needed.

q. Additional items if necessary.

COUNCIL ON PUBLIC HIGHER EDUCATION

PROPOSAL FOR INITIATION OF A NEW GRADUATE OR PROFESSIONAL PROGRAM

Submitted by

____

Institution Submitting Proposal

________________________________ ________________________________

College, School or Division — Department(s) or Area(s)

A NEW PROGRAM LEADING TO:

________________________________ ________________________________

Degree — Academic Specialty or Area

Proposed Starting Date

Approved by:

Board of Regents on (Date)____________________

President

(Signature)______________________________(Date)____________________

Date received by the Council on Public Higher Education____________________

Date and manner of review by the Council____________________________

____

Council Action: Approved____________________ Disapproved____________________

Other______________________________(Date)____________________ available to meet the needs of the new program, indicating what new acquisitions will be required for library development.

5. Describe how this program relates to the institution's academic organization.
6. If the program is in an area in which professional certification or accreditation is available, indicate the basic achievements necessary to meet such requirements. If the institution plans to seek such certification or accreditation, indicate the approximate date.
7. Discuss the sources and extent of advice and consultation which have been used in formulating organizations enjoying widespread recognition in the field.

D. Program costs

1. Project the estimated expenditures for the remainder of the current biennium, and for the following biennium, for the proposed program, including faculty, administration, library, research and teaching supplies, internship and clinical opportunities, travel expenses, secretarial and technical assistance, computer assistance, and other related costs.
2. Identify the sources of revenue, including amounts which are available, or are expected to be available, to support the program during the remainder of the present biennium and for the next biennium. Describe any special grants which may be sought to support this program.
3. If financial aid to students will be necessary to maintain enrollment in the program, indicate what financial aid is anticipated.

E. Appropriateness of program for institution

1. Discuss the appropriateness of the program in relation to the statutory role and scope of the institution.
2. Describe the relationship between this proposed program and other programs in the institution.
3. Show how the proposed program relates to the overall educational efforts of the institution.

The basic procedures used in the curriculum review process are appropriate for handling proposals for new programs. In addition to answers to questions included in the review process, information is needed about proposed texts, existing or to be acquired bibliographical materials, and procedures for evaluating the new program. Remember, too, that projected student interest and enrollments are sometimes overestimated. Vested interests often make it difficult for the involved faculty group to objectively judge the content, distinctiveness of the offerings, and expected student enrollment.

Policies are needed to expedite the screening process. These might cover the following:

1. limitations on duplication and overlapping with other offerings
2. reasonable relationships between time and credit requirements
3. objectives that support institutional philosophy
4. format for delineating content
5. bibliographic and other needed resources
6. evaluation procedures

As more and more innovative ideas appear, no professional educator dares ignore the need to examine such developments as: quarter systems, 4–14 calendars with unique four-week winter term offerings, the tremendous potential in media and technology, broad-based seminars, interdisciplinary freshman seminars to replace large broad survey classes, study abroad, community experiences, cooperative education and internships, and credit for numerous varieties of experiential learning.

Whatever is done, the view should be both long range and reasonable. Expectations should be in line with available resources. Only frustration can result if great time and effort are put into proposals that bear no chance of being implemented because they are not financially feasible.

Steps in Curriculum Development

In his classic *Basic Principles of Curriculum and Instruction,* Ralph W. Tyler raises four

APPLICATION FOR NEW COURSE

1. Submitted by College of ______________________________ Date __________

2. To be offered in Department or Division of ______________________________

3. The proposed designation and catalogue description of this course:

   (a) ______________________________ (b) ______________________________
   Departmental prefix and number — Title

   (c) ______________________________ (d) ______________________________
   Lecture/Discussion hours per week — Laboratory hours per week

   (e) ______________________________ (f) ______________________________
   Studio hours per week — Credits

   (g) Course description:

   (h) Prerequisites (if any): ______________________________

   (i) May be repeated to a maximum of __________ credits (if applicable)

4. To be cross-listed as ______________ , ______________________________
   Prefix and number — Signature, Chairman, cross-listing Department

5. Course to be offered (a) ______________ (b) ______________ (c) ______________
   Fall Semester — Spring Semester — Summer Term

6. Will the course be offered each year ______________, less frequently ______________
   (Explain, if not annually):

7. Why is this course needed?

8. (a) By whom will the course be taught? ______________________________

   (b) Are facilities for teaching the course now available? ______________________________

   If not, what plans have been made for providing them? ______________________________

   ____

9. What enrollment may be reasonably anticipated? ______________________________

(OVER)

10. Will this course serve students in the Department primarily?________________

Will it be of service to a significant number of students outside the Department?________

__________ . If so, explain: ____________________________

11. Check the category most applicable to this course:

____ traditional as generally offered in corresponding departments in other universities

____ relatively new, now being widely established

____ not yet to be found in many (or any) other universities

12. Within the Department, who should be consulted for further information about the proposed course?____________________ Extension ________

13. Attach a list of the major teaching objectives of the proposed course and outline and/or reference list to be used.

Signatures of Approval:

Department Chairman________________________ Date________

Dean of the College________________________ Date________

Date of Notice to Faculty of Proposed Course: ____________________
(To be Done When Course is Approved by Dean of the College)

Chairman, Undergraduate Council*____________________ Date________

Chairman, Graduate Council*____________________ Date________

Chairman, Academic Council for Medical Center*________________ Date ________

Chairman, Senate Council________________________ Date________
(Notice to Faculty)

Effective Date: ____________________________

ACTION OTHER THAN APPROVAL____________________

*If applicable, as provided by the Rules of the University Senate.

MINOR CHANGE REQUEST*

1. Submitted by College of ______________________________ Date ______________

   Division and/or Department of ______________________________

2. Change requested:

   (a) From:

   (b) To:

3. Statement of justification for this change:

4. Requested by ______________________________ Date ______________
   (Department Chairman)

5. Approved by ______________________________ Date ______________
   (Dean of the College)

Senate Council action ______________________________ Date ______________

*To be prepared in duplicate as provided by the Rules of the University Senate as stated on Page 17, Changes in Courses, g. as follows:

"Minor changes in courses are those changes which are restricted to any one or more of the following: (1) change in number within the same hundred series; (2) editorial change in description which does not imply change in content or emphasis; (3) editorial change in title which does not imply change in content or emphasis; (4) change in prerequisite which does not imply change in content or emphasis.

Minor changes in courses may be made in the following manner: The chief administrative officer of the originating unit will execute *two* copies of the minor change form, transmit them to the Dean of his college, if the originating unit is within a college. If the Dean approves, he will sign the two copies and transmit them to the Senate Council. If the Senate Council agrees that the change is minor, it will notify the Registrar's Office and the originating unit that the change has been approved. The Registrar's Office will make the editorial changes in catalogue material necessitated by the minor change."

APPLICATION FOR CHANGE IN EXISTING COURSE

1. Submitted by College of ______________________________ Date ____________

   Department or Division offering course ______________________________

2. Type of change(s) proposed:

   (a) Present course prefix and number __________ Proposed prefix and number __________

   (b) Present title ______________________________

   New title ______________________________

   (c) Present credits ______________ Proposed credits ______________

   (d) Change in lecture-laboratory ratio ______________ TO: ______________

   (e) Effective date of change ______________________________

3. To be Cross-listed as ______________________ ______________________

   (Departmental prefix and number) (Signature, Chairman Department requesting cross-listing)

4. Proposed change in catalogue description:

   (a) Present description:

   (b) New description:

   (c) Prerequisite for the course as changed: ______________________________

5. What has prompted this proposal?

6. If there are to be significant changes in the content or teaching objectives of this course, indicate changes:

7. What other departments could be affected by the proposed changes?

8. Within the Department, who should be consulted for further information on the proposed course change? ______________________________ Extension ____________

Signatures of Approval:

Department Chairman ______________________________ Date ____________

Dean of the College ______________________________ Date ____________

Date of Notice to Faculty of this proposal ______________ (to be done when Dean approves)

Undergraduate Council* ______________________________ Date ____________

Graduate Council* ______________________________ Date ____________

Academic Council for Medical Center* ______________________________ Date ____________

Senate Council ______________________ Date of Notice to Faculty ____________

ACTION OTHER THAN APPROVAL: ______________________________

*As appropriate in accordance with the Rules of the University Senate.

APPLICATION TO DROP A COURSE

1. Submitted by College of ________________________ Date ____________
2. Department and/or Division of ________________________
3. Title of course ________________________ Effective date: ____________
   (for drop)
4. Why is the course to be dropped?

5. Has this course been taken by a significant number of students of other departments?
   (a) List the College(s) or Department(s) from which student enrollment in this course has come, if known.

   (b) What provision has been made for meeting the needs of these students?

   (c) Is this course in current use in any of the Community Colleges? ____________
6. Within the Department, who should be consulted for further information about this proposal?

   ________________________ Extension ____________

Signatures of Approval:

Department Chairman ________________________ Date ____________

Dean of the College ________________________ Date ____________

Date of Notice to Faculty of this proposal ________________________
(to be done when proposal is approved by Dean of College)

Chairman, Undergraduate Council* ________________________ Date ____________

Chairman, Graduate Council* ________________________ Date ____________

Chairman, Academic Council for the Medical Center* ________________________
Date ____________

Chairman, Senate Council ____________ Date of Notice to Faculty ____________

Effective Date: ____________

ACTION OTHER THAN APPROVAL ________________________

*As appropriate in accordance with the Rules of the University Senate.

fundamental questions. The answers provide four basic steps for curriculum development.

1. What educational purposes should the school seek to attain?
2. What educational experiences can be provided that are likely to attain these purposes?
3. How can these educational experiences be effectively organized?
4. How can we determine whether these purposes are being attained? [9]

While Tyler's work has been oriented more toward elementary and secondary school curriculum construction, the questions are so logical in content and sequence that they are appropriate for curriculum work at the post-secondary school level.

Goals and objectives that reflect the institutional mission and goals are needed at the college, division, and department levels. Once these have been established, faculty members (because of their expertise in specific areas) should find it relatively easy to determine the content to be covered in meeting the objectives. It may be more difficult, particularly for the traditionally minded, to identify the most appropriate educational experiences. Effort is needed to avoid the lecture syndrome. A variety of approaches including individual research, class discussion, individualized learning packets, various technological devices from overhead projectors to computers, field trips, and workshops should be used.

Organization of these experiences into courses follows. A question to be asked is whether the usual three- or four-credit course is always the most appropriate. One- and two-credit units might serve the purpose better for some experiences while, for others, the full course is needed and, for still other learning experiences, a two- or three-semester sequence should be considered. Other possible questions are: Which courses are prerequisites for others? Where would interdisciplinary approaches be most appropriate? What is the best sequence for content? What experiences are the best for student acquisition of the desired content?

Evaluation

Too often, academic programs have been continued for years without much attention being given to the actual outcomes of these programs. While colleges and universities and their faculty have studied almost everything, the impact that they and their programs have upon their own students has been neglected. Periodic and careful assessments are needed.

An often omitted but most important component of every proposal for program revision or for a new program is an evaluation plan. Some of the questions and approaches described in the following material may be applied to these proposals, but are also useful for a continuous ongoing review process.

Some specific questions include:

1. Is the curriculum in accordance with the stated philosophy and purposes?
2. Does it reflect breadth and depth in terms of institutional resources?
3. Does the program reflect internal continuity with an appropriate sequence of offerings?
4. Does it reflect the changing interests of students?
5. Does it reflect the changing needs of the society served?
6. Are the desired results being obtained? To what degree are the desired changes taking place in students?
7. What aspects of the curriculum are effective and which need improvement?

A comprehensive evaluation process should also include an examination of the institutional organization along the following lines:

1. Does the current structure support the continued development of new ideas for courses and programs?

2. Does the current structure lend itself to the promotion, development, and exploration of new curriculum areas?
3. Does the current structure foster interdisciplinary approaches, experimentation, innovation, and communication?

Actually, there are numerous approaches to program evaluation. One developed by Eugene Craven identifies four areas: extensiveness, effectiveness, efficiency, and benefit. Extensiveness is a quantitative measure in that it includes data such as the number of student majors, courses, and degrees earned in a particular program. Efficiency is also quantitative since it involves the maximization of outputs given a certain level of inputs and resources leading to cost data such as the average cost of a student credit or per student major. Effectiveness and benefit are qualitative. Effectiveness relates program outputs to program objectives including identifying the desirable level of quality and criteria for measuring. Benefit has to do with the longer range value or impact of the educational outcomes to individuals, society, or scholarly inquiry.[10] It is here that difficulty arises in establishing measurable objectives in a valid, meaningful way.

Dressel suggests approaches different from the traditional "definition of objectives and assessment of student progress relative to them." His approaches "focus on processes and rationale" based on his supposition that curriculum evaluation and revision through assessment of student performance are simply not possible unless curriculum outcomes are defined in broad terms which transcend individual courses.[11]

Dressel's four approaches include historical and philosophical validation, which is inadequate because of its subjectivity. A second approach starts with the rationale—the assumption and principles—upon which the curriculum is based. This approach is through specification of the process and experiences as derived from the original rationale and desired outcomes. The third approach is process oriented. Numerous questions are asked such as: Are the various types of courses described offered? Do students fulfill these requirements as stated? Is there evidence that students and faculty understand and accept the rationale? Does understanding of the fundamental nature of the discipline emerge from the program? What behaviors or tasks provide evidence of success?

Dressel's fourth and final approach is qualitative—the extent to which the curriculum is current in offerings, content, bibliography, and instructional techniques and methodology. The number, quality, and sequence of the offerings are examined. Adequacy of faculty preparation and facilities are some of the other considerations.[12] While Dressel refers to this approach as a qualitative one, it is obvious that some of its aspects are quantitative. Also, a number of the questions to be answered are related to the standards of the various accrediting groups. If this approach is used, the standards might be an appropriate starting point. The reader is referred to Dressel's *Handbook of Academic Evaluation* for a thorough discussion of procedures and instruments for assessing curriculum outcomes in terms of student performance.

The implications of change on students, staff, cost effectiveness, faculty morale, institutional credibility, and future growth or even lack of growth and a decline must be a final consideration in the total review process.

FACULTY AND STUDENT ROLES

Faculty consider questions of curriculum to be within their authority. This has been more a matter of tradition than on the basis of institutional by-laws. Faculty are recognized as experts in their fields, which they believe makes them more familiar than administrators with the rationale for any curriculum change. Faculty members are affected by curriculum change that also emphasizes the need for their involvement in curriculum matters.

Some means must exist for encouraging and facilitating student contributions. A number of institutions have developed mechanisms for student involvement in decision making. While this involvement may be limited only to those areas which have a direct effect upon students or have been cut back as the student protest movement dissipated, it is obvious that curriculum is one area which should be of great concern to students.

Role of Faculty

Several reasons for faculty involvement in curriculum matters have already been cited. There is another. Because curriculum development should take place at the department level and faculty are traditionally department oriented, they should bear the major responsibility. If faculty are not involved, it is almost futile to expect implementation of academic policies and any changes in offerings and degree requirements.

Faculty attitude has a tremendous impact on curriculum change. Some faculty view teaching as a static process and resist change. Others, deeply involved in research, see teaching as secondary in importance and fail to expend the necessary time and effort needed to keep it vital and adaptive to changing circumstances. Still others are overly concerned with their own security and working conditions. As a result, long-range curriculum plans may not exist, or if they do, may be more beneficial to faculty interests than to the interests of students.

Faculty serving on committees involved in curriculum reform must be committed to their task as well as to the welfare of the institution. Their view must be completely objective as they work with curriculum objectives and the means for achievement of these objectives. At all times, they must work toward obtaining understanding and concurrence through two-way communication with other faculty. The majority of the faculty must concur with the outcome if any modification of curriculum is to take place or a new program introduced.

Although curriculum has been delineated as a faculty responsibility in some collective bargaining agreements, the 1977 study by Dan Adler disclosed no significant changes in the pattern of participation by faculty represented by a bargaining agent in decision making related to curriculum and new educational programs. The most significant changes appeared among institutions where faculty had voted against representation by a bargaining agent. In these instances, there was an increase from 6 percent to 40 percent in joint action with the administration on Curriculum Determination and from 37 percent to 61 percent in joint action on New Educational Programs.[13] There was a corresponding decrease in the lesser Determination roles as shown in Figures 8–1 and 8–2.

Sandeen expresses a concern that the recent growth of collective bargaining on campuses might even become a block to curriculum reform. It is possible that instead of being concerned with campus-wide educational programs for students that may involve the "breaking down" of departmental barriers, faculty may further isolate themselves into their own departments, secure with the contents of their contract.[14]

The importance of a vital, concerned faculty cannot be stressed enough if higher education is to retain its integrity. Only through a vital curriculum and its continued adaptability will institutions survive. Curriculum change should not be based on power as was some of that implemented because of the student movement of the 1960s. It should be based on educational

CURRICULUM

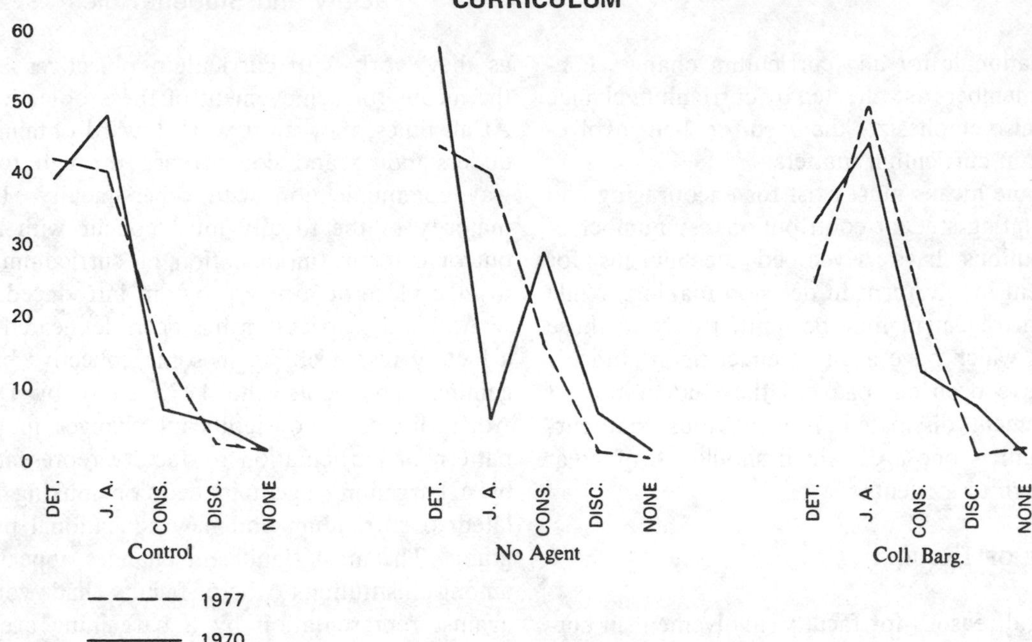

Dan L. Adler, *Governance and Collective Bargaining in Four-Year Institutions 1970–1977*, Monograph No. 3 (Washington, D.C.: Academic Collective Bargaining Information Service, 1977), p. 21.

NEW EDUCATIONAL PROGRAMS

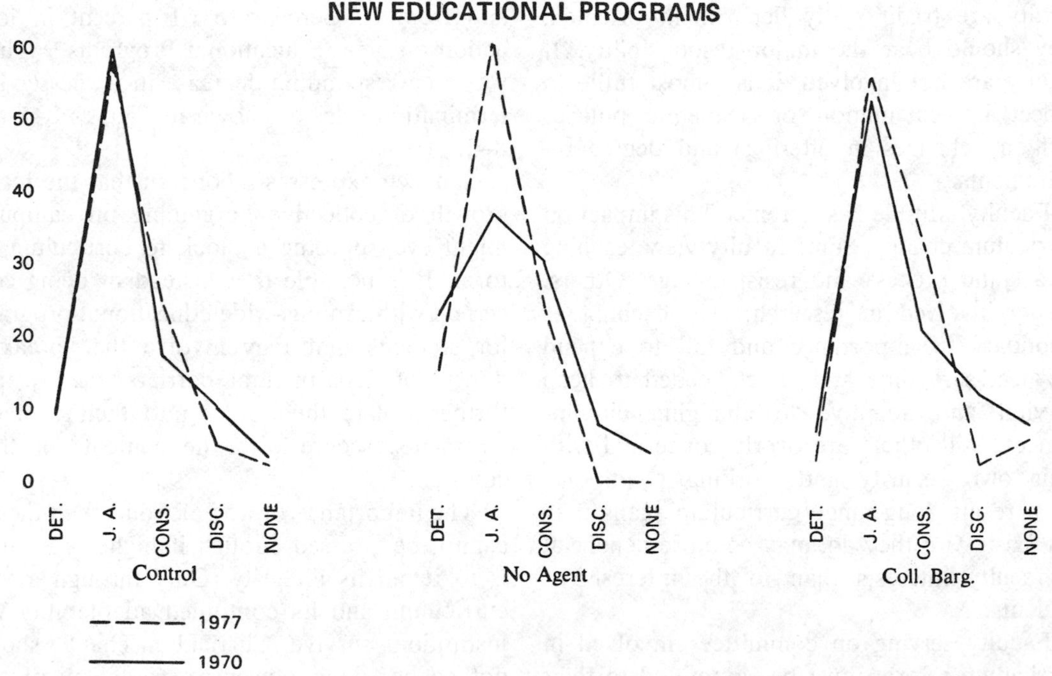

Dan L. Adler, *Governance and Collective Bargaining in Four-Year Institutions 1970–1977*, Monograph No. 3 (Washington, D.C.: Academic Collective Bargaining Information Service, 1977), p. 22.

theory and knowledge. Faculty possess that theory and knowledge.

Role of Students

Faculty and administrators should be aware that students do have legitimate concerns, complaints, and criticisms about curriculum matters. It is also true that students are not subject matter experts, are limited in disciplinary knowledge, and may not really know what is needed for their fullest development. However, student attitudes tend to reflect current societal values and their concerns are immediate. Their opinions should be sought in matters of curriculum and academic policy because of the unique perspectives they may bring to the discussions resulting from their youth and their position as consumers. The most appropriate point for student input is at the department level where the curriculum process generally begins.

THE ADMINISTRATIVE ROLE

As a result of faculty involvement in governance, the authority in colleges and universities appears to be more diffused than in other organizations. However, administrators may still wield considerable influence in curriculum change by means of their attitudes. Cooperation between administrators and faculty is needed, not complete control by one or the other. An administrator's role should be one of leadership and support as required by circumstances followed by assumption of responsibility for the ultimate approval and implementation of proposals.

Leadership Role

There is potential for conflict between the concept of faculty authority and responsibility for curriculum planning and administrative concern and responsibility for the instructional program. A suitable organization with clear delineation of faculty responsibility combined with skillful administrative leadership should result in the desired consequences acceptable to students, faculty, and administrators. Faculty and students may need to be prepared for change; administrators can help them develop the needed readiness and overcome passive resistance to change. Persuasion may be necessary to convince others of challenges and new opportunities that lie ahead. The mode of operation is vital since it is a major factor in whether an institution remains stagnant or moves ahead.

Hefferlin, in his previously mentioned study, found some interesting differences in perception among administrators, department chairpersons, and professors on the issue of initiative for recent changes in the programs of their institutions. To summarize: 45 percent of the time, administrators named administrators as initiators of change while department chairpersons and professors named administrators only 29 percent of the time; chairpersons identified chairpersons as initiators 15 percent of the time while administrators and professors identified them 4 to 7 percent of the time respectively. Another disparity existed where professors rated themselves 43 percent of the time but administrators rated professors 29 percent.[15]

Hefferlin concluded that both administrators and faculty members tend to conceive of themselves as the primary source of curriculum improvement. Each group sees itself as critical in the process, and as less reactionary and obstructionist than the other. Since they hold such disparate views of their own leadership and initiative, it is understandable that they become competitive and defensive.[16]

The leadership role of deans and chairpersons must be more that of a strategist in order to achieve the desired results. If faculty are unwilling to assume the initiative for academic change, the administrator's role may become awkward. Ability as a strategist will become even more important when the conscientious forward-looking administrator finds it necessary to assume the initiative in order to preserve curriculum integrity. The ability to persuade others to work toward change is essential if obsolescence is to be avoided.

Supportive Role

From a practical standpoint, curriculum activity should be coordinated with the budget and existing facilities. This means that faculty interests must be reconciled with administrative concerns. Administrators have a responsibility for providing projections and proposed resource commitments including short- and long-range budgetary projections. The curriculum proposal itself should include the total budgetary requirements starting with a "zero-base" rather than projecting only the needs that are additional to existing resources. This approach is preferable because it produces the information required for the newer budgetary procedures. The concept of "zero-base budgeting" is discussed in further detail in Chapter 9.

Curriculum workers need resources of several kinds. They should have available the services of an individual or office to provide needed historical and current data. This same office could determine the financial and other implications of proposals under consideration. Clerical support for the total effort is also needed. Funds are needed for communicating with and traveling to other institutions to observe and obtain information about their efforts. Workshops and training sessions are important for stimulating awareness of social and educational needs as well as providing inservice experience for the development of faculty competencies. Where appropriate, faculty should be provided with released time for extensive participation in curriculum development during the academic year and with compensation for any work done during unscheduled summer periods.

Throughout, the administrator who is truly interested in curriculum change will help to establish the necessary climate by supporting and encouraging discussion. Experimentation should be encouraged and assistance provided for those involved to reduce their hesitancy about change because they fear the unknown.

Decision Making Role

After a faculty committee and students have spent numerous hours in developing a curriculum proposal, a veto by the chairperson or the dean can have a devastating effect. If administrators keep communication channels open and provide appropriate information, faculty should be responsible enough to work toward developing proposals that will be feasible for implementation. A responsible faculty will not ignore implementation restrictions which force administrators into making unpopular decisions. Thus, administrative rejection of proposals should be infrequent and disagreement kept to a minimum. Previously described supportive attitudes and actions on the part of the administrators should be effective in reducing or removing completely the possibility of negative administrative actions.

The administrator who has played the leadership and supportive roles well will find making a decision regarding approval or nonapproval relatively simple. There should be little or no reason to disapprove the proposal. If for some unexpected reason implementation must be postponed or canceled, all concerned should be informed immediately of the action and the reasons for it. Whether the decision is positive or negative, it must be communicated immediately. No proposals should lie on some desk for days or even weeks on end. The individuals who spent many hours developing them deserve the consideration of a prompt decision.

Deans and Chairpersons

In addition to the roles just discussed that both deans and chairpersons play, each may wield influence at a particular level. Their impact will vary depending upon the personality of the individual as well as the specific organization for curriculum development adopted by the institution.

The test of the dean lies in his or her ability to provide the leadership needed even though it might be in opposition to the will of strong division and department chairpersons desiring independence and autonomy. It is the strong dean who is able to bring members of departments together for exploration and development of interdepartmental activity ultimately resulting in better ways to meet student and societal needs. No one is in a better position than the dean for identifying the basic issues since the dean has the total college program in view. Faculty collaboration and support may be sought through lectures by the dean and, in some instances, outside resource people. Finally, as an exofficio member of appropriate committees, the dean or the designated associate or assistant dean may exert a discrete yet effective influence. Extreme caution must be exercised within this arrangement so that faculty do not get a feeling they are being manipulated.

Because of the relative autonomy of departments, chairpersons may also be effective in the development of interdisciplinary approaches through persuasion of their own faculty followed by persuading chairpersons and faculty of other disciplines to participate. In the long run, however, the best approach might be through general college committees that cross departmentally defined areas.

A chairperson must be an individual who gains satisfaction from helping colleagues to grow, enriching the department and the discipline, and encouraging creative ideas as well as translating these ideas into action.

Cooperative, honest interaction and mutual trust must exist between the chairperson and the dean. Rather than being primarily concerned with furthering their own division, department, or school, a balanced consideration is necessary as they work with faculty members in evaluating, revising, and developing courses and programs.

SUMMARY

The primary focus of a college or university should be its educational purposes and the curriculum which is the means for achieving them. Curriculum change or lack of change is influenced by a number of factors. The emphases for which funding from external sources is available have an effect on institutional decisions as do the increasing constraints being placed by coordinating agencies and boards. Institutional size with the accompanying specialization and autonomy of departments are other deterrents, particularly where the development of interdisciplinary offerings is involved. Decreasing opportunities for bringing in new faculty with new ideas is another factor. Finally, new kinds of students with different ideas about what they want from higher education and who differ in their abilities from those of the "traditional students" make adjustments in institutional philosophy and programs necessary if the new populations are to be accommodated.

Cumbersome governance mechanisms can be a major deterrent to curriculum improvement. The organization must provide an exciting and vital environment with a mechanism for responding quickly when the need arises to reorganize programs and structures.

Curriculum should be viewed as the total range of influences upon students from the academic program to incidental, informal contacts with faculty. A comprehensive and responsive statement of philosophy including statements of mission and goals provides the base or point of beginning for the curriculum development process. While the most difficult to develop, program and instructional objectives and accompanying criteria for measuring achievement are needed. A circuitous process involving continuous program review is most desirable.

Faculty and students both have a role to play in curriculum development with that of faculty being a major one. If faculty are viewed as the experts in their fields, it is logical that they should bear major responsibility for curriculum development. While students are usually limited in knowledge related to a specific discipline, they do have legitimate concerns about curriculum matters. Also, student attitudes tend to reflect current societal values which along with their position as consumers make it appropriate for them to become involved particularly at the department level.

The administrative role in curriculum development involves leadership, support, and decision making. The leadership responsibility ideally is more that of a strategist than an initiator. The ability to persuade others to work toward change is essential. Administrative support involves both establishing a climate that encourages change and providing the necessary resources. Any changes must ultimately be approved by the responsible administrator prior to implementation. If the leadership and supportive roles have been played well, a positive decision should naturally follow.

ENDNOTES

1. Arthur Sandeen, *Undergraduate Education: Conflict and Change* (Lexington, Mass.: D. C. Heath, 1976), p. 13.
2. JB Lon Hefferlin, *Dynamics of Academic Reform* (San Francisco: Jossey-Bass, 1969), p. 111.
3. K. Patricia Cross, *Beyond the Open Door* (San Francisco: Jossey-Bass, 1971), p. 165.
4. Hefferlin, *Dynamics of Academic Reform,* p. 18.
5. Commission on Higher Education of the Middle States Association of Colleges and Schools, *Characteristics of Excellence in Higher Education and Standards for Middle States Accreditation,* Philadelphia, 1978, p. 7.
6. John G. Bolin, "Six Criteria for Better Goals," *Improving College and University Teaching* 21 (1973): 245–247.
7. Sinclair Goodlad, *Conflict and Consensus in Higher Education* (London: Hodder and Stoughton, 1976), p. 13.
8. G. Ben Lawrence and Allan L. Service, eds., *Quantitative Approaches to Higher Education Management: Potential, Limits, and Challenge,* ERIC/Higher Education Research Report No. 4, 1977 (Washington, D.C.: ERIC/AAHE, 1977), p. 49.
9. Ralph W. Tyler, *Basic Principles of Curriculum and Instruction* (Chicago: University of Chicago Press, 1950).
10. Eugene C. Craven, "Information Decision Systems in Higher Education: A Conceptual Framework," *Journal of Higher Education* 46 (March/April, 1975): 135.
11. Paul L. Dressel, *Handbook of Academic Evaluation: Assessing Institutional Effectiveness, Student Progress, and Professional Performance for Decision Making in Higher Education* (San Francisco: Jossey-Bass, 1976), p. 316.
12. *Ibid.,* 314–315.
13. Dan L. Adler, *Governance and Collective Bargaining in Four-Year Institutions 1970–1977,* Monograph No. 3 (Washington, D.C.: Academic Collective Bargaining Information Service, 1977), p. 17.
14. Sandeen, *Undergraduate Education: Conflict and Change,* p. 15.
15. Hefferlin, *Dynamics of Academic Reform,* pp. 75–76.
16. *Ibid.,* p. 104.

CHAPTER 9

Planning, Programming, and Budgeting

In order to cope with financial problems, higher education must look for ways to increase revenue by expanding the pool of students from which it draws and, at the same time, decrease expenses. Effective management systems are essential. In the past, even poor job performance has sometimes been overlooked because of concern for the welfare of the individual involved despite the detrimental effects upon students. There will be a growing reluctance on the part of funding agencies to increase income until higher education manages its operations more efficiently and provides evidence of increased productivity. A real challenge faces colleges and universities as they work toward not just maintaining, but improving the quality of their programs and faculty for meeting the needs of students and scholarship within the constraints of relatively fixed or, in some instances, diminishing resources. The following is an overview of several planning and budgeting approaches that are being employed for the purpose of improving management decisions.

MANAGEMENT BY OBJECTIVES

While a cost-conscious public is demanding that colleges and universities seek ways to improve management of their resources, there has been increasing emphasis upon the development and utilization of scientific management systems in the business world. As a result, a variety of new administrative and managerial concepts and tools are being adapted for use in higher education from those originally developed for use in large business organizations and federal agencies. Among these is the concept of Management by Objectives or MBO.

WHAT IS MBO?

MBO has been described as a means for working more effectively with people and includes procedures that make explicit the goals and objectives of each major component of an institution and a timetable for their realization.[1] As discussed in Chapter 8, objectives are detailed statements containing criteria which enable evaluation of goal attainment. They are more tangible and can be reached in a shorter time than goals. Each objective should cover only one issue and should be reasonable. The objectives should be in written form and reflect responsibility for completion. Goals are less detailed statements than objectives but, at the same time, are more explicit than statements of mission which serve as the most general statement of program policy direction.

All three are similar in nature, but differ in the degree of detail and level of operation. One broad mission statement may be supported by specific measurable objectives. Objectives and goals at the departmental level should support and contribute to those at the collegial level and assist in directing the institution toward accomplishment of its stated mission. All must be both realistic and attainable with a stress on precise objectives and results in place of the broader approach of activities and functions.

Members of a department should identify and define objectives for an academic year for themselves as individuals and for the department as a whole that are compatible with the overall institutional goals and objectives. Each administrator in the hierarchy works with the individual to whom he or she reports to reach agreement on specific objectives. Priorities and timetables are established as well as the achievement of agreement on the resources needed. Evaluative criteria must be included to enable determination of the extent to which the objectives have been accomplished at the end of the established period of time and expected results should be in terms of quality, quantity, and cost. It must be possible to assess the contribution of each unit and the individuals within it based on the previously established major areas of responsibility. Throughout, emphasis should be on self-appraisal and self-direction.

To illustrate specifically: a department chairperson might establish the following goal with the accompanying specific objectives for a ten-month academic year.

> Completion of a comprehensive review of the undergraduate programs and if found desirable, preparation of revised programs for implementation at the beginning of the next academic year. (Assuming that the institutional mechanism is responsive and will facilitate change not hinder it.)

a. Identification of a core of individuals responsible for completing the process (September 1)
b. Review of departmental philosophy, its compatibility with that of the institution, appropriateness for current circumstances, and revision if necessary (September 30)
c. Comprehensive evaluation of undergraduate offerings (January 31)
d. Completion of proposal for program revision where needed (March 1)
e. Completion of necessary approval for revision including making changes resulting from feedback during the approval process (April 30)
f. Completion of administrative details for implementation of changes as of September 1 (June 15)

By establishing a timetable, checkpoints make it possible for the department chairperson to assess progress toward completion of the total process while evaluating his or her own effectiveness and leadership in getting the job done. At the same time, opportunity is provided for the dean to periodically review with the chairperson the progress made and difficulties encountered and to offer the chairperson advice and assistance where needed.

Harvey recommends a procedure in which each administrator becomes accountable for one-year objectives that are tied and coded directly to goals and objectives of the institution. Quarterly reviews are scheduled with the individual's immediate superior as well as a final evaluation session at the end of the one-year period. Before the one-year period begins, the two administrators also agree on the peers and subordinates (also students, faculty, and staff) to be asked to rate the administrator on his or her efficiency and effectiveness at the end of the academic year. Use of the scale in Chapter 3, pages 52 to 54, is recommended. At the end of the full year, the administrator and his or her immediate superior develop a consensus as to placement on a scale based on the percentage of the objectives achieved.

This constitutes about 80 percent of the total evaluation with the rating sheet results comprising the remaining 20 percent or so. Harvey also suggests that this approach be tied into a salary/bonus system.[2]

Utilization of the MBO approach should lead to more explicit institutional, collegial, and departmental objectives that are compatible with the institution's mission and goals. Another result is the establishment of criteria by which the accomplishment of the objectives can be judged. There are a number of additional specific advantages for the administrator and the institution including:

- Administration
  Clarified job responsibilities
  Greater freedom of operation
  Better communication upward, downward, and laterally
  Identification and remediation of weaknesses
  Fairer appraisal and evaluation
- Institution
  Clarification of the institutional mission and a focusing of resources on appropriate goals
  Better basis for setting priorities
  Fairer wage program is possible
  Better morale among the staff
  Increased communication
  Opportunity for new administrative structures
  Better planning
  Management by exception rather than by crisis
  Improved administrative efficiency
  Can save money [3]

While the MBO approach does show some promise in improving administrative effectiveness, there are some attendant disadvantages.

- It is difficult to quantify much of what we do in education
- MBO takes time, particularly in getting started
- Some arbitrary decisions need to be made
- MBO can become a giant verbal game and paper shuffling exercise
- MBO does not control ethics or morals [4]

To the above might be added the disadvantage of the length of time needed to properly implement the system as illustrated by Harvey's recommended steps for doing so.

1. Develop an implementation plan and strategy.
2. Develop a model for your institution.
3. Clarify the program structure. (Example: NCHEMS)
4. Educate the staff and develop skills.
5. Clarify all job descriptions.
6. Review or develop the institutional mission, goals and objectives.
7. Use expert consultant help.
8. Obtain a staff commitment for implementation.
9. Allow time for a trial and a "debugging" period. (One year)
10. Allow enough time for proper implementation. (Two to five years)
11. Plan to develop a system of administrator evaluation with built-in rewards and punishments.[5]

MBO can be of great assistance in clarifying institutional mission, establishing priorities, improving planning, improving administrative efficiency, clarifying job responsibilities, providing a fair appraisal and evaluation of performance, improving the use of resources, and improving communication. On the other hand, unsuccessful utilization of the concept will result from:

> . . . forcing unrealistic objectives on subordinates, ignoring feedback, emphasizing techniques rather than results, failing to reward those who achieve, having objectives but no plan for implementation, trying to quantify everything, omitting periodic reviews, assuming that all is well, and refusing to delegate authority necessary for carrying out the objectives.[6]

While management science is widely applicable to many institutions, difficulties are arising in its application to education because education is not profit oriented and there is no precise means for measuring its product. Objectives tend to be imprecise and the faculty autonomous since they plan their own work and procedures without supervision. Responsibility for academic and administrative affairs is diffused by the involvement of Boards of Trustees, administrators, faculty, students, and alumni. However, it appears that the increasing pressures of collective bargaining may make college and university management more like business management in authority and responsibility. In business, management retains its authority and responsibility for planning and directing the enterprise. In higher education, it may become impossible to retain dual management authority and responsibility due to an adversary relationship resulting from collective bargaining.

While improved planning is needed and better data may lead to more informed decision making, improvement in higher education ultimately depends upon the faculty member's performance in the classroom and laboratory. Time alone will prove the extent to which managerial concepts from the business world may be successfully applied to higher education.

MANAGEMENT INFORMATION SYSTEMS

Effective managerial planning requires information broader in scope and less detailed than that required for the actual management or operational activities. Management information systems (MIS) are an outgrowth of advancements in computer science and one of the tools for providing decision makers with better information upon which to base their judgments. No amount of data, however, will eliminate the need to consider personal, social, and political factors including the impact of proposed decisions on people affected by them. It will still be necessary to arrive at conclusions only after weighing alternatives, balancing consequences, and exercising judgment.

MIS

MIS "refers to the process and procedures by which raw data are organized into information useful for administrative decision making."[7] Much of the data exists but must be collected and stored in a format that will make possible its retrieval for both planning and administrative control. Resulting reports present and summarize the various individual elements as required. Precise and accurate data are essential to insure consistency and quality but only data needed to reach a decision should be accumulated. Often, too much data or the wrong kind is collected because it is easily available. The criterion should be, "What is it important to know?"

Craven relates the concept of management information systems to decision making as

> . . . any method that provides the right decision maker with the right information in the right form at the right time so as to facilitate the decision-making process in pursuit of organizational and/or personal goals and objectives. This notion of an information decision system is based upon the view of decision making as a process involving such steps as (1) the recognition and definition of a problem or issue to be resolved; (2) analysis and evaluation of the problem; (3) establishment of criteria by which alternative solutions or courses of action will be evaluated; (4) initial gathering of data regarding various facets of the problem; (5) identification of alternative courses of action relative to the problem and an evaluation and selection of the preferred course of action; and (6) implementation of the selected alternative.[8]

Craven then identifies three types of decision-making activities for which information is needed. The first of these is operational or the day-to-day detailed transactions such as payroll, accounting, purchasing, disbursing, and inventory requiring routine reports usually in a fixed format. The second activity, that of management, involves decisions providing for general control of routine operations. Needed information is derived from operational data but in less detail. It includes management analysis and special reports required for monitoring, coordinating, or controlling operational functions, for responding to ad hoc requests from those involved in planning, and for providing reports to outside agencies. The third activity is planning for which information is needed in a very concise form indicating broad trends pertinent to an issue or problem.[9]

Lawrence and Service give recognition to three similar types of activities through their definition of three levels of information systems: (1) an operational data system; (2) a management information system; and (3) a planning and management system. All three are frequently included in references to a management information system.[10]

Systems and Subsystems

The National Association of College and University Business Officers recommends three major systems with related subsystems including the typical examples below:

1. Resource Management Information
   a. Personnel
   b. Facilities
   c. Equipment, supplies, and materials
   d. Finances
2. Student–Sponsor–Patron Information
   a. Students
   b. Government, industry, and foundations
   c. Alumni, parents, and patrons
   d. Participants, clients, and patients
3. Program Management Information
   a. Instruction
   b. Research
   c. Public services
   d. Academic support
   e. Student services
   f. Institutional support
   g. Operation and maintenance of plant
   h. Scholarships and fellowships [11]

The systems are a means for collecting and storing data and providing reports to meet organizational and programmatic needs. Historical and current data about the above are needed including student records, enrollment data, course demand data, facility planning data, personnel information, and environmental data that Craven defines as descriptive of the economic, demographic, and sociopolitical trends in the state or region.[12]

In addition to storing the data base, a complete system provides: information generated from the data in the form of historical profiles, comparisons, calculations, and projections; analytical tools including program profile models, enrollment projection models, flow models, and resource requirement simulation models; evaluation procedures involving extensiveness criteria, effectiveness criteria, efficiency criteria, and benefit criteria; and decision making procedures influenced by demands, supports, and constraints.[13]

Implementation

To implement a management information system, several components are required. Some decision-making body must be established to determine the kinds of information needed, make possible the accumulation and availability of the needed data, and provide the information for decision making in a usable format. The total system must make it possible to produce information that not only transcends organizational lines but also subsystem boundaries. It must be responsive to organizational and programmatic requirements for information and provide consistent support for the planning process.

Several approaches to initiating a system are possible. The first is an applications one in which individual components such as payroll, personnel records, student records, and registration and enrollment are developed and implemented one at a time. As a result, integration may be lacking and changes will become necessary to make the pieces fit together for a total system. A second possibility is to design the entire system in advance and implement the components all at the same time. The difficulty with this approach is the possibility that too many problems can occur simultaneously. A combination of the two is most feasible. The overall system should be designed in advance with the individual components implemented individually by priority with each one fitting into the others.

A simple example of the possibilities of MIS is a student data system that is capable of providing department chairpersons with a summary of the number of students enrolled in each departmental program, their status as full- or part-time students, the level at which they are in their programs, and other pertinent data. This information makes it possible for department chairpersons to schedule specific courses with the needed number of sections and to allocate faculty resources more knowledgeably. The same information may be shared with chairpersons of departments providing service courses for the same students. The data being used here for operational purposes also provide information for planning by making it possible to determine trends in the student population and project the nature of future populations and the resources that will be needed.

Additional applications of comprehensive management information systems are discussed in the section on planning and budgeting.

PLANNING AND BUDGETING SYSTEMS

In the past, it has been customary for departments to analyze their own needs and to build institutional budgets from these departmental requests. Changing circumstances require that the end product or output now be used to determine departmental needs. In other words, the output is the goal in the planning process, programs needed to produce that output are evaluated, and the needs of the departments to attain desired goals are then determined. Some of the recent thinking and approaches to planning are summarized in the following material.

PLANNING

Planning is "the act of identifying, specifying, and selecting alternative goals, objectives, and courses of action for accomplishing the mission or broad, overall purpose of the institution." [14] Effective planning is interactive, enabling its participants to coordinate their plans with the plans of others. Since many institutional problems are people problems, it will also involve as many individuals as feasible and appropriate which enhances the commitment and provides support for the goals and objectives of the institution.

Successful planning is in itself a planned process; its organization should reflect total institutional commitment. Some responsible individual should be appointed to coordinate planning by individual units and the resources provided, including provision of an adequate data base.

A master plan is essential to the success of the total process. It should be more detailed for the earlier years and become more general as the years pass. Master plans frequently cover a ten-year period and include a projection of available resources that may be applied to projected objectives, programs, staffing, and facilities needs. Academic objectives are established first, followed by supporting service objectives. Objectives and proposed program changes must be reviewed annually in terms of their relevancy to the philosophy and objectives of the institution since the master plan must be kept current if it is to be of any use at all. A more detailed discussion of goals and objectives is in Chapter 8.

Finally, planning must be integrated with the management function, including budget development and reporting, and be in terms of achievement so that a comprehensive evaluation component is possible. It is essential that the evaluation process be an integral part of the plan itself thus creating a continuous cycle in which the several activities take place concurrently.

Areas to be considered in the master plan include the three traditional activities found in higher education: instruction, research, and public service. An individual institution may include in its mission statement instruction alone, instruction and research, or public service, or all three. Faculty salaries and workload, student/faculty ratios, staffing patterns, class size, and estimated increases in costs for salaries, employee benefits, utilities, supplies, equipment, improvements, and new programs are examples of additional considerations when establishing a master plan. Alternative courses of action must also be explored including their effect on costs based upon changes in (a) goals, objectives, and programs, (b) policies, and (c) organizational structures.

One might combine the above approach with one recommended by Gamso. For each of the three activities above, goal setting and budgeting should be integrated with respect to:

> Academic Planning—Developing a mix of academic programs that will serve student needs and best utilize available faculty talent. Planning concerns include (1) program excellence, (2) comprehensive course and program offerings, (3) curricula responsive to student needs, and (4) personnel improvement through faculty development opportunities, pay increases, tenure policies, and such.
>
> Facilities Planning—Building and maintaining an inventory of classrooms, laboratories, and office space.
>
> Financial Planning—Distributing financial resources equitably. Academic and facility planning requirements must be balanced with the need for administrative services, such as libraries, computer centers, and business offices.[15]

Simulation Models

As stated before, higher education is struggling with defining its outcomes. Many cannot be described in the quantitative terms needed for the fullest and most productive application of the newer planning techniques. Nevertheless, computerized simulation models can be quite useful when examining alternatives. These models provide a means for examining numerous approaches to the allocation of resources by displaying how changes in one variable affect the other variables, thus clearly illustrating the impact of several possible decisions.

Detailed quantitative data of various kinds are needed regarding students, programs, faculty, facilities, and finances. Not only student enrollment data are needed but also their majors, level, and average course load. As for program information, kinds of data include the number of courses and sections of each offered by a particular department in addition to the size of enrollment in each section. Similar detailed information is needed about faculty and facilities, plus cost information on items such as salaries and supplies, as well as the expected revenues described in the section on planning.

The *RRPM Guide* by Gamso includes references to a number of generalized planning models. Among these are the most widely used models identified in 1976 by Plourde of the University of Massachusetts following his survey of 394 campuses known to be utilizing or evaluating planning models. They are:

1. *Resource Requirements Prediction Model,* available from the National Center for Higher Education Management Systems (NCHEMS)
2. *Comprehensive Analytical Methods for Planning in University/College Systems (CAMPUS)* produced by Systems/Dimensions Limited of Canada
3. *Higher Education Long-Range Planning/Planning Translator (HELP/PLANTRAN)* supported by the Midwest Research Institute
4. *System for Evaluating Alternative Resource Commitments in Higher Education* available through Peat, Marwick, Mitchell, and Co.[16]

PPBS

The underlying concept of PPBS (Planning, Programming, Budgeting Systems) or PB (Program Budgeting) is based on research by the Rand Corporation. PPBS was initially introduced in the Department of Defense under Robert McNamara and then mandated for governmental use by President Johnson in 1965. While, for various political reasons, PPBS has been abandoned by the federal government, its basic concepts are still being discussed and, on some campuses, implemented in some form.

PPBS is designed for long-range planning and budgeting (five to ten years). It serves as a means for developing goals and objectives, planning programs for achieving them, and determining the resources needed to achieve them. It is a planning technique only, not an operational one. Administrators are beginning to approach accountability and administrative responsibility pragmatically since it becomes easier to provide the cost accounting or cost effective approaches demanded by the proportionately dwindling resources for higher education. The process ultimately leads to the conventional departmental budget for operation and control.

PPBS is based on the general idea that budgetary decisions should be made by focusing on output categories such as goals, objectives, and end products instead of inputs such as personnel and equipment. It lays stress on estimating the total financial cost of accomplishing the identified objectives. It relates expenditures to results, program by program, then department by department. In short, a program budget is a budget arranged according to institutional purposes for programs and not organizational units. A format using both the object or line item approach and the PPBS approach provides a tremendous tool in that the major units of classification within the total budget are programs while expenditures for each program are broken down according to object categories.

Andrew and Robertson have pointed out that the appeal of PPBS for higher education lies in its concept of:

1. selecting specific objectives and systematically analyzing, in terms of costs and benefits, various courses of action to attain those objectives—planning;
2. deciding on specific courses of action (programs) and providing for review and control—programming; and
3. translating planning and programming decisions into specific financial plans—budgeting.[17]

In addition, an institution need not change its fiscal or academic operating procedures to implement PPBS.

The PPBS Process

While the concept of PPBS provides a framework for the accounting, planning, analysis, and measurement processes in an institution, each institution will have to adapt the framework for application within its own structure. Its success depends upon how successfully it can be incorporated into the daily operating and financial control systems of the particular college or university. Robert Ross implies that the steps used in implementing PPBS are common sense:

1. Identify your objectives
2. Specify the things that have to be done to achieve the objectives
3. Identify what goes into, what is done with, and what comes out of each activity
4. Compare what you have with what you want
5. Analyze alternative ways to achieve the desired objectives
6. Analyze and evaluate alternatives; resources required, how used, and results expected
7. Implement and evaluate the alternative selected
8. Change objectives and solutions in light of evaluation and repeat the process.[18]

While a total system may not be PPBS in the strictest sense, the approach can be useful in providing information for internal analysis, comparison, and decision making by establishing and clarifying the resources required for program implementation and determining the cost of achieving the identified objectives. It makes possible an analysis of alternative program possibilities in terms of anticipated costs and expected benefits. While the process makes extensive use of computers and computer technology, the human element is needed in the final decision making process.

As stated in the National Association of College and University Business Officers' publication on *Budgets and Budgetary Accounting,* "program budgeting cuts across conventional departmental lines and measures the performance of a program in terms of its output." Cost-benefit/cost-effectiveness as employed in program budgeting "may be considered as a measure of the extent to which a general program accomplishes its objectives and is related to benefit which may be considered as the utility to be derived from a given program." [19]

The system enables "an institution to make its decisions in terms of total programs rather than on a departmental basis, which is possible because the programs relate to end products rather than to the administrative organization or function of the institution." [20]

Hatley estimates that it would take an "average of three years to make the full transition from a traditional input-oriented fiscal planning methodology to one which is output-oriented, such as program budgeting." [21]

Formula Budgeting

Formula budgeting is a technique whereby a formula is applied to determine the financial needs or dollar allocation for each activity in order to enable it to accomplish its institutional mission. Formulas are most often based on enrollment data and credit-hour production. A limitation in using the technique lies in that its most equitable application would be in the area of instruction alone. To apply it accurately to all aspects of the research and public service functions of colleges and universities is almost an impossibility within the current sophistication of the approach.

Instructional costs are determined by developing a full-time equivalency (FTE) student enrollment projection and establishing a student–faculty ratio that is then used to determine the number of FTE faculty positions required. Total teaching salaries are calculated by multiplying the number of positions by the anticipated average salary. Varying percentages are added for other direct teaching expenses including clerical support, supplies and equipment, general administration, library, physical plant maintenance, research, and public service.

Estimated revenues are compared with the

needed amounts that were determined through the formula process. The gap between the two must then be closed by a process of budget cutting and/or seeking additional funds from appropriate sources, private or public.

The major use of formulas has been at the state level for the purpose of analyzing budget requests and allocating state funding support. Institutional application has been more frequent in the preliminary stages of the budget preparation process than in actual budget allocation because of the dependence on quantitative data.

Zero-Base Budgeting

Zero-Base Budgeting was developed by Peter Phyr and a managerial team in the late 1960s and used at the Texas Instruments Co. in the early 1970s. It was given increased attention by President Carter who applied it to the Georgia State Government during his tenure as governor of that state.

Zero-Base Budgeting is actually a planning system or process for budget planning. It forces each unit to reexamine its objectives, priorities, and the various alternatives available for achieving them on an annual basis. Harvey describes two basic elements of the system:

> Decision Unit—An element within a budget around which decision packages can be developed. A Decision Unit can be a program, activity, cost center (a unit or natural grouping of activities), or sub-unit of a budget which lends itself to Zero-Base Budgeting analysis.
> Decision Package—A document which specifies the costs and analysis of an alternative approach to funding a Decision Unit. The key to effective Zero-Base Budgeting is in clearly delineating various decision packages and selecting the best one for each area based on institutional objectives and priorities. There are usually at least three decision packages developed for every Decision Unit.[22]

Following identification of decision units, decision packages are developed by each unit's administrator(s). Various alternatives need to be costed out since at least three packages should be developed to cover various funding levels: minimum, maintenance, and desired. Harvey suggests the possible decision units below. Deans and chairpersons would select the units that fit into their particular organizational plan as their starting point for Zero-Based Budgeting. Following the list of decision units, Table 9–1 displays the steps in the process as perceived by Harvey.

This particular approach, which is a partial adaptation of programmed budgeting, can be a traumatic one for an administrator since it raises the question of whether a department should even have a claim on the budget. It utilizes nothing from prior budgets so that it requires starting from zero each year in developing a new budget. Each operating unit must justify from the ground up all aspects of its current expenditure pattern in addition to any increases. In actuality, each must justify its existence annually.

While the final budget is prepared in the traditional manner, strict implementation of the zero-base concept is impossible. The concept does encourage better management of an institution's resources. The difficulty lies in that the reductions or additions it calls for cannot always be accomplished immediately because it involves personnel, an area in which negotiated contract requirements frequently spell out processes and time periods for personnel actions of various kinds including termination and relocating or retraining.

Advantages and Disadvantages of New Budget Systems

The new budget systems have both advantages and disadvantages over the traditional approach. By providing for the establishment of institutional goals and objectives, planning will be more systemized and an improved allocation of resources for accomplishing goals and objectives should result. Decisions related to priority setting, planning, and evaluation will be more informed. A more accurate determination of the cost of operation should be possible, which will provide information in a format that is meaningful for both internal use and for interested external parties including legislative bodies, foundations, and supporting alumni. Expenditures are identified more directly making it possible for the institution to monitor its programs and supporting operations and evaluate results more accurately. Finally, the process requires that more people be involved in preparation of the budget. While very few will actually be in a decision-making position, the input obtained in the total consultation process from planning to evaluation will be invaluable. An indirect result might be better staff morale and a cost-conscious staff.

On the other hand, the new approaches present disadvantages that might lead to questioning their feasibility. The initial structuring and implementation require a shift in thinking. It is difficult to force an academic community to explicitly define its goals and objectives. How should output be identified and measured in the cognitive and affective areas? Is credit-hour production a legitimate measure of output? How can programs for measurement of output and identifying costs be defined when programs are interrelated more often than not? Many programs are not self-contained, that is, they depend on other departments and divisions within the institution for what are termed service courses.

Neither PPBS nor MBO have proved to be totally practical and applicable as administrative systems. Zero-Base Budgeting, the newest of the three, will most likely follow the same pattern. However, just as the concept of program planning and evaluation (PPBS) and the establishment and measurement of objectives (MBO) remain from the two earlier systems, the concepts of annual program review and costing alternatives appear to be the most likely ones that will remain after institutions have had extensive experience with Zero-Based Budgeting. Each system, in its own way, has brought institutions a step closer to improving the relationships between their objectives and their budgets.

Training administrators and supporting personnel for dealing with any new approach is essential to successful implementation. This is time consuming and expensive as is actual operation of a new budget system. An institution must determine whether the advantages outweigh additional expenditures. Also, as with any computer supported operation, more paper work is required and tremendous amounts of data become available, much of which can be meaningless and unnecessary. If a new approach to planning and budgeting is under consideration, careful thought must be given to exactly what it is expected to accomplish, its benefits over the previous system, feasibility of implementation including resources needed, careful structuring of the system to eliminate expensive and time-consuming procedures that yield useless data, and a process for evaluating the effectiveness of the system. Last, but not least, is the need to design an organization for supporting it.

Long-Range Budgeting

Some kind of permanent, systematic budgeting process is needed to avoid "crash" or last minute budgeting. A four or five year budget cycle is sufficient to accommodate cyclical fluctuations in income and a short enough time period to plan realistic future budgets which are in line with the priorities established in the long-range planning process.

Long-range budget work makes it possible

CHECKLIST OF POSSIBLE DECISION UNITS

INSTRUCTION

Divisions or Departments (Each Separately)
Courses (By Course or Similar Course Grouping)
Academic Administration
Instructional Support
"Special Academic Chairs"
Computer-Assisted Instruction
Faculty Development
Development of New Instructional Techniques
Continuing Education
Summer Session
Overseas Programs
Remedial or Developmental Education
Sabatical Leaves
Off Campus Centers (By Center)

LEARNING RESOURCE CENTER

Administration
Cataloging
Photocopy and Microfilm
New Book Purchases
Subscriptions
General Service (Checkout, Reference, etc.)
Book Binding

STUDENT SERVICES

Admissions
Student Records
Registration
Financial Aid
Student Activities
Lecture-Concert Series
Counseling
Placement
Residence Halls
Intramurals
Intercollegiate Athletics
College Union
Testing and Evaluation
Health Services
Graduate Admissions
Student Orientation
Student Judicial Affairs
Student Recruitment

ADMINISTRATION

Office of the President
Executive Management
University Relations
Alumni Relations
College Information Services
Computer Services
Institutional Research
Legal Services
Professional Development
Board of Trustees
Endownment Management
Planning Coordination
Program Evaluation

BUSINESS AFFAIRS

Accounting
Purchasing
Building Maintenance
Grounds Maintenance
New Construction
Campus Police
Campus Fire Department
Trust Funds
Preventative Maintenance (Equipment)
Auxiliary Services (By Separate Service)
Personnel
Facilities Planning and Development
Cash Flow Management
Payroll
Controller's Office
Annual Audit
Fringe Benefits

L. James Harvey, *Zero Base Budgeting in Colleges and Universities* (Littleton, Col.: Ireland Educational Corporation, 1977), p. 42.

ZERO-BASED BUDGETING PROCESS

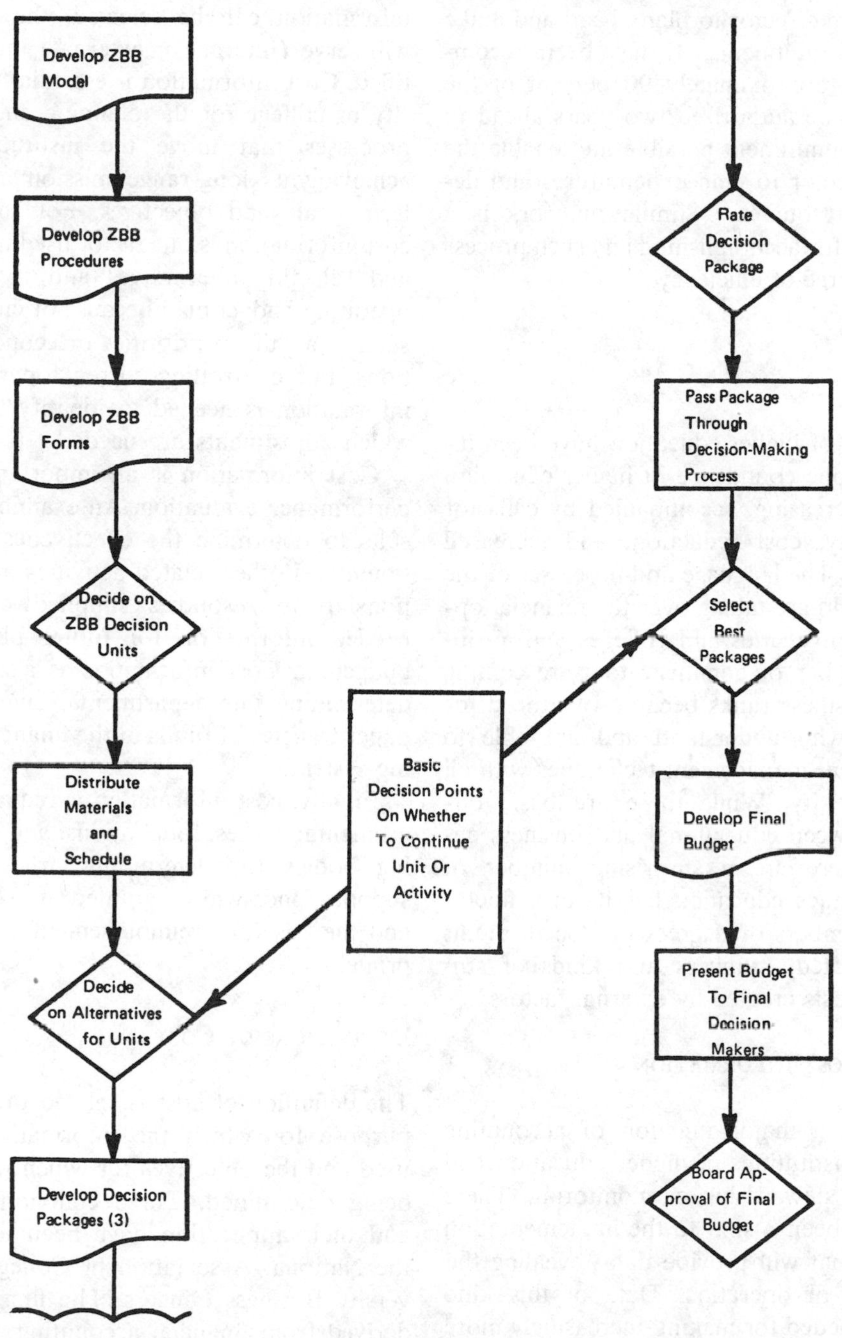

L. James Harvey, *Zero Base Budgeting in Colleges and Universities* (Littleton, Col.: Ireland Educational Corporation., 1977), p. 11.

for a program director to plan ahead and make necessary commitments. It has been recommended that approximately 90 percent of the expenditures be authorized two years ahead to make this commitment possible and enable the program director to plan expenditures and depend upon resources.[23] Simulation work is a requirement for accomplishing any such process with any degree of efficiency.

COSTING

As the costs of higher education have been increasing, public confidence in higher education has been decreasing, accompanied by calls for accountability, cost reduction, and increased productivity. The language and processes of the business world are taking over the financial operation of universities and colleges and an increasing number of administrators are coming from the business ranks because of a need for individuals who understand and are able to initiate current management techniques with all their complexity. While there are basic differences between educational and business enterprises, there are a surprising number of similarities since education has its own fluctuations in numbers of degrees produced, credit hours generated, numbers and kinds of students, and costs created by external factors.

Need for Cost Information

In the past, a major function of accounting systems in institutions of higher education had been one of stewardship or monitoring. There has recently been a shift to the implementation of systems that will provide data revealing the actual costs of operation. Data of this kind are sorely needed for making increasingly more difficult decisions regarding resource allocation in a more cost-effective way.

Before appropriate methods of obtaining cost information can be selected, the purposes it will serve (internal or external) must be identified. Cost information is essential to a university or college for the planning and budgeting processes that move the institution toward achieving its long-range mission and shorter-term goals and objectives. For this purpose, cost information is one factor used in examining and selecting alternatives and modifying the operating budget plan because of circumstances such as a shift in priorities or economic conditions. For controlling current operations, cost information is needed to identify the areas in which adjustments are needed.

Cost information is an important aspect of performance evaluation. An examination of results to determine the effectiveness of educational and other related activities and the relationship to resources supplied can provide needed information for future planning and budgeting. Cost information is also useful for determining interdepartmental charges for the paper transfer of funds in the financial accounting system.

Finally, cost information is required by governmental bodies, foundations, and other granting bodies for determining whether or not support funds will be granted, in what amount, and the basis for reimbursement where appropriate.

Definitions of Cost

The definition of cost is related to the specific purpose for which the information is to be used and the objectives for which the costs are being determined. Three common definitions and their application have been identified by the National Association of College and University Business Officers. The first of these is derived from financial accounting:

> Financial accounting is concerned with recording, classifying, summarizing, and ana-

> lyzing financial data. The financial accounting definition treats cost as the amount or equivalent paid or charged for something of value.[24]

While financial accounting "involves obtaining unit cost information, cost accounting involves obtaining costs primarily by organizational unit and function"[25] and leads to the second definition:

> Cost accounting is concerned with accumulating, classifying, summarizing, interpreting, and reporting the cost of personnel, goods, services, and other expenses incurred to determine unit costs. Expenses incurred during a specified period, as defined by financial accounting, are the prime ingredients of cost accounting for cost determination purposes. The costing process is designed to assign or allocate costs to particular units of service provided. The costs derived may be actual costs or may be other costs such as replacement, projected, or imputed costs.[26]

The third definition is taken from the field of economics in which

> . . . cost can be viewed from the "macro" or "micro" point of view. The macro definition of cost typically considers society as a whole rather than focusing attention on a particular institution. For example, the economist considers opportunities sacrificed by the community at large as societal costs external to the institution. On the other hand, the micro definition of cost used in economics focuses on the activities of an organization. This definition, in addition to considering expired cost (expense), may include other costs such as replacement, projected, or imputed costs. This latter definition is similar to that often used in cost accounting.[27]

No single one of the three definitions will satisfy the differing need for cost information since, as stated below, the definition depends upon the purposes for which the information will be used. This results in differences in cost information which can be confusing to the average faculty member and the neophyte administrator.

Kinds of Cost

Five basic kinds of cost may be employed depending on the intended use of cost information. These include historical, projected, standard, replacement, and imputed.[28] Most cost information has been acquired from an historical approach based upon the historical average cost of services. Historical cost information is based upon actual expenditures for salaries, materials, services, and utilization of facilities. Historical data are useful for examining what has been accomplished and relating its cost to the expectations for achievement. They can be helpful in decision making but, of course, do not take into consideration changes in policies, programs, or economic conditions.

Projected cost is an estimation of costs to be incurred in the future. The estimate is based upon historical data and anticipated changes including student enrollments, programs, faculty workload and salaries, and economic conditions.

A standard cost is a predetermined cost generally used for comparison purposes particularly in nonacademic areas such as plant operation and maintenance. Based on historical experience, judgment, and possible studies specifically for that purpose, estimates of expected unit costs are developed which are then periodically compared with actual costs. The analysis of the estimated and actual costs becomes a basis for evaluating the operating performance of those responsible for incurring the costs.

The name itself explains replacement cost as one incurred when facilities must be constructed or acquired to replace existing ones, or replacement of services and materials is needed. Such costs are not reflected in the accounting system but must be considered in budget planning because of the effects of rising costs. Institutions are utilizing assets purchased in the past, but the original cost of those assets misrepresents replacement costs. For this reason, replacement costs should be determined at the current or future market level to reflect the effects of inflation, or in a few instances, deflation.

The fifth and last kind of cost to be considered is an imputed cost that does not involve disbursement of cash at any time but is related to "potential resources that would have been available to an institution, but that were foregone because one alternative was chosen over another." [29] Imputed costs are important considerations in weighing the advantages of one particular alternative over another in the decision-making process.

Other kinds of cost terminology that the administrator should be familiar with include direct and indirect costs. A direct cost is one that can be readily associated with a specific project, organizational unit, or some other identifiable unit. If the unit is an academic department, faculty salaries are a direct cost of that department while expenses of the library, plant operation and maintenance, and various central administrative offices are indirect costs.

Cost Analysis

Traditionally, academic leaders in higher education have directed their efforts toward objectives reflecting institutional missions and ideals while the business managers accounted for funds and were responsible for the ongoing operation. While administrators were concerned about cost per credit hour, a specific program, cost per full-time student, or some such unit, answers have not always been as precise as they should. In addition, the data obtained generally dealt with the historical average cost of services based upon various cost-allocation procedures. Administrators are "now beginning to understand that different management problems call for different kinds of cost information" and are developing cost concepts that may be drawn upon to explain what other types of cost analysis are available to educational administrators and appropriate uses for them.[30]

Cost is a factor that must be considered both in making day-to-day decisions and in long- and short-range planning. Alternatives must be explored including the economic consequences of each. Cost information is essential for answering questions such as: Where are resources going? What costs would be eliminated by dropping a particular program and would such a reduction be short term or long range and accumulative? or What would be the cost for adding a new program?

For example, what must be considered in establishing a new program and how may cost analysis assist? Determination must be made of the initial costs needed to start the program and the transitional operating costs each year until it becomes self-supporting. The number of students needed to make the program a viable one and the availability of the needed student population is another consideration. From the present base, additional needs and cost for items including faculty, support staff, library, and building space must be projected on a long-range incremental basis. This can be accomplished only with full financial information including not only direct and indirect costs but also how different variables might influence the cost.

Difficulties in Cost Determination

It must be recognized that

> while costs appear to increase more or less directly in proportion to rising enrollment, they never decrease directly with falling enrollment. Understanding the fixed nature of many costs in the short run, and how they

> can be changed in the short run, will be a requirement for institutional management if many colleges and universities are to survive, particularly in periods of enrollment decline.[31]

This makes fixed and variable cost analysis essential. Many costs are "fixed" such as those for operating the Admission Office, physical plant maintenance, and a professor's salary that remains the same whether he or she has a class of thirty or fifteen students.

Administrators must continue to seek long-range ways to decrease fixed costs where possible. One example is cutting cleaning schedules so that facilities are cleaned less frequently in addition to which cleaning takes place during the day to avoid additional night salary rates. The establishment of centralized copy centers and computer service units are other examples, but these necessitate the establishment of recharge prices.

It is difficult to analyze costs in higher education because of the interaction among instruction, research, and other activities in addition to an interdependence of programs in serving students and joint resources upon which a number of departments depend. However, continuing effort must be made to clarify the relationship between cost and various levels of activity and how different variables influence cost while recognizing that, in education, cost is not directly related to volume or productivity and the focus is on processes, not products.

NCHEMS

A classification structure for program definition that is useful in costing and has received wide acceptance has come out of the National Center for Higher Education Management Systems (NCHEMS) which is part of the Western Interstate Commission for Higher Education (WICHE). In addition, the Center's *Cost Analysis Manual* provides a method for calculating the full cost per unit of service, information that can be useful for some internal management purposes as well as some kinds of public reporting. The system is concerned mostly with the cost of curricular programs including direct costs such as instructors' salaries and indirect costs such as administrative services and physical plant. Direct cost may also be derived by course.

The NCHEMS approach helps to determine where resources are going, the effect of dropping certain programs on current costs, and whether such a reduction would be only short term or long range and accumulative. The system makes it possible to distinguish whether budgetary variances have been caused by spending and/or inflation, new programs, curricular changes, or variances in student enrollment.

While such cost simulation schemes are helpful, academic policy and equity must outweigh cost consideration where feasible.

THE BUDGET

For the administrator, preparation of the annual budget is the most important administrative job of the year. An institutional budget is a management instrument. It may be considered a policy document also because it reflects institutional priorities and changes in academic direction. Many institutions are requiring preliminary budgets covering five- or ten-year periods. To develop these budgets, it is necessary to collect historical data about the institution to detect and interpret trends and assumptions that must be made about the future economy and the future of higher education.

Focus of the Budget

A budget is a plan expressed in words, numbers, and dollars. It reflects decisions that have been made about revenues, expenditures, and educational programs. Baldersion emphasizes the relationship between expenditures and priorities as follows:

> The budgeted expenditure pattern reflects the priority status of programs and functions. Year to year changes in the allocation for a given activity may be made because of shifts in earmarked revenues (control of the volume of an activity by the funding source), to offset price inflation that is eroding the real basis of support (influence of market events), because enrollment interest has shifted toward some fields and away from others (influence of student demand), or because an activity is assigned a changed priority (control according to institutional objectives). What is at stake, then, is the type and direction of control exerted over what the university is doing.[32]

Traditional annual operating budgets are constructed along organizational lines and emphasize expenditures. Each departmental budget provides for personnel compensation, supplies and expenses, and capital expenditures. The budget is an instrument for fiscal operation and control and can be described as object or line item since these reflect items for which checks are written to pay bills. Line items are separately labeled categories while an object class is a standard classification for each type of budgeted resource. An object category might be labeled clerical supplies while a line item within that category would be identified as duplicating paper.

In these budgets, almost nothing is indicated about the way expenditures are helping to achieve the major goals and objectives of the institution. The traditional type of budget tends to strengthen the status quo or existing programming since preparation of a line item budget generally involves little or no discussion about program goals, efficiency, and budgeting standards.

The deficiency of the approach can be seen, for example, in an application of the budgeting standard concept involving determination of the extent of the resources needed per unit of work load. This could be applied to establishing the number of faculty slots based on the number of full-time students. Weighting would be used for converting part-time students to a full-time equivalent. For some institutions, weighting might be needed also for those taking advanced graduate work as compared to undergraduate students.

The approach is incremental and assumes that the current budget is accurate and uses it as a starting base. Changes are made by increasing and decreasing line items and object categories as seems desirable in light of immediate plans and availability of resources.

This form of budget is still needed for actual operation of an institution but by using computers may be restructured along program lines making it possible to look at the costs of different programs. Thus, information becomes available for decision making regarding the most effective use of funds. It is essential that the annual operating budget be coordinated with the long-range institutional plan.

Development of the Budget

While a particular current year budget is being implemented and administered with control, the budget for the upcoming year must be prepared, defended, negotiated, and adopted. For purposes of developing the educational budget, there is a need to coordinate economic and educational criteria. Educators often do not possess sufficient knowledge of and experience with pertinent economic concepts and their implications. Administrators at the dean's office level and department and division chairmen cannot afford to be ignorant in this area and must continually be working toward finding a workable combination of efficiency and effectiveness.

Prior to beginning budget development at any level, certain policy decisions must be made and guidelines established which are communicated to deans, directors, and department heads. These provide guidelines for the administrators involved and should include information about salary and wage increases, the status of specific programs (elimination, reduction, retaining the status quo, or improvements in selected programs), anticipated enrollments, and staffing standards. Any indication of changes in work load along with the economizing adjustment each unit is expected to absorb should also be included in the guidelines.

While administrators from the central offices are most aware of institutional priorities and the overall resource situation, the budget process must begin at the level of the individual academic and administrative units. The process becomes a lengthy one as the budget is developed and moved through the various review channels. If all levels possible are involved in establishing objectives and planning, development of the budget and the ensuing analysis will not be seen as a threat. Involvement of faculty and students provides for them a beneficial learning experience while they, in turn, might provide a valuable resource for research and problem analysis. A controversial decision is more likely to be accepted if it represents the conclusions of a group of concerned faculty rather than outsiders or administrators alone. The same might be said for student participation.

In preparation of the document at the collegial level, the process begins at the departmental level with individual program input. This input is gathered together by the department chairperson who, in turn, develops the departmental budget for the dean who reviews it and determines not only whether it fits within the previously established guidelines but also whether the proposed expenditures are sufficiently and appropriately supported by back-up materials. The college budget is submitted to the specified review agency where a "hearing" is held and questions raised related to programs, efficiency, and unmet needs. In some instances, negotiation will be required followed by modification, as the central authority for the budget attempts to reconcile competing claims. The modification may require additional involvement at the department level.

Following approval of the budgets prepared by each of the units and colleges, the material is incorporated into a comprehensive institutional budget for presentation to and final approval by the responsible body whether it be a board of trustees or a governmental agency. The budget is "set" and the funds encumbered.

Budget Adjustments

Universities and colleges have absorbed tremendous growth sometimes to an almost unbelievable extent. Retrenchment is much more difficult to effect. While the amount of reduction (expressed in either percentage or dollar amounts) is one consideration, the length of time over which the adjustment will take place must also be determined. It may be necessary to cut back or phase out some programs to make funds available for new ones which better meet current student needs. It is possible, too, that some existing programs should be adapted and expanded in light of new needs.

Balderston describes four budgetary adjustment strategies which include:

1. Enriching or reducing budgetary standards such as student/faculty ratios and standards for building maintenance.
2. Proportional adjustment of dollar budgets which allows for distributing to each relevant unit the same percentage magnitude of downward adjustment or, as an alternative, distributing of resources on some work load base such as FTE enrollment.
3. "Every tub on its own bottom," a concept

popularized by Nathan Pusey, a former president of Harvard University, in which each decentralized school or major program (tub) is made responsible for generating its own operating revenue (bottom) through grants, contracts, gifts, and even tuition income

4. Budgetary adjustment according to selective program priorities which requires differential treatment for different programs and areas of activity [33]

A combination of these strategies might be desirable as would using different approaches at different times according to circumstances. The first approach can be accomplished without a detailed academic judgment and without threatening any specific programs, departments, or organizational units.

A strategy of proportional downward adjustments may, on the surface, appear to be the most equitable for all concerned, but if used too often might lead to crippling a particular unit to the point where it must close. The procedure can be detrimental to the level of performance and morale. It also ignores the concept of priority based on accomplishment of institutional objectives and will eventually lead to a general weakening of all programs.

While the Pusey concept has been an interesting one, it is not feasible. Its only advantage would be its motivational push toward obtaining outside funds and the recruitment of additional students. Seeking additional students for increasing enrollment purposes only can be detrimental to the academic quality of an institution. The concept also ignores the interrelatedness and interdependence of departments, particularly at the undergraduate level, and ignores the additional costs incurred by decentralization of adjunct services.

Budgetary adjustment according to selective program priorities

> requires assessment of the program commitments of the institution and comparison of the resource costs and apparent efficiency of each one with what it delivers, quantitatively and qualitatively, toward the objectives of the university." [34]

It can be the most upsetting approach in that it requires differentiated treatment and might even lead to reorganization. In order to implement, much comparative data are required and the capability for analyzing it in addition to which the necessary academic and fiscal decisions cannot be made independently.

The Decision-Making Process

Each institution must develop for itself the most appropriate process for decision making based on its own needs, organization, and the circumstances surrounding them. Decisions are becoming increasingly interdependent, and financial stringencies require that mistakes become increasingly unacceptable.

Institutional values are of extreme importance as is the necessity for informed decision making. When budgetary decisions are being considered, public hearings should be held to provide faculty and students opportunities to express their views. Another strategy is that of establishing advisory committees for preparation of the budget. Both kinds of activity should be implemented at the departmental and collegial levels. Besides broadening the information base for decision making, involvement in the process of as many as possible will develop in faculty and students a feeling that they have had an opportunity to participate and express their views, which should lead to a better understanding of reasons for cutbacks and an increased acceptance of the necessary decisions. A continuous process of consultation with the various groups involved should also lead to an improvement in the planning process for the ensuing years.

Regardless, higher education is being forced to determine the programs and activities that can be supported by available resources. Because everyone is being affected to some extent, every resource for support and decision making must be utilized.

Implementation

When the budget document has been approved, the financial pattern for the educational function of the institution and each of its units has been established. Administration of the budget becomes decentralized. The dean is delegated control over expenditures and may exercise discretion in switching around funds if warranted since it is impossible to foresee every contingency that may or will arise during the life of a particular budget. Money allocated for a specific category may not be used for a purpose other than indicated without special permission. As an example, funds may not be diverted from the salary allocation to purchase supplies.

Control must be exercised to insure that expenditures do not exceed allocations and that actual revenues meet the anticipated levels. If it becomes obvious that estimated revenues will not be realized, the budget must be periodically and formally revised by appropriate modification of objectives, activities, and resource allocation.

The fiscal year (July 1 to the following June 30) is the most common time period within which a budget is applicable. Each department head has primary responsibility for controlling expenditures within a unit and must keep in mind that allocated funds must last throughout the entire fiscal year. Expenditure accounts should be audited at least quarterly but preferably on a monthly basis. Through close monitoring, the department head is able to see that salaries for staff appointments and expenditures for supplies, for example, do not exceed the amount appropriated. Recently, it has become common for the monitoring to be accomplished through computerization of the budget. In these instances, it is still advisable for the department chairperson to have a departmental monitoring system as a cross-check until the computerized statements are completely accurate and received when due. This caution is mentioned because of the number of institutions where faulty data due to human error have been distributed, particularly when the computer has been a fairly new addition to the operation of the institution.

Each unit is responsible for its own portion of the total budget and the head of that unit is responsible to some individual above him or her in the administrative hierarchy. It is not uncommon for a dean to delegate budget matters to a collegial business manager, an administrative assistant, or an associate dean. Responsibility for monitoring the total institutional budget is usually attached to a central office which might be that of the controller or a vice president for finance.

SUMMARY

Colleges and universities are adapting a variety of concepts and tools originally developed by business organizations and governmental agencies for use in the interrelated activities of planning, programming, and budgeting. Among these is MBO or Management by Objectives which involves the establishment of objectives that are compatible with the institution's mission and goals. Setting priorities and development of criteria for judging the degree of accomplishment of the objectives are part of the system.

Planning for the accomplishment of the objectives, whether it be short range or long term, requires extensive information that is broader in scope and less detailed than that required for operational activities. A comprehensive management information system

(MIS) is a tool for organizing pertinent data into useful information for both planning and decision making.

New procedures for budget development require that the expected output or end product be the basis for determining budgetary needs. Computer simulation models are useful for examining the possible effects of alternative courses of action. The basic concepts of PPBS (Planning, Programming, Budgeting Systems) have been adopted on some campuses for long-range planning and budgeting activities. This system has a particular advantage in that it can be incorporated into the daily operating and financial control systems of a particular college or university. Decisions can be made in terms of total programs rather than on a departmental basis.

Formula budgeting is another technique, but it is more frequently used in the preliminary stages of budget preparation. It is most often based on enrollment data and credit hour production which makes it obvious that its most equitable application is in the instructional area since no acceptable means for translating institutional research and service functions into quantitative terms has yet been found.

A third approach is Zero-Base Budgeting which forces each organizational unit to literally start from zero to justify its existence. Strict implementation of the concept is impossible. The same is true of each of the alternative approaches to budgeting. Despite their inadequacies and disadvantages, application of the useful aspects of the newer budget techniques will result in more systematized and improved allocation of resources, more informed decisions, more accurate cost information, and a more accurate monitoring of the institution's programs and supporting operations and evaluation of their results.

An important aspect of performance evaluation is cost information. Previously, the major function of accounting systems had been one of monitoring. A shift to systems that provide data revealing actual operational cost has taken place since cost information is needed for the newer planning and budgeting processes.

A budget is a management instrument for fiscal operation and control, but it also reflects institutional priorities related to programs and functions. The budget development process begins at the department level with the dean responsible for determining whether the department's proposal fits within the previously established guidelines and if the proposed expenditures are adequately supported. The college budget is then forwarded for processing through the remaining steps required by a particular institution. Once the budget is approved and adopted, each administrator becomes responsible for monitoring activities and expenditures within the parameters specified in the budget document.

ENDNOTES

1. Daniel H. Perlman, "New Tools and Techniques in University Administration," *Educational Record* 55 (1974): 38.
2. L. James Harvey, *Managing Colleges and Universities by Objectives* (Littleton, Col.: Ireland Educational Corp., 1976), pp. 75–76.
3. *Ibid.,* p. 20–22.
4. *Ibid.,* p. 23.
5. *Ibid.,* p. 25–27.
6. Harry Rajala, Donn B. Stansbury, Florence Pyle, and Gary Rankin, "Management by Objectives," *College and University* 49 (1974): 540.
7. Perlman, "New Tools and Techniques in University Administration," p. 38.
8. Eugene C. Craven, "Information Decision Systems in Higher Education: A Conceptual Framework," *Journal of Higher Education* 46 (March/April 1975): 127.
9. *Ibid.,* p. 128–129.
10. G. Ben Lawrence and Allan L. Service,

Quantitative Approaches to Higher Education Management: Potential, Limits, and Challenge, ERIC/Higher Education Research Report No. 4 (Washington, D.C.: ERIC/AAHE, 1977), p. 28.

11. National Association of College and University Business Officers, *College and University Business Administration,* Third Edition (Washington, D.C., 1974), p. 25.
12. Craven, "Information Decision Systems," p. 132.
13. *Ibid.,* p. 132–138.
14. National Association of College and University Business Officers, *College and University Business Administration*, Third Edition (Washington, D.C., 1974), p. 13.
15. Gary Gamso, *The RRPM Guide: A Primer for Using the NCHEMS Resource Requirements Prediction Model* (RRPM 1.6), Technical Report 104 (Boulder, Col.: National Center for Higher Education Management Systems, 1977), p. 3.
16. *Ibid.,* p. 12.
17. Lloyd D. Andrew and Leon Robertson, "PPBS in Higher Education: A Case Study," *Educational Record* 54 (1973): 60.
18. Robert F. Ross, "You and the Common Sense of PPBS," *Educational Technology* 13 (1973): 57–59.
19. National Association of College and University Business Officers, *College and University Business Administration,* Third Edition (Washington, D.C., 1974), p. 159.
20. *Ibid.,* p. 4.
21. Richard V. Hatley, "Coordination of Economic and Educational Criteria in Budget Development," *Urban Education* 7 (1973): 320.
22. L. James Harvey, *Zero-Base Budgeting in Colleges and Universities* (Littleton, Col.: Ireland Educational Corp., 1977), pp. 5–6.
23. Joseph A. Maciarello and Willard F. Enteman, "A System for Management Control in Private Colleges," *Journal of Higher Education* 45 (1974): 604.
24. National Association of College and University Business Officers, Administrative Service (Washington, D.C.: 1975), Chapter 4:5, p. 3.
25. *Ibid.,* p. 4.
26. *Ibid.,* p. 3.
27. *Ibid.,* p. 4.
28. *Ibid.,* p. 4.
29. *Ibid.,* p. 5.
30. Daniel D. Robinson, "Some Thoughts on Cost Information in Higher Education," *Management Controls* 23 (New York: Peat, Marwick, Mitchell, 1976): 130.
31. Daniel D. Robinson, "Understanding the Financial Data (Health) of Colleges and Universities—Standards and Interpretation," *Management Controls* 23 (1976): 143.
32. Frederick E. Balderston, *Managing Today's University* (San Francisco: Jossey-Bass, 1974), p. 220.
33. *Ibid.,* p. 221–225.
34. *Ibid.,* p. 225.

CHAPTER 10

Accreditation

The accreditation of educational institutions began in this country in the early 1900s with the more specialized professional accreditation being initiated by the American Medical Association in 1905. Accreditation was originally based on meeting established well-defined standards that were largely quantitative. The standards are now becoming much more qualitative with the major focus on whether or not an institution is achieving its own goals. To illustrate, the Commission on Higher Education of the Middle States Association of Colleges and Schools has issued a statement that

> The accreditation of an institution is in part an affirmation that the institution has established conditions and procedures under which its purpose and objectives can be realized and that it appears in fact to be accomplishing those purposes. Accreditation rests on the integrity with which institutions conduct their educational endeavors and the orderly procedures they have established for ensuring the quality of those endeavors.[1]

There are a number of accrediting agencies of various kinds: state, regional, and professional. All provide impetus for the institutional self-study which may well be the real value of the entire process. A self-study requires faculty to inspect the educational program of the entire institution, school, and department. Following completion of the self-study, the on-site team visit and the culminating report often seem anticlimactic.

REASONS FOR ACCREDITATION

The major focus of the accreditation process is the quality of the educational program. Harold Orlans lists the following additional uses for accreditation: state institutional and professional licensing requirements; the need of educational definitions for statistical and administrative purposes; the need to articulate the programs of secondary and higher educational institutions and to assess the standing of students transferring to domestic and foreign institutions; and the wish to distinguish reputable institutions from others with which they do not wish to be associated.[2] The arguments in favor of the accreditation processes far outweigh those against.

PROGRAM QUALITY

Accreditation was originally a sorting process for the purpose of identifying those institutions that were not considered good enough for the "seal of approval." More recently, the emphasis has been on assisting institutions in identifying areas needing improvement and on the outcome of educational programs rather than the educational process.

Because great variation exists in the kinds and quality of the numerous programs in higher education, a major purpose of accreditation is to promote and insure at least a minimum level of quality. While some accreditation recognition is voluntary such as that by the regional associations and some professional groups, those who do not obtain it could be "in trouble." One reflection of program quality is found in the acceptance of the institution's courses and degrees. Accreditation provides the recognition that makes it possible for other members of the accrediting group to accept courses in transfer or accept degrees for admission to graduate school.

Accreditation also assures the student that his or her diploma and credits will be recognized; serves as a means for informing those who employ institutional graduates or examine graduates for admission to professional practice about the quality of the training received by the graduates; raises standards within professions such as medicine and teaching; and helps to provide prospective students and their parents with some guidance for selection of institutions.

Eligibility for Funding

Both public and private agencies see accreditation as an objective means for controlling access to funds and are making increasing use of it as a requirement for eligibility for funds. Institutional eligibility is the major recognition needed for funding rather than individual program review. In 1968, The U.S. Office of Education established the Accreditation and Institutional Eligibility Staff, which has since become the Division of Eligibility and Agency Evaluation. At this level, almost sixty accrediting agencies are recognized.

Criticisms of the Accreditation Process

Almost all degree-granting institutions are accredited by the regional accrediting associations. As a result, one might say that accredited schools are of minimal quality only and accreditation is not a sign of the educational quality it is purported to be. The criticism here is that the agencies are not selective enough.

Another criticism of accreditation is the belief held by some that it prevents flexibility and discourages innovation. This might be a carryover from the earlier accreditation processes that were quantitative and emphasized things and money. The criticism may also be a result of instances where accreditation has been wrongly used by administrators and faculty who are unwilling to change or experiment and argue that any change in curriculum or teaching methods would endanger accreditation. Institutions should be free to experiment and innovate. The accreditation process helps insure that experimentation and innovation do not become excuses for shoddy education.

ACCREDITING AGENCIES

Other than state agencies for accreditation, accrediting agencies have been largely created by the colleges and universities themselves. Accreditation may be tied to some form of control such as the program approval approach to teacher certification. In addition to state agencies, there are six regional associations and, as mentioned previously, almost sixty professional organizations. The function of the regional associations is institutional accreditation through a focus upon the entire institution. The professional agencies focus on programs or parts of the institution and may require regional or institutional accreditation as a prerequisite. Large universities may be accredited by as many as twenty different agencies.

State Approval

Because the Tenth Amendment to the Constitution delegates educational authority to the state, the state has the authority for issuing charters to degree-granting institutions. The state establishes minimum legal and fiscal standards. The major area for state program approval is teacher education programs. Under the program approval process, preparation programs for teachers and other educational professionals are reviewed on a regular basis. Where specific preparation programs have been approved (elementary teacher, guidance counselor, secondary school principal), the state certification office will issue the appropriate certificate upon institutional recommendation without the need for submission of supporting credentials. Over half the states reciprocate in issuing teaching credentials to graduates of approved out-of-state programs.

Because institutions of higher education must be state approved, states have the power to regulate and conduct periodic inspections of institutions for the purpose of determining whether or not they meet the established criteria. While patterns vary from state to state, a unique one exists in New York where the Board of Regents of the University of the State of New York approves the various curricula in higher education institutions of that state.

Regional Accreditation

Regional accreditation groups were generally active on the secondary school level first. Colleges then joined together to protect themselves and to have a means for dealing with colleges of a very poor quality.

Dressel summarizes the purposes of the regional accrediting agencies as follows:

> Colleges and universities have banded together in six regional accrediting associations to establish procedures which (1) certify to the general public, to government, and to other institutions the minimal qualifications of the institutions accredited; (2) provide limited protection against degree mills and disreputable educational practices; (3) provide counsel and assistance to new and developing institutions moving toward accreditation; (4) encourage improvement in institutions by a review of activities, by development of recommendations regarding program quality, and by preparation of guidelines for assessing educational effectiveness; (5) encourage continuous self-study and evaluation; (6) provide a basis for assuring that institutions are worthy of assistance from various federal programs; and (7) provide some protection to institutions against threatened encroachments on their autonomy, which might also destroy educational quality.[3]

There are six regional associations each of which covers specific states.

Middle States Association of Colleges and Schools: Canal Zone, Delaware, District of Columbia, Maryland, New Jersey, New York, Pennsylvania, Puerto Rico, Virgin Islands

New England Association of Colleges and Secondary Schools: Connecticut, Maine, Massachusetts, New Hampshire, Rhode Island, Vermont

North Central Association of Colleges and Secondary Schools: Arizona, Arkansas, Colorado, Illinois, Indiana, Iowa, Kansas, Michigan, Minnesota, Missouri, Nebraska, New Mexico, North Dakota, Ohio, Oklahoma, South Dakota, West Virginia, Wisconsin, Wyoming

Northwest Association of Secondary and Higher Schools: Alaska, Hawaii (secondary schools only), Idaho, Montana, Nevada, Oregon, Utah, Washington

Southern Association of Colleges and Secondary Schools: Alabama, Florida, Georgia, Ken-

tucky, Louisiana, Mississippi, North Carolina, South Carolina, Tennessee, Texas, Virginia
Western College Association: California, Hawaii (colleges only)

While all the groups have the same general purposes, they may follow different procedures. Their policies also vary. For example, Middle States does not work through state committees while in the South, association policy and state educational issues become enmeshed. In addition, the Middle States Association dropped the word secondary from its name as it has broadened its activities to include specialized and professional schools, proprietary institutions, and elementary and intermediate schools.

A major change in activity has been the move from use of a specific set of more or less quantitative statements that were used as guidelines to broader standards. These are applied to an examination of the institution's goals and the institutional means for achieving them. The standards are not static, but flexible and responsive to changing conditions and circumstances.

Other areas being examined are the rather common ten-year interval between accreditation cycles and the relationship between institutions and their off-campus programs. As for the former, change has become so frequent and rapid that accredited institutions may change character completely during the ten-year cycle making the original accreditation no longer valid. In the latter case, there is particular concern about the sudden proliferation of off-campus programs which differ in the nature of the student population, purposes, procedures, and program quality, all of which may affect the validity of an institution's accreditation.

Professional Associations

While the regional associations review the overall quality of the total institution, the specialized agencies restrict themselves to reviewing specific programs. Examples include business, law, library, medicine, and teacher education. The corresponding accrediting organizations are the American Association of Collegiate Schools of Business, American Bar Association, American Library Association, American Medical Association, and the National Council for the Accreditation of Teacher Education. Standards are established by the professional associations, which if met by the school make it more likely that its graduates will pass any examinations required for licensing than will graduates of nonaccredited schools.

SELF-STUDY

The preferred and most common preparation for an accreditation review is the institutional self-study defined by Dressel as

> . . . a planned and organized inquiry by the staff of an institution into the total effectiveness of institutional operations. In a complete self-study, all sectors of the institutional community become involved in a review and evaluation of purposes and goals, selection and utilization of personnel, modes of operation, past and present activities and accomplishments, and future role in relation to societal needs. The first purpose of the self-study is to achieve an understanding of the institution, to determine its strengths and weaknesses relative to institutional purposes and social responsibilities. The second purpose is to revitalize and update goals and operations in order to improve the performance and quality of output of the institution.[4]

A comprehensive self-study reviews institutional purposes and goals followed by an examination of the relationship between those purposes and goals and institutional programs, resources, and prospective resources. It forces the institution to look at itself critically, including its environment and the appropriateness of its statement of objectives.

Values of the Self-Study Approach

While a self-study is generally launched in preparation for a visit by an accreditation team, the study is a valuable instrument for planning and provides a means for continuing research into day-to-day operations. The process requires that an institution study itself on a continuous basis. It must be constantly assessing its strengths and weaknesses, evaluating its outcomes, and planning and working toward the strengthening of its endeavors. The self-study report becomes a valuable instrument for institutional improvement in addition to serving the needs of an accrediting commission. It is obvious that the process should be coordinated with the planning and budgeting efforts described in the previous chapter.

It is possible that the effect of the self-study process upon faculty may be more valuable than the set of recommendations received. Because the process stimulates professional discussion, it can lead to changes and program development that faculty otherwise might not have initiated. In addition, those who participate extensively will develop a greater degree of insight into the problems of the institution.

Content of the Study

The self-study process should begin with an examination of the mission of the institution along with a reexamination of its statement of objectives to determine their appropriateness. While this area of coverage is handled at the institutional level, the individual colleges, divisions, and departments should review their activities in light of the institutional analysis to determine how they fit into the larger picture.

A comprehensive self-study covers at the very least: philosophy, human and financial resources, organization and administration, curriculum, instructional methods and facilities, equipment and supplies. More emphasis is needed on educational outcomes. The difficulty lies in defining the outcomes and determining the means for evaluating them. It must be possible to define what students should know and be able to do as a result of their educational experiences and to measure their achievement toward meeting these objectives.

The completed self-study should describe the institution in detail, identify its strengths and weaknesses, and outline its plans for remedying the weaknesses, and any other future development plans.

Dressel provides an extensive outline in his *Handbook of Academic Evaluation* which focuses on outcomes and which would be helpful in a self-study process. Under each of the six major areas, a series of questions and guidelines for study provide extensive direction which in combination with any additional information required by the accrediting association should produce a thorough and useful self-study report. The areas covered are:

A. Determining institution purposes, goals, and educational objectives
B. Measuring educational and other outcomes
C. Evaluating learning experiences in terms of desired outcomes
D. Evaluating the adequacy and utilization of resources in terms of desired outcomes—types of resources
E. Evaluating the planning and decision-making processes in terms of desired outcomes
F. Interpreting objectives, means of attainment, and evidence of accomplishment to new faculty, to students, and to the public.[5]

Self-study activities should not be sporadic and initiated only when an accreditation review is scheduled. More valuable is a "rolling review process"

> . . . in which several topics or areas of study are regularly studied at intervals. For example, a five-year rotation might use the following emphases: undergraduate curriculum—offerings and requirements, general and liberal education; instruction and faculty advising; admissions, student personnel services, instructional services, library, physical facilities; research, graduate education; community service, extension; purposes, role, governance, organization, budget.[6]

Procedure for Self-Study

When organizing for self-study, the question arises: Should a new committee be established or should an existing one be used? While a new committee may be more objective, time might be lost if its members do not possess sufficient background. The advantages of both are possible if committee membership includes individuals with little or no previous involvement with the area under study as well as some who have experience. Care should be taken that the more experienced are interested, capable, and prestigious so that the findings of the study bear some weight. The self-study can be the most influential of all mechanisms for bringing about change.

As discussed in an earlier chapter, administrative appointment and election of committee members each have their weaknesses. A compromise might be nominations of large numbers from which the responsible administrator selects. Committee membership should include not only representatives of the unit under study but also representatives from other units that utilize its offerings. Alumni and, where appropriate, community members should be included. A fairly large committee is needed to distribute the work load in some manageable fashion. The guidelines distributed by the accrediting association will provide a pattern for assignment of specific tasks.

The chairperson should be an individual already well established on the career ladder of the institution. He or she must have the respect of all members of the faculty and administration in addition to possessing the capability for organizing large groups and inspiring group members to accomplish a large comprehensive task. Some capabilities in institutional research should be a requirement.

The charge should stipulate the specific coverage and the time period within which the study is to be completed. It is also important that the individual or individuals to whom the report goes be specified. In this way, the report could be structured according to areas of administrative responsibility. Finally, it should be specified whether or not the committee will be responsible for monitoring implementation of its recommendations.

The self-study process includes a variety of activities: examination of numerous documents; review and analysis of policies and procedures; interviews with administrators, faculty, staff, students, alumni, and employers of graduates; a tour and examination of facilities; surveys and others.

Key people on the committee should be responsible for writing sections of the report covering the areas for which they have responsibility. The chairperson for the total effort is responsible for coordinating the final report. It might be helpful to utilize a small nucleus of the committee to review the report for omissions, inconsistencies, and lack of clarity, all of which must be resolved before submission of the report.

The report must not be critical in its approach. To accomplish its purpose, it must be constructive and forward looking with an emphasis upon future growth. All data included must be relevant and provide the basis for the recommendations. There is no place for opinion.

Finally, the report must be realistic in relation to available resources. A document full of ideas is totally worthless if there is no possibility for implementation due to lack of resources.

Administrative support is essential. The institution must recognize the need and value for comprehensive self-study activity and be willing to finance it accordingly. The committee chairperson and key committee members need released time to coordinate the activities of the larger group and the subcommittees. Clerical support is essential as is the support of institutional research offices. Finally, the results of a self-study cannot be valid unless full administrative support is provided in the form of needed information as well as encouragement.

THE TEAM ON CAMPUS

Although time consuming and costly, accreditation status is sought by institutions voluntarily. A major tradition of the process has been an on-site visit by a "team" for the purpose of assessing the quality of programs, staff, and resources. Team visits, which usually follow the self-study, are initiated by institutional invitation. If the process and results of the visit are to be of any value, time and effort must be spent on planning the visit and adequate financial resources must be budgeted.

Because the expenditure of resources is so enormous, institutions are experimenting with joint visits by several accrediting groups on campus concurrently. This reduces the amount of preparation, the number of disruptive visits on campus, and the extra burden placed upon administrators and faculty by accreditation activities. One college of education combined the visits of the National Council for the Accreditation of Teacher Education and the State Department of Education program approval visit with the institutional review by the regional association. While the period of the on-site visit was an extremely busy one, only one set of materials had to be prepared and the college was able to return to normal operation for several years.

Planning Considerations

It is not unusual for the chairperson of the accrediting team to make one or more campus visits for establishing schedules, discussing procedures, identifying individuals to be interviewed, and determining the kinds of documentation that should be available. Because of the many small details to be handled, an institutional contact person is needed to coordinate the planning activities and the team visit. At the college level, this might be one of the assistant or associate deans aided by an administrative assistant.

Interviews are generally scheduled with all chairpersons and program directors as well as any persons playing a coordinating role. Representative groups of faculty, students, and alumni should be involved. Some accrediting groups request scheduling observations of classroom instruction, visits to off-campus sites including field experience locations, tours of facilities, and an opportunity to examine instructional materials and library resources. Maximum use must be made of time that is really minimal for a huge task.

Arrangements must be made for meals, housing, and adequate facilities for team meetings. An opening reception involving team members and key administrators is a means for all to become acquainted on an informal basis. Some "working meals" that provide additional time for discussion among team members and administrators should be scheduled. Meals during the latter part of the visit might be for team members alone, thus providing additional time for needed discussion among themselves.

While housing is frequently off campus, a campus headquarters is needed. The facility must be large enough to serve as a meeting room for the entire team and provide space where all might prepare a draft of their observations and recommendations prior to leaving the campus. In the same location, all relevant documents should be made available for examination for the duration of the visit. Finally, the area must provide complete privacy.

The institutional representative should work with the representative of the accrediting agency to develop instructions for gathering relevant data and preparing the most appropriate documentation for its presentation. The quantity should be limited by determining precisely what is needed. If not limited, the amount of information available could be overwhelming. The documentation must be prepared with care so that it represents the institution adequately, appropriately, and correctly. Useful information includes enrollment figures, demographic descriptions of student populations, and descriptive information about staff, programs, instructional resources, physical facilities, institutional and administrative organization, and financial resources.

Some of the documentary information should be forwarded to team members prior to their visit. This should be done in sufficient time to allow at least two weeks for examination of the material. Team members will then arrive with the necessary background information for making their on-site activities more productive.

Ultimately, the success of the results of the accreditation process depends upon the caliber and competence of the team members. Some are able to approach the task analytically and identify strengths and weaknesses within the brief span of time allowed. Others tend to use their own institutions as a frame of reference which narrows their perspective and reduces the objectivity of the results. In-service training for team members is not an unrealistic concept. While a brief orientation session may be conducted by the team chairperson, much more is really needed to prepare members for asking the appropriate questions, applying the standards, and preparing a written report with the expression of concerns and, where appropriate, recommendations for improvement. Weaknesses in the process should be kept in mind when reviewing the final report submitted by any accreditation agency.

THE REPORT

While there is concern about the validity of accreditation procedures and their attendant control upon institutions, no other more appropriate method has yet been developed. The current approach utilizing a kind of self-regulation is certainly preferable to federal regulation. Continued effort is being made toward development of an approach that is more qualitative and that assesses outcomes more than processes. Meanwhile, colleges and universities should use the process and culminating reports in working toward institutional improvement, since they are the best approach yet devised.

Accreditation Status

> In the final analysis, accreditation depends upon the credibility of the description and analysis of significant facets of the institution's functions and operations in relation to some notions about quality education.[7]

The accrediting commission of the specific agency involved is responsible for the ultimate decision regarding accreditation status. To arrive at this conclusion, examination of the self-study results, team report, and any other information available takes place. The Middle States Association defines the decision thus:

> "Accreditation decision" means the action taken by each Commission in approving or

rejecting any application for accreditation, refusing to accredit an application, reaffirming or withdrawing the existing accreditation of a member, or reducing the period during which an existing accreditation previously had been approved.[8]

INSTITUTIONAL ANALYSIS OF THE REPORT

Upon receipt, the report should be read immediately by the administrators, department chairpersons, and the members of the self-study committee. The purpose for this review is to identify any discrepancies between information in the report and actual circumstances. In addition to possible weaknesses in team members, other restraints of the on-site visit must be remembered. The amount of time may have been insufficient; a team member may have had difficulty in eliciting information from some staff members; or institutional data may have been too sparse. If discrepancies do exist or there has been a misinterpretation of the data, contact should be made with the accrediting agency for resolution of the specific problem.

After the recommendations have been reviewed by administrators and appropriate faculty, written responses to them should be gathered and organized for forwarding to the accrediting agency. The institutional response should describe the action to be taken regarding each recommendation and reasons given if it is determined that one or more recommendations should not be implemented.

The self-study should have brought about some changes even before the on-site visit. However, it is not unusual for administrators to find the accreditation report also helpful in bringing about desirable change. It is possible that the report may reflect ideas and concerns expressed by administrators to team members.

If the total process beginning with initiating the self-study has been managed with the responsible committee seeking suggestions and reactions to its deliberations, there should have been created a climate of receptivity toward recommendations made as a result of the study. The ultimate success of a self-study and the accreditation visit is reflected in the action taken on the ensuing recommendations.

SUMMARY

The focus of accreditation has shifted from an earlier emphasis on quantitative standard to the quality of educational programs. Accreditation serves to promote and insure at least a minimum level of quality and is used by public and private agencies as one requirement for funding eligibility. State agencies, six regional associations, and almost sixty professional organizations are involved in accreditation activities.

Prior to the campus visit by a team, an institutional self-study involving a review of the institutional purposes and goals and the relationship between them and the programs, resources, and prospective resources must be submitted. A continuous self-study effort that focuses upon outcomes is a valuable instrument for planning and institutional research. Involvement of highly respected, forward looking faculty will make the findings of any study more acceptable to other faculty, but all faculty should be involved or consulted in some way during the process. The same is true for representative groups of students and alumni.

The campus visit by the team selected to represent the accrediting agency may seem anticlimactic. Detailed planning is needed, though, so that the efforts of the team members are as productive as possible. The process is not without weaknesses, but it and the culminating reports with their recommendations are important to comprehensive planning efforts.

ENDNOTES

1. Commission on Higher Education and the Middle States Association of Colleges and Schools, *Accreditation, Special Programs, and Off-Campus Educational Activities,* (December, 1977), p. 1.
2. Harold Orlans, *Private Accreditation and Public Eligibility* (Lexington, Mass.: D. C. Heath, 1975), p. 6.
3. Paul L. Dressel, *Handbook of Academic Evaluation: Assessing Institutional Effectiveness, Student Progress, and Professional Performance for Decision Making in Higher Education* (San Francisco: Jossey-Bass, 1976), p. 405.
4. *Ibid.,* p. 401.
5. *Ibid.,* p. 419–422.
6. *Ibid.,* p. 430.
7. Joseph J. Semrow, "Towards Maximizing the Analytical Aspects of the Evaluating/Accrediting Process," *North Central Association Quarterly* 49 (1974): 284.
8. Middle States Association of Colleges and Schools, *By-Laws,* Article IX, Section 2a, (1976).

Selected Bibliography

ALM, Kent G.; EHRLE, Elwood B.; and WEBSTER, Bill R. "Managing Faculty Reductions." *Journal of Higher Education* 63 (1977): 153–163.

ANGELL, George W.; KELLEY, Edward P., Jr.; and Associates. *Handbook of Faculty Bargaining: Asserting Administrative Leadership for Institutional Progress by Preparing for Bargaining, Negotiating, and Administering Contracts, and Improving the Bargaining Process.* San Francisco: Jossey-Bass, 1977.

ASTIN, Alexander W. *Academic Gamesmanship.* New York: Praeger Publishers, 1976.

BALDERSTON, Frederick E. *Managing Today's University.* San Francisco: Jossey-Bass, 1974.

BALDRIDGE, J. Victor. *Power and Conflict in the University: Research in the Sociology of Complex Organizations.* New York: Wiley, 1971.

BALDRIDGE, J. Victor; CURTIS, David V.; ECKER, George; and RILEY, Gary L. *Policy Making and Effective Leadership.* San Francisco: Jossey-Bass, 1978.

BEGIN, James P. "Statutory Definitions of the Scope of Negotiations: The Implications for Traditional Faculty Governance." *Journal of Higher Education* 49 (1978): 247–260.

BELKNAP, Robert L. and KUHNS, Richard. *Tradition and Innovation.* New York: Columbia University Press, 1977.

BOWER, Cathleen P. and RENKIEWICZ, Nancy K. *A Handbook for Using the Student Outcomes Questionnaires.* Boulder, Col.: National Center For Higher Education Management Systems, 1977.

BRANN, James and EMMET, Thomas A., eds. *The Academic Department or Division Chairman: A Complex Role.* Detroit: Belamp Publishing, 1972.

BRUBACHER, John S. and RUDY, Willis. *Higher Education in Transition.* 3rd ed. New York: Harper and Row, 1976.

CARNEGIE COMMISSION ON HIGHER EDUCATION. *A Digest of Reports of the Carnegie Commission on Higher Education.* New York: McGraw-Hill, 1974.

CARR, Robert K. and VAN EYCK, Daniel K. *Collective Bargaining Comes to the Campus.* Washington, D.C.: American Council on Education, 1973.

CENTRA, John A. *Renewing and Evaluating Teaching.* San Francisco: Jossey-Bass, 1977.

———. "Types of Faculty Development Programs." *Journal of Higher Education* 49 (1978): 151–162.

CHEEK, Logan M. *Zero-Base Budgeting Comes of Age.* New York: American Management Association, 1977.

The Chronicle of Higher Education. Washington, D.C. The Chronicle of Higher Education, Inc.

COHEN, Michael D. and MARCH, James G.

Leadership and Ambiguity. New York: McGraw-Hill, 1974.

CONRAD, C. "University Goals: An Operative Approach." *Journal of Higher Education* 45 (1974): 505–515.

CROSS, K. Patricia. *Beyond the Open Door.* San Francisco: Jossey-Bass, 1971.

DECKER, C. Richard and FLETCHER, Alan D. "Campus Committees: Values and Hazards." *Educational Record* 54 (1973): 226–230.

DOYLE, Kenneth O. *Student Evaluation of Instruction:* Lexington, Mass.: D. C. Heath, 1975.

DRESCH, Stephen P. "A Critique of Planning Models for Postsecondary Education: Current Feasibility, Potential Relevance, and a Prospectus for Further Research." *Journal of Higher Education* 46 (1975): 245–286.

DRESSEL, Paul. *College and University Curriculum.* Berkeley, Calif.: McCutchan, 1968.

———. *Handbook of Academic Evaluation: Assessing Institutional Effectiveness, Student Progress, and Professional Performance for Decision-Making in Higher Education.* San Francisco: Jossey-Bass, 1976.

DRESSEL, Paul L. and FARICY, William H. *Return to Responsibility: Constraints on Autonomy in Higher Education.* San Francisco: Jossey-Bass, 1972.

DRESSEL, Paul; JOHNSON, F. Craig; and MARCUS, Philip M. *The Confidence Crisis: An Analysis of University Departments.* San Francisco: Jossey-Bass, 1970.

DUDGEON, Paul J. "Administrative Implications of Innovative Instructional Design and Delivery in Higher Education: An Experienced Based Checklist of Ideas, Comments and Questions." *Educational Technology* 76 (1976): 47–49.

DYKES, Archie R. *Faculty Participation in Academic Decision Making.* Washington, D.C.: American Council on Education, 1968.

EHRLE, Elwood B. "Selection and Evaluation of Department Chairmen." *Educational Record* 56 (1975): 29–38.

GAFF, Jerry G. *Toward Faculty Renewal: Advances in Faculty Instructional and Organizational Development.* San Francisco: Jossey-Bass, 1970.

GARBARINO, Joseph W. "Precarious Professors: New Patterns of Representation." *Industrial Relations* 10 (1971): 1–20.

GARBARINO, Joseph W. and AUSSIEKER, Bill. *Faculty Bargaining: Change and Conflict* (A Report Prepared for the Carnegie Commission on Higher Education and the Ford Foundation). New York: McGraw-Hill, 1975.

GENOVA, William J.; MADOFF, Marjorie K.; CHIN, Robert; and THOMAS, George B. *Mutual Benefit Evaluation of Faculty and Administrators in Higher Education.* Cambridge, Mass.: Ballinger, 1976.

GOODLAD, Sinclair. *Conflict and Consensus in Higher Education.* London: Hodder and Stoughton, 1976.

HAIGHT, Mike and MARTIN, Ron. *An Introduction to the NCHEMS Costing and Data Management System.* Technical Report No. 55. Boulder, Col.: National Center for Higher Education Management Systems, 1975.

HARVEY, L. James. *Managing Colleges and Universities by Objectives.* Littleton, Col.: Ireland Educational Corp., 1976.

———. *Zero Base Budgeting in Colleges and Universities.* Littleton, Col.: Ireland Educational Corp., 1977.

HAWES, Leonard C. and TRUX, Hugo R., IV. "Student Participation in the University Decision-Making Process." *Journal of Higher Education* 45 (1974): 123–134.

HEFFERLIN, J B Lon. *Dynamics of Academic Reform.* San Francisco: Jossey-Bass, 1969.

HEINLEIN, Albert C., ed. *Decision Models in Academic Administration.* Kent: Kent State University Press, 1974.

HENDERSON, Algo D. *Training University Administrators: A Programme Guide.* Belgium: UNESCO, 1970.

HENDERSON, Algo D. and HENDERSON, Jean Glidden. *Higher Education in America: Problems, Priorities, and Prospects.* San Francisco: Jossey-Bass, 1975.

HEYNS, Roger W. "Our Best Defense Against

Government Regulation." *Educational Record* 58 (1977): 350–356.

"The Invitational Seminar on Restructuring College and University Organization and Governance." *Journal of Higher Education* 42 (1971): 421–542.

KAPLOWITZ, Richard A. *Selecting Academic Administrators*. Washington, D.C.: American Council on Education, 1973.

KEMERER, Frank R. and BALDRIDGE, J. Victor. *Unions on Campus*. San Francisco: Jossey-Bass, 1976.

KIEFT, Raymond; ARMIJO, Frank; and BUCKLEW, Neil. *A Handbook for Institutional Academic and Program Planning: From Idea to Implementation*. Boulder, Col.: National Center for Higher Education Management Systems, 1978.

KIRKWOOD, Robert. "The Myths of Accreditation." *Educational Record* 54 (1973): 211–215.

LAHTI, Robert E. *Innovative College Management: Implementing Proven Organizational Practice*. San Francisco: Jossey-Bass, 1975.

LAWRENCE, G. Ben and SERVICE, Allan L., eds. *Quantitative Approaches to Higher Education Management: Potential, Limits, and Challenge*. Washington, D.C.: ERIC/AAHE, 1977.

MAUER, George J., ed. *Crisis in Campus Management: Case Studies in the Administration of Colleges and Universities*. New York: Praeger, 1976.

MCGANNON, J. Barry. "Academic Dean: Dimensions of Leadership." *Liberal Education* 59 (1973): 277–291.

MCGRATH, Earl J. *Should Students Share the Power?* Philadelphia: Temple University Press, 1970.

MCHENRY, Dean E. and Associates. *Academic Departments*. San Francisco: Jossey-Bass, 1977.

MCKEACHIE, Wilbert J. "Memo to New Department Chairmen." In *The Academic Department or Division Chairman: A Complex Role* edited by James Brann and Thomas A. Emmet. Detroit: Belamp, 1972.

MILLER, Richard I. "The Academic Dean." *Intellect* 102 (1974): 234–244.

MILLETT, John D. "Higher Education Management Versus Business Management." *Educational Record* 56 (1976); 221–225.

———. *New Structures of Campus Power*. San Francisco: Jossey-Bass, 1978.

———. *Strengthening Community in Higher Education*. Management Division, Academy for Educational Development, Inc., 1974.

MOOD, Alexander M. *The Future of Higher Education: A Report Prepared for the Carnegie Commission on Higher Education*. New York: McGraw-Hill, 1973.

MORTIMER, Kenneth P. "The Dilemmas in New Campus Governance Structures," *Journal of Higher Education* 42 (1971): 467–498.

NATIONAL ASSOCIATION OF COLLEGE AND UNIVERSITY BUSINESS OFFICERS. *College and University Business Administration*. 3rd ed. Washington, D.C.: 1974.

ODIORNE, George S. *Management Decisions by Objectives*. Englewood Cliffs, N.J.: Prentice-Hall, 1969.

PATTERSON, Kenneth D. "The Administration of University Curriculum." *Journal of Higher Education* 38 (1967): 438–443.

POLLAY, Richard W.; TAYLOR, Ronald N.; and THOMPSON, Mark. "A Model for Horizontal Power Sharing and Participation in University Decision-Making." *Journal of Higher Education* 47 (1976): 141–157.

PULLIAS, Earl V. "Ten Principles of College Administration." *School and Society* 100 (1972): 95–97.

———. "College and University Administration: Ten More Principles." *Intellect* 101 (1973): 428–431.

PYHRR, Peter A. *Zero-Base Budgeting: A Practical Management Tool For Evaluating Expenses*. New York: Wiley, 1973.

RAJALA, Harry; STANSBURY, Donn B.; PYLE, Florence; and RANKIN, Gary. "Management by Objectives." *College and University* 49 (1974): 539–546.

RICHARDSON, Richard C., Jr.; BLOCKER, Clyde E.; and BENDER, Louis W. *Governance for the Two Year College*. Englewood Cliffs, N.J.: Prentice-Hall, 1972.

RICHMAN, Barry M. and FARMER, Richard N. *Leadership, Goals, and Power in Higher Education.* San Francisco: Jossey-Bass, 1974.

RILEY, Gary L. and BALDRIDGE, J. Victor. *Governing Academic Organizations: New Problems, New Perspectives.* Berkeley, Calif.: McCutchan, 1977.

ROACH, James H. L. "The Academic Department Chairperson: Functions and Responsibilities." *Educational Record* 57 (1976): 13–23.

ROBUSTELLI, Joseph A. and ERICSSON, Carl W. "Developing a Performance Appraisal Form for University Support Personnel." *Journal of the College and University Personnel Association* 16 (1975): 3–9.

ROOD, Harold J. "Legal Issues in Faculty Termination." *Journal of Higher Education* 63 (1977): 123–152.

SANDEEN, Arthur. *Undergraduate Education: Conflict and Change.* Lexington, Mass.: D. C. Heath, 1976.

SEMROW, Joseph J. "Analytical Aspects of the Evaluating/Accrediting Process." *North Central Association Quarterly* 49 (1974): 283–290.

SIKES, Walter W.; SCHLESINGER, Lawrence E.; and SEASHORE, Charles N. *Renewing Higher Education from Within.* San Francisco: Jossey-Bass, 1974.

SOLES, James R. "Information: Missing Ingredient in University Governance." *Educational Record* 54 (1973): 51–55.

SOMMERFELD, Richard and NAGELY, Donna. "Seek and Ye Shall Find: The Organization and Conduct of a Search Committee." *Journal of Higher Education* 45 (1974): 239–252.

WALTER, Robert L. *The Teacher and Collective Bargaining.* Lincoln, Neb.: Professional Educators Publications, Inc., 1975.

WERGIN, Jon F.; MASON, Elizabeth J.; and MUNSON, Paul J. "The Practice of Faculty Development, An Experience-Derived Model." *Journal of Higher Education* 47 (1976): 289–308.

Author Index

Subject Index